Spanish: Listening   Speaking   Reading   Writing

SPANISH

Listening Speaking
Reading Writing

Guillermo Segreda   *Manhattanville College, New York*

James W. Harris   *Massachusetts Institute of Technology*

HARCOURT,
BRACE
& WORLD, INC.

New York   Chicago   San Francisco   Atlanta

Maps by J. P. Tremblay

PICTURE CREDITS

p. 4, Carl Frank, Photo Researchers; p. 20, Columbia Artists Management, Inc.; p. 40, Bernard G. Silberstein, Rapho-Guillumette; pp. 60, 78, Mauro Mujica; p. 98, UPI; p. 118, Frederic Lewis, Inc.; p. 134, Dennis J. Cipnic; p. 152, 252, United Nations; p. 168, Pan American Union; p. 186, Edith Reichman; pp. 202, 270, Jane Latta; p. 220, Ernst Jahn; p. 236, Pan American Airways.

ACKNOWLEDGMENT IS GIVEN TO HARCOURT, BRACE & WORLD, INC., FOR USE OF THE FOLLOWING MATERIALS:

"Catalina y San Antonio," from *A-LM Spanish*, Level Two, copyright © 1970.
"La esquina," slightly adapted from *A-LM Spanish*, Level Two, copyright © 1970.
"Se necesita sirvienta," slightly adapted from *A-LM Spanish*, Level Two, copyright © 1970.
"América y los americanos," slightly adapted from *A-LM Spanish*, Level One, copyright © 1969.

ISBN: 0-15-583048-1
LIBRARY OF CONGRESS CATALOG CARD NUMBER: 72-113710

PRINTED IN THE UNITED STATES OF AMERICA

Preface

This book is the outgrowth of a number of ideas developed over years of teaching elementary Spanish and participating in the preparation of other modern language textbooks. Its significant innovations have produced good results and have seemed well worth being made available to other teachers and students of Spanish.

The text has been carefully planned to include all the basic phonology, grammar, vocabulary, and cultural information necessary for comprehending, speaking, reading, and writing first-year Spanish in a book short enough to be covered comfortably in a single year's course of three class hours a week. Listening comprehension and speaking are stressed from the outset. Chapter 1 presents and drills many of the major phonological problems without becoming highly technical. The remaining 15 chapters contain listening passages (described below), basic dialogs with appropriate cultural notes, related supplementary vocabulary, drills on pronunciation, grammatical explanations and exercises, and reading selections. Grammatical explanations are limited to giving the student a mastery of essential generalizations: they are brief, with just enough detail to teach the point. By not being subjected to the frustrating confusion of grammatical minutiae, the student receives a simple, straightforward background of the fundamentals and a firm preparation for further study. Users of the accompanying workbook will find there additional exercises for developing and reinforcing writing skills.

Spanish: Listening, Speaking, Reading, Writing includes largely the kinds of essentially audio-lingual teaching devices most teachers have become accustomed to in recent years. A special and unique feature, however, is the listening passage preceding each lesson. Completely in Spanish, each passage (read from the Instructor's Manual by the instructor or played on the tape, with a parallel English translation in the textbook for the student to consult as he listens) discusses some aspects of culture related to the basic dialog, presents the dialog situation, and concludes with a list of the grammar points of the lesson. The listening passage immerses the student in spoken Spanish that goes beyond what he is expected to learn for active use, but is sufficiently limited in structure and vocabulary to ensure its aural comprehension for the most part. The superior student is thus encouraged to try to increase his understanding of spoken Spanish, while the less gifted student, relying to a greater degree on the translation, will also profit from the exposure. The listening passages are an integral part of the conception and pedagogical method; nevertheless the book can be used effectively without them, or they can simply serve as additional reading material or material for dictation or for other writing exercises.

Although many people have helped to inspire the present content and form of this book, we are especially grateful to Dr. S. N. Treviño, formerly of the Foreign Service Institute of the Department of State, for his personal encouragement during the preparation of the manuscript, and to Professors Dwight L. Bolinger of Harvard University, Roger M. Peel of Middlebury College (formerly of Yale

University), Robert Brody of Columbia University, and W. F. Byess of the University of Tennessee for their constructive suggestions. We are also greatly indebted to Professor H. Ernest Lewald of the University of Tennessee for his valuable suggestions for cultural material, his collaboration on some of the listening passages, and his contribution of the reading *El Index de los mayas*. And finally, our thanks go to our students of the last several years at Manhattanville College, the Massachusetts Institute of Technology, and Harvard University; their suggestions and comments on previous versions of these materials helped make *Spanish: Listening, Speaking, Reading, Writing* the distinctive book we believe it to be.

GUILLERMO SEGREDA

JAMES W. HARRIS

Contents

Chapter 3   41

Chapter 4   61

Chapter 15   253

Chapter 16   271

Appendix   286

Vocabularies   295

Index   321

Listening Passage for Chapter 1
English Translation

First read the English translation of the listening passage. Then listen carefully, only glancing at the English, as the same passage is read to you in Spanish. The letters in parentheses will help you to pinpoint any specific fragment of the passage that you may wish to follow particularly closely. You should not expect to understand every word of the Spanish. Rather, you should concentrate on getting your ear "tuned in" to it, while grasping as much of the meaning as you can. Literal translations of some Spanish words and phrases which would sound odd in English are given in parentheses.

Part 1
Introduction

(A) Good morning, good afternoon, or good evening, (Mr. or Miss) student. Listen and pay (put) close (much) attention, please. (B) The first part of this chapter contains explanations and exercises on the pronunciation of the Spanish language. (C) (The) Good pronunciation is one of the bases for (of the) success in the study of a language. The acquisition of correct habits of pronunciation from the moment in which one begins to study is an enormous aid for making rapid and efficient progress through-

out the course. Your initial efforts in this respect are, then, of great importance.

(CH) The acquisition of (a) good pronunciation is not an impossible feat. But it does require concentration, patience, and perseverance. Once correct habits of (the) pronunciation have been formed, the study of (the) Spanish can become (be converted to) a pleasant and relatively easy task.

TO BE FOLLOWED BY
LISTENING RECOGNITION EXERCISE

The Sounds of (the) Spanish

(D) These passages which you read in English and then listen to in Spanish have two purposes: First, to provide certain information relating to the language; second, to serve as an initial step toward the pronunciation exercises. If you can "tune your ear" to the sounds and to the rhythm of the Spanish language, you will be better prepared to produce these sounds and this rhythm correctly.

(E) In general, the sounds of (the) Spanish are quite different from the sounds of (the) English. There are a few Spanish sounds which are practically the same as (equal to) certain English sounds; but the majority are different,

1

and some do not have the least resemblance to any English sound. In this chapter you are going to learn the pronunciation of all the Spanish vowels and some of the consonants.

TO BE FOLLOWED BY
LISTENING RECOGNITION EXERCISE

(The) Spanish Vowels

(F) (The) Spanish has only five vowels. These are: *a, e, i, o, u*. Listen again: *a, e, i, o, u*. Each one of these vowels, naturally, has been repeated many times in this lesson. (G) The Spanish vowels are always spelled (written) the same way. The sound [a]* is always written with the letter *a*, the sound [e] is always written with the letter *e*, the sound [i] is always written with the letter *i*, etc. There exists one trivial exception, which will be mentioned below.

(H) (The) Spanish vowels are always pronounced the same, whether they are in stressed or unstressed syllables. Unlike (to the contrary of the) English vowels, Spanish vowels are always (pronounced in a manner) short, tense, and clear. For example, the English word ''no'' is pronounced [nóuu], with the *o* drawn out until it changes to a kind of [u]. The same word in Spanish is pronounced [no]. Listen again (another time) and observe how short the *o* is: [no, no]. Listen once again (one time more)

---

*Brackets [ ] will be used to distinguish sounds from letters.

and observe how the *o* does not lose its quality (of *o*): [no, no].

TO BE FOLLOWED BY
LISTENING RECOGNITION EXERCISE

Part 2
(*The*) Vowels and (*the*) Rhythm

(I) The English speaker who is learning (the) Spanish has greater difficulty with the unstressed vowels than with the stressed vowels in (of) Spanish. The problem comes from (the) English. In English, all (the) unstressed vowels are generally pronounced alike, at least in unguarded speech (the ordinary language of the people). Listen to the unstressed vowels underlined in the following words.

usu<u>a</u>lly   vow<u>e</u>l   diff<u>i</u>culty

pr<u>o</u>nounce   caref<u>u</u>l

(J) In Spanish, on the other hand (in change), all (the) unstressed vowels are pronounced exactly the same as the corresponding stressed vowels. Furthermore, the sound that all unstressed vowels generally have in English does not occur at all in Spanish, ever. Listen very carefully (with much care) to the following Spanish words. Both (the two) are very long and have several unstressed vowels, which are underlined. Notice how every unstressed *a* always has the very clear [a] sound, every unstressed *e* the sound [e] equally clear, etc.

<u>a</u>nti<u>a</u>m<u>e</u>ric<u>a</u>nizad<u>a</u>ment<u>e</u>   p<u>a</u>r<u>a</u>lel<u>e</u>píp<u>e</u>d<u>o</u>

(K) The principal cause of the difference between (the) English and (the) Spanish in the pronunciation of (the) unstressed vowels is (the) rhythm. The usual rhythm of the English language is uneven. That is to say, in English, (the) stressed vowels are relatively long while (the) unstressed vowels are relatively short and tend to disappear. In contrast (change) the usual rhythm of (the) Spanish is even. All (the) vowels have the same length, whether or not they are stressed. Thus (the) unstressed vowels are not shortened or pronounced in a relaxed manner, and they do not tend to disappear, as occurs in English.

(L) Listen one more time to (the) paragraphs I, J, and K. As you are (go) listening, concentrate your attention on the even rhythm of (the) Spanish and on the clear pronunciation of all the vowels, unstressed as well as stressed.

TO BE FOLLOWED BY
LISTENING RECOGNITION EXERCISE

Part 3
Sounds and Letters

(LL) In this course, you will begin to study from the start both (the) pronunciation and (the) spelling. This can be done more effectively in Spanish than in other languages. The reasons are that Spanish uses roman letters (characters), the same as (the) English; (then that) the Spanish alphabet is almost the same as the English alphabet; (also that) several of the letters represent the same, or nearly the same, sound in Spanish and in English (*m*, *n*, *s*, and *f*, for example); and, finally, (that) the Spanish spelling system is excellent.

(M) Spanish has one of the simplest spelling systems in (of) the world. Once you learn a few simple rules, you will know how to pronounce any (whatever) word you see written, although you may never have heard it before. You will also know how to spell (write) correctly any word you hear, although you may never have seen it written before, with the exception of a few consonant sounds which, for historical reasons, have more than one spelling (way of being written).

(N) An alphabetical system that is the same or almost the same for both languages presents, however, a serious problem for the student. This is his inevitable tendency to forget that the letters of Spanish do not represent the English sounds to which he is accustomed. This tendency is particularly strong in words of the same or similar spelling (writing) in both languages and of the same or nearly the same meaning. For example, the word *animal* is spelled (written) the same and means the same in both languages, but in Spanish it is pronounced [animál]. In [animál] the *n* and the *m* have almost the same sound as the *n* and the *m* of (the) English, but the *l*, all the vowels, the stress, and the rhythm are quite different.

TO BE FOLLOWED BY
LISTENING RECOGNITION EXERCISE

Chapter 1

The Sounds of Spanish

PRONUNCIATION EXERCISES

Vowels. Listen and repeat. Mimic what you hear as precisely as you can.

1. [a]. Note that Spanish [a] is not produced as far back in the mouth as the vowel in English "con," nor as far front as that in English "can." Spanish [a] is, so to speak, between these two English vowels.

        a   a   a   a
        ma-má   Pa-na-má   ma-ña-na[1]

2. [e]. Make Spanish [e] short and clipped. It should *not* rhyme with the name of the English letter *a*, which is long and assumes the quality of "ee" at the end.

        e   e   e   e
        sé   ne-ne   e-se

3. [i]. Spanish [i] is also short and tense. Notice carefully how it differs from the name of the English letter *e*.

        i   i   i   i
        sí   Li-li   Mi-si-si-pi

4. [o]. Spanish [o] does not rhyme with the name of the English letter *o*. Round your lips at the beginning of Spanish [o] and keep them in exactly the same position. Spanish [o] does not acquire the quality of "oo" in "pool" at the end, as the most similar English sound does.

        o   o   o   o
        no   co-mo   lo-co

5. [u]. Make Spanish [u] short and tense. Round your lips at the beginning (more than for [o]) and keep them that way.

        u   u   u   u
        u-na   lu-na   A-ca-pul-co

[*To be followed by* LISTENING PASSAGE, *Part 2*]

---

[1]The letter ñ (*eñe*) represents a sound similar to English *ny* in "canyon."

PRONUNCIATION EXERCISES

1. Vowels and rhythm. Listen and repeat each of the sentences below. These sentences are divided into syllables rather than into words to help you imitate the correct even spacing of Spanish syllables. As you repeat, try to maintain exactly the rhythm and speed of the voice you hear. Do not worry now about remembering the vocabulary. Make an attempt to pronounce the consonants, but concentrate on the vowels.

[a]:	Va-pa-ra-Pa-na-má.[2]	(*He's headed for Panama.*)
	Va-la-ca-sa-ma-ña-na.	(*He's going to the house tomorrow.*)
	(H)as-ta-ma-ña-na-na.[3]	(*See you tomorrow, Ana.*)
[e]:	Sé-que-Pe-pe-sel-je-fe.[4]	(*I know that Pepe's the boss.*)
	Dé-me-se-que-so.	(*Give me that cheese.*)
	El-ne-ne-sel-je-fe.	(*The baby is the boss.*)
[i]:	Di-ce-Li-li-que-sí.	(*Lily says yes.*)
	Mi-si-si-pi-e-sa-sí.	(*Mississippi is like that.*)
	Di-fi-ci-lí-si-mo.	(*Very difficult.*)
[o]:	Co-mo-co-mo-lo-co.	(*I eat like crazy.*)
	No-no-no-no-no-y-no.	(*No, no, no, no, no, and no.*)
	Al-fon-so-y-yo-no-so-mos-ton-tos.	(*Alfonso and I aren't stupid.*)
[u]:	U-na-mu-no-e-sú-ni-co.	(*Unamuno is unique.*)
	Tú-tú-tú-tú-tú-y-tú.	(*You, you, you, you, you, and you.*)
	Tú-u-sas-mu-cho-tu-plu-ma.	(*You use your pen a lot.*)

2. Diphthongs and syllables. A Spanish word usually has as many syllables as it has vowels. Thus, *no* has one vowel and one syllable, *Lili* has two vowels and two syllables, and so on. However, when unstressed *i* or *u* occurs next to another vowel, it does not form a separate syllable. For example, *bien*, stressed on the *e*, has only one syllable; *bueno*, stressed on the *e*, has two syllables. As a reminder, we will sometimes write unstressed *i* next to another vowel as [y], as in [dyárya] (*diaria*); and unstressed *u* next to another vowel as [w], as in [bwéno] (*bueno*).

Combinations of [y] or [w] and another vowel are called *diphthongs*. In Spanish, syllables containing a diphthong are of the same short duration as syllables containing only a simple vowel.

Listen and repeat the following words, which contain the diphthongs indicated. Do not let the presence of the diphthongs interfere with even rhythm and clear pronunciation of unstressed vowels.

[wa]: Juan, cuán-do, cuá-les, a-gua

[we]: bue-no, lue-go, sue-ño, jue-ves, a-bue-la, es-cue-la

[wi]: fui, cui-da-do, Lui-si-ta

[ya]: ru-bia, gra-cias, dia-ria, es-tu-dia, lim-pia-di-ta

[ye]: bien, quién, mie-do, vie-ja

[yo]: Dios, a-diós, no-vio, su-cios, E-mi-lio

[yu]: ciu-dad

[*To be followed by* LISTENING PASSAGE, *Part* 3]

---

[2] The letter *v* is pronounced [b], as in "boy."   [3] The letter *h*, except in the combination *ch*, is always silent.
[4] The letter *j* is pronounced like the *ch* of "Bach."

PRONUNCIATION EXERCISES

1. *r* between vowels. Three of the Spanish consonants that give English speakers the most trouble are *t, d,* and *r.* The pronunciation of Spanish *r* (*ere*), [r], is totally unlike that of any kind of *r* heard in normal American English. There is, however, a very common sound in English which works very well for Spanish [r], although it is not spelled *r* in English. This is the sound of the *t* (or *tt*) and the *d* (or *dd*) in words like "Betty," "Eddie," "ladder," "caddie," "got it," and so on, in casual pronunciation. Listen to the similarity of the English *t*'s and *d*'s to the Spanish *r*'s in the following words.

better	Vera (*a proper name*)	cotter	cara (*face*)
Eddies	eres (*you are*)	pot of tea	para ti (*for you*)

Listen and repeat the following words and phrases. Pay particular attention to [r]. Most of the words in the pronunciation exercises appear in the basic material of the first few chapters. You need not memorize their meanings at this time.

hora	(*hour*)	pero	(*but*)	cara	(*face*)
ahora	(*now*)	para	(*for*)	señora	(*lady*)
mujeres	(*women*)	estar aquí[5]	(*to be here*)	americana	(*American*)
mejores	(*better*)	mira	(*look*)	lotería	(*lottery*)

Now repeat the following sentences, all of which contain several occurrences of [r]. Make them all sound like the first *t* in "I got it." These sentences are divided into syllables rather than into words to remind you to keep the rhythm even.

No-sé-qué-(h)o-ra-e-sa-(h)o-ra.	(*I don't know what time it is now.*)
Las-mu-je-re-son-me-jo-res.	(*Women are better.*)
¿Pe-ro-pa-ra-qués-ta-ra-quí?	(*But what's the purpose of being here?*)
Mi-ra-la-ca-ra-de-la-se-ño-ra-me-ri-ca-na.	(*Look at the American lady's face.*)

2. The consonant *d*. In Spanish, the letter *d* (*de*) stands for two distinct sounds. At the beginning of an utterance or after a pause, and after *l* or *n*, Spanish *d* is pronounced [d], much like the English *d* of "dog," "day," and "adopt." Listen and repeat the following words.

el de	(*that of*)	dispénseme	(*excuse me*)
dónde	(*where*)	después	(*afterwards*)
cuándo	(*when*)	domingo	(*Sunday*)

In all other positions, Spanish *d* is pronounced [đ], almost like the *th* of "mother," "lather," and "then." Listen to the similarity between English *th* and Spanish *d* in the following words; repeat only the Spanish words.

mother	moda (*fashion*)
either	ida (*departure*)
soothing	suden (*perspire*)
lather	lado (*side*)
than	Adán (*Adam*)

---

[5] The combination *qu* is pronounced [k]; the *u* is silent.

A word naturally does not appear in the same context every time it is used. For example, the word *dónde*, "where," might be used in the sentence ¿*Dónde estás?*, "Where are you?" In this case, the first *d* occurs after silence (let's suppose), and is accordingly pronounced [d]. But *dónde* might also be used in *No sé dónde*, "I don't know where." Here the first *d* of *dónde* does *not* occur after silence (or after *n* or *l*), and is accordingly pronounced [đ]. Listen and repeat the following examples, in which *d*'s in the same word are pronounced differently according to context. As a reminder, all *d*'s pronounced [đ] are underlined.

de Juan	(*John's*)	casa de Juan	(*John's house*)
dónde	(*where*)	de dónde	(*from where*)
delgada	(*slender*)	la delgada	(*the slender one*)
domingo	(*Sunday*)	qué domingo	(*what a Sunday*)

We must stress the correct pronunciation of Spanish *d* for the following reason. Mispronunciation of some Spanish sounds, for example [r], results in a strong foreign accent, but does not necessarily lead to a failure of communication. Mispronunciation of Spanish *d*, however, may easily result in misunderstanding. You have already been given a clue as to the reason: English *d* (or *dd*), in words like "Eddie" and "ladder," sounds like Spanish [r]; therefore, if you incorrectly use an English *d*-sound in Spanish words like *todos*, "all," and *modos*, "ways, manners," you will actually be saying *toros*, "bulls," and *moros*, "Moorish." This can produce utter nonsense; for example, the very common expression *de todos modos*, "anyway," might come out *de toros moros*, "of Moorish bulls."

We will give you additional practice pronouncing Spanish [đ]. In the following words, the *d*'s pronounced [đ] are underlined as a reminder. Listen and repeat.

nada	(*nothing*)	ocupado	(*occupied, busy*)
parecidos	(*similar*)	preocupado	(*worried*)
ciudad	(*city*)	miedo	(*fear*)
usted	(*you*, singular)	vida diaria	(*daily life*)
ustedes	(*you*, plural)	idea	(*idea*)
cansada	(*tired*)	desocupada	(*unoccupied, free*)
todavía	(*still*)	estudia	(*he studies*)
limpiadita	(*cleaning*)	Facultad de Derecho	(*Law School*)
todos	(*all*)	pedacito	(*piece*)
enamorado	(*in love*)	cuidado	(*care*)

3. The consonant *t*. Spanish *t* (*te*) is quite different from English *t*, and mispronunciation of it is one of the most obvious and unattractive characteristics of a foreign accent. Spanish *t* differs from English *t* in two principal respects. First, for Spanish *t*, the front part of the tongue is pressed against the back of the upper teeth, *not* against the gum ridge above and behind the upper teeth as in English. You may think a fraction of an inch could not matter very much, but you will hear the difference in a moment. Second, Spanish *t* is *never* followed by a puff of air (technically, *aspiration*) as English *t* frequently is.

To appreciate the effect of mispronounced *t*'s and to familiarize yourself with the sound of Spanish *t*, listen to a Spanish speaker mispronounce English by using Spanish *t*'s.

You take too much time, Tom.
Take two tokens, Tina.
It takes two to tango.

Listen again to these sentences, and if you are not shy, imitate the Spanish speaker's foreign accent. This is an excellent way to learn to pronounce Spanish correctly.

In pronouncing the following words, concentrate on the *t*'s, but do not neglect the pronunciation of previously learned vowels, *r*'s, and *d*'s, and the maintenance of an even rhythm. Listen and repeat.

Terán	(*a proper name*)	tengo	(*I have*)
todavía	(*still*)	tiene	(*he has*)
tal	(*such*)	temprano	(*early*)
tipo	(*type, guy*)	tú	(*you*)
todos	(*all*)	té	(*tea*)
tiempo	(*time; weather*)	también	(*too*)
tan	(*so*)	tomamos	(*we drink*)

Now listen and repeat the following sentences.

Los-ti-cos-no-to-ma-mos-té.	(*We Costa Ricans don't drink tea.*)
Yo-no-ten-go-tan-tos-tan-gos.	(*I don't have so many tangos.*)
Tan-tos-ton-tos-to-man-te-qui-la.	(*So many fools drink tequila.*)

Useful expressions

Practice the following short dialogs until you have memorized them. Learn the names of the "characters."

I

	Los personajes son: B (be larga) y v (be corta)[6]		The characters are: B and v
B.	Buenos días, ¿cómo está?	B.	Good morning (days), how are you?
V.	Estoy bien, gracias, ¿y usted?	V.	I'm fine, thanks; and you?
B.	Bastante bien, gracias.	B.	Quite well, thank you.
V.	Con permiso.	V.	Excuse me (with permission).
B.	Cómo no.	B.	Of course (how not).

II

	c (ce) y z (zeta)[7]		c and z
C.	Buenas tardes; tome asiento, por favor.	C.	Good afternoon; take a seat, please.
Z.	Gracias. ¿Y cómo sigue el profesor Campos?	Z.	Thank you. And how's Professor Campos coming along?
C.	Según el médico, muy mal.	C.	According to the doctor, very poorly.
Z.	Cuánto lo siento.	Z.	I'm very sorry (How much I regret it).

---

[6] The letters *b* and *v* are pronounced the same and are distinguished only in writing. An informal way of identifying these letters is to call *b*, *b larga* ("long *b*") and *v*, *b corta* ("short *b*").

[7] The letter *z* is pronounced [s], as in "say."

G (ge) y J (jota)		G and J
G. ¿Quién habla inglés aquí?		G. Who speaks English here?
J. Yo hablo un poco, ¿por qué?		J. I speak a little, why?
G. ¿Cómo se dice "me alegro" y "mañana por la mañana"?		G. How do you say "I'm glad" and "tomorrow morning"?
J. "I'm glad" y "tomorrow morning".		J. "I'm glad" and "tomorrow morning."
G. Gracias.		G. Thanks.
J. De nada.		J. You're welcome (of nothing).

REJOINDERS

We shall call any appropriate reply to a question or statement a *rejoinder*. Give rejoinders to the following questions and statements. Make them as short or as long as you like, but stay within the bounds of what you think you can say more or less correctly and without too much fumbling.

EXAMPLE: El profesor Campos sigue mal.
Cuánto lo siento.
Me alegro.
Cuánto me alegro.
No no no. Según el médico, sigue muy bien.

1. Buenos días.
2. Gracias.
3. ¿Cómo está usted?
4. ¿Habla usted inglés?
5. ¿Cómo se dice "tomorrow"?
6. ¿Y "tomorrow morning"?
7. Y usted, ¿habla español?
8. ¿Cómo se dice "characters"?
9. ¿Son los personajes letras o personas?
10. ¿Con quién habla "be larga"?
11. Y "jota", ¿con quién? ¿Y "ge"?
12. Usted, tome asiento, por favor.
13. ¿Cómo se dice "good afternoon" en español?
14. ¿Cómo se dice "how are you"?
15. Según el médico, el profesor Campos sigue bastante bien.
16. Yo estoy muy mal.
17. Yo estoy muy muy muy bien.
18. Con permiso.

PRONUNCIATION EXERCISES

r **before a consonant.** If you have mastered Spanish *r* between vowels, you may have no trouble with *r* before a consonant, although many people find the latter more difficult. Spanish *r* before a consonant is pronounced [r], just as it is between vowels—never like English *r*. The following trick is often helpful: To approximate the Spanish sound [r] before a consonant, as in *suerte*, think of the sound of English *t* (or *d*) in a word like "sweater" followed rapidly by a consonant, as in the nonsensical "sweat a tay." A rapid pronunciation of "sweat a tay" actually sounds much more like *suerte* than the same word pronounced with an English *r*.

Listen to the following combinations of English words and nonsense syllables and notice how similar they sound to real Spanish words. Just listen; do not repeat.

sweat a tay	suerte (*luck*)	cot a loss	Carlos (*Charles*)
mot a tess	martes (*Tuesday*)	be Eddie ness	viernes (*Friday*)
tot a they	tarde (*afternoon; late*)	me Eddie cole is	miércoles (*Wednesday*)

The following words and phrases have *r* before a consonant. Concentrate on pronouncing Spanish [r] correctly by associating it with the sound of English *t* in words like "sweater."

martes	(*Tuesday*)	Carlos	(*Charles*)	gorda	(*fat*)
miércoles	(*Wednesday*)	hermano	(*brother*)	verde	(*green*)
perdón	(*pardon*)	verdad	(*truth*)	tarde	(*afternoon, late*)
viernes	(*Friday*)	por favor	(*please*)	corbata	(*necktie*)
porque	(*because*)	conversar	(*to converse*)	por qué	(*why*)

Listen and repeat the following sentences.

Por-fa-vor-Car-los-mi-cor-ba-ta.	(*Please Carlos, my tie.*)
¿Por-qué-mar-tes?	(*Why Tuesday?*)
¿Por-qué-no-miér-co-les?	(*Why not Wednesday?*)
Car-lo-sy-Mar-ta-so-n(h)er-ma-nos.	(*Charles and Martha are brother and sister.*)

Numbers

Números

1	u-no	11	on-ce	21	vein-tiu-no
2	dos	12	do-ce	22	vein-ti-dós
3	tres	13	tre-ce	23	vein-ti-trés
4	cua-tro	14	ca-tor-ce	30	trein-ta
5	cin-co	15	quin-ce	31	trein-ta-yu-no
6	seis	16	die-ci-séis	32	trein-tay-dos
7	sie-te	17	die-ci-sie-te	40	cua-ren-ta
8	o-cho	18	die-cio-cho	50	cin-cuen-ta
9	nue-ve	19	die-ci-nue-ve		
10	diez	20	vein-te		

A. **Dieciséis** (16), **diecisiete** (17), **dieciocho** (18), and **diecinueve** (19) are actually *diez y seis*, "ten and six," *diez y siete*, "ten and seven," and so on, but they are customarily written as one word, as shown.

B. **Veintiuno** (21), **veintidós** (22), **veintitrés** (23), and so on through **veintinueve** (29) are actually *veinte y uno*, "twenty and one," *veinte y dos*, "twenty and two," and so on. These may be written either way, but the one-word spelling is more common. The final *e* of *veinte* is dropped in the one-word forms, in both spelling and pronunciation.

C. No other compound number is written as one word: *treinta y uno* (31), *treinta y dos* (32), *cuarenta y tres* (43), *cincuenta y nueve* (59), and so on.

COUNTING ALOUD

1. Count the people in your class.
2. Count the chairs.

3. One student counts from 1 to 10, the next one from 11 to 20, etc.
4. One student counts in even numbers to 10, the next one from 12 to 20, etc.
5. Repeat exercise 4 with odd numbers.
6. One student counts in fives from 5 to 25, the next one from 30 to 50.
7. Count in tens to 50.

The alphabet

In the preceding listening passages you have heard the names of the letters through *n*. The complete alphabet follows. Listen and repeat.

El alfabeto

a	a	f	efe	l	ele	p	pe	u	u
b	be	g	ge	ll	elle	q	cu	v	ve
c	ce	h	hache	m	eme	r	ere	w°	doble ve
ch	che	i	i	n	ene	rr	erre	x	equis
d	de	j	jota	ñ	eñe	s	ese	y	i griega
e	e	k°	ka	o	o	t	te	z	zeta

° These letters occur only in a few words that Spanish has borrowed from other languages.

Sound-letter correspondences

Spanish has one of the best spelling systems in the world; most letters represent only one sound, and most sounds are represented by only one letter. The following are the principal classes of exceptions:

Letters representing more than one sound

	Before a consonant	*Before* a, o, *or* u	*Before* e *or* i
c	[k] crema, acto	[k] catorce, cómo, cuánto	[s] once, gracias
g	[g] gracias, enigma	[g] gana, gorda, gusto	[h][8] general, lógico
gu	[gu] gusto, según	[gw] lengua, antiguo	[g] sigue, guitarra

---

[8] Like the *ch* in "Bach."

Also, *h* (*hache*) alone is always silent (*h*ora, a*h*ora, *h*ermano, pro*h*ibición), but the combination *ch* is always pronounced just as in English "church" (*ch*ico, mu*ch*acho). Incidentally, *ch* is considered to be a single letter, *che*, in Spanish. It comes between *c* and *d* in the alphabet, and words are alphabetized accordingly; for example, *chico* comes after *cuánto*.

In short, the pronunciation of any Spanish word is always completely given by the spelling (aside from a few proper names, which aren't actually Spanish). There are no ambiguities; *h* alone is always silent, *ch* is always as in "church," *c* before *e* is always [s], *c* before *a* is always [k], and so on.

Sounds represented by more than one spelling

Sound	Spellings	Examples
[b]	*b* or *v*	*b*ueno, *b*aja, tam*b*ién; *v*iejo, *v*erde
[h]	*g* or *j*	*g*emelos, *g*ente; mu*j*eres, me*j*ores
[s]	*c*, *s*, or *z*	on*c*e; *s*í, ca*s*as; *z*apato, die*z*
[y]	*ll* or *y*	*ll*amo, e*ll*a, a*ll*í; *y*o, *y*a, o*y*e

In general, you cannot predict the spelling of Spanish words that have any of the sounds [b, h, s, y] or are spelled with a silent *h*; the spelling must simply be memorized. The situation is not really as bad as it may sound, however, since in an extremely large number of cases Spanish spelling may be deduced from English spelling. A tiny sample follows.

ENGLISH	SPANISH	ENGLISH	SPANISH
alpha*b*et	alfa*b*eto (*not* alfaveto)	*J*esus	*J*esús (*not* Gezúz)
*v*alid	*v*álido (*not* bálido)	difference	diferencia (*not* diferensia)
*h*abit	*h*ábito (*not* _ávito)	expression	expresión (*not* expreción)
*h*onor	*h*onor (*not* _onor)	*z*one	*z*ona (*not* sona)
*g*eneral	*g*eneral (*not* jeneral)	cas*t*le	cas*t*illo (*not* caztiyo)

General spelling rules

It will be extremely helpful if from the very start you memorize thoroughly the following completely regular spelling conventions.

A.   **Combinations of [k] or [g] and a vowel**

Sounds⟶	[a]	[e]	[i]	[o]	[u]
↓	Spelled:				
[k]	ca	que	qui	co	cu
[g]	ga	gue	gui	go	gu

Remember that *ce* and *ci* are pronounced [se] and [si], and that *ge* and *gi* are pronounced [he] and [hi]. Also, the sequence *qu* is used only before *e* and *i:* [ke] and [ki]; [kw] is always spelled *cu*, never *qu: cuota, cuestión, ecuación.*

B. The letter *z* is never written before *e* or *i* except in *zeta* (the name of the letter *z* itself) and in a few other words borrowed from other languages. For example, *diez,* "ten," is spelled with a final *z*, but this *z* changes to *c* before *i* in *dieciséis,* "sixteen"—literally "ten and six"—and all the following "teens."

C. The sound [i] is always spelled *i* except in the word *y,* "and," and when unstressed at the end of a word: *muy,* "very"; *doy,* "I give"; *Paraguay.*

D. Spanish never uses *ph* for [f] nor *ch* for [k]; for example, "telephone" is *teléfono* and "technology" is *tecnología*. Also, double letters are not used to represent a single sound; for example, "difference" is *diferencia,* "expression" is *expresión,* "recommend" is *recomendar,* and "illegal" is *ilegal.* (Remember that *ll*, pronounced [y], is considered to be a single letter, different from *l; rr (erre)* will be discussed later.) There are a few exceptions, most of which involve prefixes; for example, *in + numerable* gives *innumerable.*

Regional differences in pronunciation

You are of course aware that English is not pronounced exactly the same throughout the English-speaking world. The same is true of Spanish. In neither case, however, are regional differences in pronunciation any great barrier to communication. The Spanish described in this book is typical of the great majority of Spanish speakers, and would be accepted and understood anywhere. It would be very time-consuming—and not very useful—to list here a large number of minute and inconsequential regional variations in Spanish pronunciation. Instead, we shall give only the three most striking differences.

A. In southern Spain and all of Latin America, the letter *z* in any position and the letter *c* before *e* or *i* are pronounced [s], as in English "say." In northern and central Spain only, *z* in any position and *c* before *e* or *i* are pronounced like *th* in English "think." Thus, most speakers pronounce *casa* and *caza* alike: [kasa]; but in northern and central Spain *casa* is [kasa] while *caza* is [katha]. This pronunciation is a characteristic of what is known as Castilian Spanish.

B. In parts of Spain and most of Latin America, the letter *ll* is pronounced [y], as in English "yes." In other parts of Spain and isolated pockets of Latin America, *ll* is pronounced similar to *lli* in English "million." Thus, most speakers pronounce *cayo* and *callo* alike: [kayo]; but for a minority of speakers *cayo* is [kayo] while *callo* is roughly [kalʸo].

C. In several areas, notably around the Caribbean, *s* before a consonant or at the end of a word is reduced to an aspiration—like English *h*—in normal unguarded speech. Thus, in these areas *gasta* may be heard as [gaʰta] and *las casas* as [laʰ kasaʰ].

Useful expressions

1. Practice the following dialog until you have learned it by heart.

H (hache) y s (ese)	H and s
H. Hola, "ese", ¿qué tal? ¿Qué hay de nuevo?	H. Hi, "S," how are things? What's new (What is there of new)?
S. Nada. ¿Cómo se escribe "ahora", con o sin hache?	S. Nothing. How do you spell (write) "ahora" (now), with or without an *h*?
H. Con hache.	H. With an *h*.
S. Gracias, hasta luego.	S. Thanks, so long (until then).

2. Learn the following additional expressions.

Cierre la puerta, el libro	*Close the door, the book*
Abra la ventana	*Open the window*
Buenas noches	*Good evening* or *good night*
Hasta mañana	*See you tomorrow (until tomorrow)*
Adiós	*Good-bye*

REJOINDERS

1. Buenos días (buenas tardes).
2. ¿Qué tal, cómo está usted?
3. ¿Qué hay de nuevo?
4. ¿Habla usted español?
5. ¿Cómo se escribe "nuevo", con *b* larga o *b* corta?
6. ¿Cómo se dice *nine*? ¿Y *new*?
7. ¿Cómo se escribe "dice", con *c* o con *s*?
8. ¿Cómo se escribe "ahora"? ¿Y "hablo"?
9. ¿Cómo se escribe "diez"?
10. ¿Y "favor"?

The written accent mark and stressed syllables

We will use the word "stress" to refer to the relative prominence of syllables in *pronunciation*, and the expression "written accent" to refer to the mark ' which occurs over some vowels in Spanish *spelling*. We use two different words to avoid confusion, since the stress of a Spanish word is not always indicated by a written accent. In Spanish, unlike English, the location of the stressed syllable of a word is always predictable from the spelling, according to the following rules.

A. If a word has a written accent, the syllable with the written accent is stressed. Read aloud the following examples.

simpática	todavía	después	órdenes	azúcar	inglés
antipática	lotería	adiós	lógico	fácil	café
miércoles	Jiménez	también	sábado	difícil	según

B. If a word has no written accent and ends in any consonant except *n* or *s*, the *last* syllable is stressed. Read aloud the following examples.

usted	animal	profesor	mujer	español
ciudad	escribir	reloj	estoy	lugar

C. If a word has no written accent and ends in *n*, *s*, or a vowel (that is, every word not covered by rules A and B), the *next-to-last* syllable is stressed. Read aloud the following examples.

buenos	americano	ocupados
escribe	delgada	bastante
dicen	apellido	personajes

Cognates

Having studied and, hopefully, mastered some of the problems of the Spanish system of pronunciation and writing, you are now ready to dig into a vast reservoir of Spanish words that you already "almost" know. These are cognates, Spanish words that have at least some resemblance to English words in the way they are pronounced, very similar spellings, and the same meanings as the corresponding English words.

Here is a list of just a few, taken from the listening passage of this chapter. They have been separated into syllables to help you maintain an even rhythm when you pronounce them.

res-pec-to	prác-ti-ca-men-te	mo-men-to
a-ten-ción	re-pe-ti-da	le-tras
im-po-si-ble	con-tra-rio	i-na-cen-tua-do
e-jer-ci-cio	con-so-nan-tes	re-la-ja-do
pro-gre-so	di-fi-cul-tad	per-se-ve-ran-cia
rá-pi-do	len-gua-je	al-fa-be-to
e-fi-cien-te	fi-nal-men-te	o-cu-rre
re-quie-re	sis-te-ma	ca-rác-ter
há-bi-tos	ex-cep-ción	re-pre-sen-tan
re-la-ti-va-men-te[9]	his-tó-ri-co	ro-ma-no
pa-sa-je	cla-ro	co-rrec-ta-men-te
di-fe-ren-te	ten-den-cia	lon-gi-tud

---

[9]The suffix *-mente* corresponds to the English adverb-forming suffix *-ly*. When *-mente* is added to an adjective, the adjective keeps its original stress and the first syllable of the suffix is also stressed: *relativamente*.

Listening Passage for Chapter 2
English Translation

Read the English translation of the listening passage. This passage contains two parts. One refers to the basic dialog, which you are going to learn afterwards, and explains certain cultural matters related to this conversation; the other simply mentions the grammar points of the chapter. Then listen closely as the passage is read to you in Spanish. The numbers in parentheses will help you to pinpoint any specific fragment of the passage that you may wish to follow in the text as you listen.

(*The*) *English Classes at the Cultural Center*

(1) The Cultural Center is an educational and cultural institution established by the United States Information Agency—an administrative agency subordinate to the Department of State—in Spain and in each one of the countries of Latin America with which the United States maintains diplomatic relations. (2) Said institutions are sponsored jointly by the United States and the governments of these countries as a means to bring closer the relations between the peoples of Latin America and Spain and the North American people. (3) The cultural activities offered by these institutions are numerous and varied: There are lectures, films, art exhibits, concerts, dances, etc. But undoubtedly the

principal activity is (are) the English courses, which everybody (all the world)—men, women, old and young (children)—wants to attend.

(4) Today is the first day of classes at the Colombian–North American Cultural Center, which is situated in the city of Bogotá, capital of the Republic of Colombia. (5) In one of the classes the students are waiting for the teacher. One of them, Emilio Fonseca, is curious (has curiosity) to know who the teacher is and asks another student who is sitting beside him (at his side). (6) This other young man, whose name is Carlos María and his last name Terán Marín—Carlos María Terán Marín—explains to him that he doesn't know her name (last name), but that she is an American (young) woman. Emilio is glad to know that the teacher is a woman and not a man; according to him, women are better teachers than men. (7) He also wants to know what she's like (how she is). Carlos María explains to him that she's very pretty, blonde, with green eyes (eyes green). But that's not exactly what Emilio wants to know. He wants to know how she is as a teacher. Carlos María explains to him that she's a little strict but very good—so they say.

(8) (The) Colombians, and particularly (the) "bogotanos," that is (to say), the people from Bogotá, are well known (have fame) for being very formal in their personal relations and in their manner. Emilio and Carlos María give us a demonstration of this when they introduce each other (one to the other) with a great deal of ceremony, and when Carlos María then presents his sister, Luz María, who is seated next to him (at his side).

(9) Emilio greets Luz María with great formality and then, to make conversation, comments that Carlos María and his sister look (are) very much alike and asks if they are twins. But they're not; they're just brother and sister. (10) Carlos María notices that Emilio speaks with an accent that is not "bogotano" and asks him where he's from. Emilio is from Barranquilla, one of the most important seaports of Colombia, located on the north coast of the country.

Grammar Points

First, (the) agreement in gender and number between nouns, articles, and descriptive adjectives; second, position of (the) descriptive adjectives with respect to the noun; third, personal subject pronouns; fourth, the present tense of the verb **ser** (to be); fifth, interrogative words; and sixth, (the) formation of negative sentences with the particle **no**.

TO BE FOLLOWED BY
LISTENING RECOGNITION EXERCISE

Basic Dialog

Las clases de inglés en el Centro Cultural

E. *Emilio*   CM. *Carlos María*   LM. *Luz María*

I

E. Perdón, ¿sabe usted quién es el maestro?
CM. No sé su apellido, pero es una señorita americana.
E. ¡Qué bueno! Las mujeres son mejores como maestras. ¿Cómo es ella?
CM. Es muy bonita, rubia, de ojos verdes...
E. Sí, pero como maestra, ¿qué tal es?
CM. Ah, perdón. Dicen que es un poco estricta, pero muy buena.

II

E. Mi nombre es Emilio Fonseca, a sus órdenes.
CM. Carlos María Terán Marín, mucho gusto. Mi hermana, Luz María.
E. Encantado, señorita. ¡Qué parecidos son ustedes! ¿Son gemelos?
LM. No, somos hermanos nada más.
CM. ¿De dónde es usted, Emilio? Usted no es bogotano, ¿verdad?
E. No, soy de la costa, de Barranquilla.

< *El Ballet Nacional de Chile representando*
la obra Calaucán

(The) English Classes at the Cultural Center

E. *Emilio*   CM. *Carlos María*   LM. *Luz María*

I

E.   Excuse me, do you know who the teacher is?

CM.   I don't know her last name, but she's an American lady.[1]

E.   That's good;[2] women are better as teachers. What's she like?[3]

CM.   She's very pretty, blonde, with green eyes[4]. . . .

E.   Yes, but as a teacher, what's she like?[5]

CM.   Oh, excuse me. They say that she's a little strict, but very good.

II

E.   My name is Emilio Fonseca, how do you do.[6]

CM.   Carlos María Terán Marín, it's a pleasure.[7] My sister, Luz María.

E.   Delighted (miss). How much alike you two look! Are you twins?

LM.   No, we're just[8] brother and sister.[9]

CM.   Where are you from, Emilio? You're not a "bogotano,"[10] right?[11]

E.   No, I'm from the coast, from Barranquilla.

CULTURAL NOTES

A.   **A sus órdenes, mucho gusto,** and **encantado** (or **encantada**) are expressions frequently used to acknowledge introductions.

B.   Both men and women commonly have María as a second given name: Carlos María, Luz María.

C.   At least in official records, a person's family name is always his father's last name followed by his mother's maiden name. Some people omit the mother's maiden name in informal use; others retain it at all times. In the dialog, Emilio Fonseca prefers the short version of his last name, whereas Carlos María Terán Marín uses both names. If Carlos María should decide to use only one last name, it would be Terán, not Marín. On a visit to the United States, he would probably soon drop his mother's name to avoid being called "Mr. Marín."

PRONUNCIATION EXERCISES

r **after a consonant.** This *r* has exactly the same sound as the *r* between vowels and before a consonant. It is a single tap of the tongue against the gum ridge right above and behind the upper teeth. It is just as easy to learn to pronounce the *r* after a consonant as it was in the other two positions. Listen and repeat each combination of English letters and words and the corresponding Spanish word in the two columns below. Notice, however, that the first of the two letters is in brackets. This means that you are to pronounce the sound that letter represents. But the letter *d* that follows is not in brackets. This means that you are to say the *name* of the letter *d*, "dee." Then say the word that follows. Pronounce the three items fast and in very close succession.

---

[1] Miss, young woman.   [2] What good.   [3] How is she?   [4] Of eyes green.   [5] What such is?   [6] At your orders.   [7] Much pleasure.   [8] Nothing more.   [9] *Hermanos*, plural form of *hermano* (brother), refers to *hermano* and *hermana* (sister).   [10] Native of Bogotá.   [11] Truth.

[t]-d-stay	triste	(*sad*)	[g]-d-toe	grito	(*scream*)
[p]-d-mow	primo	(*cousin*)	[b]-d-Joe	brillo	(*shine*)
[k]-d-men	crimen	(*crime*)	[f]-d-toe	frito	(*fried*)

Now listen and repeat the following words with the same combination of a consonant plus *r*; many of them have other vowels besides *i* after the *r*. All the words in the first group appear in the basic materials of the first four chapters, so no English translation is necessary at this time.

gracias	estricta	trabajar	entramos
compra	treinta	escribe	hombre
maestro	trece	alegres	madre
tres	negro	frío	traje
cuatro	francés	prisa	sombrero
abra	otros	padre	preocupado

COGNATES
opresión	promesa	brusco	fruta
franco	tren	Francia	Africa[12]
Cristo	principal	fraternal	profesor

SUPPLEMENT

New vocabulary items are to be studied and memorized in context, within the framework of the related basic phrase or sentence, as shown in the example.

EXAMPLE: ¿Quién es el maestro?
muchacho
¿Quién es el muchacho?

I

¿Quién es el maestro?
alumno	*student*
muchacho	*boy*
chico	*boy*

Es una señorita.
una señora	*a (married) lady*
una mujer	*a woman*
un señor	*a gentleman*
un hombre	*a man*

¿Cómo es ella?
Cuál	*which (one)*

---

[12] *Africa* is stressed on the first syllable, and thus technically should have a written accent on the initial *A*. To avoid printing problems, however, accent marks are usually not written on capital letters.

Es muy bonita.

fea	*homely, ugly*	joven	*young*
alta	*tall*	mala	*bad, mean*
baja	*short, low*	simpática	*nice, pleasant, cute*
grande	*big*	antipática	*unpleasant*
pequeña	*short, small*	delgada	*thin, slender*
nueva	*new*	gorda	*fat*
vieja	*old*	tonta	*dumb, silly*

De ojos verdes

pelo negro   *black hair (hair black), brunette*

II

Mi hermana, Luz María

prima	*cousin*
amiga	*friend*
novia	*sweetheart, girlfriend*

¿De dónde es usted?

qué país	*what country*
qué lugar	*what place*
qué ciudad	*what city*

¿Son gemelos?

primos	*cousins*
amigos	*friends*

Las clases de inglés[13]

francés	*French*
español	*Spanish*

DIALOG AND SUPPLEMENT CHECK

SENTENCE RECALL

Say the dialog phrase or sentence in which each of the following words or phrases occurs.

EXAMPLE: el maestro
        ¿Sabe usted quién es el maestro?

apellido	Emilio Fonseca	americana
rubia	Carlos María Terán Marín	costa
las mujeres	gemelos	cultural
estricta	parecidos	bogotano
nada más	verdes	ojos

SENTENCE COMPLETION

Complete the following sentences by saying many complimentary or uncomplimentary things about the person named.

---

[13] Names of languages and nationalities are always written with lower-case letters.

EXAMPLE: La maestra es _____ .
        La maestra es una señorita (mujer, señora, etc.) **muy bonita, muy buena, muy joven,** etc.

1. Luz María es _____ .
2. Mi maestra es _____ .
3. Mi hermana es _____ .
4. Mi amiga es _____ .
5. Mi prima es _____ .
6. Mi mamá es _____ .

ITEM SUBSTITUTION

Repeat each of the following sentences, substituting a related word or phrase for the part in italics. If books are closed, your teacher will repeat the item at the end of each sentence.

EXAMPLE: No sé su *apellido,* pero es una señorita americana.
        No sé su *nombre,* pero es una señorita americana.

1. Perdón, ¿sabe usted quién es *el maestro?*
2. Pero como maestra, *¿qué tal es?*
3. Usted no es *bogotano,* ¿verdad?
4. Dicen que es *un poco* estricta.
5. ¡Qué parecidos son ustedes! ¿Son *gemelos?*
6. Es muy bonita, rubia, *de ojos verdes...*
7. No, somos *hermanos* nada más.
8. Es mi *hermana,* Luz María.

QUESTIONS

1. ¿Cuál es el apellido de Emilio?
2. ¿Cuál es el nombre completo de Carlos María?
3. Y usted, señorita, ¿cuál es su nombre? ¿Y su apellido?
4. ¿Sabe Carlos María el apellido de la maestra de su clase?
5. ¿Sabe usted?
6. ¿Cómo es la maestra de Emilio, bonita o fea?
7. ¿Es ella americana?
8. Y como maestra, ¿qué tal es ella?
9. ¿Son ustedes dos gemelos?
10. Y usted, señorita, y usted, señor, ¿qué son, hermanos, o amigos nada más?
11. Usted y usted, ¿son parecidos o no?
12. Según Emilio, ¿cómo son Carlos María y su hermana?
13. ¿De dónde son Carlos María y su hermana, de Colombia o de Venezuela?
14. Y ustedes, ¿son de los Estados Unidos[14] o de Canadá?
15. ¿Es Emilio bogotano o de la costa?
16. ¿Es su novia bonita o fea? ¿Grande o pequeña? ¿Gorda o delgada? ¿Vieja o joven? ¿Simpática o antipática? ¿Inteligente o tonta?

[*To be followed by* LISTENING RECOGNITION EXERCISE]

---

[14] United States.

Grammar

1. *Gender of nouns and modifiers*

Nouns

Masculine	*Feminine*
maestro	maestra
señor	señora
hombre	mujer
libro	ventana
nombre	clase

A. English commonly uses two entirely different nouns to distinguish male and female persons of the same category, for example, "brother" and "sister," "gentleman" and "lady," "man" and "woman." Also, other devices such as "male teacher" and "female teacher" are sometimes used. Spanish, on the other hand, typically uses the endings *-o* (masculine) and *-a* (feminine) for sex distinctions of this sort, for example, *maestro*, "male teacher," and *maestra*, "female teacher."

B. The ending *-a* is also used for the feminine counterpart of many nouns whose masculine form ends in a consonant, for example, *señor*, "gentleman," and *señora*, "lady."

C. In Spanish—as in English—there are also a number of masculine–feminine pairs made up of entirely different words, for example, *hombre*, "man," and *mujer*, "woman."

D. Unlike English, Spanish classifies as masculine or feminine *all* nouns, whether or not they refer to persons. For example, *libro*, "book," is masculine; *ventana*, "window," is feminine. In the case of nouns which do not refer to persons, "masculine" and "feminine" are only grammatical terms; Spanish speakers do not conceive of books as being somehow male and windows female. As a rule, nouns ending in *-o* are masculine and those ending in *-a* are feminine, regardless of what they refer to. Among the exceptions are *día*, "day," masculine, and *mano*, "hand," feminine.

E. Many nouns end in a consonant or some vowel other than *o* and *a*. Their gender is, in general, unpredictable. It must therefore be memorized, for example, that *nombre*, "name," is masculine and *clase*, "class," is feminine. In these cases it is often helpful to remember an article or some other modifier (see below).

GENDER SUBSTITUTION

Give the feminine counterpart of the following masculine nouns.

EXAMPLE: maestro
            maestra

amigo	chico	señor	primo	hermano	español[16]
alumno	muchacho	gemelo	novio	francés[15]	inglés[17]

---

[15] Frenchman. The feminine forms *francesa* and *inglesa* do not require a written accent since the stress falls on the next-to-last syllable. (See page 15.)   [16] Spaniard.   [17] Englishman.

Articles

	Masculine	Feminine
Definite	**el** libro *the book*	**la** clase *the class*
Indefinite	**un** libro *a book*	**una** clase *a class*

F. The Spanish definite (**el, la**) and indefinite (**un, una**) articles have forms for each gender and agree with the nouns they modify.

ARTICLE SUBSTITUTION

Read the following list of words, repeating each word and changing the definite article to the indefinite article, or vice versa.

EXAMPLES: la clase   un ojo
una clase **el ojo**

el inglés	la hermana	un permiso	un apellido
un perdón	la noche	una mujer	el gemelo
la clase	una tarde	la mañana	el nombre
el día	un hombre	un primo	el señor

Adjectives

Masculine	Feminine
1. un hombre **bueno** *a good man* 2. un chico **italiano** *an Italian boy*	una mujer **buena** *a good woman* una chica **italiana** *an Italian girl*
3. el chico **inglés** *the English boy*	la chica **inglesa** *the English girl*
4. el libro **grande** *the big book* 5. un maestro **joven** *a young (male) teacher*	la ventana **grande** *the big window* una maestra **joven** *a young (female) teacher*

G. Adjectives always agree in gender (masculine or feminine) with the nouns they modify.

H. Many adjectives end in *-o* or *-a*: *-o* when they modify a masculine noun, *-a* when they modify a feminine noun (examples 1 and 2).

 I. Adjectives of nationality that end in a consonant (unlike *italiano, -a*) add *-a* when they modify a feminine noun (example 3).

J. All other adjectives are invariable (examples 4 and 5).

K. As illustrated in all the examples above, descriptive adjectives normally follow the noun they modify.

EXPANSION WITH GENDER SUBSTITUTIONS

Give the form of the opposite gender for each of the nouns and modifiers contained in the following expanding phrases and sentences. Note that Spanish does not usually use a comma after the next-to-last word in a series (*alta, rubia y delgada*).

1. Una señora alta
    Un señor alto
    Una señora alta y rubia
    Un señor alto y rubio
    Una señora alta, rubia y delgada
    Una señora alta, rubia, delgada y simpática
    Una señora alta, rubia, delgada, simpática y joven

2. Mi amigo gordo
    Mi amigo gordo y tonto
    Mi amigo gordo, tonto y feo
    Mi amigo gordo, tonto y feo, pero simpático

3. El maestro es americano.
    El maestro es americano o inglés.
    El maestro es americano, inglés o italiano.
    El maestro es americano, inglés, italiano o español.
    El maestro es americano, inglés, italiano, español o francés.

4. La maestra es una mujer joven.
    La maestra es una mujer joven y alta.
    La maestra es una mujer joven, alta y delgada.
    La maestra es una mujer joven, alta, delgada y simpática.

5. ¿Es su novio muy gordo y muy bajo?
    ¿Es su novio muy gordo y muy bajo y muy feo?
    ¿Es su novio muy gordo y muy bajo y muy feo y muy viejo?
    ¿Es su novio muy gordo y muy bajo y muy feo y muy viejo, pero muy inteligente?

REPLACEMENT

For each word replacement, make all changes necessary to maintain agreement in gender between the noun and its modifiers. Follow the example.

1. El maestro es americano.   EXAMPLE
    La_____   La maestra es americana.
    _____ simpático.   El maestro es simpático.
    __ chica _____   La chica es simpática.
    _____ joven.   La chica es joven.
    El _____   El chico es joven.

28

2. La ciudad es muy bonita.
   El país _____
   _____ pequeño.
   __ clase _____
   El lugar _____

3. ¿Es una clase grande?
   _____ centro _____
   _____ enorme?
   _____ puerta _____
   _____ alta?
   _____ hombre _____

WRITTEN TRANSLATION

This is your first written assignment. Do not worry too much at this time about spelling errors, but be sure that you make the proper gender agreement between nouns and modifiers, and that you place the adjectives in the proper position.

1. A large city[18] and a small country[19]
2. The tall man and the short woman
3. A Spanish lady and a French man
4. The good place and the bad place[20]
5. A fat boy and a slender girl
6. The young girl and an old woman
7. The tall, slender girl is the French teacher (teacher of French), but she's not French.
8. The short, blonde lady with (the) green eyes is the English teacher, but she's not English.
9. The city of Bogotá is a very nice place.
10. Colombia is a very large country.

SENTENCE COMPLETION

Describe each of the following people, providing as many details as you can imagine. Concentrate on making the correct gender agreement with each subject.

1. Emilio Fonseca _____.
   Emilio Fonseca es un chico colombiano, alto, de pelo negro, etc.
2. La hermana de Carlos María _____.
3. La maestra de Carlos María _____.
4. Mi primo _____.
5. El amigo de mi hermana _____.
6. El maestro de francés _____.
7. Mi novia _____.

QUESTIONS

1. Señorita, ¿es su mamá alta o pequeña?
2. ¿Y su papá?
3. ¿Cómo es usted, señor? ¿Alto? ¿De ojos verdes? ¿Nada más?
4. ¿Verdad que su maestra es muy simpática?
5. ¿Qué es mejor en un hombre, el pelo negro o el pelo rubio?
6. Y en una mujer, ¿qué es mejor?
7. ¿Es la maestra de Emilio fea, gorda y antipática?
8. ¿Y cómo es la hermana de Carlos María?

[*To be followed by* LISTENING RECOGNITION EXERCISE]

---

[18] *Fem.*   [19] *Masc.*   [20] *Masc.*

2. *Plural of nouns and modifiers*

In addition to gender agreement, Spanish nouns and their modifiers show agreement in number. The formation of the plural in Spanish is the same for nouns and adjectives, and almost the same for articles.

	Nouns		**Adjectives**	
Singular	amigo	lugar	verde	mejor
Plural	amigos	lugares	verdes	mejores

Articles

	Definite		*Indefinite*	
	MASC.	FEM.	MASC.	FEM.
Singular	el	la	un	una
Plural	los	las	unos	unas

A. Singular nouns and adjectives ending in a vowel add -*s* to form the plural; those ending in a consonant add -*es*.

B. All of the forms of the articles follow the same pattern as nouns and adjectives, except for the masculine singular *el* and *un*. The usual English equivalent of *unos, unas* is "some."

EXPANSION WITH NUMBER SUBSTITUTIONS

Give the plural form of each of the following expanding phrases and sentences. *Note:* The plural of the verb form *es* is *son.*

1. El lugar es grande.
   Los lugares son grandes.
   El lugar es grande y viejo.
   El lugar es grande, viejo y feo.
   El lugar es grande, viejo, feo y malo.

2. Una maestra americana
   Una maestra americana, muy estricta
   Una maestra americana, muy estricta, pero buena
   Una maestra americana, muy estricta, pero buena y simpática

3. ¿Un hombre gordo?
   ¿Un hombre gordo y pequeño?
   ¿Un hombre gordo, pequeño y feo?
   ¿Un hombre gordo, pequeño, feo y tonto?

4. El americano es alto, ¿verdad?
   El americano es alto y gordo, ¿verdad?
   El americano es alto, gordo y rubio, ¿verdad?
   El americano es alto, gordo, rubio y joven, ¿verdad?

5. Sí, la maestra es una señorita.
   Sí sí, la maestra es una señorita muy bonita.
   Sí sí sí, la maestra es una señorita muy bonita: baja y rubia.
   Sí sí sí sí,[21] la maestra es una señorita muy bonita: baja, rubia y gorda.

QUESTIONS

Answer with complete sentences.
   1. ¿Son Carlos María y Luz María primos?
   2. ¿Son gemelos?
   3. ¿Son Carlos María y su hermana americanos o colombianos?
   4. ¿Y Emilio es colombiano? ¿Y Luz María?
   5. En general, ¿son las chicas francesas bonitas?
   6. ¿Son las mujeres buenas como maestras, en general?
   7. ¿Son los hombres buenos como maestros?
   8. ¿Son los hombres mejores que las mujeres como maestros?
   9. ¿Son ustedes dos hermanos, primos o amigos?
  10. ¿Son las maestras de inglés en el Centro Cultural de Bogotá americanas, inglesas o francesas?

3. *Subject pronouns*

Singular		Plural	
yo	*I*	nosotros, -as	*we*
tú	*you*		
usted	*you*	ustedes	*you*
él	*he*	ellos	*they*
ella	*she*	ellas	

vosotros, -as	*you*

A. Subject pronouns are normally omitted in Spanish, as can be seen from the following dialog lines.

No sé su apellido.	(*I*) *don't know her last name.*
Es muy bonita...	(*She*) *is very pretty . . . .*
¿Son gemelos?	*Are* (*you*) *twins?*
No, somos hermanos.	*No,* (*we*) *are brother and sister.*

---

[21] A series of *sí*'s or *no*'s spoken at a rapid pace one after the other, meaning emphatic approval or denial, is a common pattern among Spanish speakers.

Use of subject pronouns indicates emphasis.

Yo no sé su apellido.   I *don't know her last name* (but maybe somebody else does).
Ella es muy bonita.   She *is very pretty* (but her sister is a dog).
Nosotros somos hermanos.   We *are brother and sister* (but they are cousins).

B.   There are two words for "you" (singular), **tú** and **usted.** You should form the habit of using *usted,* since the use of *tú* places the speaker on an intimate basis with his listener, roughly equivalent to addressing a person by his first name in English. The acceptability of *tú* varies considerably from region to region, in accordance with differences in age, social position, degree of intimacy, and so on, among speakers. Because of this variation, you should not attempt to use *tú* freely until you have gained considerable proficiency in Spanish and have become acquainted with the relevant cultural patterns.

C.   The "familiar" plural form **vosotros**[22] is not used in everyday conversation or writing in Latin America, where **ustedes** is used as the plural of both *tú* and *usted.*

D.   The feminine plural forms *nosotras, vosotras,* and *ellas* are used only to refer to a group composed exclusively of females. In all other cases the masculine form is used.

E.   The English subject pronoun "it" has no commonly used Spanish counterpart: *¿Quién es?,* "Who is it?"

NOUN–PRONOUN CORRELATION

Listen to each of the following basic sentences of this and the preceding chapter. Then repeat the sentence, substituting a subject pronoun for each subject noun or adding one when the subject is not mentioned.

1. Buenos días, ¿cómo está?
    Buenos días, ¿cómo está usted?
2. ¿Cómo sigue el profesor Campos?
    ¿Cómo sigue él?
3. Es muy bonita.

4. Las mujeres son mejores que los hombres.
5. Pero como maestra, ¿qué tal es?
6. ¡Qué parecidos son ustedes! ¿Son gemelos?
7. No, somos hermanos nada más.
8. No, soy de la costa.

4. *Present tense of* ser, *to be*

yo	soy	*I am*
tú	eres	*you are*
usted ⎫	es	*you are*
él, ella ⎭		*he, she, it is*
nosotros, -as	somos	*we are*
ustedes ⎫	son	*you are (plural)*
ellos, ellas ⎭		*they are*

vosotros, -as	sois	*you are*

[22]The verb, object pronoun, and possessive adjective forms corresponding to *vosotros* will be shown but not included in the pattern drills. Your teacher will decide whether or not to add these forms.

Note that *usted* and *ustedes,* although they mean "you," take *third* person verb forms, like "he," "she," "it," and "they."

PARADIGM PRACTICE

Say the forms of the verb **ser** several times. This will enable you to do more effectively the pattern drills that follow. Say the forms alternately with and without the subject pronouns, thus:

First time	*Second time*
yo soy	soy
tú eres	eres
usted es, él es, ella es	es
nosotros somos	somos
ustedes son, ellos son, ellas son	son

PERSON–NUMBER SUBSTITUTION

Follow the example. Make sure that you also make the correct agreement between nouns and modifiers.

1. ¿Cómo es la *maestra,* simpática?
    (hombres)
    ¿Cómo son los hombres, simpáticos?
    (maestro, Luz María, señora, él, ella, francesas, ingleses, yo)
2. ¿De dónde es *usted?*
    (tú, nosotros, ustedes, su papá, ellos, yo)
3. *Yo soy de Colombia.*
    (los hermanos Terán Marín, Emilio, yo, nosotros, mi primo, usted, ustedes)

5. *Interrogative words*

qué	*what*	cuál, -es	*which (one)*
cómo	*how*	quién, -es	*who, whom*
dónde	*where*	por qué	*why*
cuánto, -a, -os, -as		*how much, how many*	

A. Listed above are the most common interrogative words in Spanish. The drills that follow will give you oral practice with them.
B. **Qué** used as an exclamatory word before an adjective corresponds to English "how."
    ¡Qué bueno!   *How nice!*
    ¡Qué parecidos!   *How similar!*

C. **Cuál** has a plural form, as does **quién.**

¿Cuál es?	*Which (one) is it?*
¿Cuáles son?	*Which (ones) are they?*
¿Quién es?	*Who is it (are you)?*
¿Quiénes son?	*Who are they (you)?*

D. **Cuánto** agrees in number and gender with the noun it modifies. Note that English uses "how much" for the singular, but "how many" for the plural.

¿**Cuánto** pelo?	*How much hair?*
¿**Cuánta** agua?	*How much water?*
¿**Cuántos** paises?	*How many countries?*
¿**Cuántas** novias?	*How many girlfriends?*

E. All interrogative words have a written accent on the stressed syllable.

F. In Spanish, prepositions always precede interrogative words.

¿**De** dónde es usted?	*Where are you from?*
¿**Con** qué se escribe "centro", con *s* o con *c*?	*How (With what) do you spell* centro, *with (an)* s *or with (a)* c?

YOU ASK THE QUESTIONS

Use interrogative words in questions that could elicit each of the following replies.

1. La maestra es de los Estados Unidos.
   ¿De dónde es la maestra?
2. Yo soy de México.
3. Mi nombre es José.[23]
4. Mi apellido paterno es Jiménez.
5. Mi apellido materno es Jijón.
6. Mi nombre completo es José Jiménez Jijón.[24]
7. Soy bueno, simpático, pequeño, y de pelo verde y ojos feos.
8. Yo soy alumno del Centro Cultural de Baja California.
9. Hay[25] seis alumnos en mi clase: mi papá, mi mamá, mi hermano, mi amigo Pedro, mi prima Luisa y yo.
10. Mi maestra de inglés es una señorita inglesa.
11. Ella es una chica gorda y muy baja, pero muy bonita.
12. Ella y yo somos novios.

SUBSTITUTION

Notice the use of *qué* as "how." Make sure that the adjectives agree with the nouns they modify.

1. ¿Mi novia? ¡Qué bonita es!
   ¿El Centro Cultural? ¡_____!
   ¿Las clases de español? ¡_____!

2. ¿El Profesor Campos? ¡Qué simpático es!
   ¿Los hermanos Terán Marín? ¡_____!
   ¿Nosotros? ¡_____!

---

[23] Use "which," not "what." [24] Make sure that you are pronouncing these *j*'s like the *ch* of the word "Bach." [25] There are.

3. ¿Los profesores americanos? ¡Qué estrictos son!
   ¿El profesor de francés? ¡_____!
   ¿Tú? ¡_____!
   ¿El papá de la chica? ¡_____!

[*To be followed by* LISTENING COMPREHENSION–SPEAKING EXERCISE]

6. *Negative sentences with* no

¿Es o no es el maestro?	*Are you or aren't you the teacher?*
No, no soy.	*No, I'm not.*

A. Any affirmative sentence, whether declarative or interrogative, can be made negative by placing the particle **no** before the verb.

B. *No* is also used alone, like *sí*. Therefore, when a question is answered with *no* first, followed by a negative verb construction, two *no*'s may occur in a sequence.[26]

AFFIRMATIVE ⟶ NEGATIVE

1. Usted es francés.
   Usted no es francés.
2. Yo soy de la capital.
3. Bogotá es la capital de Chile.
4. Es una ciudad muy grande.
5. Los colombianos somos muy simpáticos.
6. ¿Es usted americano?
7. ¿Habla usted español?
8. Ustedes son unos alumnos muy buenos.

EMPHATIC DENIAL

Answer the following questions with a rapid sequence of three *no*'s followed by a complete negative statement.

1. Perdón, ¿es usted el profesor de español?
   No no no, yo no soy el profesor de español.
2. ¿Es la ciudad de Nueva York la capital del estado?
3. ¿Son ustedes buenos en español?
4. ¿Es Rusia un país pequeño?
5. ¿Son las mujeres mejores que los hombres?
6. ¿Somos usted y yo parecidos?

CONVERSATION STIMULUS

The whole class answers by giving a full-utterance response[27] to each of the following questions, salutations, and information statements. You may agree or disagree with the information statements by starting your reply with *Sí, señor (señorita),...* or *No, señor,...* Your instructor will signal the yes and no

---

[26]Three, four, or five *no*'s in rapid sequence are also used by native speakers to indicate emphatic denial. See footnote 21 on page 31.

[27]A full-utterance response is a complete, meaningful phrase, which may or may not be a grammatically complete sentence.

answers. Don't be shy; let yourself go along with the others in the class, even if the first time you can give only a fraction of the correct answer. Follow the examples below.

1. Buenos días, señores (señoritas), buenos días.
   Buenos días, profesor, buenos días.
2. Yo soy un profesor estricto, ¿verdad?
   No señor, usted no es un profesor muy estricto.
3. ¿Son ustedes alumnos buenos?
4. Ustedes son de los Estados Unidos.
5. Bogotá es una ciudad muy bonita.
6. Carlos María y Luz María son bogotanos.
7. Bogotá es la capital de Venezuela.
8. Los Centros Culturales son instituciones muy importantes.
9. Luz María Terán Marín es la novia de Emilio Fonseca.
10. En los Estados Unidos hay ciudades viejas y ciudades nuevas.
11. Carlos María y su hermana son de la ciudad de Barranquilla.
12. Barranquilla es uno de los puertos principales de Colombia.
13. ¿De qué país son ustedes?
14. ¿Son las mujeres mejores estudiantes que los hombres?
15. Ustedes y yo somos amigos, ¿no es verdad?
16. Estados Unidos es un país muy grande y muy bonito.
17. La capital del estado de Nueva York es la ciudad de Nueva York.
18. Los americanos son muy simpáticos.
19. La clase de español es muy mala.
20. Perdón, ¿quién es el maestro de español?

Reading and Performing

Read the following dialogs several times each until you familiarize yourself with the lines and can put some feeling into them. Then close your books and try to act out each situation, without necessarily repeating all the lines verbatim.

Un alumno nuevo

PIRI. *Pirimpimpín*[28] PROF. *Profesor*

PIRI. Con permiso, buenas tardes.
PROF. Buenas[29], ¿qué tal[30]?
PIRI. Muy bien, señor, gracias. Perdón, ¿es usted el profesor de filosofía?
PROF. A sus órdenes.
PIRI. Yo soy uno de los nuevos alumnos. Mi nombre es Pirimpimpín Soto.
PROF. Ah, mucho gusto. ¿De dónde es usted, Pirimpimpín? Usted no es colombiano, ¿verdad?
PIRI. No, señor, soy peruano. Perdón, señor, ¿es verdad que usted es un profesor muy estricto?
PROF. ¡No no no no no, no es verdad, no es verdad!
PIRI. ¡Qué bueno, cuánto me alegro! Su clase es por la mañana, ¿no?
PROF. No, por la tarde.

---

[28]Pirimpimpín is a nickname. It is used here so that you will practice pronouncing a series of unstressed *i*'s, every one of which must sound as distinct and clear as the stressed *i* in the last syllable.

[29]*Buenas* (or *buenos*) alone is a common and less formal way of responding to any of the "good..." greetings (*buenos días; buenas tardes, noches*).

[30]"Hi," "How are you?"

PIRI.   Ah... Bien, con permiso, profesor, mucho gusto[31], hasta mañana, con permiso, por favor.

PROF.   Cómo no. Hasta luego.

Con Luis y Ana, sus nuevos amigos

PIRI.   Pst, Luis, ¿quién es la chica de pelo rubio y ojos verdes? ¡Qué fantástica, qué fenomenal, qué...!

LUIS.   Es mi hermana.

PIRI.   Oh, perdón.

LUIS.   ¿Por qué? ¡ANA! ¡ANA!

PIRI.   No, por favor, yo soy muy tímido.

ANA.   ¿Sí, Luis?

LUIS.   Pirimpimpín, mi hermana Ana.

PIRI.   Encantado, señorita. Pirimpimpín Soto, a sus órdenes.

ANA.   Mucho gusto.

Por la tarde, con Ana

PIRI.   Usted y su hermano son muy parecidos. Pero usted es mucho más bonita.

ANA.   Gracias, ¡qué simpático es usted!

PIRI.   Y su nombre es muy bonito, Ana.

ANA.   Mi nombre completo es Ana de los Angeles[32].

PIRI.   ¿Ana de los Angeles qué? ¿Cuál es su apellido?

ANA.   Montenegro. Ana de los Angeles Montenegro.

PIRI.   ¿Montenegro qué?

ANA.   Montenegro De Gaulle.

PIRI.   ¿De Gaulle? ¿Su mamá es francesa?

ANA.   No, ella es colombiana, pero de origen francés. Dicen que es descendiente de un hombre muy famoso en la historia de Francia.

Por la noche, con Ana

ANA.   Pirimpimpín, ¿cómo son las chicas peruanas?

PIRI.   Unas son altas, otras[33] son bajas, otras son gordas, otras son simpáticas, otras antipáticas...

ANA.   ¿Qué más?

PIRI.   ¿Qué más qué? Nada más. Ah, sí, son muy bonitas.

ANA.   ¿Muy *muy* bonitas?

PIRI.   Sí, pero ustedes las colombianas son muy muy *muy* bonitas.

[*To be followed by* LISTENING COMPREHENSION–SPEAKING EXERCISE]

---

[31] *Mucho gusto* can be used not only as "How do you do?" but also as "Very happy to have met you."

[32] *Angeles* is stressed on the first syllable.   [33] Others.

Listening Passage
for Chapter 3
English Translation

Sunday: An Outing in the Country

(1) During their summer or Easter vacations, groups of North American students usually (are accustomed to) visit some of the Latin American countries. These are short visits of two or three days in each country, but with lots of activity and fun, not only for the visitors but also for the students of the country they are visiting. The high school students and college freshmen are mainly the ones in charge of meeting and accompanying to outings and dances—in other words, those in charge of looking after (attending)—their friends from the North. (2) Right now (in these moments) there is a group (that is) visiting one of the small Central American countries, Costa Rica. Costa Rica, situated between Panama and Nicaragua, is a tiny republic of the tropics, with a population of a million and a half inhabitants. Its territorial extension is approximately half that of the state of New York. It is one of the most democratic and advanced countries in Latin America, although, like the other Central American republics, it is still an essentially agricultural country, coffee being its main product for export.

(3) The most beautiful and picturesque part of Costa Rica is the countryside, with its coffee, banana, and sugar plantations; with the poor (humble) but clean and cheerful homes of the peasants; with the impressive tropical vegeta-

tion; with the cows and the oxen and the horses and the chickens and the birds and the flowers that abound everywhere. Yes, the Costa Rican countryside is an ideal place for outings. (4) It is precisely at an outing in the country, in a place called Tres Ríos (Three Rivers), about ten or fifteen kilometers from San José, the capital, where this group of students, all girls from a high school in Florida, is right now. Accompanying them there is, naturally, a very large group of "ticos," as they call the Costa Ricans. Several of the young ladies are being waited on (attended) by two and three young men at a time.

(5) For example, over there in the shade of a magnificent (splendorous) mango tree is Vickie talking to Manuel and Jorge. Vickie says that she likes Costa Rica very much, that the outing is beautiful, and that everybody seems to be so gay. (6) Manuel then explains—jokingly, of course—that they are in a happy mood not only because they are on the outing but because the "ticos" are like that by nature; they are always cheerful people. (7) In the face of (before) such showing off (ostentation) Jorge intervenes to say that that's a lie, that the "ticos" are very dull, and that if now they look very happy it's because they, the American girls, are visiting Costa Rica.

(8) And way over there, walking by the bank of the river, we see beautiful Linda accompanied by Enrique and Hernán. It is almost one o'clock in the afternoon and Linda probably is tired from walking—although she says she isn't and she's not hungry (hasn't hunger). She says she's only thirsty (has thirst) and doesn't want to eat anything; she just wants to drink (take) something cold. (9) Enrique says that he'll be glad to go and get (with much pleasure he will bring) some Coca-Colas that are in the car. Hernán does not protest, naturally, and simply says that that's fine and that he and Linda will wait there. But Linda intervenes on behalf of poor Hernán, saying that she's not tired and suggesting that the three of them go look for the Cokes.

(10) Today is Sunday; this group of American students is going to be in Costa Rica until Tuesday. Then they're going to go to Nicaragua, where they're going to spend two days.

Grammar Points

First, the present tense of the verb **estar** (to be); second, the difference between the verbs **ser** and **estar;** third, learning how to tell time; fourth, the present tense of the verb **ir** (to go); fifth, the infinitive form of verbs; and sixth, the construction **ir a** + *infinitive* (to be going to).

TO BE FOLLOWED BY
LISTENING RECOGNITION EXERCISE

Chapter 3

Basic Dialog

Domingo: un paseo al[1] campo

VI. *Vickie*   MA. *Manuel*   JO. *Jorge*
LI. *Linda*   EN. *Enrique*   HE. *Hernán*

I

VI. ¡Qué lindo está el paseo! ¡Todos están tan alegres!

MA. Los ticos somos así por naturaleza; somos gente alegre.

JO. Mentira, Vickie, somos muy apagados. Hoy estamos alegres porque ustedes están en Costa Rica.

VI. Gracias, muy amable. Costa Rica me gusta mucho.

MA. ¿Le gusta, de veras? ¿Cuánto tiempo van a estar aquí?

VI. Hasta el martes. Luego vamos a Nicaragua. Allí vamos a pasar dos días.

II

LI. ¿Alguien sabe qué hora es? No tengo mi reloj.

EN. Es casi la una. ¿Ya tiene hambre? ¿Quiere comer?

LI. No, gracias, tengo sed solamente. Quiero tomar algo frío.

HE. En el carro están las Coca-Colas. ¿Vas a ir tú, Enrique? Linda y yo esperamos aquí, entonces.

EN. Sí, claro, con mucho gusto. Yo voy.

LI. ¿Por qué no vamos los tres? Yo no estoy cansada.

---

[1] Contraction of *a el* (to the).

Sunday: An Outing in the Country[2]

VI. *Vickie*   MA. *Manuel*   JO. *Jorge*
LI. *Linda*   EN. *Enrique*   HE. *Hernán*

I

VI.   What a nice outing![3] Everybody[4] looks[5] so happy![6]
MA.   We "ticos"[7] are naturally[8] like that; we are cheerful people.
JO.   That's not true,[9] Vickie, we're very dull. Today we are happy because you are in Costa Rica.
VI.   Thank you, that's nice of you.[10] I like Costa Rica very much.[11]
MA.   Do you like it, really? How long[12] are you going to be here?
VI.   Until Tuesday. Then we're going to Nicaragua. We're going to spend two days there.

II

LI.   Does anybody know what time it is? I don't have my watch.
EN.   It's almost one. Are you hungry[13] already? Do you want to eat?
LI.   No, thank you, I'm only thirsty.[14] I want to drink something cold.
HE.   The Coca-Colas are in the car. Are you going to go, Enrique? Linda and I will wait here, then.
EN.   Yes, of course, gladly.[15] I'll go.
LI.   Why don't the three of us go? I'm not tired.

CULTURAL NOTES

In Spanish-speaking areas Sunday is listed as the last day of the week, not the first. Rather than a day of rest, "el domingo" (morning and afternoon) is a day for festivities and all kinds of outdoor and indoor activities. People go to church, but they also go on picnics, to the stadium (the most important sports events and other spectacles take place on Sunday), dancing, to the movies, and to birthday parties. Presidential elections usually occur on Sunday, and in some countries the winners are drawn in the national lottery on that day.

PRONUNCIATION EXERCISES

The "double r." You have already studied the pronunciation of the "single *r*"; in addition, Spanish has another *r*-type sound, traditionally called "double *r*" (*erre*). This traditional name is a handy label, but it is slightly misleading on two counts: (1) the sound in question is spelled *rr* between vowels (*carro*, *perro*), but with a single *r* at the beginning of a word (*rubia*, *reloj*) and after *n*, *l*, or *s* (*Enrique*, *alrededor*, *Israel*); (2) the "double *r*" usually consists of a rapid series of three, four, or five—not just two—taps of the tongue against the top of the mouth. In extremely emphatic pronunciation there may be as many as ten or more taps.

   Normal American English has no sound even approximately like Spanish "double *r*." This sound is produced by placing the tongue in roughly the position for *t* or *d*, and then expelling air forcefully over the top of the tongue. This makes the tip—which must be relaxed—flutter like a flag. See the diagram at the top of page 43.

---

[2]Countryside.   [3]How beautiful is the outing.   [4]All.   [5]Are.   [6]In a festive mood.   [7]Nickname for Costa Ricans.   [8]By nature.
[9]Lie.   [10]Very kind.   [11]Costa Rica pleases me much.   [12]How much time.   [13]Have you hunger.   [14]I have thirst.   [15]With much pleasure.

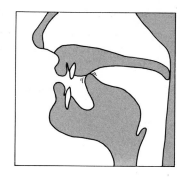

Try now to produce a series of "double *r*'s," first in long spurts and then in shorter ones. The sound should be something like an imitation of a small motor, like this:

rrrrrrrrrrrrrrrrrrrrrrrrrr
rrrrrrrrrrr rrrrrrrrrrr
rrrrr rrrrr rrrrr rrrr

Now listen and repeat the following nonsense jingle.

Erre con erre cigarro
Erre con erre barril
Rápidos corren los carros
Del ferrocarril

It is absolutely essential not to confuse "single *r*"—exactly one tap—with "double *r*"—more than one tap. For Spanish speakers, these two sounds are just as different as *t* and *d* or *m* and *n*. Many pairs of words are distinguished *solely* by the contrast between the two kinds of *r*. Listen and repeat the following examples.

caro	(*expensive*)	carro	(*car*)
cero	(*zero*)	cerro	(*hill*)
ahora	(*now*)	ahorra	(*he economizes*)
coro	(*choir*)	corro	(*I run*)
pero	(*but*)	perro	(*dog*)

Listen and repeat the following words. Since they are all included within the basic material of the first five chapters, an English translation for the words you do not yet know is unnecessary at this time.

cierre	reloj	Enrique
rubia	carro	ropa
Costa Rica	ratito	arroz

COGNATES

horrible	Rusia	cigarro	roca
terrible	Puerto Rico	errático	resto
rápido	ruinas	irritación	ocurre

SUPPLEMENT

Study and memorize the new vocabulary items in context, within the framework of related basic phrases or sentences, as in the preceding chapter.

I

Un paseo al campo

al mar	*to the sea*
al lago	*to the lake*
al río	*to the river*
a la playa	*to the beach*
a la montaña	*to the mountain*

¡Todos están tan alegres!

contentos	*happy, satisfied*
tristes	*sad*
ocupados	*busy*
preocupados	*worried*
aburridos	*bored*

Luego vamos a Nicaragua.

Después	*afterwards*
Antes	*before*
También	*also*
Siempre	*always*

¿Cuánto tiempo van a estar aquí?

estudiar	*to study*
trabajar	*to work*
hablar	*to talk*
esperar	*to wait, hope*

Allí vamos a pasar dos días.

una semana	*a week*
un mes	*a month*
un año	*a year*
un ratito	*a little while*

¡Qué lindo está el paseo!

el cielo	*the sky*
¡Qué linda está la fiesta!	*the party*
la casa	*the house*

II

Es casi la una.

apenas	*barely*

¿Alguien sabe qué hora es?

Nadie	*nobody*
Todo el mundo	*everybody*[16]

¿Ya tiene hambre?

Todavía	*still*

No, tengo sed.

calor	*hot*[17]
frío	*cold*
sueño	*sleepy*[18]
miedo	*afraid*[19]
prisa	*in a hurry*[20]

Quiero tomar algo.

hacer	*to do, to make*
decir	*to say*
ver	*to see*

Quiero tomar algo frío.

caliente	*hot*[21]

En el carro están las Coca-Colas.

En el carro está la cerveza.

la leche	*the milk*
el agua	*the water*[22]
el café	*the coffee*
el té	*the tea*
	the beer

---

[16] All the world. [17] Heat. [18] Sleep. [19] Fear. [20] Haste. [21] *Caliente* is an adjective, "hot"; *calor* is a noun. [22] Although *agua* is a feminine noun, it takes the article *el*. All other modifiers are feminine (*agua fría, las aguas*, etc.).

DIALOG AND SUPPLEMENT CHECK

SENTENCE RECALL

Say the dialog phrase or sentence in which each of the following words or phrases occurs.

Costa Rica	Coca-Colas	por naturaleza
alegres	reloj	de veras
Nicaragua	hora	hambre
apagados	martes	sed
cansada	mucho gusto	esperamos

NEXT-SENTENCE REJOINDERS

Say the dialog sentence that follows the one you hear.

1. ¡Qué lindo está el paseo!
   ¡Todos están tan alegres!
2. ¿Vas a ir tú, Enrique?
3. ¿Alguien sabe qué hora es?
4. No tengo mi reloj.
5. Mentira, Vickie, somos muy apagados.
6. ¿Quiere comer?
7. Quiero tomar algo frío.
8. ¿Cuánto tiempo van a estar aquí?

ITEM SUBSTITUTION

Repeat each of the following phrases or sentences, substituting one or more related words or phrases for the one in italics. If books are closed, your teacher will repeat the item to be substituted.

EXAMPLE: Allí vamos a pasar *un mes*.
       Allí vamos a pasar dos días.
       Allí vamos a pasar una semana.
       Etc.

1. Un paseo *a la montaña*.
2. *¿Nadie* sabe qué hora es?
3. Allí vamos a pasar *un ratito*.
4. ¿Cuánto tiempo van a *esperar* allí?
5. ¡Todos están tan *cansados!*
6. ¡Qué lindo está *el cielo!*
7. ¿Cuánto tiempo van a *trabajar* allí?
8. *¿Alguien* sabe qué hora es?
9. *Después* vamos a Nicaragua.
10. Un paseo *al río*.

QUESTIONS

1. ¿En qué país están Vickie y Linda?
2. ¿En qué parte de Costa Rica están, en una ciudad?
3. ¿Está Vickie con uno o con dos muchachos?
4. ¿Quiénes son ellos? ¿Cuáles son los nombres?
5. ¿Cómo está el paseo, alegre o triste?
6. ¿Están todos aburridos?
7. Según Manuel, ¿cómo son los ticos por naturaleza?

8. ¿Y según Jorge?
9. ¿Cuánto tiempo más van a estar las chicas en Costa Rica?
10. ¿Y adónde[23] van a ir después?
11. ¿Cuánto tiempo van a pasar ellas en Nicaragua?
12. ¿Está Costa Rica al norte o al sur de Nicaragua?
13. Y Linda, ¿con quiénes está ella?
14. ¿Sabe Linda qué hora es? ¿Por qué no sabe?
15. ¿Qué hora es en el paseo?
16. ¿Tiene hambre Linda? ¿Tiene sueño? ¿Tiene frío? ¿Qué tiene?
17. ¿Quiere ella tomar algo caliente?
18. Y usted, ¿tiene calor o tiene frío?
19. ¿Y usted no tiene hambre? ¿Qué quiere comer?
20. ¿Y usted tiene sed? ¿Qué quiere tomar, cerveza o té?
21. ¿Cómo está el día hoy, bonito o feo?
22. ¿Quiere usted ir a un paseo mañana o ahora?
23. ¿Adónde quiere ir, a un lago, a la playa o adónde?
24. ¿No le gusta a usted la clase de español? ¿De veras?
25. ¿Quiere estudiar más ahora?

[*To be followed by* LISTENING RECOGNITION EXERCISE]

Grammar

7. *Present tense of* estar, *to be*

yo	estoy
tú	estás
usted ⎱ él, ella ⎰	está
nosotros, -as	estamos
ustedes ⎱ ellos, ellas ⎰	están

vosotros, -as	estáis

PARADIGM PRACTICE

Say the forms of the verb **estar** several times. Alternate saying them with and without the subject pronouns. This will enable you to do more effectively the pattern drills that follow. The *vosotros* form should be included in this practice if your teacher wishes to include it in the pattern drills.

---

[23](To) where.

If the cue for substitution is given in English, do not say the subject or subject pronoun. Follow the example.

1. Ahora estamos aquí.
   (the girls)
   Ahora están aquí.
   (I)
   Ahora estoy aquí.
   (you and I, they, you [*fam.*],[24] Vickie and Linda, all of us)
2. Todos están tan alegres.[25]
   (yo, las alumnas, el paseo, tú, Enrique y Hernán, todos, usted y yo, él)
3. ¿Dónde está Costa Rica?[26]
   (Centroamérica, las montañas, nosotros, el mar, el río, ellos)

Concentrate not only on **estar** but on making the correct number–gender agreement between subject and modifiers. Follow the example.

1. Yo no estoy cansada.
   Jorge _____
   Jorge no está cansado.
   _____ estoy _____
   Nosotros _____
   _____ ocupadas.
   Ellos _____
   _____ estás _____
   _____ aburrido.
   Vickie y Linda _____

2. El cielo está lindo.
   __ casa _____
   _____ fantástica.
   __ paseo _____
   _____ aburrido.
   Ella y yo[27] _____
   _____ estás ___
   _____ preocupado.
   Todo el mundo __

3. ¡Qué bonito está el paseo!
   _____ montañas!
   _____ está _____
   _____ verde _____
   _____ mar!
   _____ fantástico _____
   _____ playa!

---

[24]Familiar (the *tú* form).

[25]Remember that adjectives not ending in *-o*, *-a* change form to show agreement in number but not in gender.

[26]Make sure that you are pronouncing a very strong double *r* in *Costa Rica*.

[27]If *yo* is a male, then use the masculine plural form to agree with subject.

8. *ser vs.* estar

---

estar
A. *Location*

    1. ¿Dónde **está** Bogotá? **Está** en Colombia.   *Where is Bogotá? It's in Colombia.*

    2. ¿Dónde **está** María? **Está** aquí.   *Where is María? She's here.*

B. *Condition*

    3. ¿Cómo **está** María? **Está** muy cansada.   *How is María? She's very tired.*

ser

    4. ¿Quién **es** María? **Es** una chica.   *Who is María? She's a girl.*

    5. ¿Qué **es** María? **Es** colombiana.   *What is María? She's Colombian.*

    6. ¿De dónde **es** María? **Es** de Colombia.   *Where's María from? She's from Colombia.*

    7. ¿Cómo **es** María? **Es** muy alegre.   *What's María like? She's very cheerful (a very cheerful person).*

    8. ¿Qué día **es** hoy? Hoy **es** domingo.   *What's today? Today is Sunday.*

    9. ¿Qué hora **es**? **Es** casi la una.   *What time is it? It's almost one.*

A. Both *ser* and *estar* mean "to be." For Spanish speakers, however, these two verbs are just as different as "do" and "make" (both *hacer* in Spanish) or "say" and "tell" (both *decir* in Spanish) are for English speakers.

    As shown in the chart above, *estar* is used in just two cases (a third will be added in Chapter 4): to refer to the *location* of a person or thing, and to refer to the *condition* of a person or thing at a particular time. *Ser* covers all other meanings of "to be," which are many and varied (examples 4 through 9 provide a small sample). Thus your learning task is relatively simple. When confronted with making a choice between *ser* and *estar,* you ask two questions: "Location of something?" If so, *estar.* "Condition of something at a particular time?" If so, *estar.* If the answer to both questions is "no," then *ser,* regardless of meaning. In time you will learn to make the choice automatically, without having to go through the steps of asking these questions consciously.

B. The only sentences in which either *ser* or *estar* may be used are those with predicate adjectives (examples 3 and 7). *Ser* expresses the normal, characteristic, usual classification of the subject as to appearance, personality, intelligence, size, etc. (*María es bonita, es simpática, es inteligente, es alta,* etc.). *Estar,* on the other hand, expresses the state of appearance, health, etc., that the subject happens to be in at a particular time. Obviously, the state or condition of a subject at a particular time (*estar*) may or may not coincide with the normal, characteristic classification (*ser*). This is illustrated in the basic dialog of this chapter: Manuel says that Costa Ricans are characteristically cheerful (**somos así por naturaleza**); Jorge denies this, saying that they are normally dull (**somos muy apagados**); whatever the correct facts are about the usual nature of Costa Ricans, they happen to be happy on this particular occasion because of the American girls (*Hoy **estamos** alegres porque ustedes están en Costa Rica*).

    Similar distinctions are often made in English with some word other than "be"; for example, *María **es** muy bonita, pero **está** fea en la foto,* "María is very pretty, but she *looks* ugly in the photo"; *El café **está** bueno porque **es** café bueno,* "The coffee *tastes* good because it's good coffee."

    Some predicate adjectives are normally used only with *estar.* These are adjectives that describe a situation usually thought of as out-of-the-ordinary or as a departure from a norm: *ocupado* (busy), *enfermo* (sick), *preocupado* (worried), etc.

After having carefully read the preceding discussion, listen to each of the following English sentences and decide whether the same sentence in Spanish would require the *ser* verb form or the *estar* verb form given alongside it. *Note:* Do not translate the sentences.

1. How is your mother this morning? (*Es* or *está?*)
2. Where are you from, my friend? (*Eres* or *estás?*)
3. What's that? (*Es* or *está?*)
4. Do I look okay with this hat? (*Soy* or *estoy?*)
5. What nationality is your uncle? (*Es* or *está?*)
6. What does he look like? (*Es* or *está?*)
7. You must be tired. (*Ser* or *estar?*)
8. Who is that man over there? (*Es* or *está?*)
9. Well, here we are. (*Somos* or *estamos?*)
10. You sound very intelligent today. (*Eres* or *estás?*)
11. But I am intelligent! (*Soy* or *estoy?*)
12. Sorry. Are we friends? (*Somos* or *estamos?*)
13. Don't bother me, I'm busy! (*Soy* or *estoy?*)
14. What day is today? (*Es* or *está?*)
15. What beautiful eyes she has. One is green, the other one black. (*Es* or *está?*)

PAIRED QUESTIONS

The first question must be answered affirmatively. Follow the example.

1. ¿Está usted triste?
   Sí, estoy triste.
   ¿Por qué está triste?
   Porque yo soy así por naturaleza.
2. ¡Qué estricta está la maestra hoy! ¿No?
   ¿Por qué está tan estricta?
3. ¿Está Pedro muy gordo en la foto?
   ¿Pero por qué está tan gordo?
4. ¿Están aburridos los alumnos?
   ¿Por qué? ¿Es una clase aburrida?[28]
5. ¡Qué bonita está Teresita con su vestido[29] nuevo! ¿No?
   Pero ella no está bonita por[30] el vestido nada más, ¿no?
6. ¡Qué inteligentes estamos todos hoy! ¿No es verdad?
   ¿Y por qué estamos todos tan inteligentes?

QUESTIONS

1. ¿Emilio Fonseca? ¿De la costa?
   Sí, Emilio Fonseca es de la costa.
2. ¿Vickie y Linda? ¿En Costa Rica?
   Sí, Vickie y Linda están en Costa Rica.
3. ¿Qué? ¿Casi la una?

---

[28]In this case *aburrida* means "boring."   [29]Dress.   [30]Because of.

4. ¿Usted? ¿Muy bien?
5. ¿Ustedes? ¿De los Estados Unidos?
6. ¿Carlos María? ¿Hermano de Luz María?
7. ¿Ellos? ¿Gemelos?
8. ¿Yo? ¿Americano?
9. ¿Los rusos[31]? ¿Aquí?
10. ¿Usted y yo? ¿Amigos?
11. ¿Mañana? ¿Domingo?
12. ¿Su papá? ¿Muy bien?

[*To be followed by* LISTENING COMPREHENSION–SPEAKING EXERCISE]

9. *The time of day*

¿Qué hora es?	*What time is it?*
Es la una y cuarto.	*It's a quarter past one.*
Es la una y media[32].	*It's one thirty.*
Es la una en punto.	*It's one on the dot.*
Son las dos de la mañana.	*It's two in the morning.*
Son las tres y cinco.	*It's five past three.*
Son las cuatro menos cinco.	*It's five to four.*

A. Normally, when asking the time of day, the third person singular of *ser* is used. In responding to the question, *es* is used for the hour of one, *son* for all the other hours.

B. There is no Spanish counterpart for the phrase "o'clock."

C. The feminine article is always used before the number indicating the hour.

D. The period of the day is expressed by the phrases *de la mañana, de la tarde,* and *de la noche.*

E. Fractions of the hour are generally expressed with the words *y* (and) and *menos* (less).

TELLING TIME: THE HOURS

Practice saying the hours of the day in order several times. Use *es* for the hour of one and *son* for the rest. Add the period of the day (*de la mañana, de la tarde, de la noche*).

EXAMPLE: **Es la una de la mañana. Son las dos de la mañana.** Etc.

TELLING TIME: HOURS WITH FRACTIONS

Practice saying the hours of the day plus (*y*) and minus (*menos*) all the fractions represented by five-minute intervals.

EXAMPLE: **Es la una en punto. Es la una y cinco. Es la una y diez. Es la una y cuarto (quince).** Etc.

---

[31] Russians.   [32] Half.

50

Read the following times of the day in Spanish.

It's:

5 after 8.	5 past 5.
10 a.m.	5 till 5.
9:30 p.m.	15 (a quarter) past 4.
1:15 p.m.	15 (a quarter) to 4.
2:30 a.m.	11:20 p.m.
12:10 p.m.	10 of 3.
1:25 p.m.	8:25 a.m.
7 p.m. sharp.	6:45 a.m.

10. *Present tense of* ir, *to go*

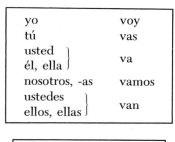

yo	voy
tú	vas
usted	
él, ella	va
nosotros, -as	vamos
ustedes	
ellos, ellas	van

vosotros, -as	vais

A. The verb endings for **ir** are the same as those for *estar*.

B. *Ir* requires the preposition *a* (to) before any noun or verb complement (*Voy a casa; allí vamos a pasar dos días*).

C. *Vamos* also means "let's go."

PARADIGM PRACTICE

Say the forms of the verb *ir* several times until you are ready to do the pattern drills that follow. Repeat the forms one time with the subject pronouns, the next time without them.

PERSON—NUMBER SUBSTITUTION

1. Tú siempre vas a la montaña, ¿verdad?
   (Jorge, Manuel y yo, los hermanos de Luz María, ustedes, alguien, yo, tú)
2. ¿Adónde van ustedes?
   (yo, Vickie y Linda, su primo, nosotros, tú)

11. *The infinitive form of verbs*

-ar	-er	-ir
estar	ser	ir
pasar	hacer	decir
tomar	comer	
estudiar	ver	
trabajar		
hablar		
esperar		

A. The infinitive is the form of a verb from which the verb takes its name. It corresponds to the English verb form that is usually preceded by the particle "to": *ser o no ser,* "to be or not to be."

B. In Spanish, all infinitives end in *r* preceded by *a, e,* or *i.* There are then three groups of verbs, as shown in the chart above. Of the three, the largest is the *-ar* group. In fact, any new verb that comes into the language is almost invariably assigned to this group.

C. The infinitive often serves as the complement, or object, of another verb.[33] Infinitive complements are sometimes preceded by the preposition *a* (*Allí vamos a pasar dos días*), sometimes not (*Quiero tomar algo frío*). The presence or absence of *a* is determined by the preceding verb (*vamos a, quiero*), not by the infinitive (*pasar, tomar*).

TRANSLATION

In all translation drills, use *usted* for "you" unless otherwise specified.

1. I want to be somebody.
2. Why do you want to study Spanish?
3. Because I want to go to Costa Rica.
4. Don't you want to work here?
5. What do you want to do now?
6. I want to say something.
7. What do you want to say?
8. I'm hungry; I want to eat something hot.
9. Do you want to see something?
10. No, I want to wait in the car.

12. *The construction* ir a + infinitive, *to be going to*

¿Cuánto tiempo **van a estar** aquí?	*How long are you going to be here?*
Allí **vamos a pasar** dos días.	*There we're going to spend two days.*
¿**Vas a ir** tú, Enrique?	*Are you going to go, Enrique?*

As in English, this construction is very frequently used to refer to the future.

---

[33] This will be taken up in more detail in Chapter 13.

PERSON–NUMBER SUBSTITUTION

If the cue is given in English, do not include the subject or subject pronoun in your response.

1. ¿Cuánto tiempo van a estar aquí?
   (we, you [*fam.*], Carlos María and his sister, Emilio, I, they, you and I)
2. Allí vamos a pasar dos días.
   (they, I, my sister, Vickie and Linda, we, he, you [*pl.*])
3. ¿Vas a ir tú?
   (nosotros, ustedes, yo, Enrique, Enrique y Hernán, todos ellos)

ALTERNATE SUBSTITUTION

1. ¿Cuánto tiempo van a estar aquí?
   _____ trabajar __
   _____ vamos _____
   ¿Por qué _____
   _____ voy _____
   _____ comer ___
   ¿Qué _____
   _____ hacer ___

2. Yo no voy a ir allí.
   Nosotros _____
   _____ comer _____
   Vickie _____
   _____ estudiar _____
   _____ vas _____
   _____ ir _____
   Yo _____

WRITTEN TRANSLATION

This is your second writing assignment. This time try to eliminate any spelling errors you may have made in your first assignment. The following are some features of spelling and punctuation you must begin to learn.

A. Spanish uses question and exclamation marks at both ends of a sentence. Those at the beginning are inverted and should be written slightly below the line, thus:

$$\text{¿——————————————?}$$
$$\text{¡——————————————!}$$

B. The sound [k] is spelled *qu* before *e* or *i*, and *c* elsewhere (see the chart on page 13). The letter *k* is used only in *ka* (the name of the letter itself) and a few other exceptional words.

C. For the use of accent marks, consult pages 15 and 16. In addition, a written accent must be used on any *i* or *u* next to another vowel when the *i* or *u* is stressed (*María, país, continúa*); on the stressed syllable of all interrogative and exclamatory words (*qué, cuánto, dónde*, etc.); and to differentiate between certain one-syllable homonyms (*si*, "if"; *sí*, "yes").

D. Now proceed with the exercise. When you translate, do not use subject pronouns every time they appear in English, but only when you think they are necessary for emphasis.

1. What a[34] beautiful day it is going to be tomorrow!
2. What are we going to do?
3. I'm going to go to a picnic in the morning and a party in the evening (night).
4. It's going to be a beautiful party!
5. Are you going to go with someone?
6. No, I'm not going to go with anyone (nobody).
7. But we're going to have a good time (to be *alegres*).

———————

[34] Do not translate "a"; just say, "What beautiful . . . !"

8. What are the ladies going to drink, tea?
9. I don't know. The men are going to drink beer.
10. Aren't you going to go, Carlos María?
11. No, I don't want to go; I'm going to study.
12. They[35] say that some very pretty English and American girls are going to be there, too.
13. Carlos María is afraid. He's not going to go because he's afraid.
14. I'm not afraid! Very well, I'm going to go and I'm going to drink lots of (much) beer, and I'm going to . . . .

QUESTIONS

Base your answers on the preceding exercise.

1. ¿Cómo va a ser el día de mañana?
2. ¿Qué van a hacer ustedes?
3. ¿Adónde va a ir usted en la mañana? ¿Y en la noche?
4. ¿Cómo va a ser la fiesta?
5. ¿Va a ir usted con alguien?
6. ¿Van a estar todos muy alegres o muy tristes?
7. ¿Qué van a tomar las señoritas?

8. Y los hombres, ¿qué van a tomar ellos?
9. ¿Va a ir Carlos María?
10. ¿Qué va a hacer él?
11. ¿Van a ir chicas bonitas o feas a la fiesta?
12. ¿De qué nacionalidad, italianas y francesas?
13. ¿Carlos María va a ir, finalmente?
14. ¿Qué va a hacer él en la fiesta?

SUBSTITUTION AND ENGLISH MEANING

Change each of the following sentences to the "going to" form. Then give the English equivalent of the new sentence.

1. ¿Quién es el maestro?
   ¿Quién va a ser el maestro?
   Who's the teacher going to be?
2. Es muy gorda.
3. Somos amigos.
4. ¡Qué lindo está el paseo!

5. Yo voy.
6. Yo no estoy cansada.
7. Linda y yo esperamos aquí, entonces.
8. ¿Quién habla español aquí?
9. Es casi la una.
10. ¡Todos están tan alegres!

[*To be followed by* LISTENING COMPREHENSION–SPEAKING EXERCISE]

CONVERSATION STIMULUS

The whole class gives a full-utterance rejoinder to each of the following statements and questions. Your teacher will signal the yes and no answers. In answering yes or no, give three very quick *sí*'s or *no*'s in sequence, and then the rest of your answer. Follow the examples below.

1. Hoy vamos a trabajar mucho, ¿no?
   ¡No no no! ¡Hoy no vamos a trabajar mucho!
2. ¿Son ustedes muy buenos alumnos?
   ¡Sí sí sí! ¡Somos muy buenos alumnos!
3. ¿En qué país están Linda y Vickie ahora?

---

[35]Do not translate.

54

4. ¿Hasta qué día van a estar allí?
5. Y luego, ¿adónde van a ir?
6. No es verdad. Ellas van a ir a México después.
7. Ustedes son muy simpáticos.
8. Yo soy muy simpático también.
9. Ustedes están en Nicaragua ahora.
10. ¿Cuántos días van a pasar las muchachas americanas en Nicaragua?
11. ¿Están Linda y Vickie contentas o tristes en el paseo?
12. ¿Son ustedes inteligentes y simpáticos por naturaleza?
13. ¿Están ustedes muy ocupados?
14. Yo estoy muy triste y muy preocupado.
15. A Vickie le gusta Manuel y a Linda le gusta Enrique.[36]

Reading

Muy parecidos

Mi nombre es Pancho, Pancho Jijón, primo hermano[37] de José Jiménez por parte de padre; la mamá de José y mi papá son hermanos, hermanos gemelos. José y yo también somos muy parecidos, excepto que él es de un temperamento muy triste y yo soy muy alegre; él es muy bajo y gordo y yo muy alto y delgado; él siempre tiene hambre y yo siempre tengo sed; él es de la ciudad y yo soy del[38] campo; él quiere estudiar inglés y yo voy a estudiar francés; a él le gusta la cerveza mexicana nada más, y a mí me gusta la cerveza americana, la cerveza francesa, la cerveza china y la cerveza japonesa.

Mañana por la noche voy a ir a la casa de José; estoy invitado a comer enchiladas y tamales[39] en su casa. Pero no vamos a tomar cerveza, vamos a tomar algo un poco más fuerte[40], tequila. Después él y yo vamos a visitar a[41] dos chicas mexicanas muy bonitas, según José. Yo estoy un poco preocupado porque soy muy tímido, pero después del tequila... ¡Quién sabe, mi amigo! ¡Vamos a pasar un ratito muy alegre mañana!

QUESTIONS

1. Pancho y José son hermanos, ¿no?
2. ¿Qué son, entonces?
3. ¿Por qué son primos hermanos?
4. ¿Son muy parecidos?
5. ¿Excepto qué? ¿Y qué más?
6. ¿Adónde va a ir Pancho mañana?
7. ¿Va Pancho mañana por la mañana, por la tarde o por la noche?
8. ¿Está invitado a comer qué?
9. ¿Van a tomar cerveza?
10. ¿Y después qué van a hacer?
11. ¿Por qué está preocupado Pancho?

---

[36]To Vickie Manuel is pleasing and to Linda Enrique is pleasing.
[37]First cousin. [38]Contraction of *de el* (from the). [39]Mexican dishes. [40]Strong. [41]The so-called "personal *a*" precedes verb objects that refer to human beings.

Performing

Read the following dialog several times until you are able to put some feeling into the lines. Then act out a similar situation, expanding the conversation with other subjects, such as asking the other person if he is hungry, etc., but leaving the names out until the very end.

Error

A. ¡Ah! ¡Francisco! Mi amigo, ¿cómo está usted?

B. ¡Ah! ¡Buenos días, mi amigo! ¡Mucho gusto! ¿Qué tal está?

A. Estoy bien, muchas gracias. Está muy bonito el día, ¿no es verdad?

B. Sí, ¡está fantástico! ¡Pero usted está muy bien! Está un poco más gordo, nada más, pero ¡está muy bien!

A. Gracias, muchas gracias. Y... ¿cómo están todos en su familia, Francisco?

B. Todos están bien, gracias. ¿Y qué tal su familia, Alfredo, cómo están todos?

A. Pero mi nombre no es Alfredo.

B. Y mi nombre no es Francisco.

A. Oh, perdón.

B. Cómo no. Con permiso.

[*To be followed by* LISTENING COMPREHENSION–SPEAKING EXERCISE]

Listening Passage
for Chapter 4
English Translation

Aspects of (the) Daily Life: In a Cafe

(1) Everywhere in almost all the cities in Spain and Latin America there are outdoor cafes. They are not only places where people go to eat or drink something. (2) With the pretext of having a cup of coffee, a soft drink, or a beer, or eating a sandwich or a dish (plate) of something (whatever thing), people—especially men—go there to chat, to discuss politics, to read the paper, and to look at the girls passing by on the street. (3) The cafe is like a free club, a social center, where the customer may spend several hours, if he so desires, without anybody protesting (and nobody protests). It is a custom, an aspect of daily life.

(4) Not always, however, is the cafe the place where one can read the paper or chat with his friends peacefully (with all tranquility). The cafe is a place where beggars, shoeshine boys, and

venders of lottery also hang around (arrive). They (these) go from table to table begging (asking for alms), offering their services, interrupting conversations, and, at times, even intervening in them. (5) Poor people! They have to live too. The trouble is that this occurs so frequently that one cannot even chat with a friend. (6) Such is the case with (of) Juan José and his friend, who enter a cafe and in a matter of a few minutes are interrupted several times—first by a woman selling lottery tickets, then by a shoeshine boy, and finally by a beggar.

(7) Juan José and his friend are talking about a girl from whom the latter orders two coffees, thinking that she is a waitress (employee). But it turns out that she's not a waitress; she's the boss's daughter. The girl, according to Juan José, is studying at the Law School of the National University, and, since she is very attractive and probably is the only woman, everybody is in love with her.

(8) The shoeshine boy interrupts to say that a guy who is looking towards Juan José's table is her boyfriend, and that he's very jealous. At the same time, the beggar appears, asking for a little something "for the love of God." Juan José and his friend become impatient (lose patience) and leave without drinking their coffee.

Grammar Points

First, the demonstratives **este** (this), **ese** (that), **esto** (this), and **eso** (that); second, the present tense of regular verbs ending in **-ar;** third, the days of the week; and fourth, the present progressive construction.

TO BE FOLLOWED BY
LISTENING RECOGNITION EXERCISE

Chapter 4

Basic Dialog

Aspectos de la vida diaria: en un café

JJ. *Juan José*   A. *Amigo*   MU. *Mujer*
L. *Limpiabotas*   ME. *Mendigo*

I

JJ.   ¿Por qué no entramos y tomamos un café?
A.   Buena idea. Mira, esta mesa está desocupada.
MU.   ¡LOTERIA! ¿Compra un pedacito[1] para el domingo, señor?
A.   No, gracias. Pst, dos cafés. ¡Pst! ¡Señorita! No oye.
JJ.   Esa no es una empleada, hombre. Es la hija del dueño.

II

L.   Están bastante sucios, señor. ¿Les doy una limpiadita?
JJ.   No. ¿Qué estás haciendo? Mis zapatos están bien.
A.   ¡Hombre! ¿No es ésa la chica que estudia en la Facultad de Derecho?
JJ.   La misma. Y todo el mundo está enamorado de ella.

III

L.   Ese tipo que está mirando para acá es el novio. Cuidado, dicen que es muy celoso.
JJ.   ¡Ah caramba! ¡Tú aquí todavía! ¡Vete o llamo a la policía!
ME.   Una limosnita, por amor de Dios...
JJ.   ¡Esto es imposible! Aquí no se puede ni hablar. ¡Vámonos!

---

[1] *Pedacito,* "small piece," comes from *pedazo* (piece) + *ito.* The diminutive suffix *-ito* is frequently added to masculine nouns, and *-ita* to feminine nouns. The final vowel of the noun is dropped when the suffix is added (*limpiada, limpiadita; limosna, limosnita*). Suffixes will be further discussed in Chapter 11.

Aspects of Daily Life: In a Cafe

JJ. *Juan José*   F. *Friend*   W. *Woman*
S. *Shoeshine boy*   B. *Beggar*

I

JJ. Why don't we go in and have a cup of coffee?
F. Good idea. Look, this table is empty.[2]
W. LOTTERY! Will you buy a ticket[3] for Sunday, sir?
F. No, thanks. Pst, two coffees. Pst! Miss! She doesn't hear.
JJ. That's not a waitress, man. She's the boss's daughter.

II

S. They look pretty dirty, sir. Shall I give them a little shine?
JJ. No. What are you doing? My shoes are okay.
F. Hey, isn't that the girl who's studying at the Law School?
JJ. The same. And everybody's[4] in love with her.

III

S. That guy looking this way is her boyfriend. Careful, they say he's very jealous.
JJ. For Pete's sake! You still here? Go away or I'll call the police!
B. Can you spare a little something, please[5] . . . .
JJ. This is impossible! You can't even talk. Let's get out of here![6]

CULTURAL NOTES

People who wait on tables are never addressed as "waiter" or "waitress" (*mesero, -a*), for this form of address tends to belittle them. A common, more dignified, and more generally acceptable term is *señor* or *señorita*. Paradoxically, however, the interjection *pst* before *señor* or *señorita* is not at all considered to be bad manners.

PRONUNCIATION EXERCISES

Syllabication and rhythm. The attainment of an even syllabic rhythm in spoken Spanish is a great aid to acquiring an even, clear, and precise pronunciation of the vowels. And this even, clear, and precise pronunciation of the five vowels—whether stressed or unstressed—is in turn the basis for the acquisition of a generally correct pronunciation of Spanish.

Reading aloud is, of course, an excellent rhythm exercise; but it will not help you much unless you know—and apply to your reading—the rules for syllable division in Spanish. By applying these rules to your spoken Spanish, you can attain the even, staccato rhythm that native speakers of Spanish have.

The rules are quite simple, although they differ from the English rules. In the spoken language they apply not only to single words but also to sequences of words uttered as a single breath group

---

[2]Unoccupied.   [3]Small piece.   [4]All the world.   [5]A little alms for love of God.   [6]Let's go away.

(*mi nombre es Emilio, adiós, buenas noches, yo no estoy cansada,* etc.). In writing, of course, the rules apply to single words only. They are listed below.

A. A single consonant between vowels always begins a syllable.

    a *s*us órde*n*es   a-*s*u-*s*ór-de-*n*es
    qué *t*al es   qué-*t*a-*l*es
    *t*odos están a*qu*í   *t*o-*d*o-*s*es-tá-na-*qu*í

B. Clusters of two consonants whose second member is *r* or *l* (*br, cr, fr,* etc.; *bl, cl, fl,* etc.) are treated as single consonants, the entire cluster going with the following vowel.

    h*abl*o mucho   (h)a-*bl*o-mu-cho[7,8]
    tan ale*gr*es   ta-na-le-*gr*es

C. Other consonant clusters are separated, the first consonant ending the preceding syllable, the second (plus *r* or *l*) beginning the next.

    el alu*mn*o   e-la-*l*u*m*-*n*o
    a sus órde*n*es   a-su-sór-de-nes
    *el m*aestro   el-ma-es-tro

D. Any vowel preceded or followed by unstressed *i* or unstressed *u* is pronounced in the same length of time as a single vowel and is contained, therefore, in one syllable. Combinations of *i* and *u* always form a single syllable.

    t*ie*ne   t*ie*-ne   b*ue*no   b*ue*-no
    ag*ua*   a-g*ua*   v*ei*nte   v*ei*n-te
    qu*ie*n es   qu*ie*-nes   c*au*sa   c*au*-sa
    c*iu*dad   c*iu*-dad   ad*ió*s   a-d*ió*s
    c*ui*dado   c*ui*-da-do   d*ue*ño   d*ue*-ño

E. If the same vowel or consonant sound occurs at the end of one word and the beginning of the next, the two sounds are normally pronounced as one single vowel or consonant, and the words are linked together.

    mi nomb*r*e *es* Cielito   mi-nom-b*r*e-*c*ie-li-to
    la*s s*illa*s s*on feas   la-*s*i-lla-*s*on-fe-as[8]
    cie*rr*e *el l*ibro   cie-*rr*e-*l*i-bro[8]

F. If the final vowel of one word and the beginning vowel of the next are not the same, they are both pronounced but are linked together.

    n*o* h*abl*a *e*spañol   no‿(h)a-bla‿es-pa-ñol
    cóm*o está e*lla   có-mo‿es-tá‿e-lla
    Marí*a o E*milio   ma-rí-a‿o‿e-mi-lio
    José *o A*licia   jo-sé‿o‿a-li-cia

You should review the six rules above before you do the following exercises and whenever you are going to do any practice reading, particularly on your own.

SYLLABICATION

Rewrite each of the following phrases or sentences in accordance with the syllable division of the spoken language. Then read it as it is divided into syllables. *Note:* Use hyphens, not slanted lines.

---

[7] Remember that the letter *h* alone represents no sound.
[8] Recall that *ch, ll,* and *rr* are single letters.

1. ¿Quién es el maestro?
2. Es una señorita americana.
3. Dicen que es un poco estricta.
4. Mi nombre es Emilio.
5. A sus órdenes
6. Somos hermanos.
7. Los ticos somos así.
8. Quiero tomar algo frío.
9. Luego vamos a Nicaragua.
10. Una visita al lago
11. ¿Qué estás haciendo?
12. Voy a llamar a la policía.

SUPPLEMENT

I

Esta mesa está desocupada.

silla	*chair*

Es la hija del dueño.

esposa	*wife*
madre	*mother*
abuela	*grandmother*
tía	*aunt*
sobrina	*niece*

II

Están bastante sucios.

limpios	*clean*

Mis zapatos están bien.

medias	*stockings*
calcetines[9]	*socks*
pantalones[10]	*pants*
cosas	*things*
gafas	*eyeglasses*

Mi camisa está bien. — *shirt*

blusa	*blouse*
corbata	*tie*
vestido[11]	*dress*
traje[12]	*suit*
sombrero	*hat*
ropa[13]	*clothes*

III

Ese tipo que está mirando para acá

para allá[14]	*that way, over there*

Es el novio.

padre	*father*
pariente	*relative*

Aquí uno no puede ni hablar.

conversar	*chat*
cantar	*sing*
fumar	*smoke*

Voy a llamar a la policía.

buscar	*to look for*

---

[9] Masc.: *los calcetines.*   [10] Masc.: *los pantalones.*   [11] In some countries men's suits are also referred to as *vestidos.*   [12] Mas *el traje;* in Chile, Ecuador, and Peru the word *terno* is preferred.   [13] *Ropa* is used as a singular noun.

[14] *Acá* differs from *aquí* in that *acá* is less precise; it means "here," "in this general area." *Allí* and *allá,* both meaning "there," differ in the same way, *allá* being less precise.

DIALOG AND SUPPLEMENT CHECK

SENTENCE RECALL

Say the dialog phrase or sentence in which each of the following words or phrases occurs.

mira	¡caramba!	empleada
limosnita	un café	mirando
¡pst!	dueño	enamorado
señor	tipo	zapatos
¡vete!	amor	policía
entramos	celoso	hablar

WORD RECALL

Give the Spanish equivalent of the following words.

love	stockings	world
go away	boyfriend	Law School
small piece	daily	life
we drink	God	a relative
in love with	doing	shoes
niece	looking	clothes

ITEM SUBSTITUTION

Repeat each of the following sentences, substituting one or more related words or phrases for the one in italics. If books are closed, your teacher will say the item at the end of each sentence.

1. Esa es *la hija* del dueño.
2. Mis *zapatos* están bien.
3. ¿Compra un pedacito para *el domingo?*
4. Aquí no se puede ni *hablar.*
5. Mi *camisa* está bien.
6. Mira, esta *mesa* está desocupada.
7. Están bastante *limpios.*
8. Voy a *buscar* a la policía.
9. Aquí uno no puede ni *fumar.*
10. Es el *novio.*

QUESTIONS

1. ¿Dónde están Juan José y su amigo?
2. ¿Van a tomar o van a comer algo?
3. ¿Van a tomar una cerveza?
4. ¿Quién es la señorita que está en el café, una empleada?
5. ¿Hay mesas desocupadas en el café?
6. Según el limpiabotas, ¿están limpios o sucios los zapatos de Juan José?
7. ¿Y según Juan José?
8. ¿Es la hija del dueño estudiante de la escuela secundaria o de la universidad?
9. ¿Estudia ella en la Facultad de Filosofía y Letras?
10. ¿En qué facultad de la universidad está ella?
11. ¿Va usted a estudiar medicina o derecho en la universidad?
12. ¿Qué va a estudiar usted?
13. ¿Cómo están sus zapatos, limpios o sucios?
14. ¿Y su camisa?
15. ¿Y su sombrero?
16. ¿Quién está mirando para la mesa de Juan José?
17. ¿Qué dicen del novio de la hija del dueño?
18. ¿Hay otras interrupciones en la conversación de Juan José y su amigo?
19. ¿Qué quiere el mendigo?
20. ¿Hay muchos mendigos en los Estados Unidos?

[*To be followed by* LISTENING RECOGNITION EXERCISE]

Grammar

13. *Demonstratives*

Descriptive adjectives (see Chapter 2) refer to some property of the noun they modify—for example, its size, shape, color, or condition. *Limiting* adjectives, on the other hand, relate the noun they modify to its environment. They may specify its position relative to the speaker, state the possessor, indicate the quantity, etc., and are classified accordingly as demonstratives, possessives, quantifiers ("many," "few," numbers), and so on.

Spanish descriptive adjectives pose two problems for the English-speaking student: gender and number agreement, and position *after* the noun they modify. Limiting adjectives pose only the problem of agreement, since they *precede* the noun they modify, in Spanish just as in English.

Demonstrative Adjectives

	this	*that*	*these*	*those*
masculine	este	ese	estos	esos
feminine	esta	esa	estas	esas

A. Note that the masculine singular forms **este** and **ese** end in *e*, instead of the expected *o*.
B. *Este*, like "this" in English, refers to something closer to the speaker than *ese* ("that"). One hint may help you remember the difference: *este* goes with *aquí*, *ese* with *allí*.

NOUN SUBSTITUTION

1. Este sombrero
    (zapatos)
   Estos zapatos
    (traje)
   Este traje
    (corbata, vestido, calcetines, medias, ropa, sombreros, cosas, blusa)
2. Ese señor
    (señora, sobrino, hijos, padre, esposo, maestras, profesora, empleado, dueños, abuela)
3. Esos días
    (domingos, mes, semana, horas, reloj, ratitos, año, minutos)
4. Esta montaña
    (cielo, lagos, mar, playas, lugares, país, ciudad, campo, mundo, vida)

Point with your finger as you do this exercise.

Este sombrero que está aquí
_____ allí
Ese sombrero que está allí
_____ cosas _____
_____ aquí
_____ señores _____
_____ allí
_____ mesa _____
_____ aquí
_____ sillas _____
_____ allí
_____ zapatos _____
_____ aquí
_____ camisa _____

Demonstrative Pronouns

este vestido y **ése**	*this dress and that one*
esas cosas y **éstas** también	*those things and these too*
¿Cuál traje quiere, **éste** o **ése**?	*Which suit do you want, this one or that one?*

C. Spanish demonstratives are sometimes used without a following noun; they then function as *demonstrative pronouns*. In English we say "these" and "those" in the plural, but "this one" and "that one" in the singular. As the above examples indicate, the Spanish singular demonstratives are just like the plurals; they are never followed by *uno*.

D. Note that there is a written accent on the stressed syllable of demonstratives not followed by a noun. This accent is purely a writing convention; it reflects no change in pronunciation.

¿ C U Á L   E S ?

Give one-word answers to the following ¿*cuál?* questions, pointing with your finger as you answer.

EXAMPLE: ¿Cuál es su corbata?
            Esta[15] (pointing).
            ¿Cuáles son mis zapatos?
            Esos.

¿su amigo?	¿ustedes?	¿mi traje?	¿su camisa?
¿la clase?	¿yo?	¿mi camisa?	¿mis alumnos?
¿sus ojos?	¿la puerta?	¿mi blusa?	¿su maestro?
¿el profesor?	¿sus zapatos?	¿mis ojos?	¿la ventana?
¿su ropa?	¿mis pantalones?	¿mi ropa?	¿su libro?

_____

[15] Notice that *Esta* does not have a written accent here because it begins with a capital letter.

Neuter Demonstratives

¡**Esto** es imposible!	*This is impossible!*
¿Qué es **eso?**	*What is that?*

E. *Esto* and *eso* never modify a noun. Consequently, they never change for number or gender and are called *neuter demonstratives*. *Esto* and *eso* are used to refer to situations, ideas, actions, etc., for which no particular noun exists (first example), and to things (not people[16]) that are identified by a particular noun only later in the sentence or discourse, if ever (second example).

TRANSLATION

1. What's this?
2. That? I don't know.
3. Is that (stuff) French or English?
4. This is Spanish!

5. Do you want this?
6. What's that?
7. What's this, coffee or tea?
8. That's Coca-Cola.

[*To be followed by* LISTENING COMPREHENSION–SPEAKING EXERCISE]

14. *Present tense of regular -ar verbs*

cantar

yo	cant	-o
tú	cant	-as
usted ⎫ él, ella ⎭	cant	-a
nosotros, -as	cant	-amos
ustedes ⎫ ellos, ellas ⎭	cant	-an

vosotros, -as	cant	-áis

A. The part of a verb to which *-ar, -er,* or *-ir* is added to form the infinitive is called the *stem.* Regular verbs, such as *cantar,* have the same stem throughout their entire conjugation.

B. The present tense endings are the same for all *-ar* verbs except *estar* (*estoy*) and *dar* (*doy*).

C. The simple present tense forms of a verb in Spanish (those illustrated in the chart above) correspond to both the simple present and the present progressive in English.

　　Juan canta bien.　　　　　　*John sings well.*
　　Juan canta en este momento.　*John is singing right now.*

D. Spanish may also use a simple present tense verb form to express the future.

　　Linda y yo esperamos aquí.　　*Linda and I will wait here.*

---

[16] If a lady were to introduce her husband by saying *Esto es mi esposo,* she would be saying something quite outrageous. The implication would be something like "This (unidentified thing) is my husband." She should say *Este es mi esposo.*

Practice saying the forms of the verbs listed below until you can do them without hesitation. Say the forms one time with the subject pronouns, the next time without them. This will enable you to do more effectively the pattern drills that follow. If your teacher wishes to add the *vosotros* form in the pattern drills, include this form in your paradigm practice.

tomar	esperar	cantar
hablar	mirar	fumar
estudiar	comprar	buscar
trabajar	conversar	llamar

PERSON–NUMBER SUBSTITUTION

If the cue is given in English, do not say the subject or subject pronoun.

1. ¿Por qué no esperan?
   (you, you and I, my niece, I, they)
2. La chica estudia en la Facultad de Derecho.
   (nosotros, ese tipo, yo, todo el mundo, ellos, la chica)
3. ¿Con quién hablan Juan José y su amigo?
   (tú, usted, el limpiabotas, la mujer y yo, Juan José y su amigo)
4. Juan José no busca a la policía.
   (yo, nosotros, el mendigo, ustedes, Juan José)
5. ¿Por qué no entramos y tomamos un café?
   (they, John, John and you, I, you and I, the girls, we)
6. Juan José y su amigo no toman el café, ¿verdad?
   (el novio de la chica, mis tíos, el mendigo, nosotros)

SÍ O NO

The whole class answers. Listen carefully to each of the following statements. Then give as long an answer as possible, indicating whether the statement is true or false. Begin your answer with *sí* or *no*.

1. Juan José y su amigo entran a[17] una casa. ¿Sí o no?
   No, ellos no entran a una casa, entran a un café.
2. Hay veinte mesas desocupadas en el café. ¿Sí o no?
3. Ustedes hablan español muy muy muy bien. ¿Sí o no?
4. Todo el mundo en la Facultad de Derecho está enamorado de la hija del dueño del café. ¿Sí o no?
5. El tipo que está mirando para la mesa de Juan José es el hermano de la chica. ¿Sí o no?
6. El amigo de Juan José compra cinco pedacitos de lotería para el domingo. ¿Sí o no?
7. La hija del dueño conversa durante una hora con Juan José. ¿Sí o no?
8. Juan José va a llamar a la policía porque el limpiabotas todavía está allí. ¿Sí o no?
9. Todo el mundo conversa con el mendigo. ¿Sí o no?
10. Alguien llama a la policía. ¿Sí o no?
11. En esta clase uno no puede ni tomar una cerveza, ni fumar, ni cantar, porque esto no es un restaurante[18] público. ¿Sí o no?
12. Ustedes son estudiantes muy buenos porque son muy inteligentes y estudian mucho. ¿Sí o no?

---

[17] The preposition *a* usually follows the verb *entrar*.

[18] The word for "restaurant" is also spelled and pronounced *restorán* and *restaurant*.

15. *Days of the week*

Días de la semana

lunes	*Monday*
martes	*Tuesday*
miércoles	*Wednesday*
jueves	*Thursday*
viernes	*Friday*
sábado	*Saturday*
domingo	*Sunday*

A. The days of the week are normally preceded by the definite article.

    Hasta **el** martes.   *Till Tuesday.*

    ¿Compra un pedacito para **el** domingo?   *Will you buy a ticket for Sunday?*

    La fiesta es **el** sábado.   *The party is Saturday.*

    Yo no trabajo **los** lunes.   *I don't work (on) Mondays.*

B. When they are listed, as in a calendar, and when they are equated with an adverb or noun of time (*hoy, ya, ahora, mañana,* etc.), the days of the week are not preceded by an article.

    Hoy es domingo.   *Today is Sunday.*

    Mañana va a ser lunes.   *Tomorrow is (going to be) Monday.*

C. The days of the week are always written with a lower-case letter.

D. Only *sábado* and *domingo* add an *s* to form the plural; the others remain the same.

    No tengo clases los sábados.   *I don't have classes (on) Saturdays.*

    Tengo tres clases los miércoles.   *I have three classes (on) Wednesdays.*

QUESTIONS

    1. ¿Cuántos días hay en la semana?

    2. ¿Cuáles son?

    3. ¿Qué día es hoy?

    4. ¿Va usted a la universidad los sábados o los domingos?

    5. ¿Qué días de la semana van ustedes a la escuela?

    6. ¿Qué día de la semana le gusta más, el sábado o el domingo?

    7. Y el lunes, ¿no le gusta?

    8. ¿Cuál le gusta a usted más, el lunes o el viernes?

16. *The present progressive*

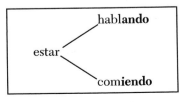

A. The present progressive construction in English consists of a form of the verb "to be" plus the present participle, the "-ing" form of a verb.

> I *am studying* now.
>
> *Are* you *sleeping?*

The present progressive in Spanish is very similar. It consists of a form of *estar* (never *ser*) plus the Spanish equivalent of the "-ing" form. This form consists of the verb stem plus -*ando* for -*ar* verbs and -*iendo* for -*er* and -*ir* verbs. Only *estar* agrees with the subject; the -*ando*/-*iendo* form is invariable.

> (Yo) **estoy estudiando** ahora.   *I am studying now.*
>
> Juan **está comiendo.**   *John is eating.*

B. The use of the present progressive in Spanish is similar to the use of the present progressive in English. There is one important difference, however. In Spanish the present progressive is used only to refer to an action *in progress at the moment of speaking.* Thus, unlike English, Spanish *never* uses the present progressive to refer to an event which will take place in the future. For example, "I'*m eating* with some friends this evening" *cannot* be translated *Estoy comiendo...* in Spanish; it can be only *Como con unos amigos esta noche* or *Voy a comer con unos amigos esta noche.*

PRESENT PARTICIPLE SUBSTITUTION

Substitute the present participle of each of the following verbs as shown in the example.

EXAMPLE: Estoy hablando.
               mirar
               Estoy mirando.

trabajar	comprar	fumar	hacer
tomar	conversar	llamar	ver
entrar	cantar	buscar	comer

CONSTRUCTION SUBSTITUTION

The whole class responds.

1. Juan José y su amigo entran ~~a~~ *en* un café.
   Juan José y su amigo están entrando a un café.
2. Llaman a la empleada.
3. En este momento entra una mujer.
4. Ahora Juan José compra un pedacito de lotería.
5. También entra un limpiabotas.
6. La abuela del dueño estudia en la universidad.
7. Los dos amigos conversan con el limpiabotas.
8. Hablan de la tía del dueño.
9. Un tipo mira para la mesa de Juan José.
10. ¡Uy[19], qué miedo! Juan José llama a la policía.

---

[19] Interjection used with expressions of fear, surprise, or displeasure.

Reading

First read each of the following selections silently for comprehension only. Then repeat each line after your instructor, paying particular attention to the following points.

1. Syllable division within groups of words (*Ba-mo-sa-lla-to-ma-ro-a-co-me-ral-go* for *Vamos allá a tomar o a comer algo*).
2. Clarity of unstressed vowels (re*p*ública).
3. Pronunciation of *d* and *t* (Facul*t*a*d* *d*e *D*erecho, in*t*eresan*t*e).
4. Single *r* (Ca*r*mencita, g*r*acias, fu*r*ioso).

Durante una clase en la Facultad de Derecho

PR. *Profesor*   AN. *Antonio, un alumno*   MA. *Mario, otro alumno*   X. *Alguien en la clase*

PR. Por ejemplo, es interesante observar que la constitución de la República Argentina...
AN. ¡Pst! ¡Mario, pst! ¿Dónde está Carmencita, tú sabes?
MA. No tengo idea.
AN. ¡Qué tragedia!
MA. Probablemente está en el café del papá. Cuando no está en la universidad siempre está allá.
AN. Vamos allá a tomar o a comer algo, después de la clase, ¿eh? Yo tengo mucha hambre.
MA. ¿Hambre? ¡Hombre! ¡Tú también estás enamorado de Carmencita!
AN. Me gusta un poco nada más.
MA. Dicen que tiene un novio, que es muy grande y ex-campeón de boxeo de México.
AN. No es verdad.
MA. Eso dicen, yo no sé. Shh, silencio.
PR. ... y entonces eso es todo por hoy, señores. Muchas gracias, hasta mañana. ¡Oh!, ¿alguien sabe dónde está Carmencita... perdón, la Srta.[20] Fernández?
X. Quién sabe, profe[21], tal vez[22] está enferma.[23]
PR. ¡Qué tragedia!

En el café del papá de Carmencita

CA. *Carmencita*   AN. *Antonio*   MA. *Mario*

CA. ¡Hola Mario! ¿Qué tal, Antonio? ¡Ah! Allá también están Arturo y Fernando y el profesor Lobo, en esa mesa. ¡Qué sorpresa!
AN. Y en esa otra mesa están Chucho, Jacinto y José. Toda la universidad está aquí. ¡Qué tragedia!
MA. ¿No va a ir a clase, Carmencita?

---

[20] Abbreviation of *señorita*.   [21] Chummy for *profesor*.   [22] Maybe.   [23] Sick.

CA. No, hoy no puedo ir; dos de las empleadas que trabajan en las mesas están quién sabe dónde. ¡Estas indias son unas irresponsables!²⁴ Bien ¿y? ... ¿Van a tomar algo? Hay una cerveza mexicana de-li-cio-sa, Carta Negra.

AN. ¿Por qué no conversa con nosotros un ratito primero? Tome asiento, después trabaja.

CA. Ay, lo siento mucho, Antonio, pero ahora no puedo, estoy muy ocupada. Más tarde tal vez, ¿eh?

MA. Carmencita, ¿quién es ese señor que está mirando para acá tan serio?

CA. ¡Ay Dios! Es mi papá. Está furioso. Rápido, ¿van a tomar algo?

AN. ¡No, no, y NOOO! ¡Vete inmediatamente o llamo a la policía!... ¡Perdón Carmencita! ¡No es a usted! ¡Es al limpiabotas! ¡Carmencita! ¡Por favor! Carmencita... ¡Qué tragedia!

CONVERSATION STIMULUS

Each of the three preceding dialogs must be read several times by different students and then acted out. You need not use the same lines each time, but be sure that the situation is the same.

[*To be followed by* LISTENING COMPREHENSION–SPEAKING EXERCISE]

QUESTIONS

The whole class answers. Give full answers, not just the present participle.

1. ¿Qué están estudiando ustedes, español o francés?
   Estamos estudiando español.
2. ¿Están trabajando mucho o poco?
3. ¿Está el profesor hablando por teléfono o hablando con los alumnos?
4. ¿Estoy yo fumando?
5. ¿Estoy comiendo?
6. ¿Están ustedes fumando?
7. ¿Están comiendo?
8. ¿Qué estamos haciendo, cantando?

QUESTIONS

Individual students answer the following questions with a progressive construction.

1. ¿Dónde estudia inglés Emilio Fonseca?
   Está estudiando en el Centro Cultural.
2. ¿Con quién conversa usted en este momento?
3. ¡Señor! ¿Por qué fuma usted ahora, en la clase? ¿No sabe usted que aquí no se puede fumar, ah?

---

²⁴A large percentage of the total population of Latin America is Indian. In some countries—for example, Argentina, Uruguay, and Costa Rica—the Indian population is almost nil; in other countries—Guatemala, Ecuador, and Bolivia, for example—Indians constitute the overwhelming majority. Since the times of the Conquest the Indians have been so oppressed in most Latin American countries that today most of them are in the lowest social and economic groups. The attitude of the upper classes toward them has been sometimes paternalistic, sometimes contemptuous; they consider the Indians today—as they have for centuries—to be dormant, docile, and lacking ambition. The expression used in the cafe by the owner's daughter is a reflection of this attitude.

4. ¡Y usted, señorita! ¿Por qué canta?
5. Ah no, ¡esto es imposible! ¿Por qué come usted, señor?
6. ¡Y usted! ¿Por qué mira para allá? ¿Por qué no mira para acá?

TRANSLATION

Use a progressive construction in the third sentence of each group only.

1. Emilio chats with Carlos María.
   Emilio is going to chat with Carlos María.
   Emilio is chatting with Carlos María.
2. They study at the Cultural Center.
   They are going to study at the Cultural Center.
   They are studying at the Cultural Center.
3. My niece always spends two weeks in Nicaragua.
   My niece is going to spend two weeks in Nicaragua.
   My niece is spending two weeks in Nicaragua.
4. Her husband smokes forty cigarettes[25] a (al) day.
   Her husband is going to smoke forty cigarettes a day.
   Her husband is smoking forty cigarettes a day.
5. Do your relatives work much?
   Are your relatives going to work much?
   Are your relatives working much?
6. I speak Spanish.
   I am going to speak Spanish.
   I am speaking Spanish.

Reading

Papá furioso, mamá ambiciosa

PA. *Papá*   MA. *Mamá*   CA. *Carmen, su hija*

PA. ¡CARMEN! ¿Con quién está usted conversando? ¿Quiénes son esos dos tipos?

MA. Ay, por Dios, Francisco, ¿por qué eres así? Carmencita no está haciendo nada malo. Está conversando con dos jóvenes muy simpáticos. ¿Qué hay de malo en eso?

CA. Son dos amigos de la universidad, dos muchachos muy decentes y de muy buena familia.

PA. ¡¡Yo no permito que mi hija...!!

MA. Shh, silencio un momento. ¿Ah, sí? ¿Qué apellido son?

CA. Gómez Castro uno y Gómez Pinto el otro. Son primos.

PA. ¡Primos o no primos, usted es mi hija y usted...!

---

[25] "Cigarette" is *cigarro* or *cigarrillo*.

74

MA. Shh, Francisco, por favor. ¿Ah, sí? ¿De los Gómez millonarios? ¿Por qué no invitas a los dos muchachos a la fiesta del domingo?

CA. ¡No, mamá!

MA. Entonces al paseo del sábado.

CA. ¡Mamá, yo tengo novio! ¡No puedo!

MA. ¡Ay, ese tipo no me gusta! ¡No no no no no, imposible! Un hombre que no trabaja, no estudia, no sabe hacer nada; cantar y comer, comer y cantar, nada más.

PA. Pero canta muy bien, ¿no crees tú, mi vida?

MA. ¡CANTA HORRIBLE! Francamente, no sé cómo mi hija, una señorita de la mejor sociedad, tan atractiva, tan inteligente, tan, tan, tan... ¿Adónde vas, Francisco? ¿Adónde vas, Carmencita? ¡Francisco! ¡Carmen!

CONVERSATION STIMULUS

Act out the basic dialog of this chapter once more. This will serve as a warm-up for fluency. Then act out the other conversations. Do not change the context of each situation, but feel free to make any changes in the lines within the limitations of the vocabulary and structure that you have learned up to this point. The situations are:

1. Aspectos de la vida diaria: en un café (*basic dialog*)
2. Durante una clase en la Facultad de Derecho
3. En el café del papá de Carmencita
4. Papá furioso, mamá ambiciosa

[*To be followed by* LISTENING COMPREHENSION–SPEAKING EXERCISE]

Listening Passage
for Chapter 5
English Translation

Appearances Are Deceiving

(1) In Latin America there are rich people, there are poor people, and there are rich people who are poor or who, if they are not really poor, at least pretend to have more than (what) they really have. (2) This third group is very numerous, more numerous than (what) one would imagine. I am in this group. We are people who go through (pass) life accumulating debts and eluding bill collectors (collectors of bills) or keeping them busy with promises of payment and all kinds of excuses. This comes about because our laws, or the judges who apply them, are not sufficiently strict in this respect. We are very sentimental, perhaps, and except in rare or extreme cases, we almost never see a man go to jail or lose prestige because of his debts. (3) Those of us who owe money here, there, and everywhere are so many that we don't really worry too much about it, because, as the saying goes, misery loves company (suffering of many, consolation of fools).

(4) Many times, in order to collect a bill, the creditor has to depend more on the skill of his bill collector than on the protection that the law itself affords him. This individual must be an expert in the art of collecting bills, a person who has tact, infinite patience, perseverance, and optimism. When the bill collector goes to a house for the first time, he knows beforehand that the person who opens the door already has

a reply ready: "Come back tomorrow," or "The master has visitors," or "They just went out," or "Come back tomorrow; the master is in the bathroom," or "He's not in; I don't know what time he'll get back (arrive)." And so it happens each time the poor fellow goes back to collect. But he goes back again and again (one and another time) without losing his patience or his good humor, or the hope of trapping his victim at last, some day.

(5) The basic dialog of this lesson presents a typical case. Here I am, the husband, in the dining room with my wife and children, making my usual comment about the fact that we owe money everywhere; but that's not really important to me. What makes (puts) me furious is this stinking lottery. I never win. This time, same as ever, NOTHING! Some day perhaps: that's everybody's hope. That's why everybody here, from the richest to the poorest, buys lottery tickets (lottery).

(6) However, notice how I, in spite of my debts, am planning (thinking) to sell my house in order to buy another one, better, much more expensive, with an enormous garden, with a swimming pool, with one bath on the first floor and two on the second, with many bedrooms, cement walls, many windows, and a beautiful red roof. (7) Notice how I also permit (give) myself the luxury of having a gardener, besides the cook and Lucrecia, the new maid. Poor Lucrecia! My wife shouts at her all the time because she doesn't know how to set the table yet. Sometimes I can't cut the meat because there aren't any knives on the table. Other times there aren't any spoons (tablespoons), or teaspoons, or napkins, or glasses. . . . Poor Lucrecia! She has to learn.

(8) Incidentally, my wife says she is going to fire the cook because she is very insolent. But that's not true. The cook only wants to know when we are going to pay her the three months' overdue salary we owe her. That's why she is very insolent, and that's why my wife wants to fire her.

Grammar Points

First, the present tense of regular verbs ending in **-er** and in **-ir**; second, some verbs of this type that are irregular in the first person— **saber** (to know), **conocer** (to know), **poner** (to put), **traer** (to bring), **salir** (to go out), **ver** (to see), and **hacer** (to do, to make); third, the construction **acabar de** + *infinitive;* fourth, the personal **a;** fifth, some uses of the definite article; sixth, the contraction **al;** seventh, the difference between the verbs **saber** and **conocer;** eighth, prepositions; ninth, the use of the infinitive after a preposition; and tenth, review of verb constructions.

TO BE FOLLOWED BY
LISTENING RECOGNITION EXERCISE

Chapter 5

Basic Dialog

Las apariencias engañan

MA. *Marido*   MU. *Mujer*   H. *Uno de los hijos*   L. *Lucrecia, la nueva criada*[1]

I

MA. Debemos dinero en todas partes, mujer. Y la lotería, como siempre... NADA. ¿Con qué corto[2] la carne?

MU. ¡Lucrecia! ¡Los cuchillos! ¡Siempre debe poner todos los cubiertos! ¿Cuántas veces...?

MA. Calma, mujer, la pobre es nueva; tiene que aprender.

MU. A propósito, voy a despedir a la cocinera también; es muy insolente. Esta mañana...

MA. No quiero saber, gracias. Y ustedes, hijitos, ninguno está comiendo. ¿Qué pasa?

II

H. ¿De veras vamos a vender esta casa, papá?

MA. Sí, pero es para comprar una más linda.

H. ¿Cuándo vamos a verla? ¿Después de comer?

MU. Tal vez. Tiene un jardín enorme y... ¡Lucrecia! ¡La puerta!

L. Creo que es el mismo cobrador del otro día.

MU. Dígale que acabamos de salir.

L. Sí, señora.——Dice la señora que acaban de salir.

---

[1] When *nuevo, -a* precedes the noun it modifies, it means "recently acquired or arrived"; when it follows, it means "recently formed or made." Similarly, *pobre* means "unfortunate," "pitiful" before a noun, but "impoverished" after a noun.
[2] From *cortar*, a regular verb.

< *Muchas familias en América Latina tienen dos y más criadas*

Appearances Are Deceiving

H. *Husband*   W. *Wife*   C. *One of the children*   L. *Lucrecia, the new maid*

I

H. We owe money everywhere, dear. And the lottery—like always, NOTHING. What do I cut the meat with?
W. Lucrecia! The knives! You must always put all the silverware (on the table). How many times . . . ?
H. Easy, dear, the poor (gal) is new; she has to learn.
W. Incidentally, I'm going to fire the cook too; she's very insolent. This morning . . . .
H. I don't want to know, thank you. And you, children, none of you is eating. What's the matter?

II

C. Are we really going to sell this house, Dad?
H. Yes, but it's for the purpose of buying a nicer[3] one.
C. When are we going to see it? After we eat?
W. Maybe. It has an enormous garden and . . . Lucrecia! The door!
L. I think it's the same bill collector as the other day.
W. Tell him we've just gone out.[4]
L. Yes, ma'am.——The lady says they just went out.

CULTURAL NOTES

A. There are three acceptable ways of referring to someone's wife: *la mujer de Pedro, la esposa de Pedro,* and *la señora de Pedro. La mujer* is rather informal; *la esposa,* a little more formal; and *la señora,* the most formal. In direct address from husband to wife, only *mujer* can be used; it is equivalent to "dear" in this case.

B. Middle-income families usually have a maid and a cook. They can afford this luxury because Latin American servants are among the most underpaid people in the world. A good cook, for instance, earns not more than $35 a month in most countries.

C. Here, the lady of the house addresses Lucrecia, the maid, with the *usted* form of the verb rather than with the familiar form *tú.* This usage varies from country to country. The maid, however, would always answer in the *usted* form.

PRONUNCIATION EXERCISES

1. The consonants *b* and *v*. The letters *b* and *v* are not distinguished in pronunciation. Spanish *v* is never pronounced with the sound of English *v*.

At the beginning of an utterance and after *n* or *m*, both *b* and *v* are pronounced [b], like English *b*. The letter combination *nv* is pronounced [mb]. Repeat the following examples.

b (be larga)	verdes	en vez de	vamos	invierno
v (be corta)	vieja	blusa	vender	en verano
buenos	bonita	bogotano	nombre	un vaso

---

[3] More beautiful.   [4] We finish going out.

After a vowel, both *b* and *v* have the sound [ᵬ], which is not found in English. The lips are brought close together so that they are almost touching, but not quite; the flow of air is not stopped even momentarily, as it is for English *b* and Spanish [b]. In the following examples, *b* and *v* in the left-hand column are pronounced [b]. In the right-hand column they have the Spanish sound [ᵬ]. As a reminder, the *b*'s and *v*'s with the unfamiliar sound are underlined. Remember that Spanish *v* is never pronounced like English *v*.

voy	me voy
vemos	debemos
bonita	qué bonita
vestido	ese vestido
bueno	qué bueno
voy	no voy
van	acaban

Practice saying the following sentences. Do not stop between words. Each sentence must be said as if it were one long word. *Note:* The English meaning alongside each sentence is given for your information and need not be learned.

Eva bebe vino blanco.	(*Eva drinks white wine.*)
¡Que viva Cubita bella!	(*Long live beautiful little Cuba!*)
Abuelita no vende la vaca blanca.	(*Granny's not selling the white cow.*)
¡Qué bueno sabe este vaso de vino!	(*This glass of wine sure tastes good!*)

In all other positions, *b* and *v* can be pronounced as either [b] or [ᵬ]. Thus, you may hear native speakers say either *cor*[b]*ata* or *cor*[ᵬ]*ata, el* [b]*aile* or *el* [ᵬ]*aile.*

2. The consonant *g*. At the beginning of an utterance and after *n*, Spanish *g* is pronounced [g], like English *g*. After a vowel, it is pronounced [ɣ], with the back of the tongue almost, but not quite, touching the roof of the mouth. In all other positions either sound is acceptable. Read the following pairs of words and phrases. Notice that the same word can have a [g] or a [ɣ], depending on what sound precedes it. The *g*'s that are pronounced [ɣ] are underlined.

gusto	mucho gusto	góndola	una góndola
grande	qué grande	gusta	me gusta
gato	ese gato	gano	nunca gano

Practice the following sentences. Each must be said as if it were one long word. The *b*'s, *v*'s, and *g*'s with the unfamiliar sounds are underlined. As a reminder, *d*'s pronounced like English *th* are also underlined (Chapter 1, pages 7 and 8).

Hugo es el abogado de Gonzalo.	(*Hugo is Gonzalo's lawyer.*)
Dice que vive en la Habana, Cuba.	(*He says he lives in Havana, Cuba.*)
Yo no digo ni hago nada.	(*I don't say or do anything.*)
Hugo y Gonzalo me ganan siempre.	(*Hugo and Gonzalo always beat me.*)

I

¡Lucrecia! ¡Los cuchillos!

el tenedor	*the fork*
la cuchara	*the spoon (tablespoon)*
la cucharita	*the teaspoon*
el plato	*the plate, dish*
la taza	*the cup*
el vaso	*the glass*
la servilleta	*the napkin*
el mantel	*the tablecloth*
la comida	*the dinner, food*

¿Con qué corto la carne?

el pan	*the bread*
la mantequilla	*the butter*
el queso	*the cheese*

¿Con qué tomo la sopa? — *the soup*

¿Con qué como los huevos? — *the eggs*

el arroz	*the rice*
el postre	*the dessert*
la ensalada	*the salad*

A propósito

Sin embargo	*however*
De todos modos	*anyway*
Por consiguiente	*therefore, consequently*
Por eso	*that's why, therefore*

No quiero saber.

beber	*drink*
vivir	*live*
escribir	*write*
prometer	*promise*
leer	*read*

Voy a despedir a la cocinera.

al jardinero	*the gardener*
conocer	*to meet, get acquainted with*
traer	*to bring*

II

Mi casa tiene un jardín enorme.

una sala	*a living room*
un comedor	*a dining room*
un patio	*a patio*
una cocina	*a kitchen*
un piso	*a floor*
un baño	*a bathroom*
una pared	*a wall*
un techo	*a roof*
un cuarto	*a room, bedroom*
una piscina	*a swimming pool*

DIALOG AND SUPPLEMENT CHECK

SENTENCE RECALL

Say the dialog line in which each of the following words or phrases occurs.

dinero	vender	hijitos	calma
carne	dígale	insolente	de veras
despedir	para comprar	jardín	cobrador

NEXT-SENTENCE REJOINDERS

Listen to each of the following dialog lines; then say the line that follows.

1. ¿Con qué corto la carne?
2. ¡Lucrecia! ¡La puerta!
3. ¿Cuántas veces...?

4. Dígale que acabamos de salir.
5. Es muy insolente. Esta mañana...

TRANSLATION

1. Lucrecia! Where are the knives? And the spoons and forks? And the cups and plates? Where is everything?
2. My house has seventeen bedrooms!
3. My house has three kitchens!
4. My house has forty-three windows!
5. By the way, my house has an enormous swimming pool.
6. However, my house has no kitchen.
7. My house has ten floors and one bath.
8. Anyway, I don't want to live there.
9. I always drink the soup with a teaspoon.
10. I always eat the dessert before and the salad afterwards.

QUESTIONS

1. ¿Quién es Lucrecia?
2. ¿Va a despedir la señora a Lucrecia?
3. ¿Por qué va a despedir a la cocinera?
4. ¿Es verdad que el marido y la mujer van a vender la casa?
5. ¿Para qué, según él?
6. Cuando la familia está comiendo, ¿quién llama a la puerta?
7. ¿Qué le dice Lucrecia al cobrador?
8. ¿Por qué no puede el señor cortar la carne?
9. ¿Con qué toma usted la sopa?
10. ¿Toma usted café en una taza o en un vaso?
11. ¿Cómo se escribe "taza", con *s* o con *z*?
12. Y "vaso", ¿cómo se escribe, con *b* o *v*?
13. ¿Hay teléfono en su casa? ¿Qué número es?
14. ¿Tiene usted una casa o un apartamento?
15. ¿Cómo es su casa, bonita o fea?

16. ¿Cuántos baños tiene?
17. ¿Tiene su casa paredes y techo?
18. Y su casa, ¿tiene puertas y ventanas?
19. ¿Es su casa de estilo español, inglés, japonés o chino?
20. ¿Quién es el dueño de su casa, usted o su papá?
21. ¿Cuál de ustedes tiene un jardín en su casa?
22. ¿Hay flores en el jardín? ¿Qué clase de flores, rosas, gladiolos, crisantemos o qué?

[*To be followed by* LISTENING RECOGNITION EXERCISE]

Grammar

17. *Present tense of regular* -er *and* -ir *verbs*

beber	vivir
beb	viv

-o
-es
-e
-emos   -imos
-en

vosotros	beb	-éis
	viv	-ís

Regular -er and -ir verbs have the same endings in all tenses, except for the *nosotros* forms of the present (-emos/-imos) and the *vosotros* present tense and command forms. (See Chapter 16 for *vosotros* command forms.)

PARADIGM PRACTICE

1. Practice saying the present-tense forms of the verbs listed, first with and then without the subject pronouns.

comer	prometer	insistir	deber
creer	vender	decidir	recibir
leer	escribir	describir	aprender

2. Practice saying the first-person plural forms of the following pairs of verbs.
   1. leer y escribir
      leemos y escribimos
   2. beber y vivir
   3. recibir y vender
   4. insistir y salir
   5. creer y aprender
   6. ver y creer

If the cue is in English, do not repeat the subject.

1. Nosotros debemos dinero en todas partes.
    (yo, el marido, el marido y la mujer, usted y yo)
2. Tal vez venden la casa.
    (I, we, these gentlemen, she, they all)
3. La cocinera come y bebe mucho.
    (el señor y la señora, todo el mundo, ustedes, yo, tú)
4. ¿Por qué no escribimos tú y yo una novela?
    (él y ella, usted, todos, nosotros, el jardinero)
5. ¿Dónde viven ellos ahora?
    (los hijos, ese pariente, el marido, la criada y yo, tú, el cobrador y la cocinera)

QUESTIONS

1. ¿Quiénes son los personajes principales del diálogo de esta lección?
2. ¿Son el marido y la mujer gente rica o gente pobre?
3. ¿Deben dinero? ¿Dónde, en una parte nada más?
4. ¿Creen ustedes que el marido es un hombre responsable o irresponsable? ¿Por qué?
5. ¿Cuántos sirvientes hay en esa casa?
6. ¿A quién quiere despedir la señora, al jardinero? ¿Por qué?
7. Si ellos venden su casa, ¿dónde van a vivir?
8. ¿Quién quiere describir la casa que ellos van a comprar?
9. ¿Quiere usted describir su casa, por favor?

18. *Verbs with an irregular first person singular form*

Infinitive	First person singular	
poner	**pongo**	*I put*
traer	**traigo**	*I bring*
salir	**salgo**	*I leave, go out*
hacer	**hago**	*I do, make*
saber	**sé**	*I know*
conocer	**conozco**	*I know*
ver	**veo**	*I see*

A. The rest of the present tense forms of the above verbs are regular.

B. The irregular forms have to be learned individually, since it cannot be predicted from the infinitive whether or not a verb has an irregular first person form. Before going on with the drills that follow, study each of the above forms in "paradigm practice" (*pongo, pones, pone,* etc.; *hago, haces, hace,* etc.).

Answer with a full sentence each time. Select the *yo* answer whenever there is a choice.

1. ¿Quién sabe más español, usted o su hermano? **Yo sé más español.**
2. ¿Quién pone más atención en la clase, usted o ella?
3. ¿A qué hora sale usted de su casa, a las ocho o a las nueve?
4. ¿Conoce usted mi casa?
5. ¿Quién hace la comida en su casa, usted o su mamá?
6. ¿Cuántas ventanas y cuántas puertas ve usted en esta clase?
7. ¿Siempre trae usted su libro de español a la clase?

PERSON–NUMBER SUBSTITUTION

1. Si no pones los cubiertos, no comes.
   (I, they, he, my sister and I, you [*pl.*])
2. Si usted no sabe la lección, no sale el domingo.
   (nosotros, los alumnos, yo, mi hija, tú, ustedes)
3. ¿Estudiamos, salimos o hacemos otra cosa?
   (you, Emilio and Luz María, I, my children)
4. ¡Ustedes! ¿Por qué no hablan o hacen algo?
   (usted, maestro, usted y yo, yo, hijitos, senorita)

[*To be followed by* LISTENING COMPREHENSION–SPEAKING EXERCISE]

19. *The constructions* tener que + infinitive *and* acabar de + infinitive

Tenemos que vender la casa.	*We have to sell the house.*
Dígale que **acabamos de salir.**	*Tell him that we just went out.*

The first of these constructions corresponds to the English "must" or "have to" before an infinitive. The second corresponds to the English expression "to have just (done)" or "just (did)."

WRITTEN TRANSLATION

Translate the following sentences, using **tener que** + *infinitive* or **acabar de** + *infinitive.*

1. Lucrecia has to learn to set the table.
2. The lady is furious; she just called Lucrecia (*a Lucrecia*).
3. She just fired the cook, too.
4. I just said that the lady just fired the cook.
5. Her husband just said that they owe money everywhere.
6. Why does he have to buy a new house, then?
7. But he just bought one with a big swimming pool.
8. "I don't have to eat if I'm not hungry," says one of his children.
9. "You have to eat, anyway," says his father.
10. But I just ate six eggs, rice, salad, bread, cheese, and butter. It's the truth, Dad, . . . almost.

Listen to the following statements. After each statement the teacher will ask *¿Qué acabo de decir?* Begin your answer with *Usted acaba de decir que....*

1. Ustedes son muy buenos y muy simpáticos. ¿Qué acabo de decir?
   Usted acaba de decir que nosotros somos muy buenos y simpáticos.
2. Ustedes comen mucho. Por eso están tan gordos.
3. Usted, señorita, hace todo perfectamente.
4. Usted no sabe dónde está Costa Rica.
5. Usted sale todas las noches. Por eso no estudia.
6. Mañana no hay clase de español.
7. Es la verdad.
8. No, es mentira.
9. Finalmente, tengo que decir una cosa.
10. Usted tiene que participar más en la clase.
11. Usted tiene que aprender el diálogo básico de memoria.
12. Usted tiene que poner más atención en la clase.

20. *The personal* a

Voy a llamar **a** la policía.	*I'm going to call the police.*
Voy a llamar un taxi.	*I'm going to call a taxi.*
Busco **a** mis primos.	*I'm looking for my cousins.*
Busco una silla.	*I'm looking for a chair.*
Estoy mirando **a** la maestra.	*I'm looking at the teacher.*
Estoy mirando la pared.	*I'm looking at the wall.*

The particle **a** normally precedes all verb objects that refer to people.

OBJECT SUBSTITUTION

Substitute each of the items listed below each sentence for the verb object of that sentence.

1. No veo a la maestra.
   (puerta)
   No veo la puerta.
2. No quiero conocer a nadie.[5]
   (la cocina, su cuarto, su familia, los hijos, nadie, nada)
3. ¿Ven ustedes el techo de la casa?
   (el jardín y la piscina, la dueña, los cuartos, la cocinera, el comedor, la señora)
4. ¿A quién[6] busca usted?
   (qué, cuál maestro, cuál piso, cuántas sillas, cuántos chicos)

---

[5]In Spanish the double negative, as in "I don't want to know nobody," is the correct form.
[6]The verb object in this case is an interrogative word referring to a person. Therefore, it is preceded by *a*.

5. ¿Qué quiere usted?
   (quién, cuánto dinero, cuánta gente, cuál silla, cuál señorita)
6. ¿Traigo a María aquí?
   (dos mesas, dos chicas, la señora, la ropa)

TRANSLATION

In Chapter 4 you learned that, unlike English, Spanish generally uses the definite article before the names of the days of the week. Review grammar section 15 on page 70. Then translate the following dialog orally, including the names of the letters that represent the speakers.

X. What's today, Friday or Saturday?
Y. Saturday, I believe.
Z. By the way, when is the party, Sunday?
X. Yes, Sunday.

21. *Some additional uses of the definite article*

Francisco quiere conocer a **la** señora Fonseca.	*Francisco wants to meet Mrs. Fonseca.*
Mucho gusto, señora Fonseca.	*Pleased to meet you, Mrs. Fonseca.*

When a person is *referred to* by his name and an accompanying title, the definite article *always* precedes the title. On the other hand, when a person is *addressed directly* by his name and title, the definite article is not used.

READING

Read the following dialog aloud.

EL. Buenas tardes, Sra. (señora) Campos. ¿Cómo sigue el profesor Campos? Oh, ¿usted no es la Sra. Campos? ¡Perdón, Sra. Fonseca!
ELLA. Y otra cosa, Sr. (señor) Curioso, mi hijo Emilio y la Srta. (señorita) Terán Marín no son novios; son amigos, nada más.

TRANSLATION

Include the names of the letters that represent the speakers.

I

H. Good morning, Mrs. Solano. Is Professor Gil here today?
J. No, Professor Gil is here on Tuesdays and Thursdays only.

G. Dr. (*doctor*) Gamboa, aren't you going to the picnic?[7]
C. The picnic is not today, it's Friday. Today is Wednesday.
G. But Mrs. Lobo says (that) it is today.
C. Mrs. Lobo doesn't know anything (nothing).

QUESTIONS

Answer each question with a single name and the appropriate accompanying title, *señor, señora,* or *señorita.* Make up a name if necessary.

1. ¿Quién es el profesor de español aquí?
   El Sr. Smith.
2. ¿Quién es el profesor de francés?
3. ¿Quién es el profesor de matemáticas?
4. ¿Quién es el profesor de inglés?
5. ¿Quién es el profesor de educación física?
6. ¿Quién es el profesor de música?
7. ¿Quién es el profesor de ruso?
8. ¿Quién es el profesor de chino?
9. ¿Quién soy yo, la Srta. González?
10. ¿Quién es usted? ¿Y él? ¿Y ella?

[*To be followed by* LISTENING COMPREHENSION–SPEAKING EXERCISE]

22. *The contraction* al

$$a + el \longrightarrow al$$

The other forms of the definite article do not contract.

OBJECT SUBSTITUTION

Remember to use the personal *a* when the substitution is a personal noun.

1. No conozco a la Srta. Malo[8].
   (Sr. Bueno)
   No conozco al Sr. Bueno.
2. Buscan a la Sra. Jiménez.
   (profesor Gil, Srta. Cuevas, Dr.[9] Caro, Padre Jesús, Madre Superiora)
3. La mujer llama a la criada.
   (jardinero, policías[10], cocinera, hija, hijo)
4. No conocemos al marido.
   (tía, maestro, patio, piscina, primo)

---

[7]Spanish uses *el picnic,* borrowed from English, as well as *el paseo.*   [8]*Malo* and *Bueno* are fairly common family names in Spanish.
[9]The abbreviation for *doctor* is the same in Spanish and English.   [10]*La policía* refers to the police force, while *el policía* and *los policías* are "the policeman" and "the policemen," respectively.

Answer with full sentences.

1. ¿De qué país es usted y qué idioma[11] habla?
2. ¿Qué idioma está estudiando ahora?
3. ¿Cree usted que está aprendiendo mucho, un poco o nada[12]?
4. ¿Qué está haciendo ese señor? ¿Y esa señorita?
5. ¡Otra vez usted! ¿Por qué está comiendo en la clase?
6. ¿Qué va a hacer usted esta noche? ¿Va a estudiar o va a salir?
7. ¿Qué día es hoy, y qué hora es ahora?
8. ¿Por qué no está usted poniendo atención?

23. saber *vs.* conocer

1. **Conozco** un lugar muy bonito.	*I know a very pretty place.*
2. ¿Quiere ir a **conocer** esa casa?	*Do you want to go to see that house?*
3. Quiero **conocer** a su prima.	*I want to meet your cousin.*
4. Emilio **sabe** quién es la maestra.	*Emilio knows who the teacher is.*
5. Luz María **sabe** hablar inglés.	*Luz María knows how to speak English.*

A. *Conocer* means "to know" in the sense of being or getting acquainted with something or someone (examples 1 and 2). *Conocer* is often used in Spanish where "see" and "meet" (a person for the first time) are used in English (examples 2 and 3).

B. *Saber* means "to know" in the sense of having factual information or data that could be communicated to someone else (example 4), or in the sense of possessing a skill—knowing how to do something (example 5). *Saber* is not normally followed by *cómo* before an infinitive.

READING AND COMPLETION

Read the following paragraph, filling in the blanks with the correct form of either *saber* or *conocer*. Do not write the answers; force yourself to try to say the correct form as you read. Don't forget the definite article before titles and the personal *a*.

Mañana vamos a ir a _____ la casa que vamos a comprar. Yo no _____ cuántos cuartos tiene, pero dice mi hermana que es muy grande. El dueño es un señor de apellido Caremango. Yo no _____ quién es él. Mi hermana _____ . Ella _____ Sr. Caremango muy bien. Mi hermana _____ todo el mundo y _____ muchas cosas. Yo _____ que ella _____ mucho y que _____ mucha gente. Ella _____ Europa y los países de Africa y _____ los nombres de las capitales de todos esos países. Francamente, mi hermana es muy inteligente.

---

[11] *Idioma* is a false cognate: it means "language," not "idiom."

[12] If your answer is *nada,* you must use a double negative construction.

24. Prepositions

Simple Prepositions

a	*to, at*	hasta	*up to, until*
con	*with*	para	*for, in order to, to*
contra	*against*	por	*for, by, through*
de	*from, of, about*	según	*according to*
en	*in, on, at*	sin	*without*
entre	*between, among*	sobre	*on, about*
hacia	*toward(s)*		

A. The prepositions given above are among the commonest in Spanish and the easiest to learn. Further details will be taken up in later lessons. The most important thing to remember about prepositions at this point is that they are never used in Spanish to end a sentence with. They must always precede their objects, even when these are question words. For example, in English we may say either "Who(m) are you talking *about?*" or "*About* whom are you talking?" but in Spanish there is just one possibility: ¿***De quién** está usted hablando?*

Compound Prepositions

antes de	*before*	delante de	*in front of*
después de	*after*	encima de	*on top of*
enfrente de	*in front of*	debajo de	*under*
detrás de	*behind*	fuera de	*outside*
cerca de	*near*	dentro de	*inside*
lejos de	*far from*	además de	*besides, in addition to*
al lado de	*beside, alongside*	en vez de	*instead of*

B. Like English, Spanish also has compound prepositions, most of which consist of an adverb followed by a preposition (usually *de*).

ADVERB	COMPOUND PREPOSITION
Está **encima.**	Está **encima de** la mesa.
It's on top.	*It's on top of the table.*

The commonest compound prepositions in Spanish are those listed above.

TRANSLATION

Don't forget the article before titles.

1. According to Professor Campos and Miss Bueno
2. In order to go
3. From Peru (*Perú*) to New York by sea
4. One must pass through the Panama Canal (*canal de Panamá*).

1. Según el profesor Campos, ¿qué?
2. ¿Quién más dice eso? ¿El profesor Campos nada más?
3. ¿Para ir de dónde a dónde?
4. Perdón, ¿por dónde debe pasar uno?
5. ¿Ah, sí? ¿Usted cree que para ir de Perú a Nueva York por mar, uno debe pasar por el canal de Panamá?

TRANSLATION

1. What is that for?
2. You! Who are you talking about?
3. What are you talking about?
4. I know! You are talking about me (*mí*)!
5. And without my permission!
6. You and you and you, against the wall!
7. Poor Lucrecia, she doesn't know how to set the table.
8. She places the glasses on top of the plates, the napkins under the cups, and the knives, forks, and spoons in front of the plates.

SÍ O NO

The whole class confirms or corrects the following statements, according to your teacher's cue. If a correction is to be made, first deny the statement and then correct it.

EXAMPLE: El profesor está al lado de la ventana.
Confirmation: **Sí, el profesor está al lado de la ventana.**
  Correction: **No, el profesor no está al lado de la ventana; está detrás de la puerta.**

1. Ustedes siempre estudian español antes de la clase y después de la clase.
2. Este libro está debajo de la mesa.
3. Ustedes están detrás del profesor.
4. Yo estoy al lado de la puerta.
5. Los alumnos están fuera de la clase.
6. Argentina está cerca de México.

25. *The infinitive after a preposition*

después de **comer**	*after eating*
su manera de **ser**	*their way of being*
sin **poner** atención	*without paying attention*
además de **estudiar**	*besides studying*

After a preposition, *only* the infinitive form of the verb is used, *never* the present participle (*-ando/-iendo*), as is usually the case in English.

1. Talking about owing money, the bill collector is here.
2. Is this water good for (*para*) drinking, Lucrecia?
3. Before selling his house, he's going to buy another.
4. What do you do, besides work?
5. This is for (*para*) María, for (*por*) being so good.[13]
6. Instead of doing that, why don't you pay attention?

QUESTIONS

Answer in complete sentences.

1. ¿Estudia usted para saber más o solamente para pasar el tiempo?
2. ¿Está usted contento con aprender un poco, nada más?
3. ¿De qué está hablando él, de ir a la playa?
4. ¿Es posible vivir sin deber dinero?
5. ¿Es bueno comprar una casa sin tener suficiente dinero?
6. ¿Qué acaba de decir él?

26. *Review of verb constructions*

1. Simple present	El marido **vende** la casa.	*The husband sells (is selling) the house.*
2. Present progressive	El marido **está vendiendo** la casa.	*The husband is selling the house.*
3. "Wants to"	El marido **quiere vender** la casa.	*The husband wants to sell the house.*
4. "Going to"	El marido **va a vender** la casa.	*The husband is going to sell the house.*
5. "Just did"	El marido **acaba de vender** la casa.	*The husband just sold the house.*
6. "Has to"	El marido **tiene que vender** la casa.	*The husband has to sell the house.*

Verb constructions in Spanish may contain a single verb form (example 1); a form of *estar* followed by a present participle (example 2); a verb form followed directly by an infinitive (example 3); a verb form followed by an infinitive, with an intervening preposition, usually *a* or *de* (examples 4 and 5); or, rarely, a verb followed by an infinitive with an intervening *que* (example 6). Verb constructions will be taken up in greater detail in Chapter 13.

---

[13]The difference between *para* and *por* will be taken up in Chapter 6.

1. ¿Qué hago ahora?
   (voy)
   ¿Qué voy a hacer ahora?
   (tiene)
   ¿Qué tiene que hacer ahora?
   (estoy)
   ¿Qué estoy haciendo ahora?
   (vamos, están, voy, debemos, quieres)
2. Compramos otra casa.
   (vamos, está, no quiere, tengo, acaban)
3. Voy a llamar a la policía.
   (tengo, debo, estamos, vamos, quiero, debes, acabo)
4. Lucrecia no sabe poner la mesa.
   (no quiere, no tiene, no está, no va)
5. No, gracias, acabo de tomar una taza de té.
   (voy, tengo, acabamos, debemos, quiere)
6. ¿Qué pasa?
   (acaba, va, está)

Reading

First read the whole passage silently. Then return to the first sentence, examining it to see what pronunciation problems it presents (word linking, *r*'s, *t*'s, *d*'s, etc.). Now read the sentence aloud slowly, keeping an even rhythm. Then go on to the next sentence.

Quito

Capital de mi país, Ecuador. Ciudad típica latinoamericana, como muchas otras construidas por los españoles durante la época colonial. En el sector viejo de la ciudad, intacto y de gran valor histórico, pueden admirarse el Palacio Presidencial, la Plaza de la Independencia, la Catedral, la Iglesia de la Compañía de Jesús y otros templos famosos por su estilo arquitectónico y decorativo. Hay otros sectores de construcción más reciente, pero no siempre de mejor construcción: uno, en el extremo norte de la ciudad, con casas residenciales modernas y de gran lujo, donde viven los ecuatorianos ricos y las familias del cuerpo diplomático; otro, en el extremo sur, donde viven, más o menos, en casas que casi no son casas, los ecuatorianos pobres y los indios, que son muchos y muy pobres. Hay también sectores residenciales en otras partes de Quito, pero especialmente en el centro de la ciudad, donde vivimos en casas de construcción modesta y relativamente viejas, los ecuatorianos que no somos ni ricos ni pobres, los ecuatorianos de la clase media, que somos muy pocos.

Quito, ciudad pintoresca del trópico, no es realmente tropical. Sus características no son típicas de una ciudad tropical. Situada allá en la alta sierra de los Andes, Quito es una ciudad de clima agradable y fresco durante el día y casi frío en las noches. No tiene el clima caliente de La Habana, Santo Domingo o Veracruz. Y su gente, los quiteños, son de carácter reservado, conservador y serio en su manera de hablar, en su manera de vestir y en su manera de ser. Allí la gente prefiere el "usted" al "tú", la ropa de estilo conservador a la ropa de brillantes colores, la moderación al exceso. Hay muchas otras ciudades grandes y bonitas en la América española. Más grandes que Quito, sí, pero más bonitas, ¡no! Quito es la mejor de todas.

Look up in a dictionary any additional vocabulary you may need to prepare a very brief discussion of each of the following points.

1. Describe in a very general way a typical Latin American city.
2. Talk about the three social classes in Ecuador.
3. Compare Quito with a "real" tropical city.
4. Prepare a twenty-second talk about your home town or any other American city.

[*To be followed by* LISTENING COMPREHENSION–SPEAKING EXERCISE]

Listening Passage
for Chapter 6
English Translation

Latin American Students Abroad

(1) Eighteen of the twenty Latin American nations—all except Brazil and Haiti—constitute the block called Spanish America. These are the former colonies of Spain, born as independent republics approximately a hundred fifty years ago, except Cuba and Panama, the babies of the family, (with) about seventy years old (of age) each. (2) Many people in the United States and (in) Europe are under the impression that these sister republics are very closely bound (united) nations, and they do not understand why they don't live all together in the same house, under the same roof, under a single government, like the fifty states which constitute the great colossus of the North.

(3) "Sisters yes! United no!" answer the Guatemalans in the face of (before) such a possibility. "Sisters yes! United no!" exclaim the Mexicans. "Sisters yes! United no!" shout the Bolivians and the Paraguayans and the Chileans and the Argentineans and the Venezuelans. . . . "What a pity!" the Great Liberator Simón Bolívar is probably (will be) saying from the great beyond; and his golden dream—a united America, one great nation—is still (continues being) only a dream.

(4) "Yes, we are terribly nationalistic," they all confess; "our fatherland and nothing else!" "Join (unite ourselves) with Venezuela? Never!" say the Colombians. "Join with Argentina? Death first!" say the Chileans. "Central America

a single country? No, thanks!'' they answer in each one of these tiny nations.

(5) Historical reasons and the formidable geographical barriers that separate these nations from one another are the principal causes of this extreme nationalistic feeling that makes impossible the realization of Bolívar's dream. (6) The curious thing, however, is that, in spite of their nationalism and (of) their wars and (of) the great (long) distances that separate them, there exists among all the Spanish American nations a true feeling of fraternity, a feeling constantly expressed in many situations and under all kinds of circumstances. An example in miniature is the case of (the) Latin American students abroad.

(7) In many of the universities in the United States, for example, there is a group—sometimes small, sometimes large—of foreign students, the majority of whom are young Spanish Americans, or Latins, as they are more commonly called. And each new Latin who arrives joins ''the group,'' the impenetrable group of Latins who always go around together, eat together, live together. (8) Here political differences cease; here there are no cultural differences; here the Mexican and the Argentinean, separated by a distance of ten thousand kilometers, discover that they are alike, that they think alike. Here there is only one nationality: Spanish American.

(9) In the basic conversation which follows we present a typical picture: a group of Latins in an American university chatting in their dormitory. There we see Miguel, a Honduran, who has just come in (returned) from the street, conversing with a Chilean. It is extremely cold (it makes an extreme cold) in the street and (the) poor Miguel's ears are (Miguel has the ears) so cold that he can't (doesn't) even feel them. Today is the first of December, and they are almost in the middle of winter (in full winter). The Chilean, poor guy, looks like he's homesick (with illness of fatherland). How he would love to be in Chile now!

(10) Over there are a Salvadoran named Sánchez and his friend Rodolfo, a Paraguayan, getting ready to go to the movies. They are in a hurry (have haste) because the movie is going to start very soon. They are worried because they are going to arrive late, but fortunately their good friend Pepe, the Panamanian, lends them his car.

(11) And in another corner of the dormitory we see a Cuban and a ''chapín'' (native of Guatemala) chatting. The ''chapín'' has a stomach ache (pain of stomach) and is also worried because they still haven't sent him his (the) check from home (the house).

Grammar Points

First, the present tense of some irregular verbs; second, pronouns after a preposition; third, the months of the year and dates; and fourth, direct and indirect object pronouns.

TO BE FOLLOWED BY
LISTENING RECOGNITION EXERCISE

97

Chapter 6

Basic Dialog

Estudiantes latinos[1] en el extranjero

MI. *Miguel*   CHI. *Chileno*   RO. *Rodolfo*   SA. *Sánchez*
PE. *Pepe*   CU. *Cubano*   CHA. *Chapín*

I

MI. ¡Qué frío hace en la calle! Parece que va a nevar. ¡Ay[2], mis orejas! Ni las siento.
CHI. Ah, cómo quisiera[3] estar en Chile. Allá estamos en pleno verano.
MI. ¿No piensas ir a tu tierra para Navidad?
CHI. ¿Estás loco? ¿Sabes cuánto cuesta el viaje?

II

RO. ¿Vas a preguntarle al panameño o no? Vamos a llegar tarde. La película empieza a las ocho.
SA. Si lo veo le pregunto. Ah, aquí viene. Hola, Pepe. ¿Quieres ir al cine con nosotros?
PE. No, prefiero quedarme. Mañana tengo un examen difícil.
SA. ¿Nos prestas el coche, entonces? Te prometo cuidarlo mucho.

III

CU. ¿Qué te pasa, chapín? ¿Estás con mal de patria?
CHA. No, es que tengo dolor de estómago. ¿Qué fecha es hoy?
CU. Primero de diciembre.
CHA. Si no me mandan un cheque pronto, no sé qué voy a hacer.

---

[1] Short for *latinoamericanos*.   [2] The interjection *ay* expresses surprise or pain.   [3] *Quisiera* is the past subjunctive form of *querer* that agrees with *yo, usted, él,* and *ella*.

Latin American Students Abroad

MI. *Miguel*　　CHI. *Chilean*　　RO. *Rodolfo*　　SA. *Sánchez*
PE. *Pepe*　　CU. *Cuban*　　CHA. *Chapín*[4]

I

MI.　It sure is cold outside![5] It looks like it's going to snow. Ow! My ears![6] I don't even feel them.
CHI.　Oh, how I'd love to be in Chile. We're right in the middle of summer[7] down there.
MI.　Aren't you planning[8] to go home[9] for Christmas?
CHI.　Are you crazy? Do you know how much the trip costs?

II

RO.　Are you going to ask the Panamanian or not? We're going to be[10] late. The picture[11] starts at eight.
SA.　If I see him, I'll ask him. Oh, here he comes. Hi, Pepe. Do you want to go to the movies with us?
PE.　No, I'd rather[12] stay here. I have a difficult test tomorrow.
SA.　Will you lend us your car, then? I promise you I'll take good care of it.[13]

III

CU.　What's the matter,[14] Chapín? Are you homesick?[15]
CHA.　No, it's just that I have a stomach ache.[16] What's today's date?[17]
CU.　December first.
CHA.　If they don't send me a check soon, I don't know what I'm going to do.

PRONUNCIATION EXERCISES

1. Spanish *l* at the end of a word. Notice how different English *l* and Spanish *l* sound at the end of a word. Listen to the following pairs of English and Spanish words.

l (letter "*l*")	él
meal	mil (*thousand*)
dell	del (*of the*)
hotel	hotel

The difference between the two *l*'s is due to the position of the tongue. In English, the tip of the tongue touches the gum ridge behind and above the upper teeth, and the body of the tongue is relaxed and low in the mouth. In Spanish, the tip of the tongue is placed against the upper teeth and the body of the tongue is tense and high. Listen again to the same pairs of words, but this time repeat each pair as you listen. See if you can feel and hear the difference between the two sounds.

　　Practice saying the following words and phrases. Remember that words ending in any consonant except *n* or *s* are stressed on the last syllable unless they have a written accent indicating a different stress.

---

[4]Nickname for a Guatemalan.　[5]In the street.　[6]Literally, outer ears.　[7]In full summer.　[8]*Pensar,* to think, to intend.　[9]To your land, homeland.　[10]Arrive.　[11]Film.　[12]I prefer.　[13]To care for it much.　[14]What's happening to you?　[15]Illness of fatherland.　[16]Pain of stomach.　[17]What date is today?

100

FAMILIAR WORDS		COGNATES		
mantel	el	animal	cultural	sensacional
muy mal	al	brutal	inicial	monumental
qué tal	fácil	anual	parcial	fenomenal
difícil	cuál	rival	personal	imparcial
español	Miguel	final	festival	continental

2. The consonant [h]. Compare Spanish [h] with the sound of English *h* (or *wh*) as you listen to the following pairs of words.

high	Jaime (*James*)
hen	gente
who goes	jugos (*juices*)
holly	jale (*pull*)
hill	Gil (*family name*)

Notice that the Spanish sound is harsher. This harshness is caused by the friction of the air passing through a narrow opening between the tongue and the roof of the mouth. You must learn to hold your tongue high when you imitate this sound, in order to create enough friction. Listen again to the same pairs of words, and then repeat each pair. See if you can feel the difference.

Imitate a Spanish speaker as he would mispronounce the following English utterances with a very strong Spanish [h] sound.

He is *h*ere.	*H*ow do you *h*ide from *h*im?
*Wh*o's *Wh*o in America.	*H*ippies *h*ave *h*epatitis.
*H*i! *H*ow are you?	*H*ello, *h*oney! I'm *h*ome!

Now practice the following words and phrases, all of which you are familiar with. The [h] should have a hard rasping sound.

japonés	jefe	hijos	jota	Jesús	mujer
jardín	Jorge	gente	ge	Jiménez	vieja
jardinero	José	joven	ojos	Jijón	trabaja

SUPPLEMENT

I

¡Qué frío hace!

buen tiempo	*good weather*
mal tiempo	*bad weather*
sol	*sunny*[18]

¡Qué frío hace en la calle!

en el centro	*downtown*
en las afueras	*in the outskirts*
afuera	*outside*
adentro	*inside*

Parece que va a nevar.

llover	*to rain*

---

[18] Masc.: *el sol,* the sun.

¡Ay, mis orejas! *la*

mis oídos *el*	*my ears (inner)*	
mis manos[19] *la*	*my hands*	
mis dedos *els*	*my fingers; my toes*	
mis brazos *el*	*my arms*	
mis piernas *la*	*my legs*	
mis pies[20] *el* *l*	*my feet*	
mis dientes[21] *el*	*my teeth*	
mi cara *la*	*my face*	
mi nariz[22] *la*	*my nose*	
mi boca *la*	*my mouth*	

Allá estamos en pleno verano.

invierno	*winter*
otoño	*fall*

Allá estamos en plena primavera. *spring*

estación	*season*

II

¿Vas a preguntarle al panameño?

contestarle	*answer*

Mañana tengo un examen difícil.

fácil	*easy*

Vamos a llegar tarde.

temprano	*early*
a tiempo	*on time*

¿Nos prestas el coche?

das	*give*

III

Tengo dolor de estómago.

dolor de oídos	*earache*
dolor de muelas[23]	*toothache*
dolor de cabeza	*headache*
dolor de garganta	*sore throat*

DIALOG AND SUPPLEMENT CHECK

SENTENCE RECALL

Say the dialog phrase or sentence in which each of the following words or phrases occurs.

calle	con nosotros	película	nevar
verano	mal de patria	el coche	cheque
Navidad	quisiera	cuidarlo	examen
viaje	fecha	al cine	quedarme
diciembre	el extranjero	panameño	tierra

---

[19]Fem.: *la mano.* [20]Masc.: *el pie.* [21]Masc.: *el diente.* [22]Fem.: *la nariz.* [23]*Muela* means "molar," but the expression *dolor de muelas* includes the front teeth as well.

Repeat each of the following sentences, substituting a related word or phrase for the part in italics. If books are closed, your teacher will say the item at the end of each sentence.

1. ¡Qué frío hace en *la sala!*
2. ¡Ay, *mis piernas!*
3. Parece que va a *llover.*
4. ¡Qué *buen tiempo* hace!
5. Vamos a llegar *a tiempo.*
6. Tengo dolor de *muelas.*
7. ¿Vas a *preguntarle* al panameño?
8. Allá estamos en plena *primavera.*
9. Mañana tengo un examen *facil.*
10. ¡Ay, *mi estómago!*

QUESTIONS

1. ¿Con quién está hablando el chileno?
2. ¿Con quién está hablando usted?
3. ¿Dónde quisiera estar el chileno ahora?
4. ¿En qué estación están los estudiantes latinos ahora?
5. ¿En qué estación estamos aquí?
6. ¿Cómo está el tiempo hoy? ¿Hace frío afuera?
7. ¿Va a ir el chileno a su tierra para Navidad?
8. ¿Por qué no va a ir a su tierra a pasar la Navidad?
9. ¿Y adónde van a ir Rodolfo y su amigo Sánchez?
10. ¿Es Sánchez un nombre o un apellido?
11. ¿Va a ir el panameño al cine? ¿Por qué no?
12. ¿Sabe usted qué película van a ver Rodolfo y su amigo?
13. ¿Van a ir ellos a pie o en coche?
14. Y el muchacho guatemalteco, ¿qué tiene, está con mal de patria?
15. Según el cubano, ¿por qué está el chapín con dolor de estómago?
16. ¿Cuál de ustedes tiene dolor de estómago?
17. ¿Alguien tiene dolor de garganta, o de oídos, o de cabeza?
18. ¿Cuáles son las estaciones del año?
19. ¿En el verano, hace frío o hace calor?
20. Señorita, ¿cuál de las cuatro estaciones le gusta más?
21. Señores y señoritas, ¿cómo está el día hoy, bonito, feo o regular[24]?
22. ¿Cómo está el tiempo? ¿Hace frío o hace calor?
23. ¿Parece que va a llover, o ya está lloviendo?
24. ¿Va a nevar, o ya está nevando?
25. Señor, ¿usted siempre llega tarde o temprano a clase?
26. ¿A qué hora sale de su casa, generalmente?
27. ¿Y a qué hora llega aquí?
28. ¿Cuál de ustedes va a ir al centro después de clase?
29. ¿Va a ir al cine? ¿Qué película va a ver?
30. ¿Va a ir a pie, en coche, en taxi, en tren, en avión[25] o en autobús?
31. ¿Vive usted en el centro o en las afueras de la ciudad?
32. ¿Cuál es el nombre de la calle y el número de la casa donde usted vive?
33. ¿Estamos dentro o fuera de la clase?

[*To be followed by* LISTENING RECOGNITION EXERCISE]

---

[24]So-so.   [25]Airplane.

Grammar

27. *Stem-changing verbs:* e ⟶ ie

pensar	**querer**	**sentir**[26]
*pien*so	*quie*ro	*sien*to
*pien*sas	*quie*res	*sien*tes
*pien*sa	*quie*re	*sien*te
pen*sa*mos	que*re*mos	sen*ti*mos
*pien*san	*quie*ren	*sien*ten

pen*sáis*	que*réis*	sen*tís*

A. The chart illustrates a large class of verbs whose stem vowel changes from *e* to *ie* in certain forms. This stem change cannot be predicted from the infinitive form; it has to be learned through practice. Notice that the change occurs only when the stress is on the stem. (In the chart, the stressed syllable is indicated by italics.) Thus, this stem change does not occur in the infinitive or in the *nosotros* or *vosotros* forms of the present tense.

B. The verbs **tener** (to have, to hold) and **venir** (to come) are like *querer* and *sentir*, except for the first-person singular forms **tengo** and **vengo**.

C. The "it" form of **nevar** (to snow) is **nieva**.

PARADIGM PRACTICE

Before proceeding with the pattern drills, do paradigm practice with the following verbs, alternating each verb form with the *nosotros* form, as suggested by the example.

EXAMPLE: empezar
    yo empiezo, nosotros empezamos, tú empiezas, nosotros empezamos, usted empieza, nosotros empezamos, él empieza, nosotros empezamos, ustedes empiezan, nosotros empezamos, ellos empiezan, nosotros empezamos

pensar	sentir	cerrar	preferir
querer	venir	tener	

---

[26] The *-ir* verbs of this class undergo an additional change. In the present participle and in certain other forms, which will be discussed later, the stem vowel changes from *e* to *i*: *sentir, sintiendo; venir, viniendo.* (The stem vowel of a verb is the last vowel in the stem of the infinitive form. For example, the stem vowel of the verb *comenzar*, to begin, is *e*.)

If the cue is given in English, do not include the subject in your responses.

1. Hola, Pepe. ¿Quieres ir al cine con nosotros?
   (Pepe y Juan, amigos, Srta. García)
2. No, prefiero ir otro día.
   (we, my sister, they, you and I, everybody, you [*fam.*], I)
3. Lo siento mucho.[27]
   (they, we, Mary, your friends, all of us, you [*pl.*])
4. ¿En qué piensan[28] ustedes?
   (el panameño, los cubanos, nosotros, el estudiante, yo, usted)
5. Ah, aquí viene Pepe.
   (yo, nosotros, los latinos, el coche, mi novia, unos americanos, los rusos y los chinos)
6. El chapín tiene dolor de estómago.
   (el profesor, yo, nosotros, su abuela, mis hijos, todo el mundo)

ALTERNATE SUBSTITUTION

Besides saying the correct verb form, you must also make the proper number–gender agreement between nouns and modifiers.

1. Mañana yo tengo un examen difícil.
   _____ difíciles.
   _____ nosotros _____
   _____ fácil.
   _____ los _____
   _____ prefiero _____
   _____ clases _____
   _____ venimos a _____

2. La película empieza a las ocho.
   Las _____
   _____ temprano.
   Nosotros _____
   _____ empiezo _____
   _____ a la una.
   _____ cerramos _____
   Yo _____

YOU ASK THE QUESTIONS

Ask questions that would elicit the following answers.

1. Nosotros queremos ir a Chile.
2. No vamos porque no tenemos dinero.
3. Yo pienso ir a mi tierra para Navidad.
4. Usted tiene dolor de pies.
5. Ellos quieren ir a Florida porque allá hace calor.
6. Nosotros preferimos ir al cine.
7. Rodolfo y su amigo quieren ir al cine.
8. La película empieza a las nueve menos diez.
9. Ustedes tienen frío porque estamos en invierno.
10. Sí sí sí, yo lo siento mucho.

---

[27]I regret (feel) it much.   [28]"To think *about*" is pensar *en* in Spanish, similar to archaic English "to think *on*."

28. *Pronouns after a preposition*

para mí	para nosotros
ti	
usted	ustedes
él	ellos
ella	ellas

para vosotros

A. With the exception of **mí** and **ti,** the prepositional pronouns are identical to subject pronouns.

B. *Con* has the special forms **conmigo** (with me) and **contigo** (with you, familiar).

TRANSLATION

1. near them
2. without me
3. according to us
4. from them

5. under you (*pl.*)
6. with me
7. towards her
8. after you (*formal*)

9. on top of him
10. behind them
11. for us
12. with her

QUESTIONS

The whole class answers, giving negative responses. Replace the nouns after prepositions with the appropriate pronouns.

1. ¿Quiere Pepe ir al cine con Sánchez y con Rodolfo?
   No, no quiere ir al cine con ellos.
2. ¿Quiere Pepe ir con el chileno?
3. ¿Quiere él ir con ustedes?
4. ¿Quieren ustedes ir conmigo?

5. ¿Quieren ustedes ir al cine con la chica mexicana?
6. ¿Estoy yo detrás de ustedes?
7. ¿Puedo yo vivir sin ustedes?
8. ¿Están ustedes hablando de mí?

QUESTIONS

Individual students answer.

1. ¿Vive usted con sus padres?
2. ¿Con quién está hablando usted en este momento?
3. ¿Y yo estoy hablando con este alumno?
4. ¿Está usted pensando en su novia?
5. ¿Quién está delante de usted?

6. ¿Vive usted lejos de su suegra[29]?
7. ¿Quiere ir al cine conmigo?
8. ¿Es fácil el español, según el profesor?
9. ¿Hay otros alumnos inteligentes en esta clase, además de usted?
10. ¿Tiene usted problemas con sus hermanos?

---

[29] Mother-in-law.

29. *Months and dates*

Meses y fechas

1º³⁰ de enero	7 de julio
2 de febrero	8 de agosto
3 de marzo	9 de septiembre
4 de abril	10 de octubre
5 de mayo	11 de noviembre
6 de junio	31 de diciembre

A. Except for the first day of the month, Spanish uses cardinal numbers for dates. The names of the months are written with lower-case letters.

B. The word order *primero de diciembre* or *diez de abril*—rather than *diciembre primero* or *abril diez*—is practically the only one used in the spoken language.

QUESTIONS

The whole class answers.

1. ¿Qué fecha es hoy?
2. ¿En cuál estación estamos?
3. ¿Cuándo empieza la primavera?
4. ¿Cuándo acaba?
5. ¿Y cuándo empieza el verano?
6. ¿Cuáles son los meses del verano?
7. ¿Cuáles son los meses del otoño?
8. ¿Cuáles son los meses del invierno?
9. ¿Cuál es la fecha de la independencia de los EE. UU.³¹?
10. ¿En qué fecha empieza el año?
11. ¿Cuál es el último día del año?
12. ¿Cuántos días hay en el mes de diciembre?
13. ¿Cuántos meses hay en el año?
14. ¿Cuántas semanas hay en el año?
15. ¿Cuántas horas hay en un día?

[*To be followed by* LISTENING COMPREHENSION–SPEAKING EXERCISE]

30. *First and second person direct and indirect object pronouns*

me (a mí)	*me, to me, for me*
te (a ti)	*you, to you, for you*
nos (a nosotros)	*us, to us, for us*

os (a vosotros)	*you, to you, for you*

A. The pronouns **me, te, nos,** and **os** serve as either direct or indirect objects of verbs.

---

³⁰Abbreviation for *primero*.   ³¹Abbreviation for *Estados Unidos*.

B. Spanish indirect objects often correspond to English phrases with "for" or "to."

   ¿Me compra el libro?   *Will you buy the book for me?*
   ¿Me trae el libro?   *Will you bring the book to me?*

   Somewhat surprisingly perhaps, Spanish indirect objects also correspond to English phrases with other prepositions, such as "from" and "on."

   ¿Me compra el libro?   *Will you buy the book from me?*
   ¿Me pone los zapatos?   *Will you put the shoes on me?*

   Context usually clarifies the intended meaning of sentences like *¿Me compra el libro?* (" . . . for me?" or " . . . from me?"). The important thing to remember is that the usual Spanish equivalents of many English prepositional phrases are single pronouns, not phrases such as *por mí, de nosotros, en ti.*

C. Object pronouns always precede a single verb. However, in verb constructions with either an infinitive or a present participle at the end (*debe llamar, está llamando*), the object pronoun may precede or follow the whole construction with no change in meaning. In writing, an object pronoun that follows the verb is always attached to it.

   Te prometo   *I promise you*

   Te voy a prometer ⎫
   Voy a prometer**te** ⎬   *I am going to promise you*

   Te estoy prometiendo ⎫
   Estoy prometiéndo**te**[32] ⎬   *I am promising you*

D. Object pronouns in Spanish are never stressed to emphasize the object of the verb, as they may be in English. Instead, the prepositional phrases **a mí, a ti,** etc. (see chart above), are added, either at the beginning of the whole sentence or at the end. Note that the unstressed object pronouns are NOT dropped when the prepositional phrases are added.

   El **nos** va a comprar la   *He's going to buy the house*
      casa **a nosotros.**   *for us (not for someone else).*
   A mí no **me** mandan dinero, *They don't send me money, they*
      sólo **a ti te** mandan.   *only send it to you.*

WRITTEN TRANSLATION

Write each sentence twice, the first time as a simple statement, the second time emphasizing the object by adding the proper prepositional phrase. If there is a choice of position for the object pronoun, place it at the end every time. Follow the example.

   1. They'll look for us.
      Ellos nos buscan; sí, nos buscan a nosotros.
      They are going to look for us.
      Ellos van a buscarnos; sí, van a buscarnos a nosotros.
      They're looking for us.
      Ellos están buscándonos; sí, están buscándonos a nosotros.

---

[32] In order to show in writing that there is no shift of stress when a pronoun is added to a present participle, a written accent is necessary: *prometiendo, prometiéndote.*

108

2. I'll call you.
   I'm going to call you.
   I'm calling you.

3. He lends me the car.
   He's going to lend me the car.
   He's lending me the car.

4. Perhaps they'll sell the house for him.
   Perhaps they're going to sell the house for him.
   Perhaps they're selling the house for him.

QUESTIONS

The *tú* form is drilled in this exercise to give you practice with the familiar object pronoun.

1. Ellos no te conocen a ti, ¿verdad?
2. ¿Y tú me conoces a mí?
3. ¿Te quiere[33] tu novia? ¿Te escribe? ¿Te llama por teléfono?
4. ¿Te conozco yo a ti?
5. ¿Quieres decirme algo?
6. Tú no estás poniéndome atención, ¿verdad?
7. ¿Tú me llamas a mí?
8. ¿Van a escribirnos a usted y a mí?
9. Si yo te espero a ti, ¿tú me esperas a mí?
10. ¿Esa chica está mirándote a ti?

[*To be followed by* LISTENING COMPREHENSION–SPEAKING EXERCISE]

31. *Third person direct and indirect object pronouns*

Direct		Indirect	
lo, la (a usted)			(a usted)
lo (a él)	le	{	(a él)
la (a ella)			(a ella)
los, las (a ustedes)			(a ustedes)
los (a ellos)	les	{	(a ellos)
las (a ellas)			(a ellas)

A. As indicated in the preceding section, the pronouns *me, te, nos,* and *os* may be either direct or indirect objects of verbs. For the third person, however, the direct object pronouns are different from the indirect object pronouns, as shown in the chart above.

---

[33] Recall that *querer* means "to love" as well as "to want."

B. The third person direct object pronouns show agreement in both number and gender with the nouns they refer to. The indirect object pronouns show agreement in number only.

	DIRECT	INDIRECT

Sí, señor,   si no **lo** llamo,   **le** escribo.
Yes, sir, if I don't call you, I'll write to you.

Sí, señora,   si no **la** llamo,   **le** escribo.
Yes, ma'am, if I don't call you, I'll write to you.

Sí, señores, si no **los** llamo,   **les** escribo.
Yes, gentlemen, if I don't call you, I'll write to you.

Sí, señoras, si no **las** llamo,   **les** escribo.
Yes, ladies, if I don't call you, I'll write to you.

C. The phrases *a usted, a él,* etc., can be used to emphasize either the direct or the indirect objects.

DIRECT

¿A María?[34] Sí, hoy la veo **a ella.**
Maria? Yes, I'll see her today.

¿A Pedro y a[35] Juan? Sí, hoy los veo **a ellos.**
Pedro and Juan? Yes, I'll see them today.

INDIRECT

¿A María? Sí, hoy le escribo **a ella.**
Maria? Yes, I'll write to her today.

¿A Pedro y a Juan? Sí, hoy les escribo **a ellos.**
Pedro and Juan? Yes, I'll write to them today.

D. To replace an indirect object noun is not the only function of the indirect object pronoun. In normal speech, the indirect object pronoun always accompanies the indirect object noun *in the same sentence.* Notice the example from the basic dialog, *¿Vas a preguntarle al panameño o no?,* which is literally "Are you going to ask *him* the Panamanian or not?" The direct object pronoun, on the other hand, is not used together with a direct object noun. Compare the objects in the following sentences.

DIRECT

Yo llamo **a María.**
I'm calling María.

INDIRECT

Yo **le** presto el coche **a María.**
I'm lending the car to María.

NOUN–PRONOUN SUBSTITUTION: DIRECT OBJECT

Repeat the sentence, substituting each of the following phrases for the part in italics. Make all changes necessary to maintain agreement in number and gender between the noun and pronoun and to adjust for the contraction of *a + el.*

1. ¡Ay, *mis orejas!* Ni las siento.
   (los pies)
   ¡Ay, los pies! Ni los siento.
   (mis piernas, este brazo, los dedos, el pelo, la cara, los ojos, la boca, esta muela, el diente malo, la garganta, esta mano, la nariz)

2. ¿Al *panameño?* Muy bien, si lo veo.
   (las chicas)
   ¿A las chicas? Muy bien, si las veo.
   (Rodolfo, el profesor, mis padres, los chilenos, mi mujer, su esposo, los hijos del dueño, usted, él, ellos, ellas)

---

[34] *¿A María?* is an elliptical question meaning, in this case, "Am I going to see María?" Presumably, the speaker is rephrasing a question someone has just asked him: *¿Va a ver a María?* ("Are you going to see María?") Since *María,* a personal noun, is understood to be the direct object of the rephrased question, the personal *a* must be included.
[35] The personal *a* must be repeated before each personal verb-object.

NOUN–PRONOUN SUBSTITUTION: INDIRECT OBJECT

1. ¿Al *panameño?* Sí, yo le pregunto.
   (los cubanos)
   ¿A los cubanos? Sí, yo les pregunto.
   (el cobrador, la cocinera, ellos, ellas, usted,
   tú, todos, todo el mundo)

2. ¿Nos prestas el coche a *nosotros?*
   (Rodolfo)
   ¿Le prestas el coche a Rodolfo?
   (Rodolfo y yo, yo, el limpiabotas, nosotros,
   tus amigos, él, ella)

NOUN–PRONOUN SUBSTITUTION: DIRECT AND INDIRECT OBJECT

1. ¿Al *panameño?* Si lo veo le pregunto.
   (mis hermanas)
   ¿A mis hermanas? Si las veo les pregunto.
   (ellos, esos señores, mis parientes, mi abuela,
   el mendigo, usted, ellas)

2. ¿A *Luz María?* ¿Va a escribirle o llamarla?
   (ellos)
   ¿A ellos? ¿Va a escribirles o llamarlos?
   (su novia, su novio, yo, nosotros, Carmencita, él, ella)

QUESTIONS

Use a complete sentence in your reply and stress the object by adding the appropriate prepositional
phrase at the end.

1. ¿A quién llama usted, al hombre o a la mujer?
   La llamo a ella.
2. ¿A quién le presta Pepe el coche, a ella o a ellos?
   Le presta el coche a ella.
3. Rodolfo no nos pregunta a nosotros si queremos ir al cine, ¿verdad?
4. ¿Usted me ve a mí o lo ve a él?
5. ¿Usted me debe dinero a mí, ¿no es verdad?
6. ¿A quién le ponen ustedes más atención, a él o a mí?

WRITTEN TRANSLATION

Don't forget the personal *a*, and bear in mind that the indirect object pronoun is used together with
indirect object noun.

1. We're going to look for[36] the doctor.
   We're going to tell the doctor.
2. Who (to whom) are you writing?
   Who (whom) are you calling?
3. We owe the cook a lot of money.
   We have to fire the cook.
4. Are you going to lend the Cuban fifty pesos?
   Are you crazy? You don't know the Cuban.
5. I want to buy a new car for my wife.
   That's why I want to sell this car to my grandmother.
6. If you tell my wife, I'll call your husband.
   I'm not going to tell your wife anything (nothing).

---

[36] Remember that *buscar* means "to look *for.*"

32. *Indirect discourse*

Direct	
A pregunta: "Ah, ¿cómo está usted?"	*A asks: "Ah, how are you?"*
B contesta: "Estoy bien, gracias."	*B answers: "I'm fine, thanks."*
A pregunta: "¿Sabe quién es el maestro?"	*A asks: "Do you know who the teacher is?"*
B dice: "No, no sé."	*B says: "No, I don't know."*

Indirect	
A le pregunta a B cómo está él.	*A asks B how he is.*
B le contesta que está bien, gracias.	*B answers that he is fine, thanks.*
A le pregunta a B si él sabe quién es el maestro.	*A asks B if he knows who the teacher is.*
B le dice que no, que no sabe.	*B says no, that he doesn't know.*

A. In speaking we rarely use direct quotations of what other people have said; normally we use indirect discourse. Notice that exclamatory words and interjections such as *ah, ¡ay!,* and *perdón* are not included in indirect quotations. The following phrases are frequently used for introducing indirect discourse.

> *For yes-no questions:*
> Le(s) pregunta si...   *He (she) asks him (her, them) if . . . .*
>
> *For questions beginning with an interrogative word:*
> Le(s) pregunta...   *He (she) asks him (her, them) . . . .*
>
> *For statements or exclamations:*
> Le(s) dice que...   *He (she) tells (says to) him (her, them) that . . . .*
>
> Le(s) contesta que...   *He (she) answers him (her, them) that . . . .*

B. If the indirect discourse contains several sentences, only the first sentence requires the introductory phrase. The subsequent sentences can be started by the conjunctions *que* (that) or *si* (if).

DIRECT

Miguel: ¡Qué frío hace! Parece que va a nevar.

Manuel: ¿Tiene hambre, Vickie? ¿Quiere comer algo?

Miguel: How cold it is! It looks like it's going to snow.

Manuel: Are you hungry, Vickie? Do you want to eat something?

INDIRECT

Miguel dice que qué frío hace, **que** parece que va a nevar.

Manuel le pregunta a Vickie si tiene hambre, (y) **si** quiere comer algo.

Miguel says that it's very cold, that it looks like it's going to snow.

Manuel asks Vickie if she's hungry, (and) if she wants to eat something.

Change the basic dialog of Chapter 2 into indirect discourse; that is, relate what the characters say. Then do the same for the basic dialogs of Chapters 3 through 6.

EXAMPLE:
First student: Emilio le pregunta a Carlos María si él sabe quién es el maestro.
Second student: Carlos María le contesta que no sabe su apellido, pero que...
Third student: Emilio le dice a Carlos que qué bueno, que las mujeres...

Reading

First read each paragraph silently; then read it aloud. Remember the three main features of word linking: a) The final consonant of a word forms a syllable with the first vowel or vowels of the following word. b) The final vowel of a word is linked to the first vowel of the following word. c) Two or more identical vowels are normally pronounced as one.

América y los americanos

"¡Todos los habitantes de este hemisferio somos americanos, no solamente la población de los Estados Unidos! ¡Porque América es Canadá, es Argentina, es todo el hemisferio occidental!"

Esta es la eterna protesta de unos pocos extremistas. No están contentos porque los americanos de los Estados Unidos parecen tener el monopolio de esta palabra[37]. Es una protesta sin mucha importancia. Técnicamente es verdad que todos nosotros somos americanos, pero la realidad es que cuando hablamos de "nacionalidad americana", de la "Embajada[38] Americana", de "astronautas americanos", de "productos americanos", sabemos muy bien que esa nacionalidad, esa embajada, esos astronautas y esos productos no son de México ni de Paraguay ni de Honduras: son de los Estados Unidos. Es simplemente una conveniencia, un término ya adoptado por los Estados Unidos y aceptado en todo el mundo, inclusive en el resto de América.

Es fácil, haciendo un pequeño análisis gramatical y aplicando un poco de lógica, descubrir una posible causa de esta "usurpación" de la palabra "americano". El término generalmente usado para denominar la nacionalidad de los ciudadanos de un país es siempre, o casi siempre, una palabra derivada del nombre principal. Así, "guatemalteco" se deriva de "Guatemala", "mexicano" de "México", "cubano" de "Cuba", "colombiano" de "Colombia", "portugués" de "Portugal", "ruso" de "Rusia", "japonés" de "Japón", "chino" de "China" y "finlandés" de "Finlandia". Todas son derivaciones obvias y lógicas. Pero, de un nombre doble y tan largo como "Estados Unidos", ¿qué palabra se puede extraer?, ¿"estadounidense"? ¡Estadounidense! ¿Es-ta-dou-ni-den-se? ¿De seis sílabas? ¿Casi siete? ¿Una palabra tan fea y difícil de pronunciar? Eso es un verdadero trabalenguas[39] y un insulto al oído. Y si esto ocurre en español, en inglés la palabra —si es que existe— derivada de *"United States"* debe ser más complicada. ¿Qué puede ser? ¿*"United Statian"?* Una catástrofe completa.

Ah, pero ellos, los "es-ta-dou-ni-den-ses", siempre tan prácticos y eficientes, resuelven el problema en un dos por tres[40], de dos maneras.

---

[37] Word. [38] Embassy. [39] Tongue twister. [40] In a jiffy.

Primero, usando las iniciales en lugar de toda la palabra: *"U.S."* (pronunciado *iu-es*) tiene un sonido melódico. Todo el mundo en los Estados Unidos está muy contento con el término *iu-es*. Y es que a la gente anglosajona le gusta mucho hablar en iniciales; quién sabe por qué —tal vez porque está más de acuerdo con su modo rápido de vida.

Sin embargo, *iu-es* no es suficiente. Ellos saben que en otras partes no nos gusta hablar en iniciales, especialmente para referirnos a una nacionalidad. Nuestros primos del Norte descubren entonces la segunda solución, un segundo nombre para su patria con fácil derivación para la nacionalidad: ¡"América"! Y de "América", "americanos". ¡Perfecto! ¡Excelente! ¡Magnífico! El resto del mundo está muy satisfecho, inclusive nosotros los latinoamericanos, a quienes la palabra "estadounidense" nos suena tan mal al oído, y hablar en iniciales, peor[41].

QUESTIONS

1. ¿Qué dicen los extremistas con respecto a la palabra "americano"?
2. Según el autor, ¿tiene mucha importancia la protesta de esos señores?
3. ¿Es verdad que todos los habitantes de este hemisferio son americanos? ¿Por qué?
4. ¿Cómo se dice *citizen* en español? ¿Cómo se escribe, con *c* o con *s*?
5. ¿De cuál palabra se deriva la palabra "ciudadano"?
6. Generalmente, ¿de dónde se deriva la palabra con que designamos la nacionalidad de los ciudadanos de un país?
7. ¿Cuál es la nacionalidad de la gente de México?
8. ¿Son todos los habitantes de México mexicanos?
9. ¿Cuál es la nacionalidad de la gente de Chile? ¿Y del Perú?[42] ¿Y de Argentina?
10. ¿Qué palabra puede ser derivada de "Estados Unidos"?
11. ¿Por qué no les gusta esa palabra a los españoles o a los hispanoamericanos?
12. ¿Cuántas palabras usan los norteamericanos para su nacionalidad? ¿Cuáles son?

[To be followed by LISTENING COMPREHENSION–SPEAKING EXERCISE*]*

---

[41] Worse.

[42] The definite article is frequently used with the names of the following countries: la Argentina, el Brasil, el Canadá, el Ecuador, los Estados Unidos, el Paraguay, el Perú, la República Dominicana, and el Uruguay. In the case of El Salvador, *El* is part of the official name of the country and must always be used.

Listening Passage for Chapter 7
English Translation

At Last They're Leaving!

(1) My name is (I call myself) Jim Davis; I'm a North American citizen living in Chile for many years. I'm married to a Chilean woman; her name is (she calls herself) Margarita. We have five children and we're very happy. I can't complain about anything. Chile is a marvelous country and I hope to stay here with my family for the rest of my life.

(2) Tonight we're having guests for dinner (to eat)—we *had*, rather (better said), because dinner ended three hours ago. Now we're in the living room chatting with them, our dear friends Napoleón Gamboa and his wife Pepita. They are Bolivian. They are old friends of ours and we are very fond of them (love them much). (3) The only thing wrong with them (bad thing that they have) is that, like typical Latins, they always arrive one or two hours late to engagements (invitations) of this type; and then that, since Pepita likes to chat so much and my wife does too, they stay for hours and hours and never leave even if you push them out (pushing them). It's true that in the course of the evening they say good-bye three or (and) four times—but they don't leave. The slightest little word added to a ''good-bye'' or to a ''thank you'' is sufficient motive to start a new theme of conversation. (4) That's why (for that) I've warned my wife that when we go to pay (make) a visit, when it's time to leave (at the hour of saying farewell) she must say only ''good-bye and thank you very much, see you tomorrow,'' and nothing else. Because if she says, for example, that the night is cold, that leads (gives place) to a ''by the way'' followed by a con-

versation that lasts at least half an hour more. Of course, my wife never pays attention (to me) to these warnings; it's like talking to the wall, because she's always full of extra little words and "by the way's" and things like (of the sort such as) "speaking of divorces, do you know that . . . ?"

(5) As for me, this business of saying good-bye in stages kills me, more so when one is as sleepy as I am (has a sleepiness like the one I have) now. Here we are in the living room, but we're not sitting; we're standing (on foot) because we're already on the second good-bye. Pepita is telling us that they have to leave because tomorrow they have to get up early. They're invited to a wedding at eight in the morning. Right away comes the "by the way" from Margarita. She says—speaking of weddings—that some friends of ours are going to get divorced because the woman is very jealous and follows her husband everywhere, and so forth and so on. And more and more details follow and nobody moves for a long while, despite my many hints and efforts to end the conversation. Finally it ends. But then comes (the) number three.

(6) We start to walk towards the door when Napoleón suddenly remembers that he has forgotten his overcoat. I run back like crazy and bring it for him. In the meantime Pepita is saying good-bye to my wife and takes advantage of the opportunity to add a small comment about the dinner, especially about the main dish, the "paella." "Delicious," according to her, and she asks Margarita for the recipe. I give my wife the eye (twist my eyes on my wife); she smiles at me and starts telling Pepita that in a very big (wide) frying pan you put a little onion and garlic—I already know the recipe by heart (memory)—and you fry it in (with) oil. Then you put in a little bit of tomato and then you put in some pieces of chicken and the rice, then you throw other things in, you cover the pan and—I don't remember the rest. There, nailed down to that spot in the living room, we spend the next twenty minutes.

(7) At last we reach the door. There Napoleón asks me how to get to (how one arrives at) the center of town. I explain to him that you go (follow) straight ahead on the street that passes in front of our house, but that it is necessary to turn right at the corner by the cemetery. Cemetery! The word reminds Pepita of something she must tell us because it's *very* interesting: "They say that . . . uh . . . what's his name"—she doesn't even remember the name of her victim—"is seriously ill and that . . . ." Jesus, Mary and Joseph! Another story! Oh no! But fortunately Napoleón is as tired as I am and doesn't let her go on. Thank God! Bravo, Napoleón!

Grammar Points

First, another group of verbs that are irregular in the present tense; second, reflexive pronouns; third, the difference between **pedir** (to ask) and **preguntar** (to ask); fourth, the prepositions **por** and **para;** and fifth, the particle **se** as (in the function of) an unspecified subject.

TO BE FOLLOWED BY
LISTENING RECOGNITION EXERCISE

117

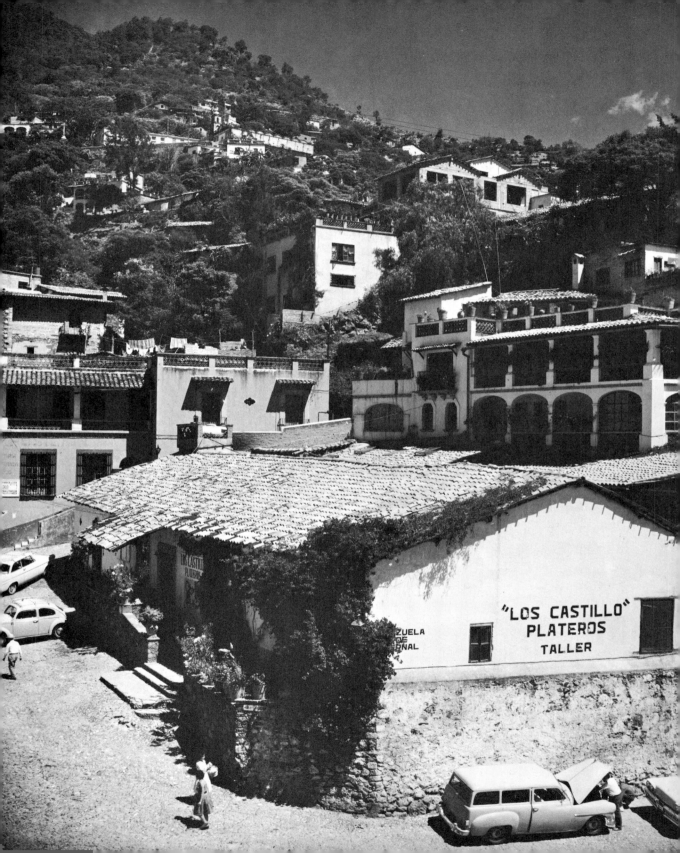

Chapter 7

Basic Dialog

¡Por fin se van!

NA. *Napoleón Gamboa*   PE. *Pepita, su esposa*
JIM. *Jim Davis*   MA. *Margarita, su esposa*

I

NA. Esta vez sí[1], Pepita, debemos irnos. ¿Por qué no te despides?
MA. Ay, ¿por qué? Mañana es feriado; no tienen que levantarse.
PE. Nosotros sí. Estamos invitados a una boda, ¡a las ocho! Se casa la hija de un peón.[2]
MA. ¿Ah sí? Y hablando de bodas, ¡Amadeo y la[3] mujer se divorcian! Dicen que ella es muy celosa.

II

NA. Bueno, ahora sí nos vamos. Muchas gracias por todo. ¡Ah! El[3] abrigo.
JIM. Ah, sí, perdón. Ya[4] se lo traigo.
PE. ¡Qué paella tan deliciosa, Margarita! Si le pido la receta, ¿me la da?
MA. Con mucho gusto. Mire: en una sartén grande se pone un poco de ajo y cebolla con...

III

NA. Para llegar al centro sigo derecho por aquí, ¿no, Jim?
JIM. No, hay que[5] doblar a la derecha en la esquina del cementerio.
PE. Ah, ahora que dice "cementerio", este, cómo se llama... está gravísimo. Esteee...[6]
NA. ¡Ah no, Pepita, por Dios! ¡Chao![7] ¡Buenas noches!

---

[1] *Sí* is used for emphasis; it is often equivalent to the use of "do" in English: "We *do* have to go."
[2] A *peón* is an unskilled manual laborer.
[3] The definite article is often used in Spanish where English uses a possessive, if it is obvious who the possessor is.
[4] *Ya* (already) is also used to imply promptness of action.
[5] *Hay que* is an impersonal expression meaning "it is necessary to."
[6] *Este*, with an extended final [e] sound, is a "fumble word," used to fill the silence while one is thinking.
[7] *Chao*, borrowed from Italian *ciao*, is commonly used in some South American countries as "so long."

At Last They're Leaving!

NA. *Napoleón Gamboa*   PE. *Pepita, his wife*
JIM. *Jim Davis*   MA. *Margarita, his wife*

I

NA. This time, Pepita, we really must go. Why don't you say good-bye?
MA. Oh, why? Tomorrow is a holiday; you don't have to get up.
PE. Yes we do. We're invited to a wedding, at eight! The daughter of one of our workers is getting married.
MA. Oh, really? And talking about weddings, Amadeo and his wife are getting divorced! They say that she's very jealous.

II

NA. Well, this time we *are* leaving. Thanks for everything. Oh, my coat.
JIM. Oh, yes, excuse me. I'll get it for you right away.[8]
PE. What a delicious *paella*, Margarita! If I ask you for the recipe, will you give it to me?[9]
MA. I'll be glad to. Look, in a large frying pan you put a little bit of garlic and onion with . . . .

III

NA. To go downtown I go[10] straight ahead this way,[11] right, Jim?
JIM. No, you have to turn right at the corner by the cemetery.
PE. Oh, now that you say "cemetery," uh, what's his name . . . is very seriously ill. Uh . . . .
NA. Oh no, Pepita, for goodness sake![12] Chao! Good night!

CULTURAL NOTES

The use of religious names in Spanish, particularly by women, is very common and is not considered blasphemous. Other common expressions, in addition to *Por Dios*, are *¡María Santísima!* (Holy Mary!), *¡Jesús!*, *¡Ave María!* (Hail Mary!), and *¡Dios mío!* (My God!).

PRONUNCIATION EXERCISES

The clusters [sya], [sye], and [syo]. In English, *c*, *t*, and *s* are usually pronounced like *sh* in words like "gracious," "nation," and "expansion." In similar words in Spanish, however, *c* and *s* are always pronounced [s], as in "say," never like *sh*.
Pronounce the following words, paying close attention to the [s] clusters.

FAMILIAR WORDS	COGNATES		
gracias	introducción	paciencia	Alicia
diecisiete	atención	social	posición
dieciocho	pronunciación	conversación	construcción
asiento	eficiente	combinación	vacaciones
Lucrecia	inicial	sección	estación
apariencia	concentración	ejercicio	internacional

---

[8]To you it I bring.   [9]To me it you give.   [10]Follow.   [11]Through here.   [12]For God's sake.

I

Debemos irnos.

acostarnos	*go to bed*
sentarnos	*sit down*

No tienen que levantarse.

vestirse	*get dressed*	quedarse	*stay*
bañarse	*take a bath, bathe*	quejarse	*complain*
lavarse	*wash*	preocuparse	*worry*
peinarse	*comb* (one's hair)	enojarse	*get angry*
afeitarse	*shave*	desmayarse	*faint*

II

¡Ah! El abrigo.

Los guantes	*the gloves*
El impermeable	*the raincoat*
La cartera	*the purse, wallet*
El paraguas	*the umbrella*

¡Qué paella tan deliciosa!

cena	*supper*
¡Qué almuerzo tan delicioso!	*lunch*
desayuno	*breakfast*

En una sartén se pone un poco de ajo.

cocina	*cook*
calienta	*heat*

Si le pido la receta...

consigo	*get*
digo	*tell*

III

Hay que doblar a la derecha.

izquierda	*left*

Está gravísimo.

enfermo	*sick*

DIALOG AND SUPPLEMENT CHECK

SENTENCE RECALL

Say the dialog line in which each of the following words or phrases occurs.

invitados	levantarse	peón
Amadeo	receta	doblar
debemos	derecho	te despides
paella	a la derecha	gravísimo
sartén	muy celosa	gusto

Make one or more substitutions within each of the following utterances.

> ¡Ah! El paraguas.
> Mañana no hay que preocuparse.
> ¡Qué comida tan deliciosa!
> Hay que doblar a la derecha.

QUESTIONS

1. ¿Quiénes son los invitados a la comida?
2. ¿Tienen que levantarse ellos temprano mañana?
3. ¿Adónde están invitados Napoleón y su señora?
4. ¿A qué hora es la boda, a las cinco de la tarde?
5. ¿Quién se casa?
6. ¿Y quiénes se divorcian?
7. ¿Por qué se divorcian Amadeo y la mujer?
8. ¿Sabe usted cocinar?
9. ¿Quién sabe cocinar arroz? Si le pido la receta, ¿me la da?
10. ¿Le gusta a usted el ajo? ¿Y la cebolla?
11. ¿Está usted furioso porque no le pregunto a usted?
12. ¿Está celoso, entonces?
13. ¿Usted no es celoso por naturaleza?
14. ¿Está él a su derecha o a su izquierda?
15. ¿Qué le pasa a ese joven, está enfermo?

[*To be followed by* LISTENING RECOGNITION EXERCISE]

Grammar

33. *Stem-changing verbs:* e ⟶ i

pe*dir*

pido
pides
pide
pedimos
piden

pedís

A. In a few very common *-ir* verbs like **pedir,** the stem vowel *e* becomes *i* in those forms in which the stress is on the stem, and in the present participle (*e.g.,* **pidiendo**). (In the chart, the stressed syllable is indicated by italics.) Thus, only the infinitive and the *nosotros* and *vosotros* forms have *e* in the stem of the verb. There is no way to predict which *-ir* verbs are like *pedir;* this must simply be memorized.

B. **Repetir** (to repeat), *seguir, conseguir, despedir,* and *vestir* are conjugated like *pedir.*

C. **Decir** is like *pedir* except that the first-person singular form has an irregularity: **digo, dices, dice, decimos, dicen, (decís).**

Alternate the *nosotros* form with each of the other forms of the following verbs.

EXAMPLE: pedir
>**yo pido, nosotros pedimos, tú pides, nosotros pedimos, usted pide, nosotros pedimos, él pide, nosotros pedimos, ustedes piden, nosotros pedimos, ellos piden, nosotros pedimos.**

seguir[13]   repetir
conseguir[13]   decir

PERSON–NUMBER SUBSTITUTION

If the cue is given in English, do not include the subject in your response.

1. Si le pido la receta...
    (we, Pepita, they, she and I, I)
2. Y Pepita sigue[14] hablando.
    (Pepita y Margarita, usted también, tú y yo, los Gamboa[15], todo el mundo)
3. ¿Dónde consigue Jim tanto dinero?
    (tú, nosotros, mis amigos, el peón, "cómo se llama", yo)
4. Si mi mujer despide a la cocinera, no consigue otra.
    (tú, nosotros, yo, "cómo se llama", ustedes, mi tía)
5. Lo digo una vez nada más; no repito.
    (A man, we, women, you [*pl.*], I, Jim, they)
6. ¿Cómo sigue el profesor Campos?
    (sus padres, la hija del peón, la situación del país, nosotros, yo, usted)
7. ¿Por qué no vistes a Juanito?
    (we, the maid, they, I, he)

[*To be followed by* LISTENING COMPREHENSION–SPEAKING EXERCISE]

34. *Some uses of reflexive pronouns*

Reflexive Pronouns

Yo	**me**	veo.	*I see myself.*
Tú	**te**	vas.	*You are leaving.*
Usted El Ella	**se**	viste.	*You (he, she) get(s) dressed.*
Nosotros	**nos**	quedamos.	*We are staying.*
Ustedes Ellos Ellas	**se**	levantan.	*You (they) get up.*

Vosotros **os** bañáis.		*You are taking a bath.*

---

[13] Remember that the *u* is not pronounced in the combinations *gue* and *gui;* its function here is to indicate that *g* is *not* pronounced [h], as in *gente.*   [14] Keeps on.   [15] The plural form of family names is rarely used in Spanish.

A. Reflexive pronouns in English are those which end in "-self" or "-selves": "myself," "himself," "ourselves," and so on. The Spanish reflexive pronouns are almost the same as the direct and indirect object pronouns. Only the third-person pronoun is different: **se** is the third-person reflexive pronoun for singular and plural, masculine and feminine.

B. The position of the reflexive pronouns is the same as that of the direct and indirect object pronouns, *i.e.*, attached to the present participle and infinitive forms or preceding the other verb forms you know.

C. Reflexive pronouns appear much more often in Spanish than in English. The reason for this is that, in general, Spanish uses reflexive pronouns wherever English does (first set of examples below), and also in a number of situations in which English does not (remainder of examples).

1. Spanish and English are parallel.

Me veo en la foto.	*I see myself in the photo.*
¿Por qué no **te** compras un paraguas?	*Why don't you buy yourself an umbrella?*

2. Spanish has a reflexive direct object, English has an expression with "get."

¿Por qué no **te** vistes?	*Why don't you get dressed? Literally, Why don't you dress yourself?*
No tienen que levantar**se**.	*You don't have to get up. Literally, You don't have to raise yourselves.*
María y Juan **se** divorcian.	*María and Juan are getting divorced (a divorce). Literally, María and Juan are divorcing themselves (each other).*

3. Spanish has a reflexive indirect object, English has a possessive adjective.

Se pone el abrigo.	*He's putting on his coat. Literally, He's putting the coat on himself.*
Se está lavando la cara.	*She's washing her face. Literally, She's washing herself the face.*

4. Spanish has a few verbs which *must* be used reflexively, although the English equivalents are not reflexive.

¿Por qué **te** quejas?	*Why are you complaining?*
¡**Se** está desmayando!	*She's fainting!*

5. Some verbs may be used nonreflexively with one meaning, and reflexively with another meaning; English uses entirely different verbs.

Vamos.	*We're going (somewhere).*
Nos vamos.	*We're leaving, getting out of here.*
Atlanta queda en Georgia.	*Atlanta is (located) in Georgia.*
Me quedo aquí.	*I'm staying (remaining) here.*

PERSON–NUMBER SUBSTITUTION

If the cue is in English, do not include the subject in your response.

1. Esta vez sí, nos vamos.
   (I, they, Pepita and I, you [*fam.*], Napoleón)
2. ¿Por qué? Ustedes no tienen que levantarse.
   (las visitas, yo, usted y su mujer, nosotros, nadie)

3. Sí, pero Pepita y yo debemos irnos.
    (ella, tú, usted, las visitas, yo, alguien)
4. Se casa la hija de un peón.
    (Jim y la chilena, yo, tú y yo, mi novia, ellos)
5. ¿Por qué no te despides?
    (we, they, Pepita and Napoleón, he, you [*fam.*])
6. ¡Amadeo y la mujer se divorcian!
    (yo, Jim y Margarita, nosotros, el profesor)
7. Ahora sí, Napoleón está poniéndose el abrigo[16].
    (yo, las visitas, tú, todo el mundo, nosotros, ellos)
8. Yo no sé si me voy o me quedo.
    (nosotros, Napoleón y Pepita, tú, Pepita, tú y yo, usted, mi mujer, mis hijos)

QUESTIONS

1. ¿Dónde están Pepita y Napoleón?
2. ¿Quiere irse a su casa[17] Napoleón o quiere quedarse?
3. ¿Por qué dice Margarita que mañana no tienen que levantarse?
4. ¿Y por qué sí tienen que levantarse ellos?
5. ¿A qué hora se casa la hija del peón?
6. Y hablando de bodas, ¿quiénes están divorciándose?
7. ¿Cuándo van a casarse ustedes?
8. ¿Para qué quiere casarse usted, para divorciarse?
9. ¿Es usted muy celoso? ¿Se enoja mucho?
10. Y usted, señorita, ¿se levanta temprano todos los días?
11. ¿Y se baña con agua fría o con agua caliente?
12. Cuando usted se viste, ¿se pone primero el zapato derecho o el zapato izquierdo?
13. Y usted, ¿es verdad que usted se pone el sombrero antes de ponerse la ropa?
14. Señor, ¿usted se afeita primero y luego se peina o viceversa?
15. ¿Cómo se llama usted?

REJOINDERS

The whole class answers, using a reflexive pronoun in each response, according to the *sí* or *no* cue given by the instructor.

1. Ustedes no quieren irse a la casa, ¿verdad?
2. Todos ustedes van a casarse mañana por la mañana.
3. Ustedes se quejan mucho, ¿verdad?
4. Ustedes llegan tarde todos los días porque no se levantan temprano.
5. Napoleón y su mujer van a divorciarse.
6. Ustedes quieren quedarse estudiando hasta las doce de la noche.
7. Yo me llamo Jesús Jiménez.
8. Yo no me enojo con mis alumnos.

[*To be followed by* LISTENING COMPREHENSION–SPEAKING EXERCISE]

---

[16]*Abrigo* is singular with both singular and plural subjects (each person puts on one coat).
[17]*Irse a (su) casa,* to leave for (one's) home.

35. pedir *vs.* preguntar

Yo no le **pido** a usted favores.	*I'm not asking you for favors.*
Yo le **pregunto** su nombre, nada más.	*I'm asking you your name only.*

A. **Preguntar** means "to ask" in the sense of inquiring or seeking information. **Pedir** means "to ask (for)" in the sense of requesting or soliciting, and also ordering something in a restaurant.

B. "To ask for" is simply *pedir;* no preposition is necessary.

WRITTEN TRANSLATION

Remember to include the indirect object pronoun together with the indirect object noun.

1. Pepita asks Margarita for the recipe.
2. Margarita asks Pepita what (which) recipe.
3. Napoleón asks his wife why she doesn't say good-bye.
4. Margarita asks why they don't stay a little while longer.
5. Napoleón asks for his coat.

36. para *and* por

para		
for (destination)	Voy **para** Panamá.	*I'm headed for Panama.*
	El dinero es **para** Juan.	*The money is for Juan.*
for (deadline)	¿Qué tenemos que hacer **para** mañana?	*What do we have to do for tomorrow?*
by (deadline)	Tiene que estar aquí **para** el lunes.	*He has to be here by Monday.*
in order to	Venden su casa **para** comprar otra.	*They're selling their house (in order) to buy another one.*
por		
for (duration)	Voy a estar en Panamá **por** tres semanas.	*I'm going to be in Panama for three weeks.*
for (exchange)	Le doy un dólar **por** el libro.	*I'll give you a dollar (in exchange) for the book.*
by (place)	Siempre paso **por** su casa.	*I always pass by your house.*
through	Vamos **por** la otra puerta.	*Let's go through the other door.*
along	¿Caminamos **por** el río?	*Shall we walk along the river?*
because	**Por** usted, voy a llegar tarde.	*Because of you, I'm going to be late.*
	Por comer tanto, tiene dolor de estómago.	*Because he ate (of eating) so much, he has a stomach ache.*
	¿Por qué?	*Why? (Because of what?)*

A. Some of the most common meanings of **para** and **por** are illustrated above. You will learn other meanings later. *Para* and *por* are tricky because both sometimes correspond to English "for." Although *por* looks and sounds a lot like "for," *para* is *much more frequently* the correct Spanish equivalent.

B. The meanings of *para* all have something in common, namely, the idea of *aim, goal, destination,* or *terminal point*. This provides a useful device for deciding whether to use *para* or *por* in many sentences. Consider, for example, "He gave me a radio for the car." If "for the car" means "to put in the car," then the car is the destination of the radio, and the Spanish would be *para el carro.* But if it means "in exchange for the car" (*i.e.,* "I gave him the car, and he gave me the radio in exchange"), then the Spanish would be *por el carro.*

C. In addition to the meanings given above, *por* occurs in a number of fixed expressions which must be learned one by one. The title of the dialog of this chapter provides an example: *por fin,* "finally," "at last."

POR OR PARA

Decide whether each of the following sentences, if translated into Spanish, would require *por* or *para*. Do not actually translate the sentences.

1. Don't go through there.
2. What do you want that for?
3. I was in China for three years.
4. Betty suffered a lot because of that.
5. Is that a present for your mother?
6. I'll come by your house at eight.
7. See what happens for not listening to me.
8. This is an assignment for Monday.
9. For the love of Mike, quiet!
10. This was meant for me.

TRANSLATION

1. Who is that for, for him or for me?
2. I work in order to have money.
3. How much do you want for your car?
4. Why do you want to work for nothing?
5. When do you leave for Caracas?
6. I am here on account of you.
7. And I'm going to tell you why and what for.
8. That's what I get (that happens to me) for being so good.

READING AND COMPLETION

As you read, fill in the blanks with *por* or *para*. Do not write in the words, so that you can do the exercise more than once.

_____ ir de Nueva York a Lima en barco[18] hay que pasar _____ el canal de Panamá. Nosotros salimos _____ Lima el domingo. ¡Qué fantástico! ¡Pensar que vamos a estar allá _____ las fiestas de Año Nuevo! Pobre Jorge, _____ no tener visa de residencia en los Estados Unidos no puede venir con nosotros. El siempre está diciendo que va a ir al Departamento de Inmigración y Naturalización _____ ver si puede cambiar[19] su visa de turista _____ una de residencia. Pero nunca lo hace.

---

[18] Boat.   [19] Change.

37. Unspecified subjects

Singular verb	
1. ¿Cómo **se escribe** "ventana"?	*How is "ventana" spelled?*
2. ¿Cómo **se hace**?	*How does one do it?*
3. **Se pone** un poco de cebolla...	*You put in a little onion . . . .*
Plural verb	
4. Aquí **se venden** sartenes grandes.	*Large frying pans are sold here.*
5. **Se necesitan** dos tazas de agua.	*You need two cups of water.*
6. **Se comen** calientes.	*People eat them hot.*

The construction *se + third person verb form* is often used in sentences in which the speaker considers it unnecessary or irrelevant to state exactly the subject of the verb. The verb usually agrees in number with the object. The most common English equivalents are passive sentences with no actor or agent indicated (examples 1 and 4), or expressions with "one," "you," "they," or "people," meaning "someone," "anybody," or "everyone" (examples 2, 3, 5, and 6). Notice examples 2 and 6, where the English object pronouns "it" and "them" have no Spanish equivalent.

REJOINDERS

Follow the examples.

1. Usted tiene que decir "buenos días" en inglés.
   ¿Cómo se dice "buenos días"?
2. Esta noche voy a hacer paella.
   ¿Cómo se hace paella?
3. Quiero escribir un libro.
4. ¿Quiere usted ir al centro, por favor?
5. Ustedes no pronuncian bien la palabra "immediately."
6. ¡Mirando la televisión y hablando por teléfono! ¡Santa María! ¡Esa no es manera de estudiar para un examen, hijito!

TRANSLATION

Use expressions with *se.*

1. How do they eat (the) paella, hot or cold?
2. And how do you make it?
3. You need many ingredients.[20]
4. First you put in a little onion and garlic.
5. Then you . . . you . . . how do you say "you add"?
6. *Se agrega.* Then you add pieces of chicken,[21] right?
7. Yes, but other things are added too.
8. How long do you cook the whole thing?[22]
9. Five hours. Then you put the paella on the table.
10. I know. Then you eat it, you wash the dishes, and that's all.

---

[20] *Ingredientes.*   [21] *Pollo.*   [22] *Todo.*

Reading

Recetas de cocina
Seviche ecuatoriano

Ingredientes:

medio kilo[23] de camarones[24]
un poquito de cebolla picada[25]
una taza de jugo de naranja[26]
media taza de jugo de limón

un poquito de salsa de ají picante[27]
salsa de tomate (un cuarto de taza)
sal y pimienta

Cómo se prepara:

En agua hirviendo[28] se ponen los camarones por aproximadamente un minuto. Luego se sacan[29] y se ponen en otro recipiente para servirse. Se agregan los otros ingredientes y eso es todo. El seviche se sirve frío con un poco de maní[30] tostado encima. Es un plato parecido al coctel de camarones americano.

QUESTIONS

1. ¿Cuál es el ingrediente principal del seviche ecuatoriano?
2. ¿Cómo se ponen la cebolla y el ajo, enteros o picados?
3. ¿Les gusta a ustedes el ajo?
4. ¿Qué cantidad se pone de jugo de naranja para medio kilo de camarones?
5. ¿Cuáles son los otros ingredientes?
6. ¿Por cuánto tiempo se ponen los camarones en agua hirviendo?
7. ¿Qué más se hace?
8. ¿Con qué se come el seviche de camarones?

Huevos rancheros mexicanos

Ingredientes:

huevos   sal
tortillas   salsa picante (de chilitos[32] y cebollitas picados y tomates molidos[33])
aceite[31]

Cómo se prepara:

Se calienta una sartén con aceite. Se pone a freír una tortilla. En otra sartén caliente con aceite se fríen los huevos. Se ponen los huevos sobre la tortilla y se agregan sal y salsa picante al gusto.

---

[23]Kilogram, equal to about 2.2 lbs.   [24]Shrimp.   [25]Chopped, diced.   [26]Orange juice.   [27]Hot pepper sauce.   [28]Boiling.
[29]*Sacar*, to take out.   [30]Peanuts.   [31]Oil.   [32]Hot peppers.   [33]Ground.

1. ¿Cuántas sartenes se necesitan para hacer huevos rancheros?
2. ¿Cuáles son los ingredientes necesarios?
3. ¿Qué se pone a freír en la primera sartén?
4. ¿Cómo se fríen los huevos?
5. ¿Dónde se ponen los huevos?
6. ¿Qué se agrega después?

Arroz con pollo centroamericano

Ingredientes:

medio kilo de arroz	dos cucharadas de mantequilla
un pollo	cebolla y ajos[34] picados
dos cucharadas de salsa de tomate	sal y pimienta

Cómo se prepara:

Primero se cocina el pollo con un poco de agua, sal, pimienta, ajos y cebolla. Luego se fríe todo en mantequilla. Después se agrega el caldo[35] del pollo, el arroz y el resto de los ingredientes. Cuando el arroz ya está cocinado, se puede agregar, si se quiere, un poco más de caldo. Se sirve con ensalada de lechuga[36] y tomate.

QUESTIONS

1. ¿Cómo se llama este plato?
2. ¿Cuáles son los ingredientes principales para la receta del arroz con pollo?
3. Después de cocinar el pollo con agua, ¿qué se hace?
4. ¿Qué se agrega al pollo y al arroz cuando están ya cocinados?
5. ¿Con qué puede servirse el arroz con pollo?
6. ¿Cuál es su plato favorito? ¿Cómo se hace?

CONVERSATION STIMULUS

Do the basic dialog of this chapter once more, but this time add more details to the story of Amadeo's divorce, the recipe for paella or some other dish, and the serious illness of "what's his name." Use your imagination.

[*To be followed by* LISTENING COMPREHENSION–SPEAKING EXERCISE]

---

[34]*Ajo* may also mean a single clove of garlic.   [35]Broth.   [36]Lettuce.

Listening Passage
for Chapter 8
English Translation

How Lucky Are Those
Who Study Spanish!

(1) Among people who study or teach foreign languages, controversies sometimes arise over whether one language is more difficult (presents greater difficulty) to study (it) and learn (it) than another. This is something very relative since it depends largely (in great part) on (what is) the native language of the student. For example, it is no doubt easier for an Argentinean to learn to speak Portuguese or Italian than it is for an American, since these are both Romance languages, like Spanish. On the other hand (for the other part), Germans can learn to speak English more easily than Frenchmen can, because English and German are languages that belong to the same Germanic family and have, therefore (by consequence), many linguistic features in common which do not exist in French, a Romance language.

(2) A direct comparison in this respect between one language and another cannot be made scientifically. One can argue for hours trying to convince his opponent, and nobody

wins. For example, is it easier for us Spanish speakers to learn to pronounce in an obscure manner the unstressed vowels of English, or for those who speak English to learn to pronounce clearly (in clear form) our unstressed vowels? It's like arguing about politics or religion—nobody wins.

(3) Only in the aspect of (the) written language is there not the least doubt as to which of these two languages is easier: Spanish, naturally. But it's this and nothing else, really, that makes many people believe (have the opinion) that English is harder to learn than Spanish—which is an inaccurate (inexact) judgment, because we must not confuse the spoken language with the written language.

(4) In the basic conversation that follows, we can observe this erroneous concept in (through) the comments of Emilio and Luz María, who, as we remember, are students at the Cultural Center in Bogotá. Both complain that English is too difficult and envy the lucky ones who study Spanish. Emilio says that English is killing him, that it is the most difficult language in (of) the world; and Luz María says that she's going crazy with the rules of pronunciation.

(5) The two of them decide to go to the bookstore to see if they can find a good grammar. There they see the book they're looking for and they point it out to the clerk. But this young lady seems to be a little dumb and she touches all the books—the gray book, the yellow book, the blue one, the purple one, this one, that one, the one that's up high, the one that's down below—all except the red one, the one on (of) grammar. At last she finds it and shows it to Luz María and (to) Emilio. But she doesn't know how much it costs. She says that she's going to (go to) ask the price and that she'll be right back. Luz María, in the meantime, says that she'll bet it's very expensive.

Grammar Points

First, the last group of verbs that are irregular in the present tense; second, the sequence of direct and indirect object pronouns; third, the possessive adjectives; and fourth, nominalization.

TO BE FOLLOWED BY
LISTENING RECOGNITION EXERCISE

133

Chapter 8

Basic Dialog

¡Qué dichosos son los que estudian español!

E. *Emilio*   LM. *Luz María*   EM. *Empleada*

I

E.   ¿De quién es este diccionario, tuyo? ¿Me lo prestas?

LM.   No es mío, pero te lo presto, si me lo devuelves.

E.   Cómo no. ¡El inglés[1] me mata! ¡No hay un idioma más difícil en el mundo!

LM.   Tienes razón. El español es mucho más fácil.

E.   ¿Tú recuerdas, Luz María, cómo se pronuncia esta palabra: erre-o-u-ge-hache?

LM.   "Rof", me parece, pero no estoy segura. Yo me vuelvo loca con las reglas de pronunciación.

E.   Vamos a la librería a ver si encontramos una buena gramática.

II

LM.   ¿Cuánto cuesta ese libro? No, el otro, más arriba.

EM.   ¿Este?

E.   El rojo, señorita, el que acaba de tocar. ¡Ese!

EM.   Ah, el de gramática. No sé el precio. Voy a preguntar. Ya vuelvo.

LM.   Apuesto a que es muy caro.

---

[1] The definite article is used with names of languages functioning as subjects of sentences. The names of all languages are masculine. Remember that the names of languages and nationalities are always spelled with a lower-case letter.

$<$ *Una librería en San José, Costa Rica*

How Lucky Are Those Who Study Spanish!

E. *Emilio*   LM. *Luz María*   C. *Clerk*

I

E. Whose[2] dictionary is this, yours? Will you lend it to me?

LM. It's not mine, but I'll lend it to you, if you return it to me.

E. Sure. English kills me! There isn't a more difficult language in the world!

LM. You're right.[3] Spanish is much easier.

E. Do you remember, Luz María, how this word is pronounced: *r-o-u-g-h?*

LM. "Rough," I believe,[4] but I'm not sure. The rules of pronunciation are driving me crazy.[5]

E. Let's go to the bookstore and see if we can find a good grammar.

II

LM. How much does that book cost? No, the other one, a little higher.[6]

C. This one?

E. The red one, Miss, the one you just touched. That one!

C. Oh, the grammar.[7] I don't know the price. I'm going to ask. I'll be right back.

LM. I'll bet[8] it's very expensive.

PRONUNCIATION EXERCISES

1. The *tio* and *tu* sequences. Because of the influence of English words like "question," where *tion* is pronounced almost like "chin," and "natural," where *tu* is pronounced almost like "chew," students tend to mispronounce the sequences *tio* and *tu* in many Spanish words. In these Spanish combinations there is no fusing of sounds: the *t* is pronounced [t], never like *ch*. It will probably help if you remember that Spanish *t* is always *dental;* that is, the tip of the tongue must be pressed firmly against the back of the upper teeth. Listen carefully to the following pairs of words.

question	cuestión
natural	natural
intellectual	intelectual

Now listen and repeat.

naturalmente	puntual	fortuna
cuestión	Portugal	impetuoso
cultural	mutuamente	fractura
intelectual	indigestión	bastión

2. *s* and *z* between vowels. In Spanish there is never a [z] sound between vowels, even when the spelling is *z*.[9] Listen to the following English and Spanish words and compare the sound of *s* or *z* between vowels.

Venezuela	Venezuela
president	presidente
visit	visitar

---

[2]Of whom; Spanish has no one-word equivalent of the interrogative "whose."   [3]You have reason.   [4]It seems to me.   [5]I'm turning myself crazy with the rules . . . .   [6]More up.   [7]The (book) of grammar.   [8]*Apostar a,* to bet on (something).
[9]In Castilian pronunciation the letter *z* is pronounced like the *th* in "think."

Now listen and repeat.

visitar	música	taza
presidente	azul	brazos
Venezuela	rosas	resultado
razón	Brasil	Jesús
presente	museo	pedazo

SUPPLEMENT

I

¿De quién es este diccionario?

	cuaderno	*notebook*
	lápiz	*pencil*
	papel	*(piece of) paper*
	periódico	*newspaper*
¿De quién es esta	revista?	*magazine*
	pluma	*pen*
	carta	*letter*

¿Me lo prestas?

regalas	*give (as a present)*
muestras[10]	*show*

Vamos a la librería.

biblioteca	*library*
tienda	*store*
oficina	*office*

Yo me vuelvo loca.

me muero de hambre	*starve*[11]

¡Qué dichosos son los que estudian español!

enseñan	*teach*
entienden[12]	*understand*

II

No, el otro, más arriba.

más abajo	*lower*

Apuesto a que es muy caro.

barato	*inexpensive*

---

[10] The infinitive is *mostrar.*

[11] Die of hunger. This verb is used both reflexively and nonreflexively; the infinitive is *morir(se).*

[12] The infinitive is *entender.*

El rojo

amarillo	*yellow*	café[13]	*brown*
blanco	*white*	anaranjado	*orange*
gris	*gray*	morado	*purple*
azul	*blue*		

DIALOG AND SUPPLEMENT CHECK

SENTENCE RECALL

Say the dialog phrase or sentence in which each of the following words or phrases occurs.

razón	loca	libro
dichosos	difícil	arriba
se pronuncia	diccionario	tocar
	precio	

ITEM SUBSTITUTION

Repeat each of the following sentences, substituting a related word or phrase for the part in italics. If books are closed, your teacher will repeat the item at the end of each sentence.

1. Vamos a *la tienda.*
2. El *azul,* señorita.
3. ¿Me lo *regalas?*
4. El *verde,* señorita.
5. No, el otro, *más abajo.*
6. ¡*Ese!*
7. Yo *me vuelvo loca.*
8. ¿De quién es *esta pluma?*
9. Vamos a *la librería.*
10. ¡Qué dichosos son los que *aprenden* español!
11. ¿Me lo *das?*
12. El *anaranjado,* señorita.

DICTATION AND COMPLETION

You will hear several incomplete dialog lines. Write each one down as you hear it, then complete it.

1. No es mío, pero...
2. Yo me vuelvo loca con las...
3. ¿Tú recuerdas, Luz María,...?
4. Vamos a la librería...
5. El rojo, señorita...
6. ¿De quién es...?

[*To be followed by* LISTENING RECOGNITION EXERCISE]

---

[13] Some speakers say *de color café;* others use *marrón, pardo, castaño,* or *habano.* There is no one universally accepted term in Spanish for "brown."

Grammar

38. *Stem-changing verbs:* o ⟶ ue

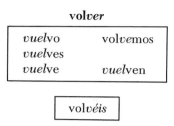

volver

*vuel*vo	vol*ve*mos
*vuel*ves	
*vuel*ve	*vuel*ven

vol*véis*

A. There is a large group of verbs in which the vowel of the stem changes from *o* to *ue*. The diphthong *ue* occurs when the stress falls on the last vowel of the stem; otherwise the stem vowel is *o*. (In the chart, the stressed syllable is indicated by italics.) This group includes *-ar*, *-er*, and *-ir* verbs. Since it cannot be predicted from the infinitive which verbs have the vowel alternation, you must simply memorize them.

B. Some of the most common verbs with the *o* ⟶ *ue* alternation are listed below.

-ar		*-er*		*-ir*	
mostrar	*to show*	devolver	*to return, give back*	morir(se)	*to die*
apostar	*to bet*	volver	*to return, go back*		
costar	*to cost*	poder	*to be able*		
encontrar	*to find*				

PARADIGM PRACTICE

Do paradigm practice with each of the verbs listed above, alternating the *nosotros* form with the other forms.

EXAMPLE: **yo muestro, nosotros mostramos, tú muestras, nosotros mostramos, usted muestra, nosotros mostramos, él muestra,** etc.

PERSON–NUMBER SUBSTITUTION

If the cue is given in English, do not include the subject pronoun in your response.

1. Un momento, ya vuelvo.
   (we, they, I, she, she and he, you [*fam.*], he and I)
2. Emilio le devuelve el diccionario a Luz María.
   (nosotros, tú, él y Pedro, "cómo se llama", todos)
3. La empleada le muestra la gramática a Emilio.
   (yo, nosotros, los empleados, todo el mundo)
4. Linda se muere de frío[14].
   (Linda y Vickie, Linda y yo, tú, usted, todo el mundo, yo)

---

[14] Is freezing to death.

5. ¿A qué hora vuelven ustedes?
   (nosotros, la empleada, tú, Emilio y Luz María, usted y yo, los empleados)
6. Si no encuentro la revista, no puedo ir.
   (we, they, you [*fam.*], you [*pl.*], she)
7. No recuerdo cómo se pronuncia.
   (we, they, I, nobody, he and I)
8. Yo nunca apuesto; no me gusta.
   (mi hermano, nosotros, ellos, tú, mis amigos)

ALTERNATE SUBSTITUTION

¿Cuánto cuesta ese libro rojo?
_____ libros ____
_____ amarillo?
_____ cuestan _____
_____ pluma ___
_____ azul?
_____ lápiz ____
_____ estos _____

INFINITIVE DRILL

Give the infinitive for each of the verb forms listed below, attaching object pronouns whenever they are given.

EXAMPLE: nos vamos   lo sabes
           irnos   **saberlo**

voy	estamos	vuelvo	comiendo	me alegro
me voy	te despides	me mata	haciendo	lo sé
es	se casa	me da	somos	quiere
lo traigo	le pido	sigo	se divorcian	viene
me muero	los devuelves	dicen	lo presto	te prometo
	tengo	nos muestra	le gusta	

39. *Sequence of object pronouns*

Me lo da (a mí).	*He gives it to me.*
Te lo da (a ti).	*He gives it to you.*
Se lo da (a usted, a ustedes). (a él, a ella). (a ellos, a ellas).	*He gives it to* { *you.* *him, her.* *them.*
Nos lo da (a nosotros).	*He gives it to us.*

Os lo da (a vosotros).	*He gives it to you.*

140

A. The most frequent combinations of object pronouns are those illustrated above. In these combinations the pronouns beginning with *l* are always second; that is, they directly precede the verb form.

B. *Le* and *les* are always replaced by *se* before another pronoun beginning with *l*.

Le traigo el abrigo.	*I'll bring him his coat.*
Se lo traigo. (*Not* Le lo traigo.)	*I'll bring it to him.*
Les doy la receta.	*I'll give you the recipe.*
Se la doy. (*Not* Les la doy.)	*I'll give it to you.*

C. The prepositional phrases *a mí, a ti, a él,* etc., may be used for emphasis or clarity, the same as they are with single pronouns.

    Este libro, ¿se lo doy **a usted, a él** o **a ella**?   *Shall I give this book to you, to him, or to her?*

D. The position of a sequence of two object pronouns with respect to the verb is the same as that of a single pronoun. That is, sequences of pronouns precede conjugated verb forms (as in the examples in the chart and in paragraph B) or they may optionally be attached to infinitives and present participles (as in the following examples).

    ¿La casa? Quiero comprár**sela,** pero   *The house? I want to buy it from*
        él no **me la** quiere vender.   *him, but he doesn't want to*
                                   sell it to me.

A sequence may *not* be split, with one pronoun going before the conjugated verb and the other after the infinitive or participle. In the present progressive construction, the object pronouns may either be attached to the present participle or come before the form of *estar.*

    ¿La casa? Están terminándo**mela.**
    ¿La casa? **Me la** están terminando.   *The house? They're finishing it for me.*

The position of stress does not shift in infinitives and participles when pronouns are attached. Thus written accents are used, as shown in the examples above.

NOUN–PRONOUN SUBSTITUTION

    1. El diccionario, ¿me lo prestas?
       (la pluma)
      La pluma, ¿me la prestas?
       (los zapatos, el lápiz, las camisas, la gramática)
    2. ¿El abrigo? Ah, sí, ya se lo traigo.
       (su ropa, los calcetines rojos, su sombrero gris, los pantalones anaranjados, la camisa
       morada, los zapatos blancos, la corbata amarilla, un doctor y un policía)
    3. ¿El diccionario? Sí, te lo presto, si me lo devuelves.
       (los zapatos, este sombrero, mis servilletas, el mantel blanco, estos cuchillos, las tazas,
       el carro, la bicicleta, mis gafas)
    4. Ese libro, señorita, ¿puede mostrárnoslo?
       (esas cosas, la casa, el jardín, la piscina, los cuartos, el comedor, la cocina y la sala, los
       baños)

READING AND RETENTION

Read the following paragraph a sufficient number of times for you to retain the details of the situation it describes. Then answer the questions that follow.

Juanito siempre les presta sus cosas a sus amigos y muchas veces ellos no se las devuelven. Y cuando él les pide algo a ellos, ellos no le dan nada. Ahora acaba de prestarle su pluma a Pedro, su diccionario a María, y en este momento Pirimpimpín le está pidiendo[15] el reloj. Estoy seguro de que Juanito también va a prestárselo y Pirimpimpín no va a devolvérselo. ¡Pobre Juanito!

Questions. Answer with complete sentences each time. Notice that if the question begins with ¿*Qué?*, your answer can include only an indirect object pronoun (first example). Otherwise, your answer should contain both a direct and an indirect object pronoun (second example). Remember to make the appropriate changes in number and gender.

1. ¿Qué les presta Juanito a sus amigos?
   Les presta todas sus cosas.
2. ¿Y sus amigos le devuelven las cosas siempre?
   No, muchas veces no se las devuelven.
3. ¿Qué le dan ellos a Juanito cuando él les pide algo?
4. ¿Qué acaba de prestarle Juanito a Pedro?
5. ¿A quién acaba de prestarle Juanito su pluma?
6. ¿Qué acaba de prestarle a María?
7. ¿A quién acaba de prestarle el diccionario?
8. ¿Qué le está pidiendo Pirimpimpín a Juanito en este momento?
9. ¿A quién le está pidiendo Pirimpimpín el reloj?
10. ¿Cree usted que Juanito va a prestarle el reloj a Pirimpimpín?
11. ¿Y cree usted que Pirimpimpín va a devolverle el reloj?
12. ¿Qué le presta Juanito a usted?[16]
13. ¿Qué les presta Juanito a ustedes?
14. ¿A quién va a prestarle Juanito su reloj?
15. ¿Pirimpimpín acaba de pedirle, va a pedirle o está pidiéndole el reloj a Juanito en este momento?
16. Si Juanito le presta algo a usted, ¿usted se lo devuelve?
17. Y si yo le presto a usted dinero, ¿me lo devuelve usted después?
18. Y si yo le pido a usted cinco dólares, ¿me los presta usted?
19. Y si le pido a usted un favor, ¿me lo hace?
20. En el diálogo de esta lección, ¿qué le pide Emilio a Luz María?
21. ¿Y Luz María le presta el diccionario?
22. ¿Va a devolverle el diccionario Emilio a Luz María?

WRITTEN TRANSLATION

Many previously discussed grammar points are drilled in the following exercise. If you are in doubt about how to translate a phrase, do not guess, but consult the appropriate grammar section.

A. What is that (that)[17] you have in your hands?
B. It is a picture (*una foto*) of the house that I'm going to give (as a gift) Luisita.
A. When is your daughter getting married?
B. In November, I believe, but I don't remember the exact date. The seventeenth, perhaps.
A. It's a very nice house. Whose is it?

---

[15] In -*ir* verbs like *pedir* (see page 122), *i* occurs in the stem of the present participle.
[16] In Spanish the double negative is the correct form. Thus you must say in Spanish, "Juanito doesn't lend me nothing."
[17] *Que* is never omitted in Spanish.

B. Do you know Dr. Campos? He is the owner. If he sells it to me cheap, I'll buy it from him tomorrow.

A. The house looks very nice. Before buying it, however, why don't you go see others?

B. What for? After seeing two or three already, I'm sure that we're not going to find a better one (one better).

A. What are you doing now? Do you want to go with me to see the house that my uncle just bought?

B. No, thanks, I don't have time now. I have to do my work for tomorrow.

[*To be followed by* LISTENING COMPREHENSION–SPEAKING EXERCISE]

40. *Possessive adjectives*

Before the noun		After the noun
mi(s) tío(s)	*my uncle(s)*	el (los) tío(s) **mío(s)**
mi(s) tía(s)	*my aunt(s)*	la(s) tía(s) **mía(s)**
tu(s) tío(s)	*your uncle(s)*	el (los) tío(s) **tuyo(s)**
tu(s) tía(s)	*your aunt(s)*	la(s) tía(s) **tuya(s)**
su(s) tío(s)	*his, her, your, their uncle(s)*	el (los) tío(s) **suyo(s)**
su(s) tía(s)	*his, her, your, their aunt(s)*	la(s) tía(s) **suya(s)**
nuestro(s) tío(s)	*our uncle(s)*	el (los) tío(s) **nuestro(s)**
nuestra(s) tía(s)	*our aunt(s)*	la(s) tía(s) **nuestra(s)**

vuestro(s) tío(s)	*your uncle(s)*	el (los) tío(s) **vuestro(s)**
vuestra(s) tía(s)	*your aunt(s)*	la(s) tía(s) **vuestra(s)**

A. There are essentially two ways of expressing possession in Spanish: with a possessive adjective, as shown in the chart, and with *de*.

Es la hija **del** dueño. *She's the owner's daughter.*

El libro es **de** Marta. *The book is Marta's.*

B. **Mi, tu,** and **su** show inflection for number only; **nuestro, vuestro, mío, tuyo,** and **suyo** show inflection for both number and gender. The biggest problem the possessive adjectives present to English-speaking students is that they agree in number and gender with the *thing possessed*, not with the possessor. Study the following examples carefully.

ONE THING POSSESSED

Esa es **su** casa.

That's his (her, your, their) house.

MORE THAN ONE THING POSSESSED

Esas son **sus** casas.

Those are his (her, your, their) houses.

C. Note that the phrases *su casa* and *la casa suya* may mean *la casa de él, de ellos, de ella, de ellas, de usted,* or *de ustedes.* When the intended meaning of *su* or *suyo* is not clear from the context, or when the speaker wishes to emphasize one possessor rather than another, the appropriate phrase with *de* is used. *Suyo* is more common when the possessor is *usted;* and *de él, de ella,* etc., more common in the other cases.

The following is a summary of the forms you should memorize for active use, although you may hear native Spanish speakers using other forms.

POSSESSOR	BEFORE NOUN	AFTER NOUN
yo	mi	mío
tú	tu	tuyo
usted	su	suyo, de usted
él	su	de él
ella	su	de ella
nosotros	nuestro	nuestro, de nosotros
ustedes	su	de ustedes
ellos	su	de ellos
ellas	su	de ellas

ITEM SUBSTITUTION

Remember that the possessive adjective agrees with the noun possessed, not with the possessor.

1. ¿De quién es este diccionario, tuyo o de ella?
   (cosas)
   ¿De quién son estas cosas, tuyas o de ella?
   (carta, lápices, revistas, periódico, pluma)
2. Ese tenedor no es suyo, es mío.
   (plato, cuchara, servilletas, manteles, gafas, taza, huevos, ensalada, pan)
3. Esta casa no es de nosotros, es de mi tío.
   (cuarto, piscina, jardines, árboles, hotel[18], cosas)
4. No sé si la librería es de él, de ella o de los dos.
   (hoteles, farmacia, dinero, coche, hijos, casa)

QUESTIONS

Answer with a possessive adjective or phrase and point with your finger as you respond.

EXAMPLE: ¿De quién son esos zapatos?
    Míos (or **suyos, de él, de María,** etc.).

1. ¿De quién son estas cosas?
2. ¿De quién es este reloj?
3. ¿De quién es esa revista?
4. ¿De quién son esas gafas?
5. ¿De quién son estos zapatos?

6. ¿Y esta cabeza?
7. ¿Y esos ojos?
8. ¿Y estas manos?
9. ¿Y esta clase?
10. ¿Y estas orejas?

---

[18] Masc.: *el hotel.*

41. *Nominalization*

1.	El libro azul y **el** (libro) **rojo**	*The blue book and the red one*
2.	Las camisas mías y **las** (camisas) **suyas**	*My shirts and yours*
3.	El libro de recetas y **el** (libro) **de gramática**	*The recipe book and the one on (of) grammar*
4.	El libro que está allí y **el** (libro) **que acaba de tocar**	*The book that's over there and the one you just touched*
5.	Un lápiz anaranjado y **uno** (lápiz) **negro**	*An orange pencil and a black one*
6.	**Esta** (chica) y **ésa** (chica)	*This one and that one*
7.	**Este** (muchacho) y **otro** (muchacho)	*This one and another one*

A. English frequently uses the word "one" or expressions such as "that which" and "those of" in order to avoid repetition of a noun. Spanish, on the other hand, simply omits the repeated noun, under certain conditions. The noun modifiers minus the omitted noun function just like the original noun phrase, and are thus said to be "nominalized."

B. Repeated nouns may be omitted if they are preceded by a definite article and followed by a simple adjective (examples 1 and 2), an adjective phrase beginning with *de* (example 3), or an adjective clause beginning with *que* (example 4).

C. Repeated nouns may also be omitted—regardless of what modifiers may follow—if they are preceded by an indefinite article (example 5), a demonstrative adjective (examples 6 and 7), or *otro* (example 7).

D. Only two changes occur in nominalized noun phrases: *un* becomes *uno* (example 5), and nominalized demonstratives have a written accent on the stressed syllable (example 6). "Another (one)" is simply *otro*, not *un otro* or *uno otro* (example 7).

READING EXERCISE

Read the following conversations, using nominalizations where appropriate to make the language more natural.

I

A. ¿Cuál casa prefiere usted, la casa del Dr. Colón, la casa de la familia Vega o la casa del jardín grande?

B. No recuerdo cuál es la casa del Dr. Colón y cuál es la casa de la familia Vega.

A. La casa de los Vega es la casa que tiene el techo rojo.

B. Ah, claro. Esa casa es la casa que me gusta más. Es la casa que cuesta más, pero es la casa más bonita.

II

C. ¡Qué confusión de libros! ¿Cuáles libros son los libros míos y cuáles libros son los libros tuyos?

CH. Los libros míos son un libro verde, un libro gris y otro libro, no recuerdo el color.

C. ¿Y adónde vas con esa corbata, hombre? ¡Esa corbata es la corbata que acabo de comprar!

CH. ¡Esta corbata no es tuya! La corbata tuya es morada; esta corbata es azul.

Answer with complete sentences, using nominalizations to avoid unnecessary repetition of the words *casa, libro,* and *corbata.*

1. ¿Cuáles son las tres casas que el Sr. A menciona?
2. ¿Recuerda el Sr. B cuál es la del Dr. Colón y cuál es la de la familia Vega?
3. ¿De quién es la que tiene un techo rojo?
4. ¿Cuál le gusta más al Sr. B?
5. ¿Es la de los Vega más cara o más barata que la que tiene un jardín grande?
6. ¿Cuáles son los libros del Sr. Ch?
7. ¿Y es la corbata que tiene el Sr. Ch la que el Sr. C acaba de comprar?
8. ¿De qué color es esa corbata?
9. Y la del Sr. C, ¿de qué color es?
10. ¿Y de qué color es la corbata de usted? ¿Y la mía?

[*To be followed by* LISTENING COMPREHENSION–SPEAKING EXERCISE]

INDIRECT DISCOURSE

Read the basic dialog of this chapter, changing it into indirect discourse. Then try to repeat parts of it in indirect discourse from memory. This is a very efficient but somewhat difficult exercise, so don't be discouraged if you can't do it fluently the first time. The exercise begins as follows.

Emilio le pregunta a Luz María de quién es ese diccionario, si es de ella. Y luego le pregunta si se lo presta.
Luz María le contesta que...

QUESTIONS

1. ¿De quién es el diccionario, de Luz María?
2. ¿Con qué condición se lo presta ella a él, si se lo devuelve pronto?
3. ¿Qué dice Emilio respecto al idioma inglés?
4. Y según Luz María, ¿tiene Emilio razón o no?
5. ¿Por qué dice ella que son dichosos los que estudian español?
6. ¿Cuál es uno de los muchos problemas que tienen los que estudian inglés, según Luz María?
7. ¿Cómo se pronuncia la palabra inglesa "hache-o-te", "jot" o "jat"?
8. ¿Usted se vuelve loco con las reglas de pronunciación del español? ¿Son fáciles o difíciles?
9. ¿Y las del inglés, cómo son?
10. ¿Cómo son los verbos en español, fáciles o difíciles de aprender? ¿Por qué?
11. ¿Cómo se escribe la palabra *gente,* con *ge* o con *jota*? ¿Y la palabra *ahora*?
12. ¿Adónde van Luz María y Emilio después?
13. ¿Qué buscan ellos allí?
14. ¿Cuál libro quieren ellos, el amarillo?
15. ¿Quieren el que está más arriba o el que está más abajo?
16. ¿El de filosofía?
17. ¿El que la señorita acaba de tocar?
18. ¿Qué va a hacer ella para saber cuánto cuesta el libro?
19. ¿Vuelve pronto?
20. ¿Apuesta Luz María a que el libro es caro o barato?

Reading

In preceding reading selections, new words were translated for you in footnotes. Perhaps you were able to guess the meaning of some of these words before you looked at the footnotes. In any event, new words will not be glossed in footnotes in the remaining reading selections. You will find that the ability to make an intelligent guess as to the meaning of a word on the basis of clues provided by its context can be very helpful in vocabulary building. As you read each selection for the first time, jot down on a separate piece of paper your guess as to the meaning of any word you are not sure of. When you have finished your preliminary reading, check the definitions given in the Spanish–English Vocabulary. Be sure not to skip this step: Some of the words may mean something quite different from what you have guessed, and some have more than one meaning. Then reread the selection in order to associate the words you have looked up with their context in the selection.

Nociones lingüísticas[19]

Nadie sabe cuántos exactamente son los idiomas que existen en el mundo, pero se calcula que el total varía entre tres mil y cinco mil. La mayor parte de ellos, sin embargo, son los lenguajes de pequeñas sociedades que se encuentran todavía en un estado primitivo de desarrollo, y hay como consecuencia miles de lenguas sobre las cuales sabemos muy poco. Estas lenguas "desconocidas" representan el habla de muchas tribus americanas, de muchos negros africanos, de muchos nativos de Australia, Nueva Zelanda, Indonesia y China y de otros pueblos asiáticos, cuya población total puede alcanzar a las dos terceras partes de los tres mil quinientos millones de personas que habitan nuestro planeta.

Las lenguas de Europa, del Mediterráneo y del Cercano Oriente, geográficamente más accesibles al análisis lingüístico, han sido clasificadas y agrupadas en "familias" de acuerdo con ciertas características similares que revelan un antepasado común.

La más grande y la más importante de estas familias es la indoeuropea, así llamada porque cubre casi toda Europa y se extiende hasta el norte de la India. Dentro de este grupo hay otras subdivisiones lingüísticas llamadas también familias. Estas ramificaciones del antepasado indoeuropeo tienen su origen en los movimientos migratorios de esta gente hacia diferentes rumbos, iniciados aproximadamente tres mil años antes de Jesucristo. Así, algunos grupos se dirigen hacia la India, y surge allí a través del tiempo el idioma sánscrito. Otros van hacia Persia, donde la lengua original de esa región se convierte en el persa antiguo. Otros llegan a la península de Grecia, y nacen con el tiempo los primeros dialectos del griego antiguo. Otros a la península italiana, y surgen las lenguas itálicas, siendo el latín una de ellas. Y otros van a las regiones escandinavas y a la Europa Occidental, originándose entonces las lenguas de la familia germánica, de la cual desciende el inglés.

Con la expansión del imperio romano a través de Europa, el latín sufre poco a poco cambios en las diferentes regiones, y se origina de esta manera otro subgrupo de idiomas llamados lenguas romances, las principales de las cuales son el español, el francés, el italiano, el portugués y el rumano.

Es obvio entonces que aunque el inglés y el español tienen el mismo antepasado, existe entre ellos una relación menor que entre dos lenguas

---

[19]In the sequences güe and güi, the dieresis (two dots) indicates that the u is pronounced. Thus, lingüístico is lin[gwí]stico, and vergüenza, "shame," is ver[gwe]nza.

romances. Sin embargo, a causa de la invasión de Inglaterra por los normandos en el año 1066, la lengua inglesa contiene gran cantidad de vocabulario y de formas gramaticales franceses y latinos, siendo por consiguiente, de la familia germánica, la más cercana al español o a cualquier otra lengua romance.

QUESTIONS

1. ¿Cuántos idiomas se calcula que hay en el mundo?
2. ¿Son todos ellos idiomas bien conocidos?
3. ¿Cuáles son dos sinónimos de la palabra "idioma"?
4. ¿Quiénes hablan todas estas lenguas sobre las cuales casi nada sabemos?
5. ¿Cuál es la población total del mundo?
6. ¿Qué parte de ese total consiste en pequeñas y primitivas sociedades?
7. ¿En cuáles regiones del mundo existen las lenguas geográficamente más accesibles al análisis lingüístico?
8. ¿Cómo se llaman los grupos en que están clasificadas estas lenguas?
9. ¿Por qué están agrupadas unas lenguas en una familia y otras en otra?
10. ¿Cuál es la más grande y la más importante de estas familias?
11. ¿Por qué se llama así?
12. ¿Cómo se originan estas subdivisiones de la familia indoeuropea?
13. ¿Cuál lengua surge de la migración hacia la India? ¿Y hacia Persia? ¿Y hacia Grecia? ¿Y hacia Italia? ¿Y hacia Europa Occidental?
14. ¿Qué ocurre como resultado de la expansión del imperio romano?
15. ¿Cómo se llama esta otra subdivisión del latín?
16. ¿Cuáles son las principales lenguas romances?
17. ¿Por qué razón contiene el inglés muchas palabras y formas de origen latino y francés?
18. Mencione usted cinco pares de palabras inglesas y españolas parecidas y, probablemente, del mismo origen.

[*To be followed by* LISTENING COMPREHENSION–SPEAKING EXERCISE]

Listening Passage
for Chapter 9
English Translation

Notes from a History Class

(1) It wasn't Columbus but the Scandinavians, five hundred years before him, who were the first Europeans who arrived at the lands of the New World. (2) It is Christopher Columbus, nevertheless, whom the world recognizes as the true discoverer of America. Columbus, unlike (differently from) his predecessors, had the good fortune to represent such an enterprising nation as was Spain at that time. (3) After Columbus' first discoveries, other explorers followed in his footsteps and discovered new lands. Then came (arrived) the conquistadors, and later on the missionaries, the settlers, and the farmers. (4) The small flat world of those days was then converted into a marvelous world, round and enormously larger. A new era was initiated for mankind, and Christopher Columbus' great feat passed into history as one of the most important events of all times.

(5) Columbus was born in Genoa, Italy, in the year 1451, of humble family. In his youth he worked as a weaver of woolen fabrics (fabrics of wool) and then he became interested in trading and navigation. He worked as a seaman on ships that sailed the Mediterranean. He was shipwrecked off (in front of) the coast of Portugal and when he arrived in that country he decided to settle (establish himself) in Lisbon, the capital. (6) He got married in Portugal and there too was born his only son, Diego. It was also in Portugal that he conceived the idea that it was possible to reach the Indies and Japan by a shorter route, (and) traveling west (towards the occident) rather than traveling east (towards the orient). (7) After many (long) investi-

gations and studies, he finally developed a plan which he presented to the king of Portugal. The project was turned down (rejected) and then Columbus went (directed himself) to the king and queen of Spain, Ferdinand and Isabella. After much doubt and hesitation the Spanish monarchs—particularly the queen—finally gave him their full support.

(8) On the third day of August of 1492 Christopher Columbus sailed (departed) from the port of Palos, in command of three small caravels with a crew of 120 men. Seven weeks later, when most of the crew were beginning to show (give) signs of despair and rebellion, one of the sailors, named Triana, sighted for the first time the lands of our continent. The date was the 12th of October, 1492.

(9) Columbus returned to Spain on the 15th of March of the following year. Then he made three more voyages. On the 25th of September, 1493, he left Spain in command of 17 ships and 1500 men. During that second voyage he discovered several islands in the Caribbean, including the Virgin Islands and Puerto Rico. (10) On his third trip he discovered the island of Trinidad and the coast of Venezuela. His last trip was in 1502. He returned to Spain in 1504 and two years later, on the 20th of May, 1506, he died in the city of Valladolid at the age of 56.

Classmates

(11) These are the notes that Cecilia, one of the characters of the dialog which follows, took during a history class. Cecilia is an excellent student, at the top (the first) of her class. She knows by heart (from memory) any date or historical fact, the length of any river, the height of any mountain, any chemical or mathematical formula, the statistics on the population or the products of any country.

(12) She is in her third year of high school (secondary) and in every subject she's taking—literature, English, French, math, history, geography, physics, chemistry, biology, psychology, and civic education—she's always the first in her class. (13) When the teacher dictates his lesson, Cecilia is always the only one who never remains behind and the one who takes the clearest notes. For this reason her classmates admire her so much and they all want to study with her for the exams.

(14) Yesterday (during the) afternoon at about two o'clock her friend Anita called her to find out if she could go and study with her, but nobody answered the phone. There was nobody home. Cecilia was out shopping.

(15) A while ago (it makes a while) Anita called again and Cecilia invited her to come to her house. Anita is going over right away.

Grammar Points

First, the preterit forms of regular verbs; second, verb forms in the imperfect, including the few that are irregular; third, the difference between the preterit and the imperfect; fourth, cardinal numbers from 60; and fifth, ordinal numbers.

TO BE FOLLOWED BY
LISTENING RECOGNITION EXERCISE

Chapter 9

Basic Dialog

Compañeras de clase

A. *Anita*   C. *Cecilia*

I

A. Aló, ¿Cecilia? Te habla Anita, ¿qué tal? Te llamé ayer pero no estabas.
C. ¡Ay qué lástima! Andaba de compras. ¿A qué hora llamaste?
A. Eran como las dos. Nadie contestó.
C. Sí, no había nadie en casa. Todos salimos ayer.
A. Ah, con razón. Yo también iba a ir al centro pero hacía mucho calor.

II

C. Y... ¿qué hay de nuevo? ¿Estudiaste para el examen de historia?
A. Un poco. A propósito, Ceci, ¿cuándo descubrió Colón la isla de Trinidad, en el segundo o en el tercer viaje?
C. En el tercero. El 31 de octubre de 1498 (mil cuatrocientos noventa y ocho).
A. ¡Qué genio! Por eso quería ir a tu casa ayer. Mis apuntes son un desastre.
C. ¿Por qué no vienes hoy? ¿A qué hora te conviene?
A. A cualquier hora. Ahora mismo si te parece.
C. Perfecto. Te espero, entonces.

Classmates

A. *Anita*   C. *Cecilia*

I

A. Hello, Cecilia? This is Anita, hi! I called you yesterday but you weren't in.

C. Oh, too bad! I was out shopping.[1] What time did you call?

A. It was about two. Nobody answered.

C. Yes, there was nobody home. We all went out yesterday.

A. Oh, no wonder. I was going to go downtown too, but it was very hot.

II

C. And . . . what's new? Did you study for the history exam?

A. A little. By the way, Ceci, when did Columbus discover the island of Trinidad, on his second or on his third trip?

C. On his third. October 31, 1498.

A. What a genius! That's why I wanted to come over to your house yesterday. My notes are a mess.[2]

C. Why don't you come over today? What time suits you?

A. Any time. Right now if it's okay with you.[3]

C. Fine. I'll be waiting for you, then.

CULTURAL NOTES

The curriculum of the secondary school system in Latin America is much broader than the U.S. high school curriculum, and a *bachiller,* or graduate of a Latin American secondary school, usually has come into contact with more fields of the humanities and sciences than most U.S. high school graduates. One of the main reasons for the wide scope of the Latin American system is that only a small percentage of secondary students are able to go on to the universities.

There are several drawbacks to this system, however. For example, since most students cannot afford to buy all the textbooks they would need for the different subjects they are studying (as many as fifteen a year in some countries), teachers must dictate their lessons in greatly condensed form and expect students to memorize everything that has been presented in class. Consequently, there is little time for laboratory and field work. However, more and more universities are now being built in Latin America, and increasing numbers of students receive government aid for higher education; the accompanying trend in the secondary schools is toward more specialized curricula.

PRONUNCIATION EXERCISES

Diphthongs with final glides. In Chapter 1 you learned that the combination of an unstressed *i* or *u* plus another vowel forms only one syllable in Spanish spoken at a normal conversational tempo. For example, *bien* has one syllable, *bueno* two. Also, as you learned in Chapter 4, a vowel followed by an unstressed *i* or *u* forms a single syllable. For example, *seis* has one syllable, *causa* two. The most common combinations of this type are given in the exercises below.

---

[1]*Andar,* literally, "to walk," is also used with the meaning of "to be out (somewhere or doing something)"; *compras,* "purchases," is a noun.   [2]Disaster.   [3]If it seems to you.

The closest English equivalent to some of these combinations may or may not be an acceptable approximation of Spanish, depending on which regional variety of English you speak. For example, one common English pronunciation of "cow" is very much like the first syllable of Spanish *causa*, but another common pronunciation of "cow" is quite different. In Spanish you must make the unstressed *i* or *u* very tense, short, and high in the mouth. Listen carefully to the following pairs of words.

I	¡ay!
boy	voy
lay	ley (*law*)
cows	causa
howl	jaula (*cage*)

Now listen and imitate the pronunciation of a native Spanish speaker as he says the following English sentences.

Boy oh boy! Why buy that blouse, Mae?
Hi, Mike! I just came from Maine.
I'm not annoyed, I am fine.

Listen and repeat the following Spanish sentences.

Soy de Buenos Aires.	*I'm from Buenos Aires.*
Hoy me voy para Europa. Muy bien.	*Today I'm leaving for Europe. Very good.*
Seis por seis no son veintiséis.	*Six times six is not twenty-six.*
¡No hay aire en el baile! ¡Auxilio!	*There's no air at the dance! Help!*

SUPPLEMENT

I

Un examen de historia

química	*chemistry*
matemáticas	*mathematics*
alemán	*German*
biología	*biology*

Pero hacía mucho calor.

viento	*windy*[4]

Te llamé ayer.

anoche	*last night*
anteayer	*(the) day before yesterday*
anteanoche	*(the) night before last*
hace unos días	*a few days ago*

---

[4] Wind.

Nadie contestó.

ganó	*won*
nació	*was born*
murió	*died*

Ahora mismo voy.

Hoy mismo	*today for sure*
Mañana mismo	*tomorrow for sure*

DIALOG AND SUPPLEMENT CHECK

SENTENCE RECALL

Say the dialog phrase or sentence in which each of the following words or phrases occurs.

octubre	mismo	apuntes
lástima	de compras	nuevo
Colón	calor	estudiaste
contestó	centro	había
	ayer	

QUESTIONS

1. ¿En qué año descubrió Colón América? ¿En qué fecha?
2. ¿Descubrió la isla de Trinidad en su tercero o en su cuarto viaje?
3. ¿Había alguien en la casa de Cecilia ayer por la tarde?
4. Según Anita, ¿hacía calor ayer o hacía frío?
5. ¿Iba a ir ella al centro ayer o al mercado?
6. ¿Con quién quería ella estudiar ayer?
7. ¿Qué quería estudiar, historia o geografía?
8. ¿Quería ella estudiar con Cecilia anoche, anteanoche o ayer por la tarde?
9. ¿Va ella a estudiar con su amiga ahora mismo o después?

[*To be followed by* LISTENING RECOGNITION EXERCISE]

Grammar

42. *The past tense*

Spanish verbs have two sets of past tense forms, the *preterit* and the *imperfect*, which refer to past time in different ways. You will learn first the two sets of forms, and then when to use the preterit and when the imperfect. It is essential for you to learn the forms thoroughly, so that they will not be a problem later, when you are concentrating on their use.

Preterit

	llamar	**comer**	**salir**
stem	llam	com	sal

llamar	comer
-é	-í
-aste	-iste
-ó	-ió
-amos	-imos
-aron	-ieron

llamasteis	comisteis	salisteis

A. Note that in the preterit forms, stress never falls on the stem. Moreover, the position of the stress is the only difference between certain forms, for example preterit *llamó*, "he called," and present *llamo*, "I'm calling."

B. For *-ar* verbs, the first person plural is the same in the preterit and the present: *trabajamos ayer*, "we worked yesterday"; *trabajamos ahora*, "we're working now."

C. Regular *-er* and *-ir* verbs have the same endings in the preterit.

D. For *-ir* verbs, the first person plural is the same in the preterit and the present: *salimos ayer*, "we went out yesterday"; *salimos ahora*, "we're going out now." This is *not* true of *-er* verbs: *comimos ayer*, "we ate yesterday," but *comemos ahora*, "we're eating now."

E. The verb *dar*, "to give," takes the endings of *-er* and *-ir* verbs in the preterit: **di, diste, dio, dimos, dieron, (disteis).**

PARADIGM PRACTICE

Before proceeding with the pattern drills, do as much paradigm practice in the preterit as possible with the verbs listed below, all of which you have learned in the present and preceding chapters.

-ar VERBS

hablar	pasar	buscar	comprar	quedarse	quejarse
tomar	esperar	preguntar	cortar	levantarse	sentarse
estudiar	trabajar	tocar	cuidar	bañarse	peinarse
entrar	mirar	llegar	encontrar	lavarse	afeitarse
empezar	conversar	mostrar	enseñar	acostarse	enojarse
cantar	fumar	ganar	regalar	casarse	divorciarse

-er AND *-ir* VERBS

comer	ver	entender	conocer	devolver	vivir
vender	aprender	nacer	deber	salir	escribir
prometer	volver	leer	creer	descubrir	(dar)

F. All the verbs listed above are regular in the preterit except for *dar*. There are, however, some spelling rules to be observed.

1. No written accent mark is required on monosyllabic forms.

> **di, dio**
> **vi, vio**

2. In the first-person singular preterit forms of *-ar* verbs, the following spelling changes occur with respect to the final consonant of the stem.

   a. $z \longrightarrow c$. It is an arbitrary rule that *z* cannot be written before *e*.

   > empezar: **empecé**

   b. $c \longrightarrow qu$. This change is required to represent the pronunciation correctly.

   > buscar: **busqué**
   > tocar: **toqué**

   The incorrect spellings *buscé* and *tocé* would represent [bussé] and [tosé].

   c. $g \longrightarrow gu$. This change, too, is needed for correct representation of pronunciation.

   > llegar: **llegué**

   The incorrect spelling *llegé* would represent [yehé].

3. The third person singular and plural endings of *-er* and *-ir* verbs, usually spelled *-ió* and *-ieron*, are spelled *-yó* and *-yeron* in verbs whose stem ends in a vowel. It is an arbitrary rule that *y* must replace unstressed *i* between vowels.

   > creer: **creyó, creyeron**
   > leer: **leyó, leyeron**

[*To be followed by* DICTATION]

PERSON–NUMBER SUBSTITUTION

1. Nosotros vendimos la casa y compramos una nueva.
   (papá, mis tíos, Napoleón, tú, los dueños, nosotros)
2. Yo leí la carta pero no la contesté.
   (mis padres, nosotros, mi novia, tú, él, todos)
3. ¿Ayer estudiaste o saliste?
   (we, I, Anita and Cecilia, the girl, they)
4. Mi marido se acostó a las nueve y se levantó a las seis.
   (mis hijos, nosotros, tú, usted, todos, todo el mundo)
5. Cuando la mujer recibió el dinero, se volvió loca.
   (él y yo, el pobre mendigo, mis parientes, la cocinera, el jardinero y la criada, tú, el marido)
6. Si te enojaste, ¿por qué no te quejaste?
   (they, María, we, the students, he)
7. María no me dio el diccionario porque no lo encontró.
   (ellos, tú, el maestro, ustedes, la empleada)
8. Yo lo busqué, lo encontré y se lo di al dueño.
   (mis hijos, alguien, nosotros, usted y ella, los alumnos)

QUESTIONS

1. ¿A qué hora llamó Anita a Cecilia ayer?
2. ¿Cecilia salió a la calle ayer o se quedó en casa?
3. ¿Estudiaron Anita y Cecilia ayer o van a estudiar hoy?
4. Cuando Anita llamó a su amiga ayer, ¿quién contestó el teléfono?

5. ¿A qué hora se levantó usted esta mañana?
6. ¿Se bañaron ustedes en agua fría o en agua caliente, o no se bañaron?
7. ¿Estudiaron ustedes español ayer?
8. ¿En qué año descubrió Cristóbal Colón América?
9. ¿Le escribió usted a alguien anteayer?
10. ¿Usted me llamó por teléfono anoche?
11. ¿Dónde aprendió usted a leer y a escribir?
12. ¿En qué mes y en qué lugar nació usted?
13. ¿Me devolvió usted el libro que le presté anteanoche?
14. ¿Qué comieron ustedes anoche a la hora de la comida?
15. ¿Entendieron ustedes o se volvieron locos con todas las cosas que les pregunté?

[*To be followed by* LISTENING COMPREHENSION–SPEAKING EXERCISE]

Imperfect

	llamar	comer	salir
stem	llam	com	sal

-aba	-ía
-abas	-ías
-aba	-ía
-ábamos	-íamos
-aban	-ían

llamabais	comíais	salíais

G. The following verbs are irregular in the imperfect.

ser: **era, eras, era, éramos, eran, (erais)**
ir: **iba, ibas, iba, íbamos, iban, (ibais)**
ver: **veía, veías, veía, veíamos, veían, (veíais)**

PARADIGM PRACTICE

Do paradigm practice in the imperfect with the following verbs.

-ar VERBS		*-er* AND *-ir* VERBS		
estar	alegrarse	seguir	ser	hacer
acabar	pensar	saber	deber	pedir
empezar	enseñar	tener	ver	irse
dar	sentarse	decir	querer	sentirse
ganar		sentir	traer	vestirse
		conseguir		

PERSON–NUMBER SUBSTITUTION

Read the following paragraph aloud. Then reread it four times, each time substituting one of the following subjects for *Rodolfo: Yo, tú, nosotros, Rodolfo y Juan.*

Cuando Rodolfo era pequeño, cuando tenía diez años de edad, más o menos, vivía en el campo. Todos los días se levantaba muy temprano y se iba a bañar al río, si hacía calor. Después de bañarse montaba a caballo[5] por horas. Cuando ya estaba cansado, se sentaba debajo de un árbol y comía los sandwiches que la cocinera le preparaba. Francamente él era muy feliz. Y lo que[6] más le gustaba a Rodolfo era que no tenía que ir a la escuela.

43. *Uses of the preterit and the imperfect*

A. Both the imperfect and the preterit refer to past activities, events, states, and conditions, but they do so in quite different ways. Essentially, the preterit views past events, etc., as noncontinuous and the imperfect views them as continuous. That is, the preterit is used to report events, situations, etc., which begin or end—or both—at some time in the past which the speaker has in mind. The imperfect, on the other hand, is used to report events, situations, etc., which neither begin nor end at the time the speaker is thinking of, but rather which have already begun and are in progress or in existence at this time.

B. The following trivial story illustrates the most important distinctions between the preterit and the imperfect. Read the entire story in English first. Then read it again, this time considering carefully the Spanish verb forms given at the right. These are the most likely equivalents of the corresponding English verb forms, in the context of the story. Comments on these equivalents follow.

Yesterday I *called* (1) a man who *had* (2) a house for sale. He *came by* (3) for me and *took* (4) me to see the house. It *was* (5) pretty old, but on careful inspection it *seemed* (6) to me to be in good condition. I *met* (7) the owner's wife. To my surprise, she *knew* (8) my wife. They *used to work* (9) in the same office. We *chatted* (10) for a while. When I *got* (11) home, my wife *was fixing* (12) supper. I *told* (13) her about the house—that it *looked* (14) like a bargain.

(1) *llamé*, pret.
(2) *tenía*, imperf. (3) *pasó*, pret.
(4) *llevó*, pret.
(5) *era*, imperf.
(6) *pareció*, pret.
(7) *conocí*, pret.
(8) *conocía*, imperf.
(9) *trabajaban*, imperf.
(10) *conversamos*, pret.
(11) *llegué*, pret.
(12) *preparaba*, imperf. (13) *conté*, pret.
(14) *parecía*, imperf.

(1) Preterit: the calling was begun and completed at the time the speaker is thinking about. (2) Imperfect: the owner neither began to have nor stopped having the house at that time. (3) and (4) Preterit: both activities were begun and completed, one after the other. (5) Imperfect: the house was already old, and continued to be so. (6) Preterit: the speaker's impression of the house came into existence as a result of the inspection, not before. (7) Preterit: the speaker's acquaintance with the owner's wife began at that moment. (8) Imperfect: the acquaintance of the owner's wife with the speaker's wife continued, having begun earlier. Compare (7) and (8) carefully. (9) Imperfect: the speaker reports a situation which existed at a previous time, not the beginning or end of this situation. (10) Preterit: the conversation is reported as an activity which began and ended, regardless of its duration, in the period the speaker has in mind. (11) Preterit: the speaker's arrival

---

[5]*Montar a caballo*, to ride horseback.   [6]*Lo que*, what, the thing that.

was completed. (12) Imperfect: the wife's activity was in progress when the speaker arrived, having begun earlier. (13) Preterit: the story of the house began and ended, no matter how long it took, during the time the speaker is now telling about. (14) Imperfect: the speaker's impression of the house was formed earlier, and continues to exist at this moment. Compare (6) and (14) carefully.

C. Spanish *consistently* distinguishes between events in progress and events that begin and/or terminate, by choosing the imperfect for the former and the preterit for the latter. English *may or may not* explicitly make the same distinction by choosing particular verb forms. For example, in (9) and (12), the expressions "used to" and "was ____-ing" clearly indicate habitual or ongoing events. However, in all other cases where Spanish has an imperfect, English has a simple past tense form ("had," "was," "knew," etc.) just as in all the cases where Spanish has the preterit. Thus, in deciding whether to use the imperfect or the preterit in Spanish, you cannot depend on English verb *forms* for a consistently reliable clue. You must think instead about the *meaning*, as illustrated and explained above.

Another striking difference between English and Spanish is that English sometimes uses completely different verbs to express distinctions that are made in Spanish by choosing the imperfect or the preterit. For example, in (7) above, the preterit of *conocer* is equivalent to "meet," that is, "begin an acquaintance," while in (8) the imperfect of *conocer* is "know," "be acquainted with." Another common verb that has different English equivalents in the preterit and the imperfect is *saber*. In the imperfect, *saber* is "know," "have factual information," while in the preterit, it is "learn," "hear," "acquire information." (The preterit of *saber* is irregular, and will be taken up in the next chapter.) You will learn other examples of this sort.

D. As a preliminary exercise on the imperfect and the preterit, go back over the basic dialog of this chapter, find all the imperfect and preterit forms, and make sure you understand the reason for using each. For example, Anita says to Cecilia, *Te llamé ayer pero no estabas.* Here, *no estabas* (imperfect) reports a state of affairs already in existence, while *te llamé* reports an act that was begun and completed during the time the speaker has in mind.

TENSE SUBSTITUTION

Read each of the following paragraphs through. Then read each one again in the past tense, substituting the appropriate forms of either the preterit or the imperfect for those in the present tense.

I

Es la una de la tarde. Estoy cansado y tengo hambre. No tengo comida en la casa. Me levanto, me afeito, me baño y me visto. Salgo a la calle. Hace un frío fenomenal. Después de andar casi un kilómetro encuentro finalmente un pequeño restaurant. Todas las mesas están ocupadas. Le pregunto al dueño cuánto tiempo tengo que esperar. Me contesta que tengo que esperar dos horas. Salgo furioso del restaurant y vuelvo a mi casa. En ese momento llega[7] mi madre del mercado. Pocos minutos después estoy yo comiendo un enorme y delicioso sandwich de jamón con queso.

II

Emilio es un alumno nuevo. El primer día él entra a la clase y se sienta al lado de Carlos María. Quiere saber quién es la maestra y entonces le pregunta a Carlos María. Carlos María no sabe el apellido de la maestra pero sabe que ella es una señorita americana.

---

[7] Either the imperfect ("was arriving") or the preterit ("arrived") is possible.

III

Vickie está en un paseo. El paseo está fantástico y todos se sienten muy alegres. Los ticos, gente alegre por naturaleza, ese día están más contentos todavía. Vickie está hablando con Manuel. Manuel quiere saber si a ella le gusta Costa Rica y cuánto tiempo va a quedarse allí. Vickie le contesta que sí, que Costa Rica le gusta mucho, pero que no puede quedarse mucho tiempo porque tiene que ir a Nicaragua. En ese instante llega Jorge e[8] interrumpe la conversación. Le pregunta a Vickie si ella tiene hambre. Manuel se enoja mucho con su amigo.

IV

El señor le debe dinero a todo el mundo. Sin embargo, va a comprar una casa más linda y más grande. La mamá empieza a explicarles a sus hijos que la casa tiene una piscina enorme y... En ese momento alguien toca la puerta[9]. Es el mismo cobrador del otro día. Lucrecia le informa que los señores acaban[10] de salir.

D I S C U S S I O N

Without rereading them, retell in the past tense the situations in each of the preceding paragraphs.

Q U E S T I O N S

1. ¿Dónde completó usted sus estudios secundarios?
2. ¿Cómo se llamaba su maestro favorito?
3. ¿Cómo era él (o ella)?
4. ¿Estudió usted historia en la escuela secundaria?
5. ¿A qué hora empezaban sus clases?
6. ¿A qué hora se levantaba usted en esos días?
7. ¿A qué hora se levantó usted esta mañana?
8. ¿Conocía usted a este señor el año pasado?
9. ¿Cuándo lo conoció?
10. ¿Dónde estaban ustedes ayer a esta misma hora?

[*To be followed by* LISTENING COMPREHENSION–SPEAKING EXERCISE]

44. *Cardinal numbers from 60*

Números cardinales

60	sesenta	400	cuatrocientos
70	setenta	500	quinientos
80	ochenta	600	seiscientos
90	noventa	700	setecientos
100	cien	800	ochocientos
101	ciento uno	900	novecientos
200	doscientos	1000	mil
300	trescientos	1,000,000	un millón (de)

---

[8] *E* is used in place of *y* when the next word begins with the sound [i].

[9] *Tocar la puerta*, to ring the doorbell or knock.

[10] The "had just" construction always uses the imperfect of *acabar*, never the preterit.

A. The conjunction *y* is always used in combinations with the multiples of ten: **sesenta y uno, ochenta y nueve.**

B. Units and tens are added directly to hundreds without *y*: **ciento treinta y ocho, ochocientos setenta y dos.**

C. From 200 on, the suffix **-cientos** changes to **-cientas** to agree with feminine nouns: **doscientos hombres, cuatrocientas mujeres.**

D. The numbers 500, 700, and 900 have the irregular forms **quinientos, setecientos,** and **novecientos.**

E. The word **mil** is not attached to *dos, tres,* etc., and, unlike the suffix *-cientos,* it remains singular: **cinco mil niños, siete mil niñas.**

F. Spanish does not use constructions like English "seventeen hundred" or "nineteen forty-five." The year 1975, for instance, can be expressed only as **mil novecientos setenta y cinco.**

G. **Millón** is a noun. Its multiples use the plural **millones.** *De* is added before another noun: **un millón de libros, cinco millones de habitantes.**

TRANSLATION

    1. Columbus discovered America in 1492.
    2. He was born in 1451.
    3. He died in 1506.
    4. There are 210 million inhabitants[11] in this country.
    5. My grandfather is (has) almost one hundred (years).
    6. Lincoln died in 1865. He was (had) 56 years old (of age[12]).

QUESTIONS

    1. ¿En qué año descubrió Colón el continente americano?
    2. ¿En qué año mataron al presidente Lincoln?
    3. ¿En qué año llegaron los astronautas americanos a la luna?
    4. ¿En qué año nació usted?
    5. ¿En qué año llegaron los primeros colonizadores ingleses al continente americano?
    6. ¿En qué año ganaron los Estados Unidos su independencia?
    7. ¿En qué año murió el presidente Eisenhower?
    8. ¿Cuál es la fecha exacta de hoy?

45. *Ordinal numbers*

Números ordinales

primero	*first*	sexto	*sixth*
segundo	*second*	séptimo	*seventh*
tercero	*third*	octavo	*eighth*
cuarto	*fourth*	noveno	*ninth*
quinto	*fifth*	décimo	*tenth*

---

[11] *Habitantes.*   [12] *De edad.*

A. Ordinal numbers above ten are seldom used in Spanish. Cardinal numbers are generally preferred. Thus, a construction like *Te he llamado quince veces* (I've called you fifteen times) is more commonly used than *Esta es la décimoquinta vez que te llamo* (This is the fifteenth time I've called you).

B. Ordinal numbers show agreement in number and gender with the noun they modify: *los **primeros** días, la **quinta** semana.*

C. *Primero* and *tercero* drop the final *o* before a masculine singular noun: *mi **primer** libro, el **tercer** viaje.*

D. Only the first day of the month is designated by the ordinal number, *primero*. Cardinal numbers are used for all the other days: ***primero** de enero, **cuatro** de julio, **treinta y uno** de diciembre.*

QUESTIONS

1. ¿Cuál es la fecha de la independencia de los Estados Unidos?
2. ¿Cuál es el primer día del año?
3. ¿En qué fecha exacta nació usted?
4. ¿En qué fecha nació Jorge Washington?
5. ¿Cuál es el primer día de la semana? ¿El segundo? ¿Cuáles son los otros?
6. ¿Cuál es el sexto mes del año?
7. ¿Qué fecha es hoy?
8. ¿Cuántos días hay en un año?

Reading

Quiénes son los latinoamericanos

Hay varias hipótesis sobre quiénes fueron y de dónde llegaron los primeros habitantes de América. Una de ellas, probablemente la de mayor fundamento, es la de que los primeros americanos fueron el producto de varios movimientos migratorios originados en el Asia y que entraron a nuestro continente procedentes de Siberia y por el estrecho de Bering, hace unos quince o veinte mil años. De allí poco a poco fueron extendiéndose hacia el sur, pasando de Alaska al Canadá, por los Estados Unidos y México y luego a través de Centroamérica a la América del Sur, llegando por fin hasta la parte sur de Chile y Argentina.

Algunos de estos grupos continuaron su vida nómada de cazadores y pescadores. Pero otros empezaron a establecerse en tierras fértiles y a interesarse en la agricultura. Se dedicaron al cultivo de varios productos vegetales, especialmente el maíz, que es todavía uno de los in-gredientes básicos en la comida del campesino latinoamericano.

La necesidad de descubrir las épocas del año más apropiadas para el cultivo de los diversos productos dio origen a la investigación de los fenómenos naturales, al establecimiento de observatorios astronómicos, y al desarrollo de las ciencias y de las artes. Así pues nacieron grandes civilizaciones indias en América, las tres más avanzadas de las cuales fueron la tolteca–azteca del valle central de México; la civilización maya en Honduras, Guatemala y la parte sur de México; y el imperio de los incas, situado en la alta cordillera de los Andes, donde hoy día están situados los países del Ecuador, Perú y Bolivia.

Cuando los primeros españoles llegaron a América, la civilización maya estaba ya casi extinta, pero la de los aztecas y la de los incas estaban en su apogeo. Los españoles, sin embargo, conquistaron a estos dos grandes imperios de una manera relativamente fácil. Pero, al contrario de los ingleses que llegaron a América con sus mujeres y sus familias, los españoles llegaron solos y se mezclaron con los indios. Apareció entonces, además del europeo (español y portugués) y del indio, un tercer elemento racial: el mestizo.

Luego llegó el cuarto componente de la población latinoamericana, el negro, importado de Africa para trabajar como esclavo en las minas, en las plantaciones de azúcar y en otras regiones donde el indio era escaso o estaba desapareciendo rápidamente. Aparecieron entonces dos nuevos elementos raciales: el mulato, resultado de la mezcla sanguínea entre blanco y negro, y, en menor escala, el zambo, producto de la mezcla entre indio y negro.

Hoy día los descendientes de otros europeos —italianos en particular, y también ingleses, alemanes, franceses y eslavos— quienes desde mediados del siglo pasado empezaron a inmigrar a este hemisferio, constituyen también una buena parte de la población latinoamericana.

El total de esta población se aproxima ahora a los doscientos setenta y cinco millones. Sin embargo, al contrario de los Estados Unidos donde el elemento europeo predomina en la mayor parte del país, la distribución etnográfica de nuestros pueblos es menos uniforme. Hay cuatro países, por ejemplo, donde predomina el elemento indio: Guatemala, Ecuador, Perú y Bolivia. En otros, como Colombia, Honduras, El Salvador, Nicaragua, Venezuela, Paraguay, Chile y México, el porcentaje de población mestiza es el más alto. En Panamá, la República Dominicana, Cuba, Haití, y en ciertas regiones de la costa de Colombia, Venezuela, Honduras, Ecuador y Nicaragua, viven gran número de negros y mulatos. En el Brasil un cincuenta por ciento de la población es también negra, mulata y zamba, y el otro cincuenta por ciento es blanca. Y finalmente, sólo en tres países, Argentina, Uruguay y Costa Rica, predomina casi en su totalidad el elemento racial de origen europeo.

DISCUSSION

Listen to each of the following statements. Some are true with respect to the preceding selection; others are false. Confirm those which are correct by repeating the whole statement and correct those which you think are false by first denying them and then changing them to make them true.

EXAMPLE: La población total de la América Latina hoy día se aproxima a los trescientos cincuenta millones. **No es verdad. La población total de la América Latina hoy día no se aproxima a los trescientos cincuenta millones; se aproxima a los doscientos setenta y cinco.**

1. Según esta hipótesis, los primeros habitantes del continente americano llegaron de Europa.
2. Los primeros habitantes entraron por la Siberia y a través del estrecho de Bering.
3. Cuando los conquistadores españoles llegaron a América, la civilización azteca ya estaba extinta.
4. Cuando los primeros españoles llegaron a América, existían solamente los dos grandes imperios: el de los aztecas y el de los incas.
5. El mulato es el resultado de la fusión racial del indio con el blanco.
6. En México predomina el elemento racial europeo.
7. En Ecuador, Bolivia, Perú y Guatemala hay más indios que negros o blancos.
8. La distribución racial de la población de Latinoamérica es muy uniforme.

[*To be followed by* LISTENING COMPREHENSION–SPEAKING EXERCISE]

Listening Passage
for Chapter 10
English Translation

Militarism in Latin America

(1) There exists a curious parallel between the epoch which followed the wars of independence in Latin America and the decades that came after the Second World War. In both instances we note the tendency towards military dictatorship, which consequently brought about (produced) suppression of political parties and individual freedom of expression.

(2) At the present time a large part of the inhabitants of the Southern Hemisphere have lost the right to live as free citizens. There exists today, as it has always existed, the case of the legally elected government that has been overthrown by a military junta—a term sadly famous throughout the entire world because of its frequent occurrence (appearance) in Latin America.

(3) What are the causes of this repeated intervention on the part of the military forces in the political field? No doubt there are a number of factors which have contributed to the phenomenon of the *caudillo* [military strong-man] and the military coup d'état. (4) For example, in countries like Paraguay, Ecuador, or Haiti there still exists a great gap between the rich and the poor classes, and there is no middle class capable of offering social and political stability. (5) In other nations, like Argentina with its strong (developed) middle class, and Peru with its large Indian population, there emerged suddenly—and dangerously for the rich classes—the vote of the masses. This brought about fear and distrust on the part of the oligarchy and,

consequently, the use of armed forces again and again.

(6) Lack of civic responsibility on the part of the ruling class, lack of educational and economic opportunities for the people (mass), and the consequent difficulty in bringing about social mobility continuously create demands which alarm those in charge of the established order. Hence constant military intervention and the enormous expense for weapons and maintenance.

Coup D'État in Andivia

(7) In the republic of Andivia—a ficticious name—there has just been a coup d'état, and the country is (finds itself) now under the command of a military junta.

(8) Sitting on a bench in Central Park in Miraflores, a small town in a province of Andivia, we find three respectable men of that community. They are don Alfredo, don Luis, and *Licenciado** Vargas. They have just heard the news on the radio and are commenting on the matter without showing (giving signs of) much alarm, an indication that this is not the first time a military junta has seized power in Andivia. (9) As we can see by the conversation among the three gentlemen, all kinds of rumors are circulating. Some say that the president was killed; others say that the president took

refuge in a foreign embassy; others, that they put him on a plane and sent him into exile. In short, nobody knows for sure.

(10) A while ago General Méndez, head of the junta, spoke on the radio. The general addressed (directed himself to) the nation to explain the reasons that obligated the armed forces to take charge—temporarily, according to him—of the government (power). Repeating the well-known and already worn-out words of other military men in Latin America, he said that the coup d'état was necessary ''in order to save the fatherland from communism.''

(11) This reasoning sounded (seemed) amusing to don Luis and his friends, because the reasons that really provoked the fall of the government legally elected by the people of Andivia were others: The president, with the support of his cabinet, attempted (wanted) to impose (establish) a small additional tax on the rich class. At the same time he proposed to Congress a reduction in the enormous budget of the armed forces. The reaction of the military was immediate.

Grammar Points

First, a group of verbs which are irregular in the preterit; second, certain affirmative and negative words; third, shortening of some adjectives; and fourth, position of the subject in statements and questions.

TO BE FOLLOWED BY
LISTENING RECOGNITION EXERCISE

*See Cultural Notes.

Chapter 10

Basic Dialog

Golpe de estado en Andivia

DON A. *Don Alfredo*   LIC. V. *Licenciado Vargas*   DON L. *Don Luis*

I

DON A. ¿Supieron[1] la noticia? ¡Cayó[2] el gobierno!

LIC. V. Sí, la oímos por radio. ¡Qué barbaridad!

DON L. Dicen que mataron al presidente. ¿Es cierto?

DON A. Nadie sabe. Algunos dicen que se refugió[3] en una embajada.

LIC. V. A mí me contó alguien que lo pusieron en un avión y lo mandaron al exilio.

DON L. ¡Qué gran tragedia! ¡Otra junta militar!

II

DON A. Hace un rato habló el general Méndez, jefe de la junta.

LIC. V. ¿De veras? ¿Qué dijo?

DON A. Dijo que el golpe de estado fue necesario para salvar a la patria del comunismo.

DON L. ¡Qué divertido! Ustedes saben cuál fue el verdadero motivo, claro.

LIC. V. Por supuesto, el nuevo impuesto a los ricos.

DON L. Y la rebaja en el presupuesto de defensa. El gobierno no cayó; simplemente se suicidó.

---

[1]Preterit of *saber.*   [2]Preterit of *caer.*   [3]Preterit of *refugiarse.*

Coup D'État in Andivia

DON A. *Don Alfredo*   LIC. V. *Licenciado Vargas*   DON L. *Don Luis*

I

DON A. Did you hear[4] the news? The government fell!

LIC. V. Yes, we heard it on the radio. Terrible!

DON L. They say the president was killed. Is it true?

DON A. Nobody knows. Some people say he took refuge in an embassy.

LIC. V. Somebody told me that they put him on a plane and sent him into exile.

DON L. That's a great tragedy! Another military junta!

II

DON A. General Méndez, the head of the junta, spoke a while ago.

LIC. V. Really? What did he say?

DON A. He said that the coup d'état was necessary in order to save the country from communism.

DON L. What a joke![5] You know what the real[6] reason was, of course.

LIC. V. Sure, the new tax on the wealthy.

DON L. And the reduction in the defense budget. The government didn't fall; it simply committed suicide.

CULTURAL NOTES

A. It should be pointed out that the diverse conditions in the twenty countries constituting Latin America make it difficult to present a general and yet accurate total political picture. The concentration and nature of political power are apt to change in these dynamic societies, which are developing at different speeds, and any overall appraisal of Latin American politics must vary from year to year. In recent times, military intervention in Latin American governments has been very frequent; yet there is a real need to differentiate among these military regimes. While some countries are run by a traditional rightist and pro-upper-class general or junta, the military leaders who overthrew the president of Peru in 1968, for example, decreed the expropriation of foreign corporations and large land-holdings in an attempt to bring about social justice and land reform that would benefit millions of destitute Indians.

B. **Don** is a title used with male first names; it is equivalent to *señor* used with last names. Thus, José Mata may be addressed as either *don José* or *Sr. Mata*. The feminine counterpart of *don* is **doña**.

C. **Licenciado** (abbreviated *Lic.*) is the title conferred on graduates of a law school in several countries. Titles such as *licenciado* and **ingeniero** (abbreviated *Ing.*) carry considerable prestige and are commonly used with last names, just like *doctor* and *professor*.

---

[4] Find out.   [5] How amusing!   [6] True.

I

¡Cayó el gobierno!
Perdió[7]   *lost*

Se refugió en una embajada.
Se metió[8]   *got inside*

La oímos por radio.
escuchamos   *listened*

Se refugió en una embajada.
una iglesia   *a church*
un edificio   *a building*

Mataron al presidente.
Derrocaron   *overthrew*

Lo pusieron en un avión.
barco   *ship*

¡Otra junta militar!
dictadura   *dictatorship*

II

El general Méndez
almirante   *admiral*
coronel   *colonel*
mayor   *major*
capitán   *captain*
teniente   *lieutenant*
sargento   *sergeant*

¿De veras? ¿Qué dijo?
trajo[9]   *brought*
hizo[10]   *did*
propuso[11]   *proposed*

Y la rebaja en el presupuesto
el aumento   *the increase*

Jefe de la junta
de la Marina   *of the Navy*
del Ejército   *of the Army*
de las Fuerzas Aéreas   *of the Air Force*

Simplemente se suicidó.
se desmayó[12]   *fainted*

DIALOG AND SUPPLEMENT CHECK

SENTENCE RECALL

Say the dialog phrase or sentence in which each of the following words or phrases occurs.

barbaridad	rebaja	se suicidó
gobierno	embajada	cierto
presidente	avión	mataron
general Méndez	impuesto	noticia
patria	supieron	exilio

ITEM SUBSTITUTION

Repeat each of the following sentences, substituting a related word or phrase for the part in italics. If books are closed, your teacher will repeat the item at the end of each sentence.

---

[7]The infinitive is *perder*.   [8]The infinitive is *meterse*.   [9]The infinitive is *traer*.   [10]The infinitive is *hacer*.
[11]The infinitive is *proponer*.   [12]The infinitive is *desmayarse*.

1. Hace un rato habló el *sargento* Méndez.
2. *Cayó* el gobierno.
3. ¿De veras? ¿Qué *propuso?*
4. Y la *rebaja* en el presupuesto
5. ¡Qué *terrible!*
6. Se refugió en una *iglesia.*
7. El general Méndez, Jefe del *Ejército*
8. ¡Otra *junta* militar!

QUESTIONS

1. ¿Es Andivia una nación verdadera o imaginaria?
2. ¿Qué pasó allí recientemente?
3. ¿Cómo cayó el gobierno?
4. ¿Son los golpes de estado raros o frecuentes en América Latina?
5. ¿Quién derrocó al gobierno de Andivia?
6. ¿Qué le pasó al presidente, lo mataron?
7. ¿Dónde se refugió él, según unas personas?
8. Y según otros rumores, ¿adónde mandaron los militares al presidente?
9. ¿Cómo lo mandaron al exilio, lo pusieron en un barco?
10. ¿Quiénes son los tres señores que estaban comentando este golpe de estado en Andivia?
11. ¿Piensan ellos que esto es una cosa buena para su patria?
12. ¿Quién es el jefe de la junta militar?
13. ¿Cuándo habló él al país?
14. ¿Para qué habló por radio?
15. ¿Cuál fue el motivo del golpe de estado, según el general Méndez?
16. ¿Cuál fue la verdadera razón, según el Lic. Vargas?
17. ¿Y cuál otra, según don Luis?
18. ¿Cómo es el gobierno de los Estados Unidos, una dictadura o una democracia?
19. ¿Cuáles son otros países democráticos del mundo?
20. ¿En cuáles países de América Latina hay gobiernos militares o dictaduras en estos momentos?

[*To be followed by* LISTENING RECOGNITION EXERCISE]

Grammar

46. *Verbs with irregular preterit forms*

The preterit forms shown below have irregularities in both stem and endings. The stems must simply be memorized, but the observations that follow the charts may be helpful.

andar	anduv-	
estar	estuv-	
poner	pus-	
saber	sup-	
poder	pud-	-e, -iste, -o, -imos, -ieron, (-isteis)
tener	tuv-	
querer	quis-	
hacer	hic-	
venir	vin-	

A. The endings of this first group are those of regular *-er* and *-ir* verbs, except that the first person singular ending is unstressed **-e** (**anduve, tuve**) rather than stressed *-í* (*comí, viví*); and the third person singular ending is unstressed **-o** (**anduvo, tuvo**) rather than stressed *-ió* (*comió, vivió*).

B. The preterit forms of *hacer* are **hice, hiciste, hizo, hicimos, hicieron, (hicisteis)**. *Hizo* is spelled with a *z* because a *c* would incorrectly indicate [íko].

traer	traj-	-e, -iste, -o, ~~-mos~~ -imos, -eron, (-isteis)
decir	dij-	

C. The preterit stems of the second group end in *j*. The endings have one peculiarity in addition to those of the first group: the third person plural ending is **-eron** (**trajeron, dijeron**) rather than *-ieron* (*comieron, tuvieron*).

ser	fui, fuiste, fue, fuimos, fueron, (fuisteis)
ir	

D. *Ser* and *ir*, the third group, have identical preterit forms with the stem **fu-**; their endings are slightly different from those of the other groups.

E. Many of the verbs listed in the charts have derivatives formed by the addition of a prefix. Derivatives usually have the same irregularities as the corresponding simple verbs. For example, **componer** (to compose; to fix) has the same endings as *poner*: **compuse, compusiste,** etc. Listed below are some common derivatives of the irregular verbs shown in the charts.

poner (puse)	*tener (tuve)*
componer *to compose; to fix*	contener *to contain*
descomponer *to decompose; to break down*	retener *to retain*
proponer *to propose*	entretener *to entertain*
reponer *to replace*	obtener *to obtain*
posponer *to postpone*	mantener *to maintain*
oponerse *to oppose*	detener *to detain, stop;* refl., *to come to a*
imponer *to impose*	*stop*

traer (traje)	*venir (vine)*
atraer *to attract*	convenir *to be suitable*
contraer *to contract; to shrink*	provenir de *to originate from*
	prevenir *to prevent; to warn*
	intervenir *to intervene*
decir (dije)	
bendecir *to bless*	
maldecir *to curse*	*hacer (hice)*
contradecir *to contradict*	deshacer *to tear down; to break up*

PARADIGM PRACTICE

You need not memorize all the compound verbs given above. You should, however, include some of them in your paradigm practice.

PERSON–NUMBER SUBSTITUTION

1. ¿Supieron la noticia?
   (we, they, you [*fam.*], I, your friend)
2. Los militares lo pusieron en un avión.
   (el general, los sargentos, usted, nosotros, el jefe, tú)
3. ¿Qué dijo el jefe de la junta?
   (tú, yo, los generales, tú y yo, ustedes, el Lic. Vargas, usted)
4. Después vino una dictadura.
   (unos coroneles, yo, nosotros, otro golpe de estado, tú)
5. El presidente no pudo hacer nada.
   (nosotros, la gente, usted, ustedes, tú, yo)
6. Yo no fui a la iglesia porque no quise.
   (mi hermano, ellos, María y Pedro, Pedro y yo, tú, ustedes)

TENSE SUBSTITUTION

Say the following sentences (based on the basic dialogs of preceding chapters) first in the imperfect tense, then in the preterit.

1. ¿Sabe usted quién es el maestro?
   ¿Sabía usted quién era el maestro?
   ¿Supo usted quién fue el maestro?
2. Dicen que es un poco estricta.
3. ¡Qué lindo está el paseo!
4. ¡Todos están tan alegres!
5. Luego vamos a Nicaragua.
6. No tengo mi reloj.
7. Quiero tomar algo frío.
8. Voy a llamar a la policía.
9. ¿Qué estás haciendo?
10. Tiene un jardín enorme.
11. ¡Qué frío hace en la calle!
12. Ah, por fin viene.
13. Estamos invitados a una boda.
14. ¡Por fin se van!
15. No es mío.
16. Tienes razón.
17. No estoy segura.
18. Voy a preguntar.
19. Es muy caro.
20. Ando de compras.
21. Mis apuntes son un desastre.
22. ¿Por qué no vienes?

174

Listen to the following statements. After each statement the teacher will ask, *¿Qué dije yo?* The whole class answers. Start your answers simply with *Que*, as in the example.

1. Yo fui al cine ayer. ¿Qué dije yo?
   Que usted fue al cine ayer.
2. Yo fui presidente de la república de Andivia.
3. Cuando era presidente ganaba[13] mucho dinero.
4. Estaba muy contento. No podía quejarme.
5. Sin embargo, tuve mala suerte.
6. Un día mis ministros y yo tuvimos una gran idea.
7. Propusimos una rebaja en el presupuesto de defensa.
8. Inmediatamente vinieron tres generales a hablar conmigo.
9. Me dijeron que yo estaba loco.
10. Yo me puse furioso.
11. Hice un gran escándalo y dije muchas malas palabras.
12. Esa misma noche me dieron un golpe de estado.
13. Mis ministros y yo tuvimos que refugiarnos en una embajada.
14. Estuvimos en esa embajada un año.
15. El embajador, pobre hombre, se volvió loco.
16. Lo pusieron en un avión y lo mandaron a su país.
17. Por fin yo pude salir de Andivia.
18. Vine a los Estados Unidos.
19. Naturalmente, traje a mi familia conmigo.
20. Los primeros días tuve dificultad en encontrar trabajo.
21. Yo no sabía hacer nada; sabía ser presidente nada más.
22. Gracias a Dios sé hablar español también.
23. Un día supe que aquí necesitaban un profesor de español.
24. Vine y hablé con el presidente —de presidente a presidente.
25. Aquí estoy ahora: su profesor, a sus órdenes.

DISCUSSION

One student relates the beginning of the story the teacher has just told. Another student continues, and then another, until the story is completed.

[*To be followed by* LISTENING COMPREHENSION–SPEAKING EXERCISE]

47. *Affirmative and negative words*

A. Negative words can be used either before or after the verb. If they follow the verb, the verb must be preceded by *no* or another negative word.

Nada me gusta. *or* **No** me gusta **nada.**	*I don't like anything.*
Nadie viene. *or* **No** viene **nadie.**	*No one's coming.*

---

[13] *Ganar* has the additional meaning "to earn."

Affirmative		Negative	
todo	*everything*	nada	*nothing, not anything*
algo	*something*		
todos, -as	*all*	nadie	*no one, not anyone*
todo el mundo	*everyone*		
alguien	*someone, anyone*		
siempre	*always*	nunca	*never, not ever*
a veces, algunas veces	*sometimes*		
una vez	*once*		
alguno(s), -a(s)	*some, someone, any*	ninguno, -a	*no, none, not any, no one, not anyone, neither one*
también	*also*	tampoco	*neither, not either*
o	*either, or*	ni	*neither, nor; not even*
hasta	*even*		

    Tampoco bailo. *or* **No** bailo **tampoco.**   *I don't dance either.*

    Nadie come **nada.** *or* **No** come **nada nadie.**   *No one eats anything.*

"Double negation" is not only not incorrect in Spanish, it is *required* when *no* precedes the verb in sentences like the examples above.

B.   When *no* precedes the verb, no other negative word may. Several negative words other than *no*, however, may precede the verb. The following example is possible, though rather extreme.

    Aquí **ninguno tampoco ni** le pide **ni** le da **nada** a **nadie nunca.**

    Nor does anyone here ever ask anyone for anything or give anything to anyone.

    (Literally, *Here no one neither neither asks nor gives nothing to no one never.*)

TRANSFORMATION

Repeat each sentence as you hear it. Then say it once more, placing the negative word after the verb.

1. ¡En esta clase ninguno estudia!
    ¡En esta clase no estudia ninguno!
2. ¡Nada están aprendiendo!
3. ¡Nunca hacen silencio!
4. ¡Tampoco llegan temprano a clase!
5. ¡Nadie pone atención!
6. ¡Esto es imposible; aquí ni se puede enseñar!

The whole class answers. Follow the example.

1. Nosotros supimos absolutamente todo.
   Nosotros no supimos absolutamente nada.
2. Yo también hice un examen muy bueno[14].
3. Todo el mundo estaba preocupado.
4. Alguien se suicidó después del examen.

5. Algunas de las alumnas se desmayaron.
6. Yo voy a pasar este curso —¡algún[15] día!
7. Bueno, o nos vamos o nos quedamos.
8. A mí todo me pasa.

NO ES CIERTO

The whole class answers. Deny the following statements about your class, beginning each denial with *No es cierto.*

1. El profesor dice que ustedes saben muchísimo.
   No es cierto, no sabemos nada.
2. Que en esta clase todo el mundo estudia.
3. Que ustedes siempre hacen silencio.
4. Que todos ponen atención.
5. Que siempre llegan temprano también.
6. Que ustedes o son muy inteligentes o estudian mucho.

WRITTEN TRANSLATION

JUAN. You don't know anybody or know anything.
LUIS. And you don't know much either.
JUAN. You don't even know who Socrates was.
LUIS. Wasn't he the one who said "I know only that I know nothing"?
JUAN. No, he never said that.

[*To be followed by* LISTENING COMPREHENSION–SPEAKING EXERCISE]

48. *Shortened modifiers*

una mujer	**un** hombre
buena mujer	**buen** hombre
mala mujer	**mal** hombre
alguna mujer	**algún** hombre
ninguna mujer	**ningún** hombre
primera mujer	**primer** hombre
tercera mujer	**tercer** hombre
gran mujer	**gran** hombre
cualquier mujer	**cualquier** hombre

---

[14] *Hacer un examen bueno,* to do well on a test.
[15] *Alguno* drops the *o* before masculine nouns. See grammar point **48.**

A. The first section of the chart above lists some adjectives which, like *uno* and the ordinal numbers *primero* and *tercero*, drop the final *o* before the singular form of masculine nouns.

B. These modifiers are shortened even when two occur together, and when they are separated from the noun.

ningún mal hombre *no bad man*
ningún otro hombre *no other man*

C. *Grande* loses its final syllable before any singular noun, either masculine or feminine; **gran** usually means "great" rather than "big." Its plural form remains unshortened: *grandes*.

D. *Cualquiera* means "anything, any one," in the sense of "whichever," "just any (old)." The shortened form **cualquier** occurs before masculine and feminine singular nouns. The plural *cualesquiera* is seldom used.

  ¿Qué vas a darle a María? *What are you going to give María?*
  Cualquier cosa.   *Any old thing.*

NOUN SUBSTITUTION

1. ¡Qué gran tragedia!
 (tragedias, hombres, almirante, capitán, jefes)
2. Esa fue una buena idea.
 (presidente, coroneles, defensa, periódico, mujer, hombre)
3. No vino ninguna mala noticia.
 (momento, persona, doctor, criada, jefe)
4. ¿Hay aquí algún problema?
 (tragedia, sargentos, alumno inteligente, maestras simpáticas, profesor de español)

TRANSLATION

1. The third week, the third man
2. A great president, but a great tragedy
3. No woman is better than I.
4. I'm not going to read just any old book.
5. Some day I'm going to write a good book.

49. *Word order*

Information Questions

¿Por qué se refugió el presidente en la embajada?

or

¿Por qué se refugió en la embajada el presidente?

Why did the president take refuge in the embassy?

A. The basic word order of "information questions"—those that begin with interrogative expressions like *qué, cómo, cuánto tiempo,* etc.—is either

$$interrogative\ expression + verb + subject + remainder$$

or

$$interrogative\ expression + verb + remainder + subject$$

as shown in the chart.

TRANSLATION

1. What does your friend want?
2. What are the other boys doing?
3. Where is your father going to work?
4. How long is the president going to be in the embassy?
5. When did General Méndez speak on (through) the radio?
6. What did the general say?

YOU ASK THE QUESTIONS

Do not include *quién* in your questions, except in constructions such as *a quién* and *con quién.* Follow the example.

1. Linda no quiere comer porque no tiene hambre.
   ¿Por qué no quiere comer Linda?
2. Linda y Vickie van a ir a Nicaragua después.
3. Emilio es de Barranquilla.
4. El chileno quisiera estar en su patria ahora.
5. Juan José compró un pedacito de lotería ese día.
6. Luz María quería estudiar con Emilio.
7. El libro de gramática costaba veinte pesos.
8. Anita llamó a Cecilia ayer.

Yes-No Questions

¿Usted supo la noticia? ¿Supo usted la noticia? ¿Supo la noticia usted?	*Did you hear the news?*

Statements

Anita te habla. Te habla Anita.	*This is Anita.*
El gobierno cayó. Cayó el gobierno.	*The government fell.*
Alguien me dijo eso. Me dijo alguien eso. Me dijo eso alguien.	*Someone told me that.*

B. As the charts show, word order is quite free in yes-no questions and statements. Subtle shifts of meaning accompany the various arrangements of the same set of words. It takes time to master all these subtleties, but the following are the crucial points:

1. Change in word order does not necessarily imply change in grammatical function (unlike "Dog bites man" *vs.* "Man bites dog" in English).
2. Whether a given string of words is a statement or a yes-no question is determined solely by intonation—rising for questions, falling for statements—and, in written sentences, by punctuation. Listen to the differences in the intonation of the following pairs of sentences.

STATEMENTS	YES-NO QUESTIONS
Anita te habla.	¿Anita te habla?
Te habla Anita.	¿Te habla Anita?

3. In general, the *end* of a statement or question is the focus of attention; it gives or asks for information which is new, important, or surprising. The beginning supplies information which is known, in the background, or taken for granted. For example, in a previous dialog one of the speakers says on the phone, *Te habla Anita.* It is obvious that somebody is speaking; therefore *Te habla* comes first. What is informative is that the person speaking is Anita, so this word comes last.

QUESTION ⟶ STATEMENT

Repeat each of the following yes-no questions; then change it into a statement by shifting from a rising to a falling intonation. Do not change the word order.

1. ¿Por fin se fueron Napoleón y Pepita? ↑
   Por fin se fueron Napoleón y Pepita. ↓
2. ¿Se quedaron Margarita y Jim conversando con ellos?
3. ¿No se refugió en una iglesia el presidente?
4. ¿No dijo nada importante el general Méndez?
5. ¿Fueron al cine ellos anoche?
6. ¿Y se acostaron temprano los niños?
7. ¿Todavía no llega el profesor a la clase?
8. ¿Siempre llega tarde él?

QUESTIONS

Answer with a full utterance, placing the subject last.

1. ¿Quién sabe más, el maestro o el alumno?
   Sabe más el maestro.
2. ¿Quién cayó, el gobierno constitucional o la junta?
3. ¿Cuántos alumnos pasaron el examen, tres o cuatro?
4. ¿Va a hablar usted o voy a hablar yo?
5. ¿Quién llamó, Anita o Teresa?
6. ¿Es la capital de Colombia Caracas o Bogotá?
7. ¿Quién estuvo más contenta en el paseo, Vickie o Linda?
8. ¿Quién tiene razón, él o yo?

Reading

Aniversario de la independencia

El día 22 de noviembre, tres meses después de que una junta militar derrocó al gobierno constitucional del país, la república de Andivia celebró con una imponente parada militar la fecha del aniversario de su independencia. Su excelencia general Antonio Méndez, Presidente Provisional, acompañado de los otros dos miembros de la junta, mariscal Napoleón Bonavena, Jefe de las Fuerzas Aéreas, y el almirante Nelson Quesada, Jefe de la Marina, pasó revista a las tropas que con impecable precisión marchaban frente al Palacio Presidencial. El desfile continuó luego hacia la Avenida de los Héroes donde casi un millón de andivianos esperaban ansiosamente desde tempranas horas de la mañana. Durante más de tres horas, estos miles de espectadores, que en su gran mayoría eran la gente del pueblo, gente pobre, desnutrida y mal vestida, vieron pasar ante sus ojos el poderío de las fuerzas armadas de su patria: tanques de guerra, cañones y otros armamentos modernos, todo tipo de vehículos de transporte, cadetes de la Academia Militar con sus relucientes uniformes y montando grandes y hermosos caballos, cadetes de la Academia Naval con sus uniformes blancos, soldados de infantería con botas negras de la mejor calidad, aviones militares volando en precisas formaciones, varias bandas militares y muchas cosas más. Fue en realidad un grandioso espectáculo que recibió la admiración y los aplausos de muchos espectadores; pero no de todos.

De regreso a su casa el hijo de uno de ellos le preguntó a su padre:

—Papá, ¿cuánto cuestan los tanques y los aviones?

—Mucho dinero, hijo.

—¿Para qué necesitamos un ejército tan grande, papá?

—Para defender a la patria.

—¿Contra quién?

—Quién sabe.

—Papá, si algún día puedes comprarme un par de zapatos, yo quiero botas, como las de los soldados.

—Está bien, hijo, algún día... tal vez...

QUESTIONS

1. ¿Es Andivia un país verdadero o imaginario?
2. ¿En qué aspecto representa Andivia la realidad de algunos países americanos?
3. ¿Está la república de Andivia gobernada en estos momentos por un gobierno constitucional?
4. ¿Cómo llegó al poder[16] la junta militar?
5. ¿Cree usted que los militares en los Estados Unidos pueden dar un golpe de estado algún día?
6. ¿Quiénes son los tres miembros de la junta militar de Andivia?
7. ¿A cuáles cuerpos de las fuerzas armadas representan los tres militares?
8. ¿Cómo celebró Andivia el aniversario de la fecha de su independencia?
9. ¿Cómo se celebra en los Estados Unidos el aniversario de la independencia?
10. ¿En qué año se independizó Estados Unidos de Inglaterra?
11. ¿Sabe usted si en América Latina hay gobiernos militares ahora? ¿En cuáles países, sabe usted?

---

[16]Came to power.

12. El día de la independencia de Andivia, ¿qué y quiénes participaron en la parada militar?
13. ¿Por dónde pasaron las tropas primero y hacia dónde continuaron después?
14. ¿Cuánta gente vio el desfile?
15. ¿Cómo era la mayoría de esa gente?
16. ¿Cree usted que los Estados Unidos deben mandar armamentos a los países latino-americanos? ¿Por qué?

[*To be followed by* LISTENING COMPREHENSION–SPEAKING EXERCISE]

Listening Passage
for Chapter 11
English Translation

News from Home

(1) When we are far from home, there's nothing nicer (more pleasant) than getting letters from the family—very long letters full of news. It doesn't matter if the news is just a repetition of the last letter, of a routine nature (character) and about the same things that happen in every home: we still haven't painted the living room; the cat's still (has continued) sick; the maid has left us and has run (gone) away with the milkman; Uncle Antonio has finally decided to start looking (put himself to look) for a job, but he hasn't found anything yet and seems very happy about it; we still haven't expressed (given) our condolences to the Mena family for don Chico's death—may he rest in peace; we've hurt Aunt Casilda's feelings (Aunt Casilda is offended) again, as usual, and she hasn't come back to visit us, etc., etc.

(2) The important thing is knowing that everybody is well and that nothing bad has happened. Then we are interested in the sensational news, good or bad, about the things that are happening in the country: that there have been many parties lately; that "Fulano" has won a hundred thousand pesos in the lottery; that "Zutano" has challenged "Mengano"* to a duel; that the cost of living has gone sky high

---

*Fulano, Zutano, and Mengano are fictitious names used much like "John Doe" or "Tom, Dick, and Harry" in English.

(to the clouds); that the university students are on strike and there have been many demonstrations and riots on the streets; that there was a great bullfight last Sunday; that the Minister of Education has resigned; that it's been raining, that it hasn't been raining . . . . In short, the longer the letters, the more we like them; and if they are interesting and full of news, after having read them once, we read them two or three times more.

(3) Sometimes, however, we get letters in which the one who is writing only talks about the things *he* has done or complains about what others have done to him, about how sick he has been or how much he has suffered, but he hardly mentions the person to whom the letter is addressed (goes directed).

(4) Such is the case of Aunt Casilda—as we can see in the dialog that follows—who has written to her nephews, Aurelio and Vicente, who are studying in Germany. (5) Being in a strange land and so far away from home (their fatherland), these fellows, like thousands of others, are always anxiously waiting for the mail. This time, however, there was (has been) only a letter from Aunt Casilda. It's nothing to be very happy about because they already know Aunt Casilda's letters, but . . . it's something (something is something).

(6) Aunt Casilda is Aurelio's godmother, and she's complaining that her godson hasn't written to her, not even to congratulate her on

(for) her saint's day. This seems to be a new complaint because Aunt Casilda has never celebrated her saint's day, only her birthday. Aurelio didn't even know there was a saint named Casilda and, consequently, a Saint Casilda's day in the calendar.

(7) At any rate, she's very hurt and mad at her nephew, she says in her letter. She's one of those people who are very touchy and who for the slightest reason are always getting mad at everybody. In her letter, Aunt Casilda also mentions that she's angry with her brother, the boys' father, because she's been very sick in bed, and everybody has come (gone) to see her and asked about her except her own brother.

(8) Oh, Aunt Casilda! She's like a little girl. But deep down in her heart (at the bottom) she's very good, better than all the other aunts. Vicente tells Aurelio that he ought to write to her congratulating her on her saint's day, but Aurelio thinks it's too late for that. Perhaps, but better late than never, says his brother.

Grammar Points

First, the present perfect; second, irregular past participles; third, impersonal forms of the verb **haber** (there to be); fourth, comparisons; fifth, some suffixes; and sixth, familiar letters.

TO BE FOLLOWED BY
LISTENING RECOGNITION EXERCISE

185

Chapter 11

Basic Dialog

Noticias de la casa

A. *Aurelio*   V. *Vicente*

I

A.   ¿No ha venido el correo?

V.   Sí, hubo sólo una carta, de tía Casilda. Está resentidísima[1] contigo.

A.   ¿Por qué? ¿Qué he hecho yo?

V.   Dice que no le has escrito, ni para el día de su santo.

A.   No le hemos escrito, mejor dicho.

V.   ¿Yo por qué? ¡Tú! Ella es tu madrina.

II

A.   Ni siquiera sabía que había una Santa Casilda. ¿Qué más cuenta?

V.   Dice que ha estado en cama y que sólo papá no ha ido a verla. Que está muy resentida con él.

A.   ¡Oh tía Casilda! Parece una chiquita: por todo se resiente.

V.   Pero en el fondo ella es muy buena, la mejor de la familia. Debieras escribirle felicitándola.

A.   Ya es tarde para eso.

V.   Quizá, pero más vale tarde que nunca.

---

[1]*Resentidísima* comes from *resentido,* which is used to describe a touchy person who is hurt and angry at someone. The suffix *-ísimo* is discussed on page 196.

News from Home

A. *Aurelio*   V. *Vicente*

I

A. Hasn't the mail come?

V. Yes, there was only one letter, from Aunt Casilda. She's very mad at you.

A. Why? What have I done?

V. She says you haven't written her, not even for her saint's day.

A. We haven't written her, you mean.[2]

V. Why me? You! She's your godmother.

II

A. I didn't even know there was a Saint Casilda. What else does she say?

V. She says she's been in bed and that Dad's the only person who hasn't come[3] to see her. She's very mad at him.

A. Oh Aunt Casilda! She's like a little girl: she gets mad about everything.

V. But deep down in her heart[4] she's very good, the best in the family. You ought to write to her and congratulate her.

A. It's too late for that.

V. Maybe, but better[5] late than never.

CULTURAL NOTES

A. Many Spanish speaking people are named for a Catholic saint and every year celebrate their saint's day in the Catholic calendar, rather than, or in addition to, their birthday. The two days do not necessarily coincide.

B. *Madrina* and *padrino* are "godmother" and "godfather," the sponsors of a child at baptism. The relationship of a *madrina* or *padrino* to his godchild (*ahijado* or *ahijada*) is usually taken somewhat more seriously in Spanish speaking countries than in the United States.

SUPPLEMENT

I

¿No ha venido el correo?

cartero	*mailman*
lechero	*milkman*

¿Por qué? ¿Qué he hecho yo?

visto	*seen*
puesto	*put*
resuelto	*decided, resolved*

Es tu madrina.

padrino	*godfather*
ahijado	*godson*

Ni para el día de su santo

cumpleaños	*birthday*

---

[2]Better said, rather.   [3]Gone.   [4]At the bottom.   [5]It is worth more.

Parece una chiquita.

    niñita   *little child*
    viejita   *little old lady*

Está muy resentida con él.

    enojada   *angry*[6]

La mejor de la familia

    peor   *worst*

DIALOG AND SUPPLEMENT CHECK

SENTENCE RECALL

Say the dialog phrase or sentence in which each of the following words or phrases occurs.

Santa Casilda	madrina	quizá
resentidísima	más vale	se resiente
muy resentida	en el fondo	ni siquiera
mejor dicho	chiquita	hubo
sólo papá	debieras	noticias

ITEM SUBSTITUTION

Substitute each of the following words and phrases for a related word or phrase in one of the basic sentences of this chapter. Repeat the whole new sentence.

EXAMPLE: *Teacher:* dicho
             Student: **¿Por qué? ¿Qué he dicho yo?**

peor	puesto	resuelto
visto	cumpleaños	enojada
cartero	padrino	dicho
niñita	lechero	escrito
ahijado	viejita	muy contenta

QUESTIONS

    1. ¿Cómo se llaman los dos hermanos que están estudiando en Alemania?
    2. ¿Recibieron ellos noticias de la casa hoy?
    3. ¿Cuántas cartas hubo?
    4. ¿De quién era la carta?

---

[6]*Enojado* differs from *resentido* in that *enojado* does not imply resentment or hurt feelings.

5. ¿Está la tía Casilda muy contenta con su ahijado?
6. ¿Por qué está resentidísima con Aurelio?
7. ¿Por qué está resentida con el papá de Aurelio?
8. ¿Por qué parece la tía Casilda una chiquita?
9. ¿Cómo es ella en el fondo, sin embargo?
10. ¿Cómo es ella en comparación con los otros parientes?
11. ¿Está usted resentido con alguien en esta clase?
12. ¿Se resiente usted por cualquier cosa?

[*To be followed by* LISTENING RECOGNITION EXERCISE]

Grammar

50. *The present perfect*

haber	+	*past participle*
he has ha hemos han		-ado, -ido

vosotros habéis -ado, -ido

A. Although both *tener* and *haber* correspond to "have," only *haber* is used with a past participle in perfect tense constructions in Spanish. The corresponding English constructions contain a form of the verb "to have" followed by a past participle.

Mucho gusto de **haber**la **conocido.**   *Glad to have met you.*
No **hemos trabajado** mucho hoy.   *We haven't worked hard today.*

B. The past participle is formed by adding *-ado* to the stem of *-ar* verbs, and *-ido* to the stem of *-er* and *-ir* verbs.

hablar	**hablado**	comer	**comido**
estar	**estado**	ser	**sido**
dar	**dado**	ir	**ido**

C. Past participles used as such are never inflected for number or gender.

El chico no ha **comido.**   *The boy hasn't eaten.*
Las chicas no han **comido.**   *The girls haven't eaten.*

190

However, past participles are often used as adjectives, just as in English, and as such are inflected for number and gender.

> Ellas han **estado** (*past participle*) muy **preocupadas** (*past participle used as adjective*).   *They have been very worried.*

D. *Haber* and the past participle are not normally separated by adverbs, as is frequently the case in English.

> Yo nunca he estado allí.   *I have never been there.*

E. Spanish has a "progressive" form of the present perfect, which is entirely analogous to the English "progressive" present perfect.

> He trabajado.   *I have worked.*
>
> **He estado trabajando.**   *I have been working.*

F. The position of object pronouns in perfect and progressive perfect constructions is the same as in the verb constructions you have already learned.

> **Se lo** he compuesto.   *I have fixed it for him.*
>
> Después de habér**selo** compuesto   *After having fixed it for him*
>
> **Se lo** he estado componiendo.   *I have been fixing it for him.*
> He estado componiéndo**selo.**

PARADIGM PRACTICE

Practice the present perfect tense with the following verbs.

dar	quejarse	tener	ser	sentirse
estar	enojarse	aprender	ir	vestirse
enseñar	sentarse	entender	irse	resentirse

PERSON–NUMBER SUBSTITUTION

1. La tía ha estado en cama.
   (yo, los niños, nosotros, todo el mundo, tú)
2. Sólo papá no ha ido a verla.
   (ustedes, su ahijado, usted y yo, sus sobrinos)
3. Es que no hemos podido.
   (I, they, she, you and I, you [*fam.*], he)
4. ¿Por qué no se ha vestido usted todavía?
   (ustedes, yo, la niñita, tú, los chicos)
5. ¿Qué han estado haciendo ustedes todo el día?
   (tú, la criada, nosotros, Vicente, yo, ellos)
6. Nada; no me he sentido muy bien hoy.
   (you, they, she, we, the maid and the cook, I)

CONSTRUCTION SUBSTITUTION

Change each sentence first to the present perfect and then to the present perfect progressive.

1. ¿Quién habla inglés aquí?
   ¿Quién ha hablado inglés aquí?
   ¿Quién ha estado hablando inglés aquí?

2. ¿La chica que estudia en la Facultad de Derecho?
3. Debemos dinero en todas partes.
4. El inglés me mata.
5. Te presto el diccionario.
6. Este año vivimos en Venezuela.
7. Yo no me quejo de nada.
8. ¿Aprenden ustedes mucho en esta clase?

QUESTIONS

Answer with a present perfect or present perfect progressive construction.

1. Hola, ¿ya comiste?
   No, no he comido todavía.
2. ¿Qué estás haciendo?
   Estudiando; he estado estudiando toda la tarde.
3. ¿Has tenido noticias de tu familia?
4. ¿Cuánto tiempo ha estado estudiando usted en esta escuela?
5. Usted ha estado progresando mucho en español, ¿no?
6. ¿Alguno de ustedes ha estado en Latinoamérica?
7. ¿Han ido ustedes al cine esta semana?
8. ¿Cuánto tiempo me han conocido ustedes a mí?

51. *Irregular past participles*

hacer	**hecho**	volver	**vuelto**
decir	**dicho**	devolver	**devuelto**
morir	**muerto**	resolver	**resuelto**
abrir	**abierto**	ver	**visto**
poner	**puesto**	escribir	**escrito**

The chart lists most of the verbs that have irregular past participles. Notice that the past participles of *volver* and *devolver* have the same irregularity. In general, verb stems have the same irregularities, with or without a prefix.

revolver	**revuelto**	componer	**compuesto**	prever[7]	**previsto**
envolver	**envuelto**	descomponer	**descompuesto**	prescribir[8]	**prescrito**

The only exceptions among the verbs listed in the chart are *bendecir,* "to bless," and *maldecir,* "to curse," whose past participles are *bendecido* and *maldecido.*

TODAVÍA NO

1. ¿Le devolvió Emilio el diccionario a Luz María?
   No, todavía no se lo ha devuelto.

---

[7] To foresee.   [8] To prescribe.

192

2. ¿Y Luz María no le dijo nada a Emilio?
   No, todavía no le ha dicho nada.
3. ¿Es verdad que ya murió Pirimpimpín?
4. ¿Vieron ustedes la película *Gone with the Wind?*
5. ¿Le escribió usted a su tía?
6. ¿Resolvieron los expertos el problema?
7. ¿Compuso el mecánico el motor del coche?
8. ¿Pusieron ustedes el dinero en el banco?
9. ¿Ya abrieron las tiendas?
10. ¿Ya le escribió Aurelio a su madrina, la tía Casilda?

CONSTRUCTION SUBSTITUTION

1. ¿Qué hace usted?
   ¿Qué ha hecho usted?
   ¿Qué ha estado haciendo usted?
2. Escribo una novela.
3. ¿Tú no pones el dinero en el banco?
4. Nosotros no vemos a nadie.
5. Mi novia me devuelve las cartas que yo le escribo.
6. Ni siquiera las abre.

QUESTIONS

1. ¿Por qué está resentida la tía Casilda con su ahijado?
2. ¿Cree usted que Aurelio no le ha escrito porque tal vez ha estado muy ocupado?
3. ¿O quizá no ha podido porque ha estado enfermo?
4. Y usted, ¿ha estado enfermo en estos días?
5. ¿Ha recibido cartas de alguien? ¿Le ha escrito a alguien?
6. Y usted, ¿qué ha hecho en estos días?
7. ¿Por qué está resentida la tía Casilda con su hermano, el padre de los chicos?
8. ¿Han puesto ustedes mucha atención hoy en la clase de español?

[*To be followed by* LISTENING COMPREHENSION–SPEAKING EXERCISE]

52. *The impersonal forms of* haber

hay	*there is (are)*
había hubo	*there was (were)*
ha habido	*there has (have) been*
va a haber	*there is (are) going to be*

A. Spanish uses the infinitive or third person singular forms of **haber** in the same way English uses "there is," "there were," etc.

Va a **haber** una fiesta.	*There's going to be a party.*
Había mucha gente.	*There were many people.*
No **ha habido** muchos problemas.	*There haven't been many problems.*

B.   The present tense impersonal form is **hay** rather than *ha*.

TRANSLATION

1. There's a party at her house.
2. There can't be a party at her house!
3. But there seems to be one now.
4. There has never been a party at her house!
5. Oh yes. There was one there last night.
6. And there's one there now.
7. And there's going to be another one tomorrow.
8. And we all are going to be there!

YOU ASK THE QUESTIONS

Include in each of your questions the form of *haber* suggested by the following statements.

1. Hay pocos turistas en las playas porque no hace mucho calor todavía.
   ¿Por qué hay pocos turistas en las playas?
2. En Andivia hubo dos golpes de estado el año pasado.
3. Sí, creo que puede haber más revoluciones en América.
4. En la historia de Bolivia ha habido más de ciento cincuenta revoluciones y golpes de estado.
5. Va a haber una fiesta en mi casa para celebrar mi cumpleaños.
6. No va a haber cerveza en la fiesta porque no le gusta a nadie la cerveza.
7. ¡Tiene que haber cerveza porque a mí sí me gusta!
8. Usted tiene mucha razón, joven. Mañana no hay clases.

53. *Comparisons of inequality*

1. Yo soy **más inteligente que** él.	*I am more intelligent than he is.*
El es **menos grande que** yo.	*He is smaller (less big) than I am.*
2. Yo tengo **más de** 100 pesos.	*I have more than 100 pesos.*
El tiene **menos de** 50.	*He has less (fewer) than 50.*
3. Necesito un vestido **más pequeño**.	*I need a smaller dress.*

A.   The most common type of comparison corresponds to the "-er than" or "more/less (fewer)...than" constructions in English. *De* is usually used for "than" before numbers (examples 2).

4. Es **el** hombre **más rico** del mundo.	*He's the richest man in the world.*
5. Esa es **la** parte **menos divertida** del libro.	*That's the least amusing part of the book.*

B. To express the notions "-est" or "most/least," Spanish uses the definite article with the noun before *más* or *menos*.

C. *De*, rather than *en*, is normally used to indicate the group of persons or things with respect to which the comparison is made (example 4).

mejor más bueno	*better*	**mayor** más viejo	*older*
peor más malo	*worse*	**menor** más joven	*younger*

D. These irregular comparatives are very common and in most cases are freely interchangeable with their corresponding *más* forms. However, **mayor** is used for comparison only among people, either young or old, whereas *más viejo* is used to compare things or old people with one another.

   With a definite article, *mejor* means "best," *peor* means "worst," etc., as in the case of regular comparatives.

COMPARISON DRILL

EXAMPLE: Luis es un buen alumno.
   First student: **Yo soy mejor que él.**
Second student: **Pero yo soy el** (*or* **la**) **mejor de la clase.**

1. Pedro es muy alto.
2. María es inteligente.
3. Jorge es muy malo.

4. Luz María es muy gorda.
5. Alfredo tiene 18 años.
6. Beatriz es muy delgada.

PROBLEMAS

I

La primera montaña tiene 900 metros de altura, la segunda tiene 1,400, y la tercera 2,500.

1. ¿Cuál es más alta que la segunda?
2. ¿Cuáles son más bajas que la tercera?
3. ¿Cuál es la más alta de las tres?
4. ¿Cuántos metros más alta es la tercera que la primera?
5. ¿Solamente cuál tiene menos de 1,000 metros de altura?
6. ¿Solamente cuál tiene más de 2,000?

II

   Tres hijos tiene doña Patricia: Alberto, que tiene 11 años de edad; Jorge, que tiene 13; y Violeta, que tiene 17. Alberto es un chico bastante bueno en la casa y en la escuela. Jorge es un diablo que no hace nada en la casa ni le gusta estudiar; no hay nadie más malo en toda la clase. Pero Violeta es una hija buenísima y siempre la primera de su clase.

1. ¿Es Alberto mayor o menor que Jorge?
2. ¿Cuál es el menor de los tres hijos? ¿Y el mayor?
3. ¿Es Violeta la mejor de su clase? ¿Y Jorge?
4. ¿Cuántos años menor que Jorge es Alberto?
5. ¿Cuántos años tienen los tres hermanos?

[*To be followed by* LISTENING COMPREHENSION–SPEAKING EXERCISE]

54. *Suffixes*

Diminutive *-ito, -cito*

silla	**sillita**
libro	**librito**
papel	**papelito**
hombres	**hombrecitos**
mujer	**mujercita**

A. The suffixes *-ito* and *-cito* add a connotation of "cute," "little," or both, to the meaning of the noun to which they are attached.

¡Qué **perrito** tan inteligente!   *What a smart puppy!*

B. The suffix *-ito, -ita* is added to the stem of nouns ending in *-o* and *-a*, and to nouns ending in *l*. All other nouns normally take the ending *-cito*. A few nouns can take either ending: *mamá*, **mamita, mamacita;** *papá,* **papito, papacito;** Juan, **Juanito, Juancito.**

Superlative *-ísimo*

bueno	**buenísimo**
mala	**malísima**
grande	**grandísimo**
fáciles	**facilísimos**

C. The suffix *-ísimo* is added to adjective stems and means "extremely." Thus, **grandísimo** is equivalent to *muy muy grande,* and **facilísimo** is equivalent to *extremadamente fácil.*

Adverbial *-mente*

aburrido	**aburridamente**
triste	**tristemente**
fácil	**fácilmente**

D. The suffix *-mente* corresponds to the adverbial ending *-ly* in English. This suffix is attached to the feminine form of adjectives with *-o, -a* endings, and directly at the end of other adjectives. When

-mente is added to an adjective, the adjective keeps its original stress, and the first syllable of the suffix is also stressed: *fácilmente.*

E. The two suffixes *-ísimo* and *-mente* can be used together: **-ísimamente.**

Este libro es malo, es malísimo, **malísimamente** escrito.	*This book is bad, (it's) extremely bad, terribly badly written.*

NOUN SUBSTITUTION

In each of the following sentences, substitute the *-ito* or *-cito* form of each of the nouns listed, making whatever other changes may be necessary.

1. Es una cosita interesante.
   (libro, cartas, lápiz, ojos, mujer, señoras)
2. ¿Y cómo están sus hermanitos?
   (ahijado, Pedro, doctor, madrina, amor, manos)
3. ¡Qué linda está la chiquita!
   (árbol, mañana, noche, paseo, abuelo, niño, madre)

ADJECTIVE SUBSTITUTION

In each of the following sentences, substitute the *-ísimo* form of each of the adjectives listed.

1. La madrina de Vicente está resentidísima.
   (contenta, triste, preocupada, enferma, alegre)
2. Esta lección es facilísima.
   (difícil, grande, corta, interesante, mala)
3. Es un lugar lindísimo.
   (verde, feo, aburrido, alto, bueno, interesante)

ADVERB SUBSTITUTION

EXAMPLE: Es una carta perfectamente escrita.
   (horrible)
   Es una carta horriblemente escrita.

1. Es una montaña fácilmente visible.
   (perfecto, verdadero, clarísimo, facilísimo, difícil)
2. Verdaderamente, no entendemos nada.
   (franco, simple, desafortunado, obvio)

55. *Familiar letters*

Openings

Querido Estimado Recordado	} Juan	*Dear John*
Queridísimo Adorado	} Juan	*Dearest John*

Closings

Muchos cariños		*Much love (affection)*	
Muchos abrazos		*Many hugs*	
Muchos besos	de tu amiga, Ceci	*Many kisses*	*from your friend, Ceci*
Muchos recuerdos		*(Many) regards*	
Besos y abrazos		*Kisses and hugs*	
Saludos		*Greetings*	

There is obviously a great variety of ways in which letters to friends can be started and closed. The words and phrases listed in the charts are some of the most common; they can be used with either the *usted* or the *tú* form of address.

Reading

Tres cartas

I

27 de noviembre, 19—[9]

Queridos papá y mamá,

Me alegro mucho de saber que todos han estado bien y que la situación económica del país ha mejorado bastante. Papá, todavía no ha llegado el último cheque y estoy casi sin un céntimo; he tenido que empeñar el reloj. No quiero preocuparlos mucho pero he tenido un poco de mala suerte en los exámenes, especialmente en el de inglés y en el de historia. Yo he estudiado mucho y no comprendo qué ha pasado. Mala suerte, eso es todo. Por lo demás estoy muy bien, un poco enfermo nada más, con el "flu", como llaman aquí a los resfríos largos y cuando uno tiene un poco de temperatura. Pero ya estoy mejor. Termino porque tengo que ir a clase.

Besos y abrazos de su hijo,

Juan

II

3 de diciembre, 19—

Adorada Julita,

¿Qué ha pasado, mi vida? ¿Por qué no me has escrito? Me siento desesperado porque tú no me has contestado mis últimas tres cartas. Tú sabes que te quiero muchísimo y no quiero nada más que

---

[9] The English form for dates—month, day, year—is also perfectly acceptable in Spanish.

estar contigo todo el tiempo. No quiero seguir estudiando; no me gusta la medicina; yo no nací para ser médico. Además, los estudios son eternos y dificilísimos. Yo solamente quiero regresar a mi patria y casarme contigo. Yo puedo trabajar en cualquier cosa. Todavía no les he dicho nada de esto a mis padres. Es un secreto entre tú y yo y nadie más. Si ellos lo saben se mueren y no sé cómo empezar a decirles. Termino porque voy a llegar tarde a clase. Por favor, escríbeme pronto, muy pronto.

Mil besos de tu novio que te adora y piensa en ti todo el tiempo,

Juan

III

18 de diciembre, 19—

Querido Juan, (Dear John,)

Recibí tu última carta, es decir, tus últimas cuatro cartas. No te he contestado hasta ahora porque he tenido que pensar mucho antes de decirte lo que te voy a decir. Por fin he resuelto no dejar pasar ni un día más y hacerlo hoy mismo porque comprendo que soy muy cruel si te hago esperar más. No sé cómo empezar.

Tú eres un hombre maravilloso que puedes hacer feliz a cualquier mujer. Sin embargo, las circunstancias nos han separado por mucho tiempo y el amor que antes sentía por ti, debo confesarte y perdón, mil veces perdón, ya no lo siento. Estoy enamorada de otro y no lo puedo remediar. Estoy segura de que tú comprenderás. No puedo escribirte más. Te deseo lo mejor de lo mejor en todos tus trabajos y estudios. Adiós.

Un abrazo y muchos recuerdos de tu sincera amiga,

Julita

CONVERSATION STIMULUS

Summarize the contents of each of the three letters.

WRITING

Write a letter of 100–150 words to any relative or close friend. Choose any topic but stay as much as possible within the grammatical structure and vocabulary you have learned up to this point.

[*To be followed by* LISTENING COMPREHENSION–SPEAKING EXERCISE]

Listening Passage for Chapter 12
English Translation

Problems of a Housewife

(1) Latin American housewives generally lead an easier (more rested) life than that of the American woman, despite the fact that there one doesn't find the household conveniences that exist in the United States. There, women don't have to get up early to dress their children, give them breakfast, and send them off to school. They don't have to cook; they don't have to wash or iron clothes; they don't have to sweep floors or clean the house. That's what the servants are for; they take care of all these jobs. (2) Housewives, naturally, direct and control the services of their employees, but in not having to do the manual labor themselves, even women of limited financial resources can live as easily as rich women. They can also lead a more active social life than an American housewife on the same economic level.

(3) Except for (excepting) the extremely poor people of the cities—those who live in what in Argentina are called "villas miseria," that is, the slums (extremely poor neighborhoods) that are so common (abound) in every Latin American city—it is rare to find a family with modest resources that doesn't have at least a cook and a maid. Families that are better-off also have a laundress and a nursemaid, and rich people also enjoy (count with) the services of a gardener, a chauffeur, and even a seamstress.

(4) Obviously, the existence of this luxury or privilege as a normal aspect of life in Latin American homes derives from the bad socio-

economic conditions prevailing in our countries, which make it possible to obtain these services at very low prices. Thus, $60 is more than enough to cover the monthly salaries of a cook, a maid, and a nursemaid in most (the majority of the) countries of Latin America. We Latin Americans are so used to having servants that we can't live without them. At least that's what we think until we come to live in the United States.

(5) The dialog that follows presents a typical scene in the life of an ordinary family. It's early in the morning and all the children are getting ready to go off to school or to their respective jobs. They all need something and they all call (direct themselves to) poor Valentina to come help them. Lili calls her first, but Lola tells Valentina not to go because she wants her to come and help her first. At the same time Toño hands her his pants and tells her to tell the laundress to press them for him. (6) In the meantime their mother is still in bed and wants to have (take) her breakfast there. So Flora shouts to Valentina to bring it to her. Finally we hear Juan asking where Valentina is. He is in the bathroom and wants Valentina to bring him a towel. He doesn't ask anybody else, only Valentina. Poor Valentina! But, as we'll see, she won't stand for it any longer; she's fed up (up to the crown of her head).

(7) One thing that the housewife does customarily (has the custom of doing) is go in person to the market to buy groceries. Usually the cook or the maid accompanies her, carrying the shopping basket. She goes to the market for two reasons: first, in order to haggle over the prices, because in Latin America one has to haggle over everything, and anybody who doesn't haggle is a fool. Second, because she fears that her servant will steal from her if she sends her alone. Nobody trusts (has confidence in) the poor servants.

(8) A few days after the scene we have just described, we find the lady of the house haggling with don Vito over the price of some grapes. She says (that at) nine pesos a kilo is impossible, and that he should let her have them (that he leave them for her) for five. Don Vito says he won't make any profit (won't earn anything), that he'll give them to her for seven; she says no, they're too expensive. Finally she offers him six. and without waiting for don Vito's reply, she tells him to give her two kilos and to put them in her basket. It is then that don Vito notices that the lady has come without the girl Valentina who always accompanies her to the market. The lady tells him not to even mention that name to her, that that dumbbell is an ungrateful so-and-so who quit her job (left the house) without giving notice (informing), and that all servants are alike.

Grammar Points

First, command forms; second, position of object pronouns in command verb forms; third, the forms of the present subjunctive; fourth, uses of the subjunctive in noun clauses.

TO BE FOLLOWED BY
LISTENING RECOGNITION EXERCISE

Chapter 12

Basic Dialog

Problemas de una ama de casa

LI. *Lili*   LO. *Lola*   TO. *Toño*   FL. *Flora*   J. *Juan*
SRA. *Señora*   DON V. *Don Vito*

I

LI.   ¡Valentina! ¡Venga a ayudarme!

LO.   No vaya, Valentina. Yo quiero que venga aquí primero.

TO.   Tome, Valentina, dígale a la lavandera que me planche estos pantalones.

FL.   ¡Valentina! ¡Dice mamá que le traiga el desayuno a la cama!

J.   ¿Dónde está Valentina? ¡VALENTINA! ¡UNA TOALLA!

II

SRA.   ¡Qué caras están las uvas, don Vito! ¿Están dulces?

DON V.   Deliciosas, señora, pruébelas[1].

SRA.   Ah no, pero a nueve pesos el kilo, imposible. Ojalá[2] que me las deje a cinco.

DON V.   No gano[3] nada, señora. A siete, por ser usted.

SRA.   A seis, ni un centavo más. Déme dos kilos. Póngalas con las demás cosas; ya vengo.

DON V.   Está bien, no discutamos[4]. A propósito, ¿dónde está la chica que le lleva siempre la canasta?

SRA.   ¿Valentina? ¡Ni me mencione a esa ingrata! Se fue sin avisar. ¡Todas son iguales!

---

[1]From *probar.*   [2]*Ojalá* comes from an Arabic expression meaning "may Allah grant." It belongs to none of the parts of speech of Spanish.   [3]*Ganar* means "to earn" as well as "to win."   [4]From *discutir.*

Problems of a Housewife

LI. *Lili*   LO. *Lola*   TO. *Toño*   FL. *Flora*   J. *Juan*
LA. *Lady*   DON V. *Don Vito*

I

LI.   Valentina! Come help me!
LO.   Don't go, Valentina. I want you to come here first.
TO.   Here,[5] Valentina, tell the laundress to press these pants for me.
FL.   Valentina! Mother says for you to bring her her breakfast in bed!
J.   Where's Valentina? VALENTINA! A TOWEL!

II

LA.   The grapes are so expensive, don Vito! Are they sweet?
DON V.   Delicious, ma'm, try them.
LA.   Oh no, but nine pesos a kilo, impossible. I hope you'll let me have them[6] for five.
DON V.   I wouldn't make any profit,[7] ma'm. Seven, since it's you.
LA.   Six, not a penny more. Give me two kilos. Put them with the rest of the things; I'll be right back.
DON V.   All right, let's not argue. By the way, where's the girl that always carries the basket for you?
LA.   Valentina? Don't even mention that ungrateful woman to me. She left and didn't let me know.[8] They're all alike!

SUPPLEMENT

I

¡Valentina! ¡Venga a ayudarme!

barrer	*sweep*
sacudir	*dust*
limpiar	*clean up*
jugar[9]	*play*

¡Valentina! ¡Una toalla!

un jabón	*a (piece of) soap*

II

¡Qué caras están las uvas!

naranjas	*oranges*
manzanas	*apples*
peras	*pears*
frutas	*fruit(s)*
verduras	*greens*
papas	*potatoes*
lechugas	*heads of lettuce*

¡Qué caros están los tomates! *tomatoes*

¿Están dulces?

amargas	*bitter*
maduras	*ripe*
verdes	*green (unripe)*
saladas	*salty*
suaves	*soft*
duras	*hard*

---

[5] Take.   [6] Leave them to me.   [7] I don't earn anything.   [8] She went away without informing.
[9] *Jugar:* juego, juegas, juega, jugamos, juegan, (jugáis).

A nueve pesos el kilo, imposible.
    la libra   *the pound*

La chica que le lleva la canasta
                 bolsa   *bag*

Ojalá que me las deje a cinco.
Espero   *I hope*

Se fue sin avisar.
                 pagar   *paying*
                 regatear   *haggling*

DIALOG AND SUPPLEMENT CHECK

SENTENCE RECALL

Say the dialog phrase or sentence in which each of the following words or phrases occurs.

kilo	ingrata	pantalones	uvas
canasta	ayudarme	a propósito	dígale
kilos	traiga	lavandera	dulces
gano	problemas	discutamos	iguales
cama	planche	desayuno	avisar

ITEM SUBSTITUTION

Repeat each of the following sentences, substituting a related word or phrase for the part in italics. If books are closed, your teacher will repeat the item at the end of each sentence.

1. ¡Qué *baratas* están las uvas!
2. Pero a nueve pesos *el kilo*, imposible.
3. ¿Dónde está la chica que le lleva siempre *la bolsa*?
4. Venga a *barrer.*
5. No *venga.*
6. ¡Qué caras están *las naranjas!*
7. ¡Valentina, *una toalla!*
8. ¡Qué baratos están *los tomates!*
9. Se fue *sin regatear.*
10. ¿Están *suaves?*

QUESTIONS

1. ¿Cómo se llamaba la sirvienta de esa casa?
2. ¿Se fue Valentina de esa casa o todavía está allí?
3. ¿Le avisó a la señora que ella quería irse?
4. ¿Adónde fue la señora unos días después?
5. ¿En ese momento estaba comprando frutas o verduras?
6. ¿Qué clase de frutas estaba comprando?
7. ¿Estaban baratas las uvas?
8. ¿A qué precio estaban?
9. ¿Qué precio acabó pagando[10] la señora?
10. ¿Qué tuvo que hacer ella para conseguir ese precio?
11. Cuando usted va a las tiendas o al mercado, ¿le gusta regatear?
12. ¿Se acostumbra[11] regatear en los Estados Unidos?

---

[10]*Acabar* + present participle, "to end up" + present participle.   [11]Is it customary.

13. ¿Cómo son las naranjas, dulces o amargas?
14. ¿Cómo son mejores las frutas, maduras o verdes?
15. ¿Cuál es la fruta que más le gusta a usted?
16. ¿Es la vida de una ama de casa norteamericana muy suave o muy dura?
17. ¿Qué tienen que hacer ellas en la casa?
18. ¿Les ayudan los hijos?
19. ¿En qué ayuda usted en su casa?
20. ¿Sabe usted cocinar? ¿Sabe barrer? ¿Lavar ropa? ¿Planchar?
21. Y usted, ¿qué sabe hacer?
22. ¿Sabe usted jugar tenis?

[*To be followed by* LISTENING RECOGNITION EXERCISE]

Grammar

56. *Commands*

The verb forms of Spanish (and of many other languages) are inflected to show *mood*. The verb forms you have learned so far are the present, imperfect, preterit, and present perfect forms of the *indicative mood*. We are now going to take up the *usted, ustedes,* and *nosotros* forms of the *imperative mood*, often called "command forms." Later in this chapter the *subjunctive mood* will be introduced.

In general, the indicative mood is used to denote assertions or denials of *fact*. The imperative mood, on the other hand, is used in *commands and requests*, that is, to express the will of the speaker to influence the behavior of another.

> Mary, please *empty* the ashtrays.
> *Leave* immediately, all of you.

When the speaker includes himself in the group whose behavior he wishes to influence, the form "let's" is used in English.

> *Let's* not *do* anything rash.

Command Forms[12]

-ar *verbs*	-er *and* -ir *verbs*	
cante (usted)	aprenda, ponga escriba, salga	(usted)
canten (ustedes)	aprendan, pongan escriban, salgan	(ustedes)
cantemos (nosotros)	aprendamos, pongamos escribamos, salgamos	(nosotros)

---

[12] The *tú* and *vosotros* command forms will be discussed in Chapter 16.

A. The endings of the command forms are like those of the present indicative, except that the "opposite" vowel is used: the endings of *-ar* verbs have *e*, and those of *-er* and *-ir* verbs have *a*. There are no exceptions.

B. The stems of the command forms are the same as the stem of the first person singular of the present indicative. Whatever irregularity occurs in this form occurs in all command forms (*yo pongo: ponga, pongan, pongamos*). Three qualifications are necessary:

1. Those *-ar* and *-er* verbs that have the vowel–diphthong alternations *e→ie* and *o→ue* do not have diphthongs when the stress falls on the ending: **piense, piensen, pensemos; cuente, cuenten, contemos; vuelva, vuelvan, volvamos.**

2. In the few *-ir* verbs that have the alternation *e→ie* in the present indicative (*e.g., sentir*), the stem vowel changes to *i* in the "let's" form: **sienta, sientan, sintamos.** In those *-ir* verbs that have the alternation *o→ue* in the present indicative (*dormir, morir*), the stem vowel becomes *u* in the "let's" form: **duerma, duerman, durmamos; muera, mueran, muramos.**

3. The five verbs whose first person singular present indicative forms do not end in *-o* have the following command forms.

> saber (sé): **sepa, sepan, sepamos**
> ser (soy): **sea, sean, seamos**
> estar (estoy): **esté, estén, estemos**
> dar (doy): **dé, den, demos**
> ir (voy): **vaya, vayan,** { **vamos** (*affirmative*) / **no vayamos** (*negative*)

C. As is the case with other verb forms, subject pronouns are used with command forms only for emphasis or politeness. The pronouns, when used, normally follow the command forms.

INFINITIVE ⟶ COMMAND

Give the specified command forms of the following verbs.

1. Usted

EXAMPLE: venir, **venga**

hablar	suponer	mirar	decir
tomar	tener	dar	ir
comer	escribir	vivir	entender

2. Ustedes

EXAMPLE: aprender, **aprendan**

oir	trabajar	discutir	estar
saber	ganar	vender	ver
ser	insultar	comprar	venir

3. Nosotros

EXAMPLE: hacer, **hagamos**

ir	barrer	recordar	prestar
entrar	planchar	jugar	vivir
leer	dar	limpiar	decir

Add an affirmative or negative command to each of the following sentences, as illustrated.

1. ¿Por qué nunca llega temprano usted?
   ¿Por qué nunca llega temprano usted? Llegue temprano, por favor.
2. ¡Ay, cómo fuma María!
   ¡Ay, cómo fuma María! No fume, María, por favor.
3. Usted no pregunta nada.
4. Y usted, Pedro, ¿no toma más café?
5. María y José, ustedes conversan tanto.
6. ¿Por qué no imitan a Margarita?
7. Ustedes no creen en mí, ¿verdad?
8. ¿Entramos y tomamos un café?
9. ¿Pero por qué no promete usted algo bueno?
10. Manuel, usted no estudia mucho.
11. Y usted, Felipe, nunca lee el periódico.
12. Señorita, ¿bailamos?
13. Señores, ¿comemos o no comemos?
14. ¿Cantamos?
15. ¿Vendemos esta casa y compramos otra?
16. En esta clase nunca leemos ni escribimos.
17. ¿Discutimos más?

QUESTIONS

Answer with a command form; do not use object pronouns.

1. ¿Voy al mercado ahora o después?
   Vaya ahora.
2. ¿Voy yo solamente o vamos usted y yo?
   Vamos las dos.
3. ¿Llevamos la canasta o la bolsa?
4. ¿Dónde pongo esto?
5. ¿Ponemos la canasta en el coche?
6. ¿Qué traigo del mercado?
7. ¿Hago yo o hace usted la lista de las compras?
8. ¿Por qué no hacemos las dos la lista, mejor?
9. Carne, verduras, leche... ¿qué más ponemos?
10. ¿Qué hago para la comida, señora, arroz con pollo o paella?

[*To be followed by* LISTENING COMPREHENSION–SPEAKING EXERCISE]

57. *Position of object pronouns in commands*

Affirmative	*Negative*
Díga**le**.	No **le** diga.
Tell him (her).	*Don't tell him (her).*
Déje**melas**.	No **me las** deje.
Let me have them.	*Don't leave them to me.*
Discutámos**lo**.	No **lo** discutamos.
Let's argue about it.	*Let's not argue about it.*
Siénten**se**, señores.	No **se** sienten, señores.
Sit down, gentlemen.	*Don't sit down, gentlemen.*
Vámo**nos**.	No **nos** vayamos.
Let's go.	*Let's not go.*

A. Object pronouns always follow the verb in affirmative commands and precede it in negative commands. When they follow, they are attached to the verb.

B. In writing, when one or more object pronouns are attached to an affirmative command form, an accent mark must be placed over the stressed syllable of the verb in order to show that the stress remains on that syllable.

C. The *-mos* ending in affirmative commands drops the *s* when the pronoun *nos* is attached to it (last example in the chart).

REJOINDERS

Your teacher will ask you whether he should do this or that. Half the class, answering together, will tell him to do it; the other half will tell him not to. Use object pronouns in your rejoinders.

EXAMPLE: *Teacher:*   ¿Le doy este libro a él?
            First half: **Sí, déselo.**
            Second half: **No, no se lo dé.**

1. ¿Abro la ventana?
2. ¿Cierro la puerta?
3. ¿Empezamos?
4. ¿Hacemos el examen?
5. ¿Se lo doy mañana, mejor?
6. ¿Me voy a mi casa?

7. ¿Me quedo, mejor?
8. ¿Nos vamos todos?
9. ¿Se lo digo al jefe?
10. ¿Me levanto?
11. ¿Me siento?
12. ¿Me acuesto?

13. ¿Me pongo el sombrero?
14. ¿Llamo a la policía?
15. ¿Nos despedimos?
16. ¿Vengo mañana?
17. ¿No vuelvo?
18. ¿Les escribo una carta?

WRITTEN TRANSLATION

Make sure to place written accents and to drop the *s* of *-mos* wherever necessary.

PANCHO. Let's stay home today, let's not go to school.

JORGE. Great idea! But what shall we tell Mom? Perhaps if we tell her there's no school today . . . . Yes, let's tell her that.

PANCHO. No, better not. Come on (let's go). Let's get up. What excuse (*excusa*) are we going to give the teacher tomorrow?

JORGE. Let's not give him any, or let's tell him that Aunt Casilda was very sick.

MOTHER. Come on, get up! You're going to be late! And don't tell me that there's no school today!

PANCHO. Valentina! Bring me a towel and a piece of soap!

JORGE. Valentina! Here (take); shine (clean) these shoes for me,[13] please.

58. *Subjunctive forms*

Present Subjunctive: *saber*

(que yo) **sepa**	(que nosotros) **sepamos**
(que tú) **sepas**	
(que él, *etc.*) **sepa**	(que ellos, *etc.*) **sepan**

(que vosotros) **sepáis**

---

[13] See grammar section **30**, part B.

The subjunctive is the third mood for which Spanish verbs are inflected (in addition to the indicative and the imperative). You already know the forms of the present subjunctive. They are the same as the command forms (*e.g., sepa usted, sepamos nosotros, sepan ustedes*), plus forms for *yo* and *tú*. The *yo* form is the same as the *usted* command form; the *tú* form adds *-s*, as in the present indicative. (The *vosotros* form has the same stem as the *nosotros* command form, and the ending *-éis* for *-ar* verbs and *-áis* for *-er* and *-ir* verbs.)

PARADIGM PRACTICE

Before taking up the uses of the subjunctive, you should be absolutely certain of the forms. Since subjunctive verb forms are nearly always preceded by *que*, it is a good idea to practice them with this word, as in the chart.

Do paradigm practice with the verbs listed below, following the examples. Make sure to include object pronouns whenever they are attached to an infinitive.

EXAMPLES: hablar: **que yo hable, que tú hables, que él hable,** etc.
comer: **que yo coma, que tú comas,** etc.
pedir: **que yo pida, que tú pidas,** etc.
irse: **que yo me vaya, que tú te vayas, que él se vaya,** etc.

venir	levantarse	quedarse	dar	barrer
decir	sentarse	quejarse	ser	sacudir
hacer	sentirse	vestirse	ir[14]	jugar
ponerse	traérselo	ponérmelo	saber	limpiar
estar	discutir	recordar	ver	haber[15]

59. *Uses of the subjunctive*

A. Perhaps the most common use of the subjunctive is one that is quite similar to that of the imperative: to express the intention to influence the behavior of another person.

1. An imperative form alone expresses the speaker's intention to influence behavior.

Cierre la puerta.   *Close the door.*

2. A subjunctive form is used when *another* verb—such as *querer* (want), *pedir* (request), *decir* (tell), or *sugerir* (suggest)—expresses the intention of one person to influence the behavior of another.

Juan *quiere* que yo **cierre** la puerta.   *Juan wants me to close the door.*
*Díga*le que me **traiga** una toalla.   *Tell her to bring me a towel.*

B. Object pronouns always precede subjunctive forms, although they follow affirmative imperatives.

Imperative: Ciérre**la**.   *Close it.*
Subjunctive: Quiere que **la** cierre.   *He wants you to close it.*

---

[14] The *nosotros* form of *ir* in the subjunctive is **vayamos** for both the affirmative and the negative forms.
[15] The subjunctive of *haber* is **haya**.

C. In addition, the subjunctive is used after verbs that indicate such emotions as sorrow, gladness, surprise, fear, hope, expectation, and doubt. Compare the use of the indicative and the subjunctive in the following examples.

Ind.:	*Creo* que **está** enfermo.	*I think he's sick.*
Subj.:	*Siento* que **esté** enfermo.	*I'm sorry he's sick.*
Ind.:	Yo *sé* que ella **viene.**	*I know she's coming.*
Subj.:	No, yo *dudo*[16] que **venga.**	*No, I doubt that she'll come.*
Ind.:	*Dice* el médico que mamá **sigue** mejor.	*The doctor says Mom is doing better.*
Subj.:	Me *alegro* que mamá **siga** mejor.	*I'm glad Mom is doing better.*
Ind.:	¿*Piensa* usted que yo **soy** rico?	*Do you think I'm rich?*
Subj.:	¿Le *sorprende*[17] a usted que yo **sea** rico?	*Does it surprise you that I'm rich?*
Ind.:	Ella *sabe* que Jorge **dice** la verdad.	*She knows Jorge is telling the truth.*
Subj.:	Ella *espera* que Jorge **diga** la verdad.	*She hopes Jorge will tell the truth* or *She expects Jorge to tell the truth.*

D. When *decir* and other verbs of communication such as *contestar* and *escribir* are used merely to convey information, they are followed by the indicative. When the same verbs express intention to influence behavior, they are followed by the subjunctive.

Dice que Jorge **viene.**	*He says that Jorge is coming.*
Le *dice* a Jorge que **venga.**	*He tells Jorge to come.*

E. Either the subjunctive or the indicative may be used after *creer, pensar,* and *suponer* in negative and interrogative sentences.

No *creo* que hoy **es** (*or* **sea**) lunes.	*I don't think today is Monday.*
¿*Cree* usted que hoy **es** (*or* **sea**) lunes?	*Do you think today is Monday?*

In affirmative sentences, however, the indicative is always used.

Creo que hoy **es** lunes.	*I think today is Monday.*

F. Except for *verdad, obvio, evidente, seguro,* and a few other expressions of truth or certainty, nouns and adjectives used with *ser* and *parecer* always call for the subjunctive.

Es
Me parece
{ necesario
una tragedia
fácil, difícil
bueno, malo
interesante
una lástima
posible, imposible
triste
mejor, peor } que Juan **vaya.**

INDICATIVE–SUBJUNCTIVE SUBSTITUTION

Make the second verb indicative or subjunctive, as required by the expression substituted at the beginning of the sentence.

---

[16] The infinitive is *dudar.*   [17] The infinitive is *sorprender.*

1. Yo creo que somos amigos.
   (es imposible)
   Es imposible que seamos amigos.
   (dudo, es verdad, es mejor, sé, me parece necesario, espero, es evidente, prefiero)
2. Ojalá que[18] Valentina no se vaya de la casa.
   (estoy seguro, es mejor, pienso, espero, es bueno)
3. Nosotros sabemos que allí hace mucho calor.
   (es probable, dudamos, nos sorprende, creemos, es verdad)
4. Dicen que yo estoy loco.
   (dudan, sienten, saben, es posible, se alegran, quieren, es verdad)
5. Usted piensa que nosotros vamos al paseo, ¿verdad?
   (usted duda, a usted le parece, usted se alegra, es importante, es absolutamente seguro, usted piensa)
6. Tú sientes que yo no tenga dinero, ¿no, María?
   (sabes, te alegras, supones, esperas, dices, a ti te sorprende, quieres, piensas, prefieres)

TRANSFORMATION

Use a sentence beginning with *El profesor quiere que* or *dice que,* followed by a subjunctive verb form, to repeat your teacher's commands. Use either the *usted* or the *tú* form in your answer. *Todos* is a signal for the whole class; include yourself when repeating the message.

1. Luis, abra la ventana.
   Luis, el profesor dice que abra(s) la ventana.
2. Juan y María, siéntense.
   Juan y María, el profesor dice que se sienten.
3. ¡Hagan silencio, todos!
   El profesor quiere que todos hagamos silencio.
4. Emilio y Luz María, no conversen tanto.
5. Usted, ¡ponga atención!
6. Vaya a abrir la puerta, Juan.
7. Quédese usted aquí, Cecilia.
8. Tráigame un vaso de agua, Pedro.
9. Présteme su libro, Alicia.
10. Jorge, dígame qué hora es.
11. Váyanse todos a la casa.
12. Vengan todos preparados para un examen mañana.

QUESTIONS

1. ¿Qué quiere Lili que Valentina haga?
2. ¿Qué quiere Toño que Valentina le diga a la lavandera?
3. ¿Qué quiere la mamá que Valentina le traiga a la cama?
4. ¿Y qué quiere Juan que Valentina le traiga al baño?
5. ¿Cree usted que la historia de Valentina es cierta, o duda que sea verdad?
6. ¿Con quién está regateando la señora después, en el mercado?
7. ¿Quiere don Vito que la señora pruebe las uvas o no quiere que las pruebe?
8. ¿A qué precio quiere ella que don Vito le deje las uvas?

---

[18] *Ojalá* may or may not be followed by *que.*

9. ¿Cuántos kilos le compra y dónde quiere que se las ponga?

10. ¿Por qué no quiere ella que don Vito le mencione el nombre de Valentina?

11. ¿Cree usted que yo sé, o duda que yo sepa jugar tenis?

12. ¿Quiere usted que yo le traiga una manzana mañana?

13. ¿Esperan las madres norteamericanas que sus hijas ayuden con el trabajo de la casa?

14. ¿Es importante que las mujeres sepan cocinar, lavar y planchar ropa?

15. ¿Creen ustedes que hay mujeres que no saben hacer nada?

16. ¿Es bueno o es malo que las mujeres tengan muchos hijos?

17. ¿Creen ustedes que hay un exceso de población en el mundo?

18. ¿Es necesario, según usted, que haya un control de la población del mundo en este respecto?

19. ¿Qué recomienda usted que hagamos?

20. ¿Quiere usted que nos vayamos a la casa o que nos quedemos aquí?

[*To be followed by* LISTENING COMPREHENSION–SPEAKING EXERCISE]

60.   *Uses of the subjunctive: structural differences*

1. El quiere **ir**.	*He wants to go.*
Juan espera **ir**.	*Juan expects to go.*
2. El quiere que Juan **vaya**.	*He wants Juan to go.*
Juan espera que él **vaya**.	*Juan expects him to go.*
3. El dice que Juan **va**.	*He says that Juan is going.*
El dice que Juan **vaya**.	*He says for Juan to go.*

A. Besides understanding how the subjunctive works in Spanish, you must learn to avoid the influence of English in certain types of constructions where Spanish uses the subjunctive. In the first pair of sentences in the chart, there is only *one* subject, and the subjunctive is not used in Spanish. In sentences like this, Spanish and English have similar constructions.

B. In the second pair of sentences, in which there are two different subjects—"Juan" and "he"— Spanish and English are structurally different. English places a noun ("Juan") or a pronoun ("him") before an infinitive, but Spanish uses the subjunctive, introduced by *que*.

C. In the first sentence of the third pair, the subjunctive is not called for because *dice* merely makes the announcement that Juan is going. Here Spanish and English are alike. The only difference is that in English the relator "that" may or may not be used, whereas in Spanish the relator *que* is always used.

In sentences like the last one, where *dice* expresses an intention to influence Juan's behavior and thus calls for the use of the subjunctive of the verb *ir*, English quite frequently uses the preposition "for" followed by a noun or a pronoun and an infinitive form.

D. It is important for you to be aware of the danger of saying totally unacceptable non-sentences like *°Yo quiero usted ir allí* (for *Yo quiero que usted vaya allí*) or *°Mamá dice por* (or *para*) *Valentina traer su café* (for *Mamá dice que Valentina le traiga el café*).

°Utterances preceded by an asterisk are incorrect.

Monday, June 18

Dear Mom,

I'm glad you[19] have a new cook and I hope you are well; I am not (well). I want you to know that I love[20] you and Dad very much, and I hope that you love me, too. I have to give you some bad news,[21] however. Do you remember when I told you that English and history were very difficult, and that I didn't know if I was going to pass or not? Well, I didn't pass. But that's not all. I didn't pass in any other subject[22] either. In other words, I flunked (stayed in) everything. I'm very sorry. I hope you won't tell anybody, except Dad. If you want me to tell him, I'll tell him, but I think it's better that you tell him. I believe it's also necessary for Julita to know. I want you to do me one favor, Mom. Tell Dad to send me a little money, if he can.

Your loving son (son who loves you),
Juan

Reading

Se necesita sirvienta

La señora Dávila estaba desesperada porque Clotilde, la criada que le había durado casi tres años —tan buena, tan servicial, tan honrada y tan limpia— se había ido a trabajar a la casa de una familia americana.

—Ingrata, después de todo lo que hice por ella —le contaba por teléfono a una amiga—. La queríamos como a una de la familia, como hija. ¡Y ni siquiera nos avisó que se iba!

—Todas son iguales —le respondió su amiga—. Y tan difícil que es hoy día conseguir una sirvienta; hay que pagarles sueldos de presidente. ¿Y sabes quién tiene la culpa? Los americanos. ¿Sabes cuánto pagan ellos a una sirvienta? ¡Veinte y hasta treinta al mes! ¡Dólares! Siento mucho que no puedas jugar canasta esta tarde. Ojalá que consigas a alguien pronto.

La señora Dávila estaba pasando una verdadera crisis. No podía tomar el café en la cama; tenía que levantarse temprano para vestir a los niños y mandarlos a la escuela; tenía que hacer las camas y arreglar la casa. Era una situación horrible. Puso varios anuncios en los periódicos pero sin resultado. Dos o tres muchachas fueron a ver el empleo pero ninguna quería trabajar por menos de cien pesos; y cuando se supo que en esa casa no ofrecían más de sesenta, no volvió nadie.

Sin saber qué otra cosa hacer, la señora Dávila puso en la ventana de la sala un rótulo que decía:

SE NECESITA SIRVIENTA

Divinidad Contreras era una humilde campesina quien nunca había salido del remoto pueblo donde vivía. Había llegado hasta el tercer grado en la escuela pero tuvo que salir para empezar a trabajar y de esta manera ayudar en la casa con unos pocos centavos más cada semana. Un día, después de muchos años de estar sembrando papas, cuidando vacas y cogiendo café, Divinidad resolvió irse a la capital a probar su suerte. Según le habían contado, era fácil conseguir un empleo de sirvienta en alguna casa y ganar así

---

[19]Use the *usted* form throughout.　[20]*Querer.*　[21]One item of news is *una noticia.*　[22]*Materia.*

más dinero que el que ganaba en su pueblo. De esa manera podía ayudar mejor a sus padres que ya estaban viejos y a su hermana que recientemente había quedado viuda y con siete hijos, el mayor de siete años de edad.

Con diez pesos en su cartera y sin más ropa que la que llevaba en un pequeño bulto de mano, se despidió llorando de sus padres, hermana y sobrinos, y subió a un viejísimo autobús repleto de indios, gallinas y cerdos, el cual dos veces por semana pasaba por ese pueblo con dirección a la capital.

Llegó allá y sin perder un minuto de tiempo empezó a caminar sin rumbo por las calles. Mirando de arriba a abajo los altos y modernos edificios de la ciudad, saltando a cada momento de un lado al otro para esquivar los coches, taxis, bicicletas y camiones, llegó por fin a una casa donde había un rótulo que decía:

SE NECESITA SIRVIENTA

Golpeó tímidamente la puerta. Nadie abrió. Golpeó más fuerte. Tampoco. Golpeó mucho más fuerte y esta vez se abrió la puerta y apareció una señora furiosa:

—¡Va a tumbar la casa! ¿Para qué cree que es el timbre? ¿Qué quiere? No tenemos limosna.

—Es que en ese rótulo dice que aquí necesitan una sirvienta.

—Ah. ¿Ha estado empleada alguna vez?

—No, señora. Acabo de venir del campo. Yo vivo en Ojo del Diablo, allá muy lejos, en la montaña.

—Sí, ya sé. Entonces ni para qué preguntarle si tiene referencias o certificado de salud.

—No, señora, ni pa qué, no tengo na más que mi persona.[23] Pero estoy sanita, señora.

—¿Qué edad tiene?

—No sé, señora; como veintiocho años.

—No parece tener más de dieciocho.

—Debe ser menos, entonces.

—¿Qué sabe hacer?

—Pues pa decirle la verdá,[24] no sé hacer mucho. Pero si me enseña, yo soy buena p'aprender.[25]

—Bueno, vamos a ver. Entre. Yo pago cincuenta al mes.

—¡Cincuenta! ¡Claro!

Y así empezó Divinidad su nueva vida y la señora Dávila su nueva crisis. Divinidad no mentía cuando dijo que venía de la montaña, y la señora no podía dejarla sola ni un instante.

—¡Divinidad, no ponga las servilletas debajo de los platos! ¡Divinidad, no ponga los dedos adentro cuando trae los vasos a la mesa! ¡Divinidad, puso una cortina en la cama!

—A mí me pareció que era una sobrecama, señora.

—¡Divinidad esto, Divinidad aquí, Divinidad allá! —Era algo de volver loca a cualquiera.

Pero Divinidad poco a poco fue aprendiendo y después de un mes ya estaba más o menos domesticada. Un día la llamó la señora para darle su primer sueldo.

—Aquí tiene, Divinidad, su cheque. Nosotros tenemos la costumbre de pagar todo con cheque. —Pero viendo que la chica miraba el pedazo de papel con cierta desconfianza, la señora le explicó lo que debía hacer:

—Lleve este cheque al banco y allí le dan el dinero. Sí, el banco es el lugar donde guardan el dinero. Este cheque es del Banco Central, el edificio grande que está frente al mercado. Vaya ahora, si quiere.

Divinidad presentó el "pedazo de papel" en una de las ventanillas, según las instrucciones de la señora. El empleado examinó por un momento el cheque y luego se lo devolvió.

—Tiene que endosarlo.

—¿Qué es eso?

—Tiene que ponerle la firma.

—¿Qué es eso?

—Escribir su nombre aquí, ¿entiende? Igual como cuando termina una carta —le explicó el cajero.

Recordando las cartas que había escrito a su casa, Divinidad tomó entonces la pluma y con todo cuidado escribió: "Besos y abrazos de su hija, Divinidad Contreras."

---

[23]*Pa* and *na*, from *para* and *nada*, are very common contractions in unguarded or substandard speech.   [24]Contraction of *verdad*.   [25]*P'* represents Divinidad's contraction of *para*.

Retell the parts of the story suggested by the following key words and phrases.

Clotilde

la culpa

pasando una verdadera crisis

anuncios en el periódico

rótulo en la ventana

humilde campesina

tercer grado

a la capital a probar su suerte

viejo autobús

nueva crisis

después de un mes

con el cheque en el banco

[*To be followed by* LISTENING COMPREHENSION–SPEAKING EXERCISE]

Listening Passage
for Chapter 13
English Translation

Individualism

(1) The belligerent attitude of the Spaniard toward the demands of the government and the community, which generally require the subordination of the individual to society, is almost legendary. But to what factors is this due? In Spain many artists, writers, and political figures, whose concept of freedom originated (was born) from a romantic impulse, are continually rebelling against the laws, many of which have been imposed by dictatorial regimes.

(2) The Latin American follows this Iberian tradition of individualism. For this reason, he does not feel he is the same as others, but rather seeks to differentiate himself from them. He leads (lives) an intensely personal life. He doesn't enjoy being organized and he isn't interested in community projects. If he crosses a dangerous bridge, he doesn't think about what's going to happen to those who cross it behind him. He knows that many laws exist, but he doesn't consider that they apply to (are for) him. Because of his attitude, he doesn't understand impersonal relationships very well and rejects them whenever he can. He feels a strong loyalty toward his family and his friends. He thinks about his personal dignity more than about the usefulness of his actions. He loves ideals (ideals enchant him) and hates the empirical method.

(3) Many examples of this individualistic

attitude can be cited (named). A clerk or a worker seldom (few times) identifies with the interests of his firm. In the government offices, people are waited on sullenly or are told to come back the next day. College and even high school students are almost always willing and ready to declare themselves on strike. Professors and deans resign from their positions for minor reasons (easily) and frequently, and high government officials do the same for any personal reason.

(4) As Don Quixote demonstrated, individualism naturally comes into conflict with the law, which is made for everybody and is based on impersonal reasons. Therefore, an automobile driver will take (give himself) the privilege of obeying his own impulses rather than the traffic laws. And when his actions have created a conflict with the law, he will find a way out (to save himself) on the basis of something very personal. If he is poor, he will avail himself of this same condition; if he is rich, he would be foolish not to take advantage of this privileged situation, since that's what one is rich for in a Latin American society.

A Case of Individualism

(5) It was approximately midnight when the taxi came to a corner where the traffic signal was red (with the red light). The taxi driver, who was in a hurry, stopped for a moment, looked both ways, and since nobody was coming, crossed the corner.

(6) Unfortunately, there was a traffic officer hidden behind a tree on the other side of the street. While the officer examined the taxi driver's license, both started to argue. The taxi driver insisted that he hadn't committed any crime since, to his way of thinking, it is illogical and absurd that a human being like him, who thinks with his head, should have to obey a stupid mechanical signal at that hour of the night and at a moment when there wasn't a soul coming down the other street. (7) Naturally, the representative of the law told him that laws are made to be respected and became very angry with the taxi driver because of his nonsensical explanations. Then the taxi driver, in his efforts to avoid punishment for his crime, appealed to the fact that he was a poor man and the father of ten children. The traffic officer wasn't moved.

Grammar Points

First, additional verb constructions; second, a group of verbs that undergo a small irregularity in the preterit and the present participle; third, the infinitive as a verb complement; and fourth, review of verb tenses and constructions.

TO BE FOLLOWED BY
LISTENING RECOGNITION EXERCISE

Chapter 13

Basic Dialog

Un caso de individualismo

o. *Oficial de tránsito*   t. *Taxista*

I

o. Su licencia de manejar, por favor. Continúe[1], ¿qué estaba usted diciendo?

t. Que yo no sabía que habían puesto una señal en esa esquina. Pero le juro[2] que yo paré primero. Si me pasé la luz, como dice usted, es porque no venía nadie del otro lado. No iba a quedarme allí toda la noche esperando el cambio de luz.

II

o. Señor, las leyes se hacen para ser respetadas.

t. Yo comprendo[3], señor oficial, pero yo soy una persona civilizada y sé pensar con la cabeza.

o. ¡No me venga con cuentos! ¡Aquí todos manejan como salvajes! ¡Vamos, sígame!

t. ¡Tenga compasión, señor! ¡Yo soy un hombre pobre, padre de diez hijos!

o. Yo también soy un hombre pobre, pero debo cumplir con mi deber. ¡Vamos!

---

[1]Command form of *continuar*.   [2]From *jurar*.   [3]From *comprender*.

A Case of Individualism

o. *Traffic Officer*   t. *Taxi Driver*

I

o. Your driver's license, please. Go on, what were you saying?

t. That I didn't know they had put a light[4] on that corner. But I swear (to you) I stopped first. If I went through the light, as you say, it's because there was nobody coming from the other side. I wasn't going to stay there all night waiting for the light to change.[5]

II

o. Sir, laws are made to be respected.

t. I understand, officer, but I'm a civilized person and I know how to use my head.

o. Don't give me that![6] Everybody here drives like savages! Come on, follow me!

t. Have a heart, officer! I'm a poor man, the father of ten children!

o. I'm a poor man too, but I must do[7] my duty. Let's go!

SUPPLEMENT

I

Yo no sabía
　　no me había dado cuenta[8]　　*hadn't realized*

Si me pasé la luz...
　　　　el alto　　*the stop sign (halt)*

Una señal en esa esquina
　　　　carretera　　*highway*
　　　　ese camino　　*road*

Es porque no venía nadie.
　　　　un alma[9]　　*a soul*

II

¡No me venga con cuentos!
　　　　tonterías　　*nonsense*

Es porque no venía nadie.
　　　　se acercaba　　*was approaching, getting close*

Yo soy un hombre pobre.
　　　　honrado　　*honest*

---

[4]Signal.　[5]The change of light.　[6]Don't come to me with stories.　[7]Fulfill.　[8]The infinitive is *darse cuenta*.
[9]*Alma* is feminine. However, the form of the definite article used immediately before all singular nouns beginning with stressed *a* (or *ha*) is *el* rather than *la*. The form of the indefinite article immediately preceding such nouns is either *un* or *una*. The plural forms are the expected ones: *las almas, unas almas*.

222

SENTENCE RECALL

Say the dialog phrase or sentence in which each of the following words and phrases occurs.

diciendo	leyes	diez hijos	deber
juro	cuentos	salvajes	del otro lado
civilizada	el cambio de luz	señal	compasión

QUESTIONS

1. ¿Se había dado cuenta usted de que hoy no es domingo?
2. ¿Se había dado cuenta el taxista de que habían puesto una señal en esa esquina?
3. ¿Estaba la luz en verde o en rojo?
4. ¿Paró el taxista cuando llegó a la esquina?
5. ¿Se acercaba alguien del otro lado?
6. ¿Ni un alma?
7. ¿Se quedó el taxista toda la noche esperando el cambio de luz?
8. ¿El oficial de tránsito le pidió dinero al taxista o le pidió su licencia de manejar?
9. ¿Sabe usted manejar coche?
10. ¿Qué debe hacer usted cuando llega a una señal de tránsito que dice "alto"?
11. ¿Qué debe hacer después?
12. Y si una luz está en rojo, ¿cuándo puede pasar?
13. ¿Por qué no puede pasar cuando la luz está en rojo?
14. ¿Las leyes se hacen para ser respetadas o para ser violadas?
15. ¿Manejan los jóvenes americanos como personas civilizadas o como salvajes?
16. Según el oficial de tránsito, ¿cómo maneja la gente en su país?
17. ¿Cuál es la velocidad máxima a que se puede manejar en una carretera grande de los Estados Unidos, 50 kilómetros?[10]
18. ¿Hay muchos accidentes en las carreteras de los Estados Unidos?
19. ¿A cuántas millas por hora maneja usted generalmente en las carreteras?
20. ¿Cuál es el equivalente de esa velocidad en kilómetros?
21. Según las leyes de tránsito, ¿a qué velocidad más o menos debe uno manejar en las calles de una ciudad?
22. ¿Son buenos los caminos en todos los estados de los Estados Unidos?
23. ¿Tiene usted licencia de manejar?
24. ¿Qué debe uno hacer para conseguir una licencia?
25. ¿Debe uno pasar un examen de manejar nada más, o es necesario también pasar uno escrito?
26. En la conversación entre el oficial de tránsito y el taxista, ¿le pide el taxista al oficial que tenga compasión de él o que cumpla con su deber?
27. ¿Por qué le dice que tenga compasión?
28. ¿Qué responde el oficial?
29. ¿Son todos ustedes personas civilizadas y honradas?
30. ¿Piensan siempre con la cabeza cuando manejan o piensan con los pies?

[*To be followed by* LISTENING RECOGNITION EXERCISE]

---

[10] One *kilómetro* equals approximately 0.6 *milla* (mile); 50 *kilómetros* is the equivalent of about 30 *millas*.

Grammar

61. *Additional verb constructions*

	Present	*Past*
PROGRESSIVE	Está diciendo *He is saying*	Estaba diciendo *He was saying*
PERFECT	Han puesto *They have put*	Habían puesto *They had put*
PERFECT PROGRESSIVE	Hemos estado pensando *We have been thinking*	Habíamos estado pensando *We had been thinking*
"IR A"	Voy a quedarme *I'm going to stay*	Iba a quedarme *I was going to stay*

A. The past progressive with an imperfect form of *estar* is equivalent to the simple imperfect with the meaning "was ...ing." The progressive construction emphasizes the notion of action in progress.

The past progressive also occurs with the preterit of *estar: estuve (estuviste, estuvo,* etc.) *diciendo.* The preterit progressive is used for action in progress during a fixed segment of time: **Te estuve diciendo eso durante tres horas,** "I was (kept on) telling you that for three hours." Its use, however, is less frequent than that of the past progressive with *estar* in the imperfect.

CONSTRUCTION SUBSTITUTION

Read the following dialog; then read it once more, this time changing the preterit and imperfect verb forms to their corresponding progressive constructions.

EXAMPLES: Vi una película.
Estuve viendo una película.

Hablaba por teléfono.
Estaba hablando por teléfono.

DIEGO.   ¿Qué hacías anoche, Pedro? Te llamé varias veces.
PEDRO.   Estudiaba en casa de Juan. Estudiamos hasta casi la una. Y tú, ¿qué hiciste anoche? ¿Viste televisión?
DIEGO.   No, hombre. Escribí unas cartas nada más. ¡Qué frío hacía! ¿no?
PEDRO.   No solamente hacía frío; nevaba y llovía en cantidades, como nunca.

AYER A ESTA HORA

Following the cues, tell what the people listed below were doing yesterday at this time.

EXAMPLE: Emilio / preguntarle / Carlos María / quién ser / maestra
Ayer a esta hora Emilio le estaba preguntando a Carlos María quién era la maestra.

1. Vickie y Linda / hablar / Manuel y Enrique
2. Nosotros / quejarnos / clase de español
3. Juan José / tomar café y mirar / hija del dueño
4. Lucrecia / aprender a / poner / mesa
5. Estudiantes latinos / conversar / dormitorio
6. Luz María / preguntarle / empleada / precio / gramática
7. Tú / no hacer nada / como siempre
8. Anita / llamar / Cecilia / teléfono
9. General Méndez / dar golpe de estado y poner / presidente / avión
10. Tía Casilda / quejarse / ahijado
11. Don Vito y la señora / discutir / precio / uvas
12. Taxista / explicarle / oficial de tránsito / ser hombre pobre / padre / diez hijos

B. The past perfect, **había comido** (I had eaten), is formed with the imperfect of *haber*. The preterit perfect (**hube comido**) is almost never used in everyday language.

The past perfect progressive is formed in the obvious way (see the chart on page 224).

TENSE SUBSTITUTION

1. ¿Qué he hecho yo?
   ¿Qué había hecho yo?
2. No le has escrito a la tía Casilda.
3. Ella ha estado muy enferma.
4. No le hemos escrito, mejor dicho.
5. Todos han estado muy preocupados.
6. Sólo papá no ha ido a verla.
7. Yo no he podido escribirle.
8. Mis amigos se han quejado de mi conducta.

TENSE SUBSTITUTION

1. ¿Qué han estado haciendo todos?
   ¿Qué habían estado haciendo todos?
2. Jorge ha estado afeitándose y peinándose.
3. Nosotros hemos estado quejándonos del español.
4. Mis padres han estado pensando ir a Europa.
5. Tú no has estado haciendo absolutamente nada.
6. Yo he estado pensando comprar una casa más grande.

REJOINDERS

1. Ahora no puedo; estoy comiendo.
   Yo creí que ya habías comido.
2. Amadeo y su mujer se van a divorciar.
   Yo creí que ya se habían divorciado.
3. Tú y yo no hemos estudiado para el examen.
4. ¡Qué barbaridad! No ha venido el doctor.
5. El tico no ha recibido el cheque de su casa todavía.
6. Están poniendo una señal de tránsito en esa esquina.
7. Las chicas se van para Nicaragua mañana.

8. Dicen que el hijo del peón se casa con Valentina.
9. Usted no le ha escrito a su madrina todavía.
10. Con permiso, tengo que bañarme.

[*To be followed by* LISTENING COMPREHENSION–SPEAKING EXERCISE]

C. The **ir a** + *infinitive* construction with the imperfect of *ir* means "was going to." In the preterit, *ir* is usually interpreted as a verb of motion.

> Iba a comer.   *I was going to eat.*
> Fui a comer.   *I went (somewhere) to eat.*

TENSE SUBSTITUTION

1. Voy a decirles una cosa.
   Iba a decirles una cosa.
2. ¿Ah sí? ¿Qué vas a contarnos?
3. ¿No va a venir nadie a la fiesta?

4. Nosotros no vamos a quedarnos aquí toda la noche.
5. Sí, pero todos van a llegar tarde.
6. ¿Y tú vas a esperarlos?

QUESTIONS

Include in your answers the same type of verb construction that appears in the questions.

1. Perdón, ¿qué iba a decir usted?
   Iba a decir que usted habla muy rápido.
2. ¿Qué estaba haciendo usted?
   Yo no estaba haciendo nada.
3. ¿Dónde había estudiado usted español antes?
4. ¿Cuál de ustedes dijo que iba a ir al centro esta tarde, usted?
5. ¿Qué estaban haciendo ustedes dos, hablando?
6. Y usted, ¿qué estaba haciendo ayer a esta misma hora, bañándose o leyendo el periódico?
7. ¿No habíamos estado pensando hacer un examen hoy, ah?
8. Usted nunca me había dicho que usted era hijo del ex-presidente de Andivia, ¿verdad?
9. ¿Iban ustedes a preguntarme algo?
10. ¿En quién estaba pensando usted en este momento, en su novia?
11. ¿No dije yo que hoy íbamos a tener un examen?
12. ¿Dije yo entonces que hoy no íbamos a tener clase?

62. *Additional stem changes in* -ir *verbs*

<table>
<tr><td colspan="2">pedir</td><td colspan="2">morir</td></tr>
<tr><td>pedí</td><td>pedimos</td><td>morí</td><td>morimos</td></tr>
<tr><td>pediste</td><td>(pedisteis)</td><td>moriste</td><td>(moristeis)</td></tr>
<tr><td>pidió</td><td>pidieron</td><td>murió</td><td>murieron</td></tr>
<tr><td colspan="2">pidiendo</td><td colspan="2">muriendo</td></tr>
</table>

A. All -*ir* verbs which have vowel alternations in the present tense—like *pedir* (*yo pido*) and *morir* (*yo muero*)—have additional alternations in the preterit and in the present participle, as shown in the charts.

B. Other verbs like *pedir* which you know are *despedir, preferir, seguir, conseguir, sentir, resentirse,* and *vestirse*. A new one is **medir** (to measure).

C. Other verbs like *morir* are *dormir* (to sleep) and *dormirse* (to fall asleep).

D. The present participles of *decir* and *venir* are **diciendo** and **viniendo**.

PARADIGM PRACTICE

Do paradigm practice with all the verbs listed in B and C above.

PERSON–NUMBER SUBSTITUTION

Change only the second clause.

1. Yo no conseguí el dinero; lo conseguiste tú.
   (ellos)
   Yo no conseguí el dinero; lo consiguieron ellos.
   (ustedes, usted, unos amigos, nosotros, alguien)
2. Tú preferiste irte; ellos prefirieron quedarse.
   (nosotros, el taxista, usted, las chicas, yo, él)
3. ¿Se resintió usted? Más me resentí yo.
   (la tía Casilda, nosotros, mi novia, tus padres, yo)
4. El no pidió nada; yo pedí un café negro.
   (ella, tú, este señor, mis amigos, nosotros, nadie)
5. Si ella durmió mal anoche, peor dormí yo.
   (el marido, los hijos, tú, nosotros, usted, ellos)
6. ¿Te dormiste en la clase? Yo también me dormí.
   (la maestra, los alumnos, nosotros, todo el mundo, él)
7. Pepe midió un metro setenta de alto[11]; yo medí lo mismo.
   (tú, ellos, Valentina, los demás, usted, nosotros)

VERB SUBSTITUTION

1. ¿Qué estaba haciendo usted, trabajando?
   (decir tonterías)
   ¿Qué estaba haciendo usted, diciendo tonterías?
   (discutir, seguirme a mí, contar cuentos, pedir limosna)
2. A mí no me pasa nada, pero Jorge está muriéndose.
   (sentir el calor, dormirse, manejar como un salvaje, discutir, decir barbaridades)
3. ¿Había estado usted tomando cerveza esa noche?
   (dormir en el parque, vestirse en la calle, maldecir, llamarme a mí, pedir dinero, morirse)

[*To be followed by* LISTENING COMPREHENSION–SPEAKING EXERCISE]

---

[11] In height.

63. *The infinitive as a verb complement*

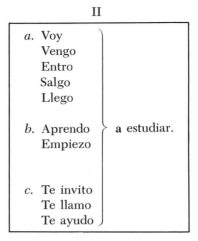

III

Acabo	**de** estudiar.
Tengo ⎱	**que** estudiar.
Hay ⎰	

A. In English, most verbs require the particle "to" before an infinitive.

$$
\text{I} \left\{ \begin{array}{l} \text{want} \\ \text{need} \\ \text{prefer} \\ \text{promise} \\ \text{hope} \\ \text{swear} \end{array} \right\} \text{ *to* study.}
$$

Only a handful of verbs omit "to."

$$
\text{I} \left\{ \begin{array}{l} \text{will} \\ \text{must} \\ \text{shall} \\ \text{can} \end{array} \right\} \text{ study.}
$$

B. Spanish is quite different: Many verbs may be followed directly by an infinitive (group I); many others require the preposition *a* (group II); and a smaller number of verbs are followed by something else, commonly *de* or *que* (group III).

C. Whether a verb belongs to one group or another is largely unpredictable and in most cases must simply be memorized. There are, however, a few helpful hints: Group II*a* contains verbs whose

228

basic meaning involves motion; the verbs in group II*b* involve beginning an activity; those in group II*c* involve participation of more than one person in an activity.

The important thing to remember is that English usually provides the *wrong* model for Spanish, since most English verbs require "to." You must try to avoid the habit of automatically inserting *a* before every infinitive in Spanish.

D. There is an important difference between *tener que* and *hay que*. *Tener que* must have a specific subject: *Tengo que estudiar* (*I* have to study); *Tienes que estudiar* (*You* have to study); and so on. *Hay que*, on the other hand, never has a specific subject. Thus, *Hay que estudiar* means "It's necessary to study," or "One's got to study."

VERB SUBSTITUTION

   1. No iba a quedarme allí toda la noche.
      (no pude)
   No pude quedarme allí toda la noche.
      (me invitaron, estaba pensando, no quise, voy)
   2. ¿De veras vas a vender esta casa, papá?
      (debes, tienes, acabas, vas, prefieres)
   3. Te prometen cuidar a los niños.
      (habían jurado, habían estado pensando, salieron, van a venir, sabían, les gustaba, van a empezar)
   4. ¿Vas a preguntarle al panameño?
      (juras, no has podido, acabas, debes, tienes, hay)
   5. La había invitado a jugar tenis.
      (está empezando, tuvo, había, no sabe, acababa, le gustaba, había aprendido)

64. *Review of verb constructions*

SUBSTITUTION

EXAMPLE: Anita habla conmigo.
      (is talking)
   Anita está hablando conmigo.
      (talked)
   Anita habló conmigo.
      (used to talk)
   Anita hablaba conmigo.
      (was talking)
   Anita estaba hablando conmigo.
      (is going to talk)
   Anita va a hablar conmigo.
      (was going to talk)
   Anita iba a hablar conmigo.

      (has talked)
   Anita ha hablado conmigo.
      (has been talking)
   Anita ha estado hablando conmigo.
      (had talked)
   Anita había hablado conmigo.
      (had been talking)
   Anita había estado hablando conmigo.
      (has to talk)
   Anita tiene que hablar conmigo.
      (has just talked)
   Anita acaba de hablar conmigo.

   1. Yo digo que no.
      (said, was going to say, have said, have just said, used to say)

2. Estos niños comen mucho.

(have eaten, ate, had been eating, are eating, have to eat)

3. Estudiamos español.

(have been studying, used to study, were going to study, are going to study)

4. ¿Le escribe usted a su tía?

(did you write, are you going to write, did you use to write, do you have to write, are you writing, have you just written)

5. Ellos no hacen nada.

(are not doing, haven't done, haven't been doing, don't have to do, hadn't done, weren't doing)

6. Tú trabajas mucho.

(have to work, have just worked, have been working, used to work, are working, were going to work, have worked)

CONVERSATION STIMULUS

Answer the following questions. Each response should be about as long as that given by the *taxista* to the *oficial de tránsito* in the second line of the basic dialog.

EXAMPLE: ¿Qué hizo usted esta mañana?

Me levanté muy temprano pensando que eran las siete. No tenía mi reloj porque se lo había prestado a Roberto. Me vestí rápidamente y fui al comedor a tomar el café. Pero cuando vi que eran apenas las seis y media, volví a mi cuarto y me acosté otra vez.

1. ¿Qué le dijo usted a su tía en la carta que le escribió ayer?
2. ¿Qué estaban haciendo todos en su casa anoche, como a las ocho?
3. ¿Por qué no es usted el primero de su clase?
4. ¿Qué contestó el taxista cuando el oficial de tránsito le preguntó por qué se había pasado la luz roja?

WRITTEN TRANSLATION

Spanish differs from English in the punctuation of dialog within prose. In particular, dashes are used instead of quotation marks. The following selection is punctuated as though it were Spanish. Observe this punctuation and imitate it in your translation.

I

—I hadn't realized it was so late —said Consuelo to her husband—. ¿Do you know what time it is? ¡It's five after four! If you don't hurry up (give yourself haste), we're going to be (arrive) late.

—¿(At) what time is the wedding? —asked Ramón.

—The wedding *was* at four o'clock.

—There's plenty of (much) time, then. I'll bet the bride hasn't left the house yet. ¿Where are my black socks? Tell the maid, what's her name, to bring me a pair and to shine (clean) these shoes for me, ¿will you (do you want), Consuelo? ¡Oh, for Pete's sake! ¡I can't wear (put on) this suit, I've gotten (am) too fat!

—Here we are at last —said Ramón—. ¿But why isn't anybody here?

—Because this is not the church.

—¿Why didn't you tell me that before?

—Because I thought you knew —replied his wife—. Besides, you were driving so fast and going through all the stop signs and everything that I was afraid (of) to open my mouth.

—Oh, don't give me that. I only went through two red lights, and I did it because nobody was coming the other way.

—But you have to respect the laws.

—¿Laws? ¿What laws? I know what I'm doing. Besides, I am Ramón Fuentes de la Torre y Gómez, the Minister of Education's first cousin.

—Okay, dear, let's not argue —said his wife impatiently—. You have to turn left at (on) this corner.

Reading

La esquina

La esquina de mi casa es mi teatro. Es una esquina muy amplia y transitada donde se cruzan calle y avenida, ricos y pobres, viejos y jóvenes, mujeres y niños, camiones y bicicletas, Cádilacs de último modelo y coches tan viejos y enfermos como yo. Sentado al lado de mi ventana paso las horas observando las muchas escenas que se desarrollan ante mis ojos, algunas interesantes, otras aburridas. La que voy a describir aquí es sobre un choque. Ocurrió ayer por la tarde, cuando ya comenzaba a oscurecer.

Acercándose hacia mi esquina por la avenida, venía un reluciente Mercedes Benz de último modelo con una elegante dama de chofer. Por la calle opuesta venía un viejísimo taxi recién pintado en brillante combinación de amarillo con verde.

La dama manejaba como manejan las mujeres: por el centro de la calle, la vista fija al frente y a velocidad moderada, sin darle importancia a otros vehículos que sonaban sus bocinas y hacían inútiles esfuerzos para pasarle por la derecha o por la izquierda.

La señal de tránsito que en grandes letras decía ALTO no produjo ningún efecto en la señora, y su Mercedes Benz entró tranquilamente a la intersección. El taxista también tenía una señal de su lado, pero como él creyó que no venía nadie por la otra dirección, le pareció absurdo parar. Ocurrió entonces lo inevitable: un fuerte y ruidoso impacto entre los dos vehículos, que segundos después se vieron rodeados de una numerosa y variada multitud. Todos o casi todos gritaban exaltadamente.

Había entre ellos niños, mujeres, señores de respetable presencia, mendigos, limpiabotas y todo tipo de vendedores ambulantes quienes, aprovechando la oportuna ocasión, anunciaban con mayor entusiasmo sus productos: ¡Helados! ¡Tamales calientes! ¡Lotería para el domingo! ¡LOTERÍAAA! Y cada uno de los presentes en aquella multitud, incluso los vendedores, limpiabotas y mendigos, parecía tener un interés personal en las causas y efectos del choque. Todos discutían y opinaban al mismo tiempo, unos a favor de la dama, otros a favor del taxista.

Yo, imitando al público de la ópera, miré con mis binóculos para observar más de cerca los detalles. ¡Ajá! ¡Allí también estaban ellos! Sí, eran ellos, los había visto en otras ocasiones y los reconocí inmediatamente, "La Pulga" y "El Santo", dos de los muchos carteristas que siempre abundan en los estadios, en las procesiones religiosas, en las corridas de toros y en toda clase de conglomeraciones públicas.

Un guardia civil, única autoridad que en ese momento circulaba por ese lugar, se acercó sin entusiasmo. Después de varios intentos pudo por fin abrirse paso entre la multitud. La dama y el taxista estaban ya en acalorada discusión:

—¡Usted tuvo la culpa, señora! —insistía el taxista—. ¡Usted se pasó el alto! ¡Hay testigos! ¡Yo soy un hombre pobre que tengo que trabajar mucho para llevarles el pan a mis hijos! ¡Mire mi pobre carro!

—¡Insolente! ¡La culpa la tuvo usted! —gritaba ella.

—¡La señora pasó primero, ella no tuvo la culpa! —exclamó vehementemente uno de los "testigos"—. ¡Yo lo vi con mis propios ojos!

—¡La vieja rica es la culpable! —gritó otro—. ¡Esa gente se cree ser los dueños de todo, hasta de las calles!

—¡Comunista! —le respondieron otros.

Intervino entonces el guardia civil exigiendo calma y menos intromisión de parte del público.

—Sus credenciales de manejar, señora —y al taxista también le pidió su licencia.

—¡Pero este hombre insolente tuvo la culpa! —exclamó ella—. ¡Hay testigos!

—Su licencia, señora, por favor —dijo el guardia con voz seca.

—No la traje. La puse en otra cartera. —Y luego, en un tono pretencioso y mirando de pies a cabeza a la autoridad, dijo: —No sé si usted se ha dado cuenta de quién soy yo. Usted está hablando con una tía del ingeniero Rafael Antonio Robles. Supongo que usted sabe quién es. Puede arreglar este asunto con él. Yo me voy.

El guardia sintió el efecto y se puso un poco nervioso, pero no queriendo dejarse intimidar ni humillar enfrente de todos, exclamó:

—Yo soy un hombre humilde, señora, y al ingeniero Robles le tengo mucha consideración y respeto. Sin embargo, usted debe comprender que yo soy la autoridad y debo proceder de acuerdo con la ley. Señora, no puedo permitirle manejar este vehículo si usted no tiene su licencia.

Pero ella no le hizo el menor caso y subió a su coche cerrando furiosamente la puerta.

—¡No la deje irse, señor guardia, tiene que pagarme! —exclamó el taxista.

Voces de protesta y de contra-protesta, brazos que se agitaban ante su cara, dedos que apuntaban directamente a su nariz; esa era la situación del infeliz representante de la ley.

—¡¡SILENCIO TODO EL MUNDO, YO SOY LA AUTORIDAD!! —exclamó con desesperación. Nadie le hizo caso y continuó el tumulto de la gente, el ruido espantoso que la elegante dama hacía con el motor de su coche, y las voces de los que vendían helados, tamales y lotería. El pobre guardia estaba perdido y sin saber qué hacer. Pero de pronto ocurrió algo que vino a sacarlo de tan precaria situación.

—¡LADRONES! ¡MI CARTERA! —gritó súbitamente un hombre de presencia distinguida y uno de los más exaltados testigos del accidente de tránsito—. ¡Me han dejado sin cartera y sin bolsillo! ¡POLICÍA! —gritaba levantando su saco para mostrar a los muchos curiosos un espacio vacío en la parte trasera de su pantalón, donde momentos antes había estado su bolsillo izquierdo... y su cartera.

—¡Allá van! —exclamó alguien, apuntando hacia "La Pulga" y "El Santo", que en ese instante pasaban como un rayo bajo mi ventana. Probablemente —yo no los vi— pero probablemente habían colaborado para dar el golpe; uno discutiendo con la víctima sobre el choque mientras el otro con gran habilidad y rapidez cortaba el bolsillo de su pantalón con una gillette.

—¡Allá van! ¡Deténganlos! ¡Policía! —gritaron otros, y todo el mundo empezó a correr tras los carteristas, incluso el guardia civil, quien alegremente obedeció al llamado, encontrando así una excusa perfecta para salir de aquel lío.

En la semi-oscuridad que ahora cubría el escenario del teatro sólo quedaron dos figuras que seguían discutiendo acaloradamente.

Prepare written answers for a class discussion.

1. ¿Por qué compara el narrador la esquina de su casa con un teatro?
2. ¿Qué tipos de personajes y de vehículos se cruzan en esa esquina?
3. ¿Son interesantes todas las escenas que se desarrollan ante sus ojos?
4. ¿Por qué está él siempre sentado al lado de su ventana?
5. ¿Qué ocurrió ayer por la tarde?
6. ¿Quién se acercaba a la esquina por la avenida?
7. ¿Puede usted describir el otro vehículo?
8. ¿Cómo manejaba la dama elegante?
9. ¿Qué hacían los vehículos que venían detrás de ella?
10. ¿Qué efecto produjo en la señora la señal de tránsito que había al final de la avenida?
11. ¿Y el taxista, por qué no paró tampoco?
12. ¿Qué ocurrió, entonces?
13. ¿De qué se vieron rodeados los dos vehículos segundos después del choque?
14. Describa usted a esa multitud y diga qué hacían todos.
15. Cuando el narrador se puso a observar con sus binóculos, ¿a quiénes vio entre la multitud?
16. ¿Quiénes eran "La Pulga" y "El Santo", y dónde abunda ese tipo de individuos?
17. ¿Quién era la única autoridad que circulaba por allí en esos momentos?
18. ¿Cuántos intentos tuvo que hacer él para abrirse paso entre la multitud?
19. ¿Qué estaban haciendo la dama y el taxista cuando el policía pudo por fin abrirse paso?
20. ¿Qué le decía el taxista a la señora y qué le decía ella a él?
21. ¿Qué hacían los otros?
22. ¿Por qué le gritaron "¡comunista!" a un tipo?
23. ¿Qué les pidió el guardia civil a la dama y al taxista?
24. ¿Qué excusa dio ella para explicar por qué no tenía su licencia?
25. ¿Qué le dijo la dama al guardia para intimidarlo?
26. ¿Quiere usted explicar la escena del choque en ese preciso momento?
27. ¿Qué empezó de pronto a gritar el señor de distinguida presencia?
28. ¿Qué le habían robado?
29. ¿Cómo no se dio él cuenta que le estaban robando la cartera?
30. ¿Cómo salió el guardia civil de tan precaria situación?

[*To be followed by* LISTENING COMPREHENSION–SPEAKING EXERCISE]

Listening Passage for Chapter 14
English Translation

The Single Woman

(1) As life changes in Latin America, women also adapt to modern times, perhaps more than men, because in the past they had much less freedom than the stronger sex. But it isn't easy to speak of *one* attitude concerning single women in Latin America, because that depends in great part on their class and social environment. Nowadays high society girls live (carry on) a fast and modern life. They don't need to work and they have time, freedom, and money to spare to flirt in convertibles, on a beach, or at an elegant party. Generally they marry well, which means that they select a husband of their same class. The newspapers with their society (social) pages full of girls in wedding gowns and with very long (last) names that become longer as they add that of the man they marry are constant evidence of this practice.

(2) But the upper class is small, whereas the lower class always constitutes the majority of the population in many Latin American countries. Among the poor people, things are quite different. Young women work, frequently from the age of twelve, whether it be as a servant, a laborer, or a peasant in the rural zones. They are considered lucky if they find a hard-working and responsible man who will treat them well. (3) A high percentage of these girls live with a man without being officially married. It is estimated that half the children born among the lower classes are illegitimate. One must read studies such as *Five Families* or *The Children of Sánchez* by the sociologist Oscar Lewis in order to understand the difficult life of these young women.

(4) There remains the middle class, which little by little is extending itself upward and downward. This class is quite synonymous with what is called the bourgeoisie, which looks after their children's morals and meddles in other people's as well. Curiously enough, their daughters are divided into two groups. The younger ones follow modern trends and are quite independent. They go out with their friends at any time, try to make (create) a professional career for themselves, and demand, in order to marry, a companion who shares their dreams. The older girls who are still unmarried are the victims of a period of transition; that is, they don't know whether to follow the norms of filial obedience and let themselves be dominated by the old traditions of their parents, or to become independent also. Most of them will choose the former. They will marry only with the family's approval, and afterwards they will accept the role of the housewife who depends completely on her husband.

(5) But at any rate, to marry is not so easy. Although there may be a great number of bachelors, many of them at the age of thirty have not finished their studies or attained an economic level which permits them to think about

marriage. And then there's the old problem with its proverb, ''a married man wants a house''; and cheap housing is lacking everywhere.

Man Marries When He Wants To, Woman When She Can

(6) In one of these upper middle class families where the traditional norms still prevail, the matrimonial possibilities and probabilities of Dolores, the still unmarried daughter, are being discussed. Gathered in the living room at this moment are, besides her parents, her older sister, fortunately already married; her younger brother, of more liberal tendencies than the rest of his family with respect to the position of the single woman; and a maiden aunt. Dolores is not present, but that doesn't matter.

(7) The aunt is worried because her niece still hasn't found a fiancé in spite of the fact that she has already passed the age of twenty, and she says that something has to be done in order for her to find a suitor. Her smart-aleck brother suggests that they light a candle to Saint Anthony, the patron saint of single girls. The aunt didn't know, however, that Dolores already has a suitor, a man by the name of Cabezas who, according to her sister, is crazy about her. The bad part is that Dolores doesn't like him because, besides being about twenty years older than she is, he is very fat. As her brother says, he must weigh about a thousand pounds. But according to her mother, Mr. Cabezas is a great catch, a very rich, decent, and honest man, from a very good family.

(8) Dolores' father agrees (is in agreement) that his daughter should accept this suitor, because the important thing in marriage is that the man have the qualities his wife has just mentioned. The aunt also agrees. According to her, women cannot afford (give themselves) the luxury of choosing too much because men are always scarce. Love is a secondary thing, she says; it grows in time. One must take advantage of the opportunities, not waste them. Like what happened to her—adds Dolores' father, her brother-in-law—who for that reason remained an old maid (stayed behind to dress up saints*). In short, the whole family, except the younger brother, agrees that Dolores should marry Mr. Cabezas. Now it's only a matter of convincing Dolores. But that will be easy.

Grammar Points

First, indicative and subjunctive forms in adverb and adjective clauses; second, the generic use of the definite article; third, contrast of the verb **gustar** with the verb ''to like''; and fourth, the article **lo**.

TO BE FOLLOWED BY
LISTENING RECOGNITION EXERCISE

---

*See footnote 14, page 248.

Chapter 14

Basic Dialog

El hombre se casa cuando quiere, la mujer cuando puede

TÍA. *Tía*   HNO.[1] *Hermano*   HNA. *Hermana*   MA. *Madre*   PA. *Padre*

I

TÍA. ¿Qué hacemos para que Dolores consiga novio?

HNO. Yo sugiero[2] que le encendamos[3] una vela a San Antonio.

HNA. No te hagas el chistoso. Dolores ya tiene un pretendiente, tía Marta, ¿no sabía? Se llama Armando Cabezas. Está loco por ella, pero a ella no le gusta.

MA. Es muy tonta porque él es un gran partido. Sólo que es un poquito gordo.

HNO. ¡Un poquito! Debe pesar mil libras. Además, es como veinte años mayor.

PA. Con tal que sea un hombre decente y honrado, eso es lo importante.

II

HNO. ¡Qué risa: Sra. Dolores de Cabezas! Además, Dolores no está enamorada. ¿Por qué no busca a alguien que sea más joven, menos gordo y que tenga otro apellido?

TÍA. ¿Con la escasez de hombres que hay aquí? Hay que aprovechar las oportunidades. El amor crece[4] con el tiempo.

PA. Vean a mi cuñada; por escoger tanto se quedó soltera.

---

[1] Abbreviation of *hermano*.   [2] From *sugerir*.   [3] From *encender* (like *entender*).   [4] From *crecer* (like *conocer*).

Altar mayor de una iglesia colonial en Ecuador

Man Marries When He Wants To, Woman When She Can

A. *Aunt*   B. *Brother*   S. *Sister*   M. *Mother*   F. *Father*

I

A. What can we do so that Dolores can catch a man?

B. I suggest that we light a candle to Saint Anthony.[5]

S. Don't be funny.[6] Dolores already has a suitor, Aunt Marta, didn't you know? His name is Armando Cabezas. He's crazy about her, but she doesn't like him.

M. She's very silly because he's a great catch. Only he's a little heavy.

B. A little! He must weigh a thousand pounds. Besides, he's about twenty years older.

F. As long as[7] he's a decent and honest man, that's the important thing.

II

B. What a laugh[8]: Mrs. Headaches! Besides, Dolores isn't in love. Why doesn't she look for someone younger, less fat, and with a different last name?

A. With the shortage of men we have here? You've got to take advantage of the opportunities. Love grows in time.

F. Look at my sister-in-law; because she was so choosy[9] she remained single.

CULTURAL NOTES

A married woman's legal name includes *de* (meaning "the wife of") before her husband's last name. Thus, if Marta Campos marries Pedro Molina, she signs her name Marta Campos de Molina, or simply Marta de Molina. She doesn't need to include the title *Sra.* in her signature, or to call herself Sra. Marta de Molina, except for reasons of emphasis: *¿Sabe usted quién soy yo? ¡Soy la Sra. Marta de Molina!*

SUPPLEMENT

I

Con tal que sea un hombre decente
                 sin vicios   *without vices*

Eso es lo importante.
         lo que cuenta   *what counts*

II

El amor crece con el tiempo.
   odio   *hatred*

---

[5] Saint Anthony is the patron saint of girls who wish to marry. (See the reading at the end of this chapter.) [6] Don't make yourself the funny one. [7] Provided that. [8] What laughter. [9] For choosing so much.

¡Qué risa!

chiste	*joke*
broma	*joke*[10]

Vean a mi cuñada.

nieta	*granddaughter*
suegra	*mother-in-law*

¿Por qué no busca a alguien que tenga otro apellido?

mejor porvenir[11]   *better future*

Hay que aprovechar las oportunidades.

olvidar	*forget*
desperdiciar	*throw away, waste*

DIALOG AND SUPPLEMENT CHECK

SENTENCE RECALL

Say the dialog phrase or sentence in which each of the following words or phrases occurs.

enamorada	menos gordo	mil libras	loco por ella
pretendiente	escasez	San Antonio	tonta
consiga	gran partido	soltera	chistoso
decente y honrado	por escoger	aprovechar	qué risa
	cuñada	cuando quiere	

ITEM SUBSTITUTION

Substitute each of the following words and phrases for a related word or phrase in one of the basic sentences of this chapter. Repeat the whole new sentence.

EXAMPLE: *Teacher:* qué chiste
             Student: **¡Qué chiste: Sra. Dolores de Cabezas!**

desperdiciar	el odio	que tenga porvenir
sin vicios	mi nieta	lo que cuenta

QUESTIONS

1. ¿Es verdad que los hombres se casan cuando quieren y las mujeres cuando pueden?
2. ¿Hay abundancia de hombres solteros aquí, o una escasez?
3. Y de chicas solteras, ¿hay abundancia?
4. ¿Cómo se llama el pretendiente de Dolores?
5. Si Dolores se casa con él, ¿cómo se va a llamar?
6. ¿Qué quiere decir "dolores de cabezas" en inglés?
7. ¿Cómo es él físicamente?

---

[10] *Un chiste* is a funny story; *una broma* is a practical joke.   [11] Masc.: *el porvenir.*

8. ¿Cuántas libras pesa él, según el hermano de Dolores?
9. ¿Quiere él a Dolores? ¿Cuánto la quiere?
10. Y Dolores, ¿está ella loca por él?
11. ¿Por qué cree la madre de Dolores que su hija debe casarse con el Sr. Cabezas?
12. ¿Es él mayor o menor que Dolores? ¿Cuántos años?
13. ¿Cree usted que una diferencia de edad de veinte años entre la mujer y el hombre tiene importancia?
14. ¿Cuántos años, máximo, debe ser el hombre mayor que la mujer, según usted?
15. ¿Qué es para una mujer "un gran partido"?
16. ¿Cuáles de ustedes están enamorados? ¿Cuándo piensan casarse?
17. ¿Se casó la tía de Dolores?
18. ¿Es ella la cuñada, la nieta o la suegra del papá de Dolores?
19. ¿Por qué se quedó ella soltera, según el padre de Dolores?
20. ¿Es una persona chistosa alguien que cuenta cosas tristes?
21. ¿Quién es el más chistoso de esta clase?
22. ¿Le gusta a usted dar bromas[12]? ¿Contar chistes?
23. ¿Olvida usted fácilmente las cosas o tiene buena memoria?
24. ¿Qué es lo contrario de "aprovechar"?
25. ¿Aprovecha usted su tiempo o lo desperdicia?

[*To be followed by* LISTENING RECOGNITION EXERCISE]

Grammar

65. *Indicative and subjunctive forms in adverb clauses*

A. In Chapter 12 you studied the use of the subjunctive in *noun clauses*. These clauses are called noun clauses because they function in sentences just like nouns and noun phrases. In the following example, the noun clause "that John pay me" functions as the object of the verb "demand," just as the single noun "payment" does.

I demand { payment.
          { that John pay me.

Adverb clauses function in sentences just like simple adverbs and adverb phrases.

I always get up { early.
               { before the sun comes up.

---

[12] *Dar una broma,* to play a joke.

240

B.

I. Adverbial expressions always followed by indicative

porque es tarde	*because it is late*
ya que } es tarde **como**	*since, inasmuch as it is late*

II. Adverbial expressions always followed by subjunctive

a menos que		*unless it is late*
antes (de) que		*before it is late*
con tal que	sea tarde	*provided it is late*
para que		*so that it is (may, will be) late*
sin que		*without (its) being late*

1. Charts I and II list some of the most common expressions that introduce adverb clauses.
2. Clauses introduced by *porque, ya que,* and *como* (chart I) always contain information that agrees with the facts in the real world. For example, one doesn't say "because it is raining" unless it is in fact raining. These clauses always contain indicative verb forms.
3. Clauses introduced by *a menos que, antes que,* and the other expressions in chart II contain information which may or may not agree with the facts in the real world. For example, if you say "I won't go *unless* Mary goes," you don't know whether Mary will go or not. These clauses always contain subjunctive verb forms.

CLAUSE SUBSTITUTION

The following exercises contain adverb clauses introduced by expressions from charts I and II, where the choice of indicative or subjunctive is automatically determined by the expression which introduces the clause. These exercises will prepare you for the explanation of the choice of indicative or subjunctive in adverb clauses introduced by a third group of expressions. Follow the example.

1. Ojalá, porque Dolores no está muy joven.
   –ser buena
   Ojalá, porque Dolores es buena.
   –tener diecinueve años
   –necesitar casarse
2. Ya que Armando es un hombre honrado, eso es lo que cuenta.
   –pesar apenas mil libras
   –ser un gran partido
   –querer a Dolores
3. ¿Qué hacemos para que Dolores consiga novio?
   –Dolores casarse
   –Dolores tener pretendiente
   –Dolores querer a Armando
   –Armando venir a verla
   –Armando proponerle matrimonio

–Dolores estar enamorada de Armando
–Dolores decir que sí
4. Con tal que Armando tenga porvenir, eso es lo importante.
  –Armando ser honrado y decente
  –Dolores no quedarse soltera
  –Armando no irse con otra
  –Armando y Dolores tener muchos hijos
5. No pueden casarse a menos que ella tenga veintiún años.
  –ella terminar sus estudios
  –ella decidirse definitivamente
  –los padres tener más dinero para la fiesta
6. No deben hacerlo sin que nadie lo sepa.
  –nosotros investigar quién es su familia
  –Dolores conocer a su suegra
  –Armando hablar con nosotros
  –nosotros saber cuándo

SUBSTITUTION–TRANSLATION EXERCISE

1. Yo no digo nada porque Armando viene.
   (provided)
   Yo no digo nada con tal que Armando venga.
   (because, before, so that, since, unless, without)
2. Ya que usted y yo somos amigos, eso no importa.
   (unless, so that, provided, since)
3. Yo no voy a ir sin que ustedes vayan.
   (because, unless, since, so that, without, before)

C.

III. Adverbial expressions followed by indicative or subjunctive

aunque es **aunque** sea	*even though it is* *even if it is, although it may be*
donde está **donde** esté	*where it (usually) is* *wherever it may be*
cuando es **cuando** sea	*when it (usually) is* *whenever it may be*
hasta que es **hasta que** sea	*until it is (as it always is)* *until (this time) it is*
tan pronto es **tan pronto** sea	*as soon as it is (as it always is)* *as soon as it is (this time)*
después (de) que es **después (de) que** sea	*after it (usually) is* *after it is (this time)*

Charts I and II illustrate the basis for the choice of indicative or subjunctive in adverb clauses introduced by the third group of expressions. Study the following pairs of sentences.

| INDICATIVE: | **Cuando sale** el sol, estoy contento. | *When the sun comes out I'm happy.* |

INDICATIVE: **Cuando sale** el sol, estoy contento.   *When the sun comes out I'm happy.*
(The sun does in fact come out regularly, and it makes me happy.)

SUBJUNCTIVE: **Cuando salga** el sol, avíseme.   *When the sun comes out, let me know.*
(The sun is *not* out now, but I want to know when it subsequently does come out.)

INDICATIVE: Nos vamos, **aunque está** nevando.   *We're leaving, although it's snowing.*
(It *is* snowing right now, but we're leaving anyway.)

SUBJUNCTIVE: Nos vamos, **aunque esté** nevando.   *We're leaving, even if it's snowing.* (I don't know whether it's snowing now or not, but we're leaving in any event.)

WRITTEN TRANSLATION

1. *Aunque*
   He wants to marry (with) her, even though she's dumb and ugly.
   He wants to marry (with) her, even if she's dumb and ugly.
2. *Donde*
   She wants to be wherever he may be.
   She's always where he is.
3. *Cuando*
   Come (to) see us when you have money.
   You never come to see us when you have money.
4. *Hasta que*
   The grandfather always waits until his granddaughter arrives.
   Today, however, he's not going to wait until she arrives.
5. *Tan pronto*
   I'll call you as soon as I have some news.
   I always call you as soon as I have some news, don't I?
6. *Después (de) que*
   I always eat after he does (eat).
   I'm going to eat after he eats.

QUESTIONS

Provide an answer that includes the phrase in parentheses. If books are closed, your teacher will give the cue. Follow the example.

1. ¿Tiene usted hambre si no come? (sí, cuando)
   Sí, cuando no como, tengo hambre.
2. ¿Va a comer tan pronto tenga hambre? (sí, cuando)
3. Su novia probablemente no sabe cocinar. ¿Va a casarse con ella de todos modos? (sí, aunque)
4. Usted no pone atención; por eso no aprende nada, ¿verdad? (sí, como)
5. Si usted sabe alguna noticia, ¿me avisa? (sí, tan pronto)
6. Como hoy es domingo, ¿podemos ir al cine? (sí, ya que)
7. ¿Cree que un joven y una chica deben casarse si están enamorados pero no tienen dinero? (sí, aunque)
8. Si Armando es un hombre decente y honrado, ¿le recomienda usted a Dolores que se case con él? (sí, con tal)

66. *Indicative and subjunctive forms in adjective clauses*

---

1. a. Busco un libro **que tiene muchas fotos.**
   b. Busco un libro **que tenga muchas fotos.**

2. a. Espero a una chica **que habla inglés.**
   b. Espero a una chica **que hable inglés.**

3. a. Hay mucha gente **que sabe hacer paella.**
   b. No hay una persona **que sepa hacer paella.**

A. *Adjective clauses* modify nouns and pronouns, just like simple adjectives and adjective phrases.

I want to study something ⎰ easier.
⎱ that won't take so much time.

B. The decision to use the indicative or subjunctive in adjective clauses is made in essentially the same way it is in adverb clauses: If the description given in the clause applies to a specific, known noun then the indicative is used; if not, the subjunctive is used.

For instance, in the (a) examples in the chart, the speaker is looking for a particular book that he knows about which has a lot of pictures, waiting for a particular girl who in fact speaks English, and referring to many people who exist and who know how to make paella. In the (b) examples, on the other hand, the speaker is looking for *any* book (he has no particular one in mind) with a lot of pictures, waiting for some girl (not yet identified and perhaps nonexistent) who speaks English, and stating that people who know how to make paella are nonexistent (thus the description "who knows how to make paella" cannot apply to anyone).

In short, the indicative is used in adjective clauses that describe nouns which exist and which have been identified or "picked out." The subjunctive is used when the described noun is unidentified, not "picked out," or nonexistent.

OPINIONS

Listen to each of the following statements. One student agrees with it, the other disagrees. Begin your responses with *Sí, yo conozco a unos (algunos)* or *No, yo no conozco a ningún(a)* or *a nadie.*

EXAMPLE: Hay muchos americanos que son millonarios.
   First student: **Sí, yo conozco a unos americanos que son millonarios.**
Second student: **No, yo no conozco a ningún americano que sea millonario.**

1. Los maestros saben mucho.
2. Las mujeres saben cocinar muy bien.
3. Hay algunos hombres que pesan más de mil libras.
4. Todas las mujeres hablan muchísimo.
5. Hay algunas personas que saben contar buenos chistes.
6. Hay hombres que son un gran partido y tienen un gran porvenir.
7. La gente inteligente pone su dinero en el banco.
8. Los latinoamericanos llegan a tiempo.

244

Follow the cues given below and write a composition about the ideal type of a woman a man wants for a wife. You may make changes or add some details if you wish to express a different opinion. Make sure you use the subjunctive in the proper places, make the necessary noun-adjective agreements, etc.

Mi tipo ideal

Yo buscar / mujer / no ser / muy viejo / y / (ella) querer tener / mucho / hijo. Yo querer / ella ser / bonito / y estar bonito / día / noche / noche / día. No ser importante / ella no tener / mucho dinero / con tal / ella quererme. Ojalá / futuro / suegra / ser simpático / y creer / yo ser / gran partido / su hija. Cuando casarnos / yo pensar invitar / mis amigos / para que / ellos venir / casa / tomar cerveza. Ojalá / ella no oponerse.

Hasta que / yo encontrar / ese tipo / mujer / yo no casarme.

[*To be followed by* LISTENING COMPREHENSION–SPEAKING EXERCISE]

67. *Generic use of the definite article*

Las mujeres son mejores como maestras.	*Women are better as teachers.*
El amor crece con **el** tiempo.	*Love grows in time.*

In Spanish the definite article normally precedes the subject noun in sentences which mention a property or characteristic of a whole group or class. In English the article is not used.

TRANSLATION

1. Money is what counts.
2. Love is good; hatred is bad.
3. All men are good.
4. Men must help other men.
5. Americans have no problems.
6. Latin Americans need money.
7. Children have to eat.
8. Clothes (*ropa*) are expensive.
9. Meat, vegetables, apples, pears, rice, eggs, butter, tomatoes . . . all food (*comida*) is very expensive.
10. Americans must help.

GENERALIZATIONS

1. ¿Cuáles hombres son malos, nosotros?
   No, los hombres en general son malos.
2. ¿Estas chicas nada más son dulces?
3. ¿Sólo este idioma extranjero es difícil?
4. ¿Sólo esas mujeres rubias y de ojos azules son bonitas?
5. ¿Cuál vida es amarga, la suya?
6. ¿Está diciendo usted que mi queridísima madre es una suegra mala y antipática?

68. *The verb* gustar

A Juan le gustan las uvas.	*John likes grapes.*
A mí me gusta María.	*I like María.*
Pero a María no le gusto yo.	*But María doesn't like me.*

A. Although **gustar** is equivalent to "like," its literal meaning is "to please, to be pleasing." Thus, Spanish says "Grapes are pleasing to Juan," whereas English says "Juan likes grapes." In other words, the Spanish subject and object are the reverse of the English.

In order to correct any tendency to say non-sentences like **Juan gusta las uvas*, it may help to remember that an indirect object pronoun (*me, te, le, nos, les*) must always be used with *gustar*, and that the preposition *a* must precede the object noun in Spanish (the subject in English): *A Armando le gusta Dolores.*

B. The third person singular and plural are the most frequently used forms of *gustar*. The first person singular is normally used only in a situation of contrast, as in the third sentence in the chart, which is in contrast with the second. The more usual equivalent of "María doesn't like me" is *María no me quiere* or *Yo no le caigo bien a María.*[13]

WRITTEN TRANSLATION

1. Pedro likes María.
   María likes Pedro.
2. Pedro and Carlos like Carmen.
   Carmen doesn't like them.
3. Dolores is going to like her mother-in-law.
   But her mother-in-law is not going to like her.
4. The children liked (*imperfect*) the maid.
   And the maid liked the children.
5. The maid didn't like (*preterit*) the lady.
   The lady didn't like the maid.
6. I hope Dolores likes her new suitor.
   Let's hope that her new suitor likes her.

TRANSLATION

Don't forget that the definite article precedes any noun subject which refers to a class as a whole.

1. I like coffee.
2. You like tea.
3. I like girls.
4. And girls like me.
5. One girl likes to go to the movies.
6. Another likes to play tennis.
7. Many don't like to do anything.
8. But Juan likes them all, anyway.

QUESTIONS

1. ¿Le gustó el desayuno esta mañana?
2. ¿Qué clase de frutas le gustan a usted más?
3. ¿Le gusta Dolores al Sr. Cabezas o el Sr. Cabezas le gusta a Dolores?
4. ¿Les gusta a todos ustedes el español?

---

[13] Literally, "I do not fall well to María."

246

5. ¿Me gustan a mí mis alumnos?
6. ¿Cuál es la película que más le ha gustado a usted en su vida?

[*To be followed by* LISTENING COMPREHENSION–SPEAKING EXERCISE]

69.   *The article* lo

Eso es **lo** importante.	*That's the important thing.*
Eso es **lo** que cuenta.	*That's what counts.*

A.   The article **lo** never precedes a noun; it is used only before adjectives that describe some aspect or part of a noun, idea, or situation. Consequently, *lo importante de una situación* can be restated as *la parte (el aspecto, la cosa) importante de una situación*. There is no English equivalent of *lo*; thus *lo importante* can be translated only as "the important thing (aspect, part, etc.)."

B.   *Lo* can also precede an adjective phrase or an adjective clause.

PHRASE: lo de la casa   *the thing about (matter concerning) the house*
CLAUSE: lo que cuenta   *the thing (part) that (that which, what) counts*

C.   Of the three constructions with *lo*, the most common are *lo* before a simple adjective (*lo bueno*) and *lo* before an adjective clause (*lo que cuenta, lo que me gusta*). Only these two are included in the following drills.

TRANSFORMATION

1. La parte mejor de la casa es la sala.
   Lo mejor de la casa es la sala.
2. La cosa importante es que sea un hombre honrado.
3. El aspecto malo de esta situación es el dinero.
4. La parte más buena de este libro es el color.
5. La parte triste en la vida de una mujer es que no puede casarse cuando quiere.
6. El aspecto más feo de la casa es que la cocina es muy vieja.
7. Todas las cosas que me gustan son caras.
   Todo lo que me gusta es caro.
8. Nadie tiene las cosas que yo tengo.
9. La parte que no me gusta de mi suegra es que habla mucho.
10. La cosa que ellos no entienden es que Dolores no está enamorada.
11. Nunca encontramos las cosas que buscamos.
12. El problema que ella menciona en su carta es terrible.

TRANSLATION

1. The important (thing) is the truth.
   What is important is the truth.
2. The best (thing) is to be honest.
   The (thing) that counts is to be honest.
3. Good (things) are expensive.
   What is good is expensive.
4. The bad (part) about this book is that it is not cheap.
   The (thing) that I don't like about this book is that it is not cheap.

Reading

Catalina y San Antonio
Una leyenda del Ecuador

En una casa grande cerca de la antigua iglesia de San Francisco en Quito vivía, hace muchos años, una viuda con su hija Catalina. Desde la edad de quince años, cuando la linda señorita fue presentada a la alta sociedad en un baile elegante y costoso, muchos pretendientes le habían pedido la mano. Pero Catalina, algo consentida y un poco orgullosa por tantas atenciones, no encontraba ningún pretendiente a su gusto. Los rehusó a todos, uno después de otro.

—Es lástima que tú, una señorita tan bella como un amanecer, no te cases —le decían a Catalina sus amigos.

—Cuidado, chica, o vas a quedarte soltera —le avisaban las amigas recién casadas.

De buen humor, Catalina escuchaba estos consejos sin seguirlos, y el resultado fue que a la edad avanzada de dieciocho años todavía no había encontrado esposo.

—Esto no puede continuar así —le dijo la buena madre a Catalina—. ¿No quieres casarte con Carlos que anoche te dio la serenata?

—¿Con ese gordo? No, mamacita. ¡Qué barril!

—Pues, no entiendo por qué no quieres a Luis que tiene una familia tan distinguida.

—No, no, es tan pálido como un muerto.

—¿Y Eduardo que es el más guapo de todos los jóvenes de la capital?

—No, no, es tan alto como un palo.

—Pues, dime, hijita, ¿quieres quedarte para vestir santos[14]?

—¡Oh, no, no! —contestó Catalina llorando—; pero, ¿qué voy a hacer cuando no encuentro a ningún pretendiente a mi gusto?

Por algunos momentos, la madre se quedó pensando. Entonces habló como si fuera inspirada:

—He oído decir que San Antonio de Padua sabe dar buenos maridos a las jóvenes que le piden devotamente este favor. Creo que debemos pedir ayuda al buen santo.

—Bueno, mamacita —contestó Catalina, secando sus lágrimas—. Vamos a rezar en seguida en la iglesia de San Francisco.

Así, día tras día, las dos, madre e hija, fueron a la iglesia a rezar al buen santo. Sin embargo, ningún pretendiente agradable se presentó. Por supuesto, la señorita se puso triste.

—Debes tener fe y paciencia, hija —avisó la madre—. Ahora tengo otra idea. En tu cuarto vamos a arreglar un altarcito con una estatua de San Antonio. Entonces, por nueve noches le rezaremos al santo, pidiéndole que te consiga un esposo a tu gusto. Sé que te dará lo que pides.

—Voy a hacerlo por obediencia —respondió Catalina, tristemente—. Pero si al fin de nueve días no me ha ayudado San Antonio, haré algo terrible, absolutamente terrible.

Así, el altarcito de San Antonio fue arreglado con flores frescas y dos velas grandes que quemaron constantemente. Aunque las dos mujeres rezaron por nueve noches, el novio del milagro no apareció.

Pacientemente, Catalina esperó unos días más. Entonces una tarde la señorita, llorando a lágrima viva, corrió al altarcito. Tomando la estatua del santo en las manos, le dijo:

—Perdóname, santo mío, pero como no me has dado un esposo, no quiero verte más.

Dicho esto, la señorita arrojó la estatua por una ventana abierta a la calle. En ese mismo momento pasaba un caballero elegantemente vestido. Y el santo cayó exactamente en la copa alta de su fino sombrero.

---

[14] The expression *quedarse para vestir santos* refers to the stereotype of the unmarried woman in Spanish speaking countries, who spends her time in Catholic churches doing various tasks, among them changing the robes of the statues of saints.

El caballero reaccionó violentamente con el golpe recibido en la cabeza. Se puso furioso. Recogiendo la estatua, fue a la puerta de la casa de donde había sido arrojada. Con su bastón llamó ruidosamente. Pronto apareció la madre.

—Arrojar una estatua a la calle es una cosa terrible, señora. Y mire cómo está arruinado mi fino sombrero que compré en París.

—Lo siento mucho, señor.

—Pues, explíqueme, señora, ¿por qué arrojó la estatua? ¿No sabe que ha cometido un gran pecado?

—Tenga paciencia, buen caballero, y se lo contaré todo.

Al final de la explicación la madre añadió:

—Pero mi hija es amable y bella, señor.

Ahora el caballero, más curioso que enojado, contestó:

—Le ruego que me disculpe, señora, que tal vez estuve un poco violento. Y ahora espero que me haga el favor de presentarme a su preciosa hija que ha sufrido mucho.

—El gusto es mío, caballero. Pase y siéntese. Esta es su casa[15] —dijo la madre, abriendo la puerta de la sala.

El señor aceptó la invitación y la madre salió en busca de Catalina. Sin entusiasmo, la señorita acompañó a su madre a la sala donde extendió la mano al caballero cuyo apellido indicaba que pertenecía a una de las familias más ricas y distinguidas del Ecuador.

El caballero quedó asombrado de la belleza de Catalina y le dijo:

—Le ruego, doña Catalina, que me considere su sincero admirador. Y permítame ser el primer servidor de su casa.

—Mi madre y yo estamos honradas con su presencia. Tendremos mucho gusto en recibirle, caballero —contestó la hija con modestia.

Después de esos discursos sinceros y entusiásticos, los tres platicaron, hora tras hora, como si hubieran sido viejos amigos. Catalina estaba encantada del buen joven amable e inteligente que acababa de volver de Europa donde había estudiado por muchos años. Y el caballero estaba encantado de la modestia y hermosura de Catalina.

Al fin del año, se casaron los jóvenes en la antigua iglesia de San Francisco, celebrando las bodas con pompa y esplendor.

Si hoy día visita la iglesia, puede ver en una de las capillas una preciosa estatua de San Antonio de Padua. Se dice que es el regalo de dos personas muy agradecidas —Catalina y su esposo.

CONVERSATION STIMULUS

Give a brief oral summary of the preceding story.

[*To be followed by* LISTENING COMPREHENSION–SPEAKING EXERCISE]

---

[15]"This is your house," the Spanish equivalent of "Make yourself at home."

Listening Passage
for Chapter 15
English Translation

Immigration and Migration

(1) The great urban centers such as Buenos Aires, Mexico City, and Sao Paulo each have a minimum population of five to six million inhabitants, and every year hundreds of thousands of people coming from the interior of the country increase this figure. Something similar occurs in almost every important Latin American city, although, unfortunately, these cities do not have the facilities to assimilate such migratory waves.

(2) At this point we should take a look at (do a little) history. Domingo Faustino Sarmiento, the famous writer, educator, and president of Argentina in the last century, said that the basic social conflict in Latin America was the struggle between civilization and the forces of unrefinement (barbarianism). According to Sarmiento's thesis, no one was interested in establishing schools, housing, or trade in the interior of the country; and consequently the prairies, jungles, and mountains remained desolate. The cities, founded almost always along the coast, grew; millions of immigrants came from Europe, particularly to the ports of the Atlantic, and settled down where there was culture and industry.

(3) Meanwhile, in the provinces of the interior, the peasants, mostly Indians and mestizos, went on cultivating their own small parcels of land or working for the owners of great haciendas or plantations. Schools and roads were not being built, and the way of life of the peasants changed little. However, despite the

high infant mortality, their number continued to increase, and when it was no longer possible to subdivide the land or work among so many, they would start moving to the cities, where they hoped to find a job and a school for their children.

(4) Unfortunately, these peasant families that get off the bus or the train, carrying their children in their arms and their cardboard boxes on their backs, come poorly prepared to face the struggle for modern life. Without money, without any technical knowledge, and in the majority of cases without even knowing how to read or write, these people have to manage any way they can. In the capital of Mexico many peasant families settle down (install themselves) in some corner of the humble room where some generous but equally poor relatives live. In the morning, after eating a tortilla and beans, they will all go around the city offering their services —the mother and older daughters no doubt as servants. In the outskirts of Buenos Aires, for instance, there are a number of the so-called *villas miseria,* a very appropriate (adequate) name for the dense clusters (conglomerations) of shacks, made of boards, sheets of tin, and canvas, where there is no electricity or running water, and where each rainfall causes a flood. There live thousands and thousands of mestizos from the north of Argentina, and Bolivian and Paraguayan Indians, all of them in search of a life that may some day offer them a little dignity, comfort, and a better future for their children.

(5) In the conversation that follows we find a peasant and his wife discussing the possibility of moving away from the place where they live. He is furious and desperate because of the drought in that region, because he is without a job, and because they have been stealing even the few chickens he has left.

(6) His wife suggests that they move to some other place, but he says that everywhere the situation is as bad as it is there, and that the only place worth (the trouble) going to would be the capital. She agrees.

(7) Now the question is where or how to get the money for the trip. The only way, he suggests, would be to sell their old cow; if they sold that cow, says he, then he could go alone first, and later send for her and the children. His wife thinks it's a good idea.

(8) And thus, like many other families before them, these poor peasants begin with great enthusiasm to make their plans, in the hope of finding a better life in the capital. They don't know what awaits them.

Grammar Points

First, the conditional; second, forms of the past subjunctive; third, the indicative and the subjunctive in clauses introduced by the conjunction **si;** fourth, comparisons of equality; fifth, position of the adverb **más;** and sixth, the use of **hace** in expressions of time.

TO BE FOLLOWED BY
LISTENING RECOGNITION EXERCISE

Chapter 15

Basic Dialog

¡Todos se van para la capital!

CA. *Campesino*   MU. *Su mujer*

I

CA. ¡Ladrones! ¡Nos robaron dos gallinas más anoche!
MU. ¡NO!
CA. ¡SÍ! ¡Si pudiera coger al ladrón, con este machete le daría! ¡Con esta sequía, sin empleo, y ahora hasta las gallinas me roban! ¡Qué vida!
MU. ¿Por qué no nos vamos a vivir lejos de aquí?
CA. Como si fuera tan fácil. Además, en todas partes la situación está tan mala como aquí. El único lugar adonde valdría[1] la pena irse sería a la capital.
MU. Chepín, el hermano del carnicero, hace más de un año que vive allá.

II

CA. Tal vez, si vendiéramos la vaca vieja, podría irme yo primero, y los traería a ustedes después, lo más pronto posible. ¿Qué dice, viejita[2]?
MU. Los chiquitos se pondrían felices[3]. ¡Ay, pero me da lástima la vaca!
CA. Esa vaca ya no sirve[4]. No da ni una botella al día.

---

[1]From *valer* (like *salir*).   [2]*Viejita* is one of the many pet names a man may use to address his wife.   [3]Singular, *feliz.*   [4]From *servir* (like *pedir*).

Everybody Is Leaving for the Capital!

P. *Peasant*   W. *His wife*

I

P. Thieves! They stole two more chickens from us last night!

W. NO!

P. YES! If I could catch the thief, I would let him have it with this machete! With this drought, no job, and now even the chickens they steal from me! What a life!

W. Why don't we go live far away from here?

P. As if it were that easy. Besides, everywhere conditions are as bad as they are here. The only place where it would be worth the trouble to go would be the capital.

W. Chepín, the butcher's brother, has been living there for over a year.[5]

II

P. Maybe, if we sold the old cow, I could go first, and I would bring you all later, as soon as possible. What do you say, honey?

W. The children would be[6] so happy. Oh, but I feel bad about the cow![7]

P. That cow is no good[8] anymore.[9] She doesn't even give a bottle a day.

SUPPLEMENT

I

¡Con este machete le daría!

palo	*stick*
esta piedra	*rock*

¡Con esta sequía!

lluvia	*rain*
humedad	*humidity*
suerte	*luck*
este polvo	*dust*

¡Ladrones!

Bandidos	*robbers, bandits*
Canallas	*scoundrels, rascals*
Sinvergüenzas	*bums*[10]
Atrevidos	*fresh (ones)*

¡Y ahora hasta las gallinas me roban!

¡Y ahora hasta los gallos me roban!	*the roosters*
cerdos	*pigs*
caballos	*horses*
bueyes[11]	*oxen*
perros	*dogs*
gatos	*cats*
pájaros	*birds*

---

[5] It makes more than a year that he lives there. [6] Become. [7] The cow gives me pity. [8] Doesn't serve (the purpose). [9] No longer. [10] Shameless. [11] Singular, *el buey.*

El único lugar adonde valdría la pena irse

mudarse   *move*

El único lugar adonde valdría la pena irse sería a la capital.

selva   *jungle*
finca   *farm*

Chepín, el hermano del carnicero

panadero   *baker*
zapatero   *shoemaker*
carpintero   *carpenter*
electricista   *electrician*
peluquero   *barber*

II

No da ni una botella al día.

un litro   *a liter*[12]

DIALOG AND SUPPLEMENT CHECK

SENTENCE RECALL

Say the dialog phrase or sentence in which each of the following words or phrases occurs.

dos gallinas más	como si fuera	carnicero	vaca vieja
hasta las gallinas	viejita	machete	lo más pronto posible
lejos	felices	situación	lástima
en todas partes	ya no	valdría la pena	botella

ITEM SUBSTITUTION

Make as many contextually related substitutions as you can for the word in italics. If books are closed, your teacher will repeat the item to be replaced.

1. El único lugar adonde valdría la pena *mudarse* sería a la capital.
2. ¡Si pudiera coger al *sinvergüenza*, con este machete le daría!
3. No da ni una *taza* al día.
4. Chepín, el hermano del *zapatero*
5. Hasta los *gatos* me roban.
6. ¡Con este *zapato* le daría!
7. ¡Con esta *lluvia*, sin trabajo... qué vida!

---

[12] Approximately 1 quart.

1. ¿Qué se robaron anoche de la casa del campesino?
2. ¿Le daría él con un zapato al ladrón, si pudiera cogerlo?
3. ¿Están estos campesinos en buena o en mala situación económica?
4. ¿Cuáles son las causas de esa mala situación?
5. ¿Está lloviendo mucho allí?
6. ¿Qué sugiere la mujer que hagan, que se queden allí o que se vayan a vivir lejos de allí?
7. ¿Y cómo está la situación en todas partes, según el campesino?
8. Según él, ¿cuál es el único lugar adonde valdría la pena mudarse?
9. ¿Por qué creen ustedes que en América Latina casi todo el mundo se va a vivir a la capital del país?
10. ¿Cuánto tiempo hace que vive allí Chepín, el hermano del carnicero?
11. ¿Qué es un carnicero, un hombre que compra carne?
12. ¿Y un zapatero? ¿Y un panadero? ¿Y un peluquero? ¿Y un ladrón?
13. ¿Ganan más dinero los electricistas que los carpinteros en este país, o ganan más o menos lo mismo?
14. ¿Cuál animal quiere vender el campesino?
15. ¿Por qué no sirve esa vaca?
16. ¿Cuánta leche da al día, diez litros?
17. ¿Tiene usted animales en su casa? ¿Qué tiene y cómo se llama?
18. ¿Qué prefiere usted, los gatos o los perros?
19. ¿Le gustan a usted los caballos?
20. ¿Cuál de ustedes sabe montar[13] a caballo?
21. ¿Son los tigres y los leones animales salvajes o animales domésticos?
22. ¿Dónde viven esos animales?
23. ¿Y en cuál continente hay muchísimos canguros?
24. ¿En cuáles continentes del mundo hay muchos elefantes?
25. ¿Es la serpiente un reptil? ¿Y el cocodrilo?
26. ¿En cuál país del mundo hay muchas cobras?
27. ¿Prefiere usted vivir en el campo o en la ciudad?
28. ¿Creen ustedes que vale la pena vivir toda la vida en una finca?
29. ¿Qué tipo de animales encuentra uno en el campo?
30. ¿En qué parte del año caen las lluvias en esta parte de los EE. UU.?
31. ¿Es la orquídea un pájaro o una flor?
32. ¿En cuáles estados hay grandes sequías algunas veces?
33. Si ustedes tienen que escoger entre la humedad y el polvo, ¿cuál prefieren?
34. ¿Creen ustedes que Estados Unidos es el único lugar donde vale la pena vivir, o creen que hay otros lugares en el mundo?
35. ¿Cómo se llama el "esposo" de la gallina?

[*To be followed by* LISTENING RECOGNITION EXERCISE]

---

[13]To mount, ride horseback.

Grammar

70. *The conditional*

trabajar comer vivir	-ía -ías -ía -íamos -ían

trabajar comer vivir	-íais

A. The conditional in Spanish is equivalent to "would + *verb*" in English.

      ¿Comería usted allí?   *Would you eat there?*

If, however, "would + *verb*" in English refers to a customary action in the past (meaning "used to"), the *imperfect, not the conditional,* is used in Spanish.

      Cuando teníamos dinero **íbamos** al cine.   *When we had money we would (used to) go to the movies.*

B. There is only one set of conditional endings for all verbs. These are the same as those of the imperfect of *-er* and *-ir* verbs, but they are attached to the infinitive rather than to the stem.

      IMPERFECT: Yo **comía** mucho.   *I used to eat a lot.*
      CONDITIONAL: Yo **comería** mucho. *I would eat a lot.*

poner	**pondría**	saber	**sabría**
valer	**valdría**	poder	**podría**
tener	**tendría**	haber	**habría**
salir	**saldría**	querer	**querría**
venir	**vendría**	hacer	**haría**
	decir	**diría**	

C. The few common *-er* and *-ir* verbs that have a slightly irregular stem in the conditional are listed in the chart.

1. Yo no trabajaría allí, ni por mil pesos.
   (nosotros/vivir)
   Nosotros no viviríamos allí, ni por mil pesos.
   (usted/comer, yo/trabajar, María/sentarse, los chicos/bañarse, ese campesino/ir, ellos/entrar)
2. ¿Comprarían ustedes una vaca vieja? ¡Nunca!
   (matar/el carnicero, vender/tú, pensar/usted en, regalar/tus amigos, cuidar/yo, conversar/el panadero con, robarse/los ladrones)
3. Dolores se casaría a las dos de la mañana, tal vez.
   (nosotros/divorciarnos, nadie/afeitarse, yo/bañarme, los panaderos/levantarse, los peluqueros/acostarse)
4. Un zapatero no haría eso.
   (nosotros/saber, tú/decir, la casa/valer, el electricista/tener, un peluquero/querer)
5. ¿A qué hora vendrías tú?
   (poder/ellos, salir/yo, querer/usted, decir/ustedes, levantarnos/nosotros, irse/ella)

TRANSLATION

1. If we sold the old cow . . .
2. I could go to the capital first.
3. My wife would stay with the children.
4. But the children would get (put themselves) very sad.
5. And they wouldn't have any milk.
6. The butcher would kill the poor cow.
7. I would feel very bad about the cow (the cow would give me much pity).
8. Besides, I couldn't sell it for more than (de) ten pesos.
9. We would have to buy another one, anyway.
10. No, I don't think we would sell the old cow.

71. *The past subjunctive*

	Third person plural preterit		*Past subjunctive*
Regular verbs	habla comie vivie		**supiera** **supieras** **supiera** **supiéramos** **supieran**
Verbs with vowel alternations	pidie murie	-ron	
Irregular verbs	estuvie pusie supie dije fue		**supierais**

A. For *all* verbs, regular or irregular, the stem of the past subjunctive is based on the third person plural form of the preterit. There are absolutely no exceptions.

B. The *nosotros* form is stressed on the third syllable from the end: *habláramos, comiéramos,* etc. All other forms are stressed on the next-to-last syllable.

C. There is an alternate set of endings for the past subjunctive in which *-se-* replaces *-ra-* in all forms; for example, **hablase, hablases,** etc., **supiese, supieses,** etc. However, for active use you need learn only the set shown in the chart, since these are far more commonly used in the spoken language in Latin America.

INFINITIVE → PRETERIT → PAST SUBJUNCTIVE

Give the third person plural forms of the preterit and the past subjunctive for each of the following infinitives.

EXAMPLE: tomar: **tomaron, tomaran**

ser	estar	traer	crecer	prometer	preguntar
pedir	deber	poner	sentir	enseñar	levantarse
decir	tener	morir	costar	robar	refugiarse
leer	saber	pesar	cuidar	enojarse	afeitarse
ir	beber	entrar	servir	vestirse	quejarse
oír	hacer	cortar	llegar	quedarse	suicidarse

PARADIGM PRACTICE

Do the complete past subjunctive paradigm of as many of the above verbs as you can. Start each paradigm form with *si.*

EXAMPLE: **si yo me levantara, si tú te levantaras, si usted se levantara, si él se levantara, si nosotros nos levantáramos, si ustedes se levantaran, si ellos se levantaran**

[*To be followed by* LISTENING COMPREHENSION–SPEAKING EXERCISE]

72. *The indicative and the subjunctive in "if" clauses*

"If" Clause	"Then" Clause
1. Si **vendemos** la vaca, *If we sell the cow,*	**llevamos** a los niños a la capital. *we will take the children to the capital.*
2. Si **vendiéramos** la vaca, *If we sold (were to sell, should sell) the cow,*	**llevaríamos** a los niños a la capital. *we would take the children to the capital.*

A. "If/then" sentences are almost identical in English and Spanish. Sentences like the first example are entirely analogous in the two languages. Note the *indicative* in both clauses. Sentences like the second example are slightly different: English uses "were to," "should," or a past tense form in the "if" clause and "would" in the "then" clause; Spanish uses the *past subjunctive* in the "if" clause and the *conditional* in the "then" clause.

B. The expression **como si**, "as if, as though," is always followed by the past subjunctive.

Como si fuera tan fácil.

As if it were so easy.

Hablas **como si** no **tuviéramos** que vender la vaca.

You're talking as though we didn't have to sell the cow.

WRITTEN TRANSLATION

1. If he comes, are you going to call me?
   If he came, would you call me?
2. If they sell the oxen, they're going to buy a horse.
   If they sold the oxen, they would buy a horse.
3. If they catch the thief, they won't tell me anything.
   If they caught the thief, they wouldn't tell me anything.
4. If you tell Mr. Coco, he's not going to mention it to anyone.
   If you told Mr. Coco, he wouldn't mention it to anyone.
5. If we go to the movies, she's not going to stay home.
   If we went to the movies, she wouldn't stay home.
6. Why don't you eat, if you are hungry?
   Why wouldn't you eat, if you were hungry?

CLAUSE SUBSTITUTION

1. Si vendiéramos la vaca vieja, seríamos muy felices.
   (tener dinero)
   Si tuviéramos dinero, seríamos muy felices.
   (ser ricos, no discutir tanto, no deber dinero)
2. Si tú no fueras tan sinvergüenza, viviríamos mejor.
   (levantarte temprano, buscar empleo, no quejarte tanto, no robar gallinas, no jugar[14] mi dinero, hacer algo)
3. Si yo te contara un cuento, no te quejarías tanto.
   (decirte una cosa, darte dinero, comprarte un caballo, traerte una criada, ser un canalla)
4. Si los chiquitos tuvieran un gato, se pondrían felices.
   (ir a la escuela, saber leer y escribir, hablar inglés, vivir en una finca, conocer la capital)
5. Si no hubiera tanta sequía, valdría la pena vivir aquí.
   (no hacer tanto calor, no haber tanto polvo, no llover tanto, no caer tanta lluvia, hacer buen tiempo)

QUESTIONS

Answer each of the following questions with a sentence containing several "if" clauses.

---

[14] Gamble.

¿Bajo qué condiciones...

    1. se casaría usted?

    Me casaría si tuviera novia, si estuviera enamorado, si yo tuviera porvenir, si ella fuera rica...

    2. viviría usted en el campo?

    3. sería usted feliz?

    4. me prestaría usted dinero a mí?

    5. estudiaría usted el idioma ruso?

    6. se casaría usted?

TRANSLATION

You talk...

    1. as if you knew everything.
    2. as if I didn't know you.
    3. as if he were a scoundrel.
    4. as if we were dumb.
    5. as if your teacher didn't like (*querer*) you.
    6. as if life were that (so) easy.
    7. as if there weren't enough problems in the world.
    8. as if you were in love.
    9. as if we didn't study enough.
    10. as if they lived in the jungle.
    11. as if man were a wild (savage) animal.
    12. as if you lived very far from here.

73. *Comparisons of equality*

Soy **tan** alto **como** él.	*I am as tall as he (is).*
Tengo **tantos** libros **como** él.	*I have as many books as he (does).*
Sé **tanto como** él.	*I know as much as he (does).*

The only differences between English and Spanish in this type of construction are (a) the gender-number agreement in Spanish between *tanto* and the noun it refers to; and (b) the lack of a Spanish equivalent for the English tags "is," "does," "would," etc.

COMPARISON DRILL

Make a comparison based on the information given.

    1. Pedro tiene cinco bueyes; Juan tiene dos.
    Pedro tiene más bueyes que Juan.
    2. El campesino tiene muchos problemas; yo también.
    El campesino tiene tantos problemas como yo.
    3. Los electricistas ganan mucho dinero; los carpinteros también.

4. El panadero tiene diez hijos; el carnicero tiene catorce.
5. El peluquero pesa sesenta kilos; su mujer pesa casi cien.
6. Aquí cae mucha lluvia; allá también.
7. Yo trabajo mucho; un caballo también trabaja mucho.
8. La vaca negra no da ni un litro de leche; la blanca da cinco.
9. Los pájaros son muy bonitos; las flores también.
10. Aquí roban mucho; en la capital también.
11. Yo tengo mucho calor; ustedes tienen menos.
12. Nosotros no pesamos mucho; el novio de Dolores pesa casi mil libras.
13. El lago está muy lejos de aquí; la montaña está más cerca.
14. El maestro llegó muy tarde a la clase hoy; los alumnos también llegaron muy tarde.
15. Los gallos cuestan cien pesos; las gallinas, veinte.

REJOINDERS WITH COMPARATIVE CONSTRUCTIONS

Compare yourself to your teacher as illustrated.

1. Yo estoy muy bien.
   Yo estoy tan bien como usted.
2. Yo me siento mal.
   Yo me siento peor (mejor) que usted.
3. Yo sé mucho.
4. Yo tengo diez hermanos.

5. Yo no sé casi nada.
6. Yo trabajo muchísimo.
7. Yo tengo cien años.
8. Yo compré muchas cosas ayer.
9. Yo he visto muchas cosas en la vida.
10. Yo soy muy tímido.

74. *The position of* más

| Anoche nos robaron **más** gallinas. | *Last night they stole more chickens from us.* |
| Anoche nos robaron dos gallinas **más**. | *Last night they stole two more chickens from us.* |

A. When *más* is the only quantifier modifying a noun, *más* precedes the noun (first example).
B. When some other quantifier precedes a noun, *más* follows the noun (second example). The usual English word order (*quantifier* + more + *noun*) is impossible in Spanish.

QUESTIONS

The whole class answers according to the cue. If books are closed, your teacher will repeat the cue answer.

1. ¿Quieren estudiar más? (una hora)
   Sí, queremos estudiar una hora más.
2. ¿Van a esperar más al maestro? (cinco minutos)
3. ¿Quieren tomar más cerveza? (una botella)
4. ¿Compró el campesino más gallinas? (ocho)
5. ¿Tuvo la mujer más hijos? (siete)
6. ¿Escribieron ustedes más cartas? (muchas)
7. ¿Quieren ustedes discutir algo más? (una cosa)
8. ¿Van a tener ustedes más vacaciones este año? (dos semanas)

1. Give me two more birds.
2. Tell me one more thing.
3. Lend me ten more pesos.
4. Wait a few (*unos*) more days.
5. Say that one more time.

6. Study a little while longer.
7. Sell me some more horses.
8. Show me one more pig.
9. Buy two more cows.
10. Don't bring one more rooster.

75. *The expressions* lo más... posible *and* ya no

Siempre salgo **lo más tarde posible.**	*I always leave as late as possible.*
Por eso **ya no** llego temprano.	*That's why I don't arrive early anymore.*

A. The expression *lo más... posible* corresponds to English "as . . . as possible." *Lo más posible,* with no other word added, means "as much as possible"; *lo menos posible* means "as little as possible."

B. *Ya no* corresponds to English "no longer," "not any more."

TRANSLATION

1. Come as soon as possible.
   I want you to come as soon as possible.
2. Get up as early as possible.
   I want you to get up as early as possible.
3. Go as far away as possible.
   I want you to go as far away as possible.
4. Bring this as near as possible.
   I want you to bring this as near as possible.
5. Talk as little as possible.
   I want you to talk as little as possible.
6. Eat as much as possible.
   I want you to eat as much as possible.

QUESTIONS

The whole class gives an affirmative answer using one of the "as possible" expressions.

1. ¿Les gustaría a ustedes vivir lejos de aquí?
   Sí, lo más lejos posible.
2. ¿Van a poner mucha atención ustedes hoy? ¿Por favor?
3. ¿Van a hablar muy poquito entre ustedes en inglés?
4. ¿Van a estudiar mucho, pero mucho, para el examen?
5. ¿Van a llegar temprano a la escuela mañana?
6. ¿Quieren que yo les haga un examen muy pronto?

1. That cow is not any good anymore (serves no longer).
2. I don't work anymore.
3. We no longer live there.
4. Don't you love me anymore?
5. They are no longer friends.
6. Don't you want any more?[15]

QUESTIONS

The whole class answers with a full sentence using *ya no*.

1. ¿Todavía da leche la vaca del campesino?
   No, ya no da leche.
2. ¿Todavía son novios Emilio y Luz María?
3. ¿Todavía saben ustedes hablar inglés?
4. ¿Todavía trabaja su papá?
5. ¿Todavía está su abuelita en la escuela?
6. ¿Todavía sirve la vaca vieja?
7. ¿Todavía me deben dinero ustedes a mí?
8. ¿Todavía están poniendo atención ustedes?
9. ¿Todavía hay tiempo para otra? ¿Una más?
10. ¿No quieren estudiar un poquititito[16] más?

[*To be followed by* LISTENING COMPREHENSION–SPEAKING EXERCISE]

76. Hace *in expressions of time*

Hace un año se fue Chepín para la capital.	*A year ago Chepín left for the capital.*
Hace un año que vive allá.	*He's been living there for a year.*

A. In a sentence where the main verb is in the past tense *hace* means "ago" (first example). In English the main verb is also in the past tense.

B. English uses the present perfect ("has lived," "has been living") to express the duration of an event that is still going on or a condition that still exists. This is expressed in Spanish by the use of

---

[15]There is no Spanish equivalent for this sense of "any"; "any more" is simply *más*.
[16]Equivalent to "teeny weeny" bit.

hace in a sentence with the main verb in the *present tense* (second example). A Spanish construction parallel to the English with the present perfect is also grammatically correct: *Ha vivido allá por un año.* However, its use is much less frequent than *Hace un año que vive allá.*

C. The whole phrase *hace* + (*time elapsed*) can occupy practically any position in the sentence.

> **Hace un año** se fue Chepín para la capital.
> Se fue Chepín **hace un año** para la capital.
> Se fue Chepín para la capital **hace un año.**
>
> **Hace un año** que vive allá.
> Vive allá **hace un año.**[17]

¿CUÁNDO?

Using *hace* in a full sentence, give an approximation of the time passed.

1. ¿Cuándo se fue Chepín para la capital?
    Chepín se fue para la capital hace más de un año.
2. ¿Cuándo mataron al presidente Kennedy?
3. ¿Cuándo descubrió Colón el continente de América?
4. ¿Cuándo nació usted?
5. ¿Cuándo empezó esta clase?
6. ¿Cuándo murió Jesucristo?
7. ¿Cuándo llegó el barco *Mayflower* a la costa de Massachusetts?
8. ¿Cuándo descendió a la luna el primer astronauta?
9. ¿Cuándo nació Jorge Washington?
10. ¿Cuándo empezó la Guerra Civil de los Estados Unidos?
11. ¿Cuándo empezó usted a estudiar español?
12. ¿Cuándo se casó usted?

TRANSFORMATION

1. Chepín ha vivido en la capital más de un año.
    Hace más de un año que Chepín vive en la capital.
2. Yo he estudiado español casi seis meses.
3. Nosotros no hemos comido por tres días.
4. Chepín no ha escrito por mucho tiempo.
5. Mi suegra ha vivido en mi casa casi catorce años.
6. Ella no me ha hablado a mí por trece años y medio.
7. Yo he sido maestro de idiomas más de cincuenta años.
8. He estado aquí casi diez años.
9. Tú y yo hemos sido amigos apenas un mes.
10. El campesino ha trabajado como un buey por dos años.
11. ¡Hola, amigo! No lo he visto por mucho tiempo.
12. ¡Por tres semanas no hemos ido al cine!

---

[17] The relater *que* is not used in this case.

Use *hace* each time.

1. How long have you been studying Spanish?
2. I started a year ago.
3. I've been studying this language for over five years.
4. I haven't written to my family in two months.
5. They called me a little while ago and asked me what was wrong (*pasar*) with me.
6. How long have they been working in this place?
7. How long have you known Dr. Campos?
8. How long have you been sick?

Reading

Un campesino ingenioso

Un campesino tenía una hermosa vaca que daba mucha leche y un perro. La vaca daba leche para sus hijos y también para venderla y comprar comida para la familia. Así vivían muy bien.

Pero un día se enfermó la mujer. Vino el doctor a verla, pero ella no se mejoró. Cada día parecía estar más enferma. El marido estaba triste y preocupado porque no sabía qué hacer para curar a su esposa.

Un día decidió ir a la iglesia a rezar a la Virgen. Le prometió a la Virgen que si le devolvía la salud a su mujer, él vendería la vaca y daría el dinero a la iglesia para los pobres. Al salir de la iglesia, el campesino le contó al sacerdote lo que había prometido a la Virgen.

—Muy bien, hijo mío —dijo el padre—, pero no te olvides de tu promesa. La Virgen castiga a los que no cumplen sus promesas.

La mujer empezó a sentirse mejor y en unos pocos días ya estaba completamente sana.

Su marido estaba muy contento, pero también muy preocupado por la promesa a la Virgen. Si vendía la vaca no tendría leche para sus hijos ni dinero para comprar la comida. Le remordía la conciencia y tenía miedo de que si no cumplía lo que había prometido, la Virgen le iba a castigar. Por fin pensó en un ingenioso plan. Llevó la vaca y el perro a una feria que había en el pueblo para vender la vaca. Pronto se acercó un señor y le preguntó:

—¿Cuánto quiere por la vaca?

—Diez pesos, señor —contestó el campesino.

—No le haga caso, señor —dijo otro señor que había llegado—. Ese hombre está loco. No sabe lo que dice. Una vaca buena como ésa vale mucho más de quinientos pesos.

—Pues es todo lo que pido por ella —agregó el campesino—, porque quiero venderla pronto.

—Bueno, la compro —dijo el primer señor, después de examinar la vaca con cuidado—. Aquí tiene el dinero.

Ya iba el señor a llevarse la vaca cuando el campesino le advirtió:

—Un momentito, señor. Quiero explicarle una cosa. La vaca está acostumbrada a estar con este perro. Si el perro no está con ella, la vaca no da leche.

—¡Qué raro! —exclamó el señor—. ¿Y cuánto quiere por el perro?

—Ah, señor, éste es un magnífico perro. Es muy inteligente. Lo vendo en quinientos pesos.

—¡Qué barbaridad, hombre! Un perro no vale tanto —dijo el señor.

—Pues éste sí —dijo el campesino—, porque si no compra el perro, la vaca no le va a dar leche.

El señor no quería comprar el perro, pero le gustaba mucho la vaca y pensó que el precio de los dos animales no estaba mal.

—Bueno, aquí tiene los quinientos pesos por el perro —dijo el señor, y se fue contento con la vaca y el perro.

El campesino se fue directamente a la iglesia y le dió al sacerdote los diez pesos que había recibido por la vaca. Así cumplió su promesa a la Virgen. Y con los quinientos pesos que había recibido por el perro se compró otra vaca.

CONVERSATION STIMULUS

Give a brief oral summary of the preceding story.

[*To be followed by* LISTENING COMPREHENSION–SPEAKING EXERCISE]

Listening Passage
for Chapter 16
English Translation

Lack of Punctuality:
Defect or Virtue?

(1) The North American visitor who has a date with his Latin American friend in a cafe at seven o'clock and has to wait for him till eight twenty no (without) doubt will get angry. Neither will he like the fact that his friend, once present, talks to him only a few inches away from his face (almost face to face), because he is accustomed to a greater distance. Perhaps the uproar (shouting) of the people in the cafe, the typical effusiveness of the Latins, and the almost interminable conversation in social gatherings will also bother him. And possibly it will displease him that without connections (the intervention of friendships) it is difficult to open a checking (running) account in a bank or to obtain the cooperation of the municipal authorities.

(2) This reaction is understandable, because the visitor judges such conduct from the point of view of his own culture. In the same way, there are thousands of Latin American students who have come to the United States and have gone back (away) after one semester because they couldn't adapt to local life.

(3) The North American must try to understand that the social structure in Latin America is different and that as a result what motivates the conduct of the Latin American is also. This doesn't mean that he must imitate that conduct. The anthropologist who studies the customs of a civilization does not necessarily utilize them for himself, but examines them, knowing that they are the result of national cultural values. If in the Latin culture sentimentalism and emotion occupy a prominent place, the gestures and phrases that seem exaggerated have their reason for being so. While in the Anglo-Saxon culture the control of emotions is a virtue, in the Latin culture such a disposition is considered (as) cold and undesirable.

(4) Returning to the question of punctuality and the lack of it, time is a subjective thing (to the) south of the Rio Grande,* because the Latin American, like Don Quixote, not only creates his own reality, but also lives comfortably within it. To arrive late is not a social crime, because time is quite elastic. The same concept prevails during a social gathering: one doesn't look at his watch, but rather lives it up (lives the hour).

(5) Where he can (it is possible for him), the Latin American considers work as an extension of his own reality, and therefore he will seek to modify it by chatting, drinking coffee, and above everything else, watching out for his social standing—in sum, by imposing an intensely personal rhythm on it. Here too time is subordinated to personal reality, and as a result, in some public offices that are open to the public

---

*In Latin America, the Rio Grande is known as the *Río Bravo.*

only from fourteen to eighteen hours from Monday to Friday, the bosses will arrive a little late and perhaps leave early too, if they feel like it (have desires). This is a privilege that only the fortunate can enjoy, but it is also an ideal that those less fortunate dream of turning into a reality (achieving) some day. Each culture has its priorities.

(6) In the dialog of this last chapter, we see poor Slim Hernández sad and disappointed because his friend Andrés, who had agreed to pick him up (come by for him) to take him to a party, stood him up (left him planted). This wouldn't have bothered Slim so much if the occasion had been different (another). After all, to be stood up (that they stand him up) is not unheard of (something of the other world). But this time it was different: Slim—everyone knows him by that nickname because he is tall and thin like bamboo—Slim was dying (crazy) to go to that party, because it was the opportunity of his life to meet Luz María Terán Marín and declare his love for her. Luz María, the beautiful former girlfriend of Emilio Fonseca, was leaving the following day for the United States on a scholarship she had won at the Cultural Center, and who knows when Slim would be able to see her again.

(7) His friend Andrés had told him to wait for him on the corner by the shoe store. Right there was where Slim waited until almost eleven, but finally he got tired and had no other recourse but to go to (put himself in) a movie. He couldn't take a taxi to go to the party because he couldn't even find out where it was. What happened to Andrés was that he was delayed a little, that was all, and when he passed by the corner it was already going on (to be) twelve.

(8) Another friend of Slim's, called (whom they call) Chino, began to tease (annoy) him and make his mouth water telling him about the party. He told him that the party had been ter-rif-ic, that they had gone all out (thrown the house out the window), that they had even hired (brought) two bands (orchestras) that played continuously one after the other. He said that Luz María had looked out of this world (simply divine), and that he had danced with her all night and she had asked (told) Chino to say hello to Slim. And poor Slim was almost crying listening to his friend. Finally Andrés intervened and told Chino to shut up.

Grammar Points

First, additional uses of the past subjunctive; second, the construction **ojalá** + *subjunctive;* third, the future tense; fourth, additional uses of **ser;** and fifth, the command forms for **tú.**

TO BE FOLLOWED BY
LISTENING RECOGNITION EXERCISE

Chapter 16

Basic Dialog

El último capítulo

FL. *El Flaco*   AN. *Andrés*   CH. *El Chino*

I

FL. Ni me digas nada. Me dejaste plantado. Ahora quién sabe cuándo tendré otra oportunidad. Ella se va mañana.

AN. Un momento. ¿No te dije que me esperaras en la esquina de la zapatería?

FL. ¿Ah sí? ¿Y dónde crees que estuve hasta casi las once? Por fin me cansé y me fui a un cine.

AN. Perdona, pero es que me atrasé un poco. No fue culpa mía.

FL. ¡Tantas ganas que tenía de ir a esa fiesta! Pero ni siquiera pude averiguar dónde era.

II

CH. ¡La fiesta estuvo fe-no-me-nal! Tiraron la casa por la ventana, no te miento[1]. ¡Dos orquestas tocaron! ¡Ah, y Luz María estaba divina!

AN. ¿Por qué no te callas, Chino?

FL. ¿Bailaste con ella?

CH. Ajá, y me dijo que te saludara.

FL. Ojalá fuera cierto. No te creo.

CH. Palabra. Lástima que no fuiste.

AN. ¡Ah, caramba! ¡Qué lata eres, Chino, de veras!

---

[1]From *mentir* (like *sentir*).

The Last Chapter

SL. *Slim*   AN. *Andrés*   CH. *Chino*[2]

I

SL.   Don't say anything to me. You stood me up.[3] Now who knows when I'll have another chance. She's leaving tomorrow.

AN.   Just a moment. Didn't I tell you to wait for me on the corner by the shoe store?

SL.   Oh yeah? And where do you think I was until almost eleven? I finally got tired and went to a movie.

AN.   Forgive me, but it's just that I was delayed[4] a little. It wasn't my fault.

SL.   I really wanted[5] to go to that party! But I couldn't even find out where it was.

II

CH.   The party was ter-rif-ic! They went all out;[6] I'm not lying. Two bands played! Oh, and Luz María looked out of this world.

AN.   Why don't you shut up, Chino?

SL.   Did you dance with her?

CH.   Uh-huh, and she told me to say hello to[7] you.

SL.   I wish it were true. I don't believe you.

CH.   I swear.[8] Too bad you didn't go.

AN.   Good grief![9] What a nuisance you are, Chino, really!

CULTURAL NOTES

The use of nicknames involving adjectives like *flaco,* "skinny," *chino,* "with slanted eyes" (literally, "Chinese"), *negro,* "dark complexioned," and *indio,* "Indian," is not offensive, and persists well beyond school age in Latin America.

SUPPLEMENT

I

¿No te dije que me esperaras...

pasaras por mí	*come by for me*

...en la esquina de la zapatería?

peluquería	*barber shop*
panadería	*bakery*
cafetería	*coffee shop*
carnicería	*butcher shop*
sastrería	*tailor shop*
tintorería	*cleaner's*

---

[2]Chinese, Chinaman.   [3]Left me planted.   [4]Got behind.   [5]So many desires I had.   [6]Threw the house out the window.   [7]Greet.   [8](I give you my) word.   [9]"For Pete's sake" and "good grief" are only two of the many possible translations of *Ah, caramba.*

Por fin me cansé.		Es que me atrasé un poco.	
me aburrí[10]	*got bored*	me adelanté	*got ahead*

II

¡Dos orquestas tocaron!		La fiesta estuvo fe-no-me-nal.	
bandas	*military bands*	El baile	*the dance*
pianos	*pianos*		
guitarras	*guitars*		
violines[11]	*violins*		
trompetas	*trumpets*		
baterías[12]	*sets of drums*		
bajos	*basses*		
clarinetes[13]	*clarinets*		
marimbas	*marimbas*		

DIALOG AND SUPPLEMENT CHECK

SENTENCE RECALL

Say the dialog phrase or sentence in which each of the following words and phrases occurs.

tendré	lata	ojalá	bailaste
ganas	te callas	esperaras	averiguar
ni siquiera	tocaron	me atrasé	por la ventana
lástima	hasta casi	zapatería	plantado
	nada	divina	

ITEM SUBSTITUTION

Substitute each of the following words and phrases for a related word or phrase in one of the basic sentences of this chapter. Repeat the whole new sentence.

guitarras	me adelanté	marimbas	carnicería
el baile	cafetería	no te engaño	trompetas

QUESTIONS

1. ¿Qué número tiene este capítulo?
2. ¿Cómo se llama?
3. ¿Dónde estaba Luz María, en un paseo?
4. ¿Cuándo se va ella?
5. ¿Por qué no fue el Flaco a la fiesta?
6. ¿Quién dejó plantado al Flaco?
7. ¿Lo ha dejado alguien plantado a usted?

---

[10]The infinitive is *aburrirse*.   [11]Sing.: *el violín*.   [12]A single drum is *un tambor*.   [13]Masc.: *el clarinete*.

8. ¿Quiere alguno de ustedes contarle a la clase cuándo y cómo fue la última vez que lo dejaron plantado?
9. ¿Dónde estuvo esperando el Flaco a Andrés?
10. ¿Hasta qué hora estuvo esperándolo allí?
11. ¿Por qué no pasó Andrés por su amigo?
12. ¿Qué hizo el Flaco entonces?
13. ¿Por qué se fue a un cine?
14. ¿Por qué no tomó un taxi para ir a la fiesta?
15. ¿Por qué no preguntó dónde era la fiesta?
16. ¿Y cómo estuvo la fiesta, según el Chino?
17. ¿Qué tiraron por la ventana?
18. ¿Cuántas orquestas tocaron?
19. ¿Sabe alguno de ustedes tocar un instrumento musical?
20. ¿Qué toca usted?
21. ¿Ha tocado alguno de ustedes en una orquesta o en una banda?
22. ¿Quiere Andrés que el Chino se calle o que siga contándole de la fiesta al Flaco?
23. ¿Bailó el Chino con Luz María?
24. ¿Cómo estaba ella, según él?
25. ¿Quién es una lata, según Andrés?

[*To be followed by* LISTENING RECOGNITION EXERCISE]

Grammar

77. *Additional uses of the past subjunctive*

I. Noun Clauses

PRESENT:	Le estoy diciendo a usted **que espere.** *I'm telling you to wait.*
PAST:	Le dije a usted **que esperara.** *I told you to wait.*

II. Adjective Clauses

PRESENT:	Busco a alguien **que sepa** cocinar. *I'm looking for someone who knows how to cook.*
PAST:	Buscaba a alguien **que supiera** cocinar. *I was looking for someone who knew how to cook.*

III. Adverb Clauses

PRESENT:	Nunca voy al cine **a menos que tenga** tiempo. *I never go to the movies unless I have time.*
PAST:	Nunca iba al cine **a menos que tuviera** tiempo. *I never went to the movies unless I had time.*

274

As illustrated in the charts, the use of the past subjunctive in noun, adjective, and adverb clauses follows the same general principles that apply to the use of the present subjunctive. The difference is that the present subjunctive refers to the *present* or the *future,* while, in general, the past subjunctive refers to the past.

Before you do the following exercises, you should review grammar sections **58, 59,** and **60** in Chapter 12, and **65** and **66** in Chapter 14 (and the accompanying exercises), which deal with the present subjunctive; and grammar section **71** in Chapter 15, which deals with the forms of the past subjunctive.

TENSE SUBSTITUTION

Change the present subjunctive forms to the past subjunctive. Remember that for all verbs, regular or irregular, the stem of the past subjunctive is based on the third person plural form of the preterit.

EXAMPLE: que estudien
           que estudiaran

1. *Clauses with* -ar *verbs*

con tal que no nos atrasemos
para que ellos no se adelanten
hasta que Catalina se canse
que Dolores se case con Armando
para que nos levantemos temprano
aunque no baile bien
que no me acueste tarde
a menos que usted cante

sin que te calles
que me esperes
tan pronto averigüemos
que no hable y no fume mucho
que me dejes plantado
que te salude
con tal que tiren la casa por
   la ventana

2. *Clauses with* -er *and* -ir *verbs,* dar, andar, *and* estar

aunque él no tenga dinero
antes que mi suegra se aburra
con tal que sea honrado
para que no digamos nada
que sepa hablar inglés
que los chicos no coman mucho
aunque haga mucho frío
que le escriban a su madre
hasta que ella se vaya
cuando venga el cartero
que vivamos muchos años
después que vaya a la fiesta

que le digan a la señora
antes que ustedes lean ese libro
que estén todos muy bien
para que me den el dinero
cuando andemos de compras
que ustedes aprendan
sin que ellos vendan la casa
hasta que salgan de la otra
tan pronto puedan
y que vayamos allá pronto
aunque él no quiera
que no me digas nada

CLAUSE SUBSTITUTION

Remember that the present subjunctive refers to the *present* or the *future,* while the past subjunctive refers to the *past.*

Noun clauses

1. No quiso que su amigo fuera a la fiesta.
       (es necesario)
   Es necesario que su amigo vaya a la fiesta.
       (dudaba, era imposible, siento, ella quería)

2. Andrés le dijo que esperara en la esquina.
   (es mejor, yo no creí, fue bueno, él quería)
3. Siento mucho que tengas tantos problemas.
   (es malo, ellos no creyeron, me alegro, fue una lástima)

Adjective clauses

1. Queremos una mujer[14] que sepa cocinar.
   (busco, no había, no encontrábamos, no conocen)
2. ¿Buscabas un hombre que tuviera experiencia?
   (quieres, encontraste, hay, necesitabas, buscas)
3. No necesito a nadie que hable francés.
   (no teníamos, no quieren, no encontré, no conozco)

Adverb clauses

1. Quiero esperar hasta que Andrés venga por mí.
   (iba a, estoy, era necesario, es imposible, estaba)
2. Nunca voy allí a menos que tenga dinero.
   (iba, estudiaba, me quedo, vuelvo, vivía)
3. Se fueron para que estudiáramos más.
   (vienen, estuvieron aquí, trajeron el libro, están aquí)

TENSE SUBSTITUTION

Shift the following sentences to the past tense. Say each segment first, then the entire paragraph. Use the past tense indicated in parentheses for the indicative verb forms, as in the example.

EXAMPLE: La madre de Dolores quiere (*imperf.*)... que su hija vaya a la fiesta,... aunque no tenga muchas ganas,... para que conozca a muchos chicos... y consiga novio... para que se case pronto.
La madre de Dolores quería... que su hija fuera a la fiesta,... aunque no tuviera muchas ganas,... para que conociera a muchos chicos... y consiguiera novio... para que se casara pronto.

1. Andrés le dice (*pret.*) al Chino... que él es (*imperf.*) una lata... y que a menos que se calle... le va (*imperf.*) a dar con un machete.
2. No me importa (*imperf.*)... que el novio de mi hija sea viejo y feo... y que no sepa bailar,... con tal que sea un hombre honrado... y tenga porvenir.
3. Le pido (*pret.*) a mi amigo... que me espere en la esquina... hasta que yo llegue,... aunque me atrase un poco... Pero como él es (*imperf.*) muy tonto,... no me espera (*pret.*)... y se va (*pret.*).
4. El campesino le dice (*pret.*) a su mujer... que no hay (*imperf.*) nadie... que tenga tan mala suerte como él,... y que cuando vendan la vaca vieja... y tengan dinero para el viaje,... todos van (*imperf.*) a irse a la capital.
5. Dice (*pret.*) el maestro... que es (*imperf.*) necesario... que pongamos atención... y estudiemos más... para que sepamos bien esto... cuando tengamos el examen final.

---

[14]The personal *a* is omitted when the speaker thinks primarily of the services rendered by the person referred to, rather than his human qualities, as in this sentence and the next. Compare, for example, the following sentences: *María quiere un médico,* "María wants a doctor," and *María quiere a un médico,* "María loves a doctor."

The teacher repeats the same questions each time, and the whole class answers. Follow the example.

EXAMPLE: *Teacher:* ¡Hablen! ¿Qué quiero yo?
         Class: **Usted quiere que hablemos.**
      Teacher: ¿Qué les dije yo?
         Class: **Usted nos dijo que habláramos.**

1. ¡Digan algo!
2. ¡Pongan atención!
3. ¡Abran la ventana!
4. ¡Cierren la puerta!
5. ¡Siéntense!
6. ¡Levántense!
7. ¡Hagan silencio!
8. ¡Váyanse a la casa!
9. ¡No vengan aquí más!
10. ¡Vuelvan! ¡Vuelvan!
11. ¡No me dejen solo!
12. ¡Quédense conmigo!

QUESTIONS

1. ¿Por qué se enojó el Flaco con Andrés el otro día?
2. ¿Le dijo Andrés a su amigo que lo esperara en la esquina de una carnicería, de una peluquería, o de una zapatería?
3. ¿Cómo se llaman los que trabajan en una peluquería? ¿Y en una carnicería? ¿Y en una zapatería?
4. ¿Qué venden en una sastrería? ¿Y en una carnicería? ¿Y en una zapatería?
5. ¿Qué hacen en una peluquería? ¿Y en una tintorería?
6. ¿Le gustaría a usted si alguien lo dejara plantado?
7. Si usted tuviera que pasar por un amigo, ¿lo dejaría plantado?
8. Bueno, pero si usted se atrasara un poco, ¿qué haría? ¿Lo llamaría a su casa para avisarle?
9. Y si él no estuviera en su casa, ¿qué haría?
10. ¿Qué podría hacer para averiguar dónde está su amigo?
11. ¿Por qué tenía el Flaco tantas ganas de ir a la fiesta?
12. ¿Para dónde se va Luz María mañana?
13. ¿Con quién bailó ella esa noche?
14. ¿Qué le dijo ella al Chino que le dijera al Flaco?
15. ¿Y qué le dijo Andrés al Chino, que se callara o que no se callara?
16. ¿Se calló el Chino o siguió contándole de la fiesta al Flaco?

[*To be followed by* LISTENING COMPREHENSION–SPEAKING EXERCISE]

78. *The construction* ojalá + subjunctive

Ojalá (que) estén aquí.	*I hope they're here (and perhaps they are).*
Ojalá (que) estuvieran aquí.	*I wish they were here (but they aren't).*

Ojalá followed by the present subjunctive means "I hope . . . ." Followed by the past subjunctive, it means "I wish . . . ." *Que* is often omitted.

1. I hope you have time.
   I wish you had time.
2. I hope you'll be my friend.
   I wish you were my friend.
3. I hope my dad will say (that) yes.
   I wish my dad would say (that) yes.
4. I hope the girl speaks Spanish.
   I wish the girl would speak Spanish.
5. I hope you'll shut up.
   I wish you'd shut up.
6. I hope you won't eat with your (the) mouth open.[15]
   I wish you wouldn't eat with your mouth open.
7. I hope they will play a "cha-cha" (*cha-cha-cha*).
   I wish they would play a "cha-cha."
8. I hope you don't have to work tomorrow.
   I wish you didn't have to work tomorrow.

79. *The future*

trabajar comer vivir	-é -ás -á -emos -án

trabajar comer vivir	-éis

A. Like the conditional, the future has only one set of endings for all verbs, regular and irregular. Also like the conditional, the future endings are attached to the infinitive rather than to the stem alone. It may be helpful to notice that, except for the *vosotros* forms, the future endings sound the same as the present indicative forms of *haber: he, has, ha, hemos, han, (habéis).*

B. The future forms are among the least frequently used verb forms in Spanish. More often than not they are replaced by the simple present or the *ir a* + *infinitive* construction. Thus the three ways of referring to the future in Spanish are the following.

Trabajo mañana.	*I'm working tomorrow.*
Voy a trabajar mañana.	*I'm going to work tomorrow.*
Trabajaré mañana.	*I shall (will) work tomorrow.*

---

[15] *Abierta.*

poner	**pondré**	saber	**sabré**
valer	**valdré**	poder	**podré**
tener	**tendré**	haber	**habré**
salir	**saldré**	querer	**querré**
venir	**vendré**	hacer	**haré**
	decir	**diré**	

C. The verbs listed in the chart, which have irregular conditional stems, have the same irregular stems in the future.

PARADIGM PRACTICE

Practice the three model regular verbs as illustrated. Then practice some of the irregular verbs.

EXAMPLE: **¿Trabajaré, comeré y viviré yo aquí?**
¿Trabajarás, comerás y vivirás tú aquí?
Etc.

FUTURE FORM SUBSTITUTION

Repeat each segment of the following paragraphs, substituting future forms for the verbs in the present tense or in *ir a + infinitive* constructions. Then repeat the whole paragraph.

1. Tenemos examen mañana y,... como probablemente yo no voy a saber mucho,... lo mejor es no ir a la clase de español.
   Tendremos examen mañana y,... como probablemente yo no sabré mucho,... lo mejor será no ir a la clase de español.
2. Pero tal vez puedo estudiar esta noche... ¡Claro! Esta noche me pongo a estudiar como loco... Leo el libro entero,... lo aprendo de memoria,... me acuesto a las tres de la mañana y... no, mejor no voy.
3. Le digo al maestro que estaba enfermo y... le voy a preguntar... cuándo puedo hacer el examen.
4. Probablemente él va a comprender mis razones y... me va a decir... que puedo hacerlo cualquier otro día... y que él me va a llamar a mi casa y... que me va a hacer un examen muy fácil.

QUIÉN SABE

Follow the examples. The whole class answers.

1. ¿Van a venir ustedes mañana?
   Quién sabe si vendremos mañana.
2. ¿Cuándo es el examen?
   Quién sabe cuándo será el examen.
3. ¿Van a ir ustedes al paseo?
4. ¿Cuánta gente va a haber allí?
5. ¿Qué van a comer ustedes?
6. ¿Quién trae las Coca-Colas?

7. ¿Cuándo llegan los estudiantes americanos?
8. ¿A qué hora van a acostarse ustedes esta noche?
9. ¿Van a volver ustedes a la escuela?
10. ¿Qué voy a hacer yo sin ustedes?
11. ¿Me invitan ustedes al paseo?
12. ¿Cuándo voy a tener otra oportunidad?

[*To be followed by* LISTENING COMPREHENSION–SPEAKING EXERCISE]

80. *Additional uses of* ser

María estaba allí.	*María was there.*
La fiesta **era** allí.	*The party was (being held) there.*

In Chapter 2 you learned that only *estar* can be used when the verb complement expresses location, for example *donde, allí, en mi casa* (first example). However, when the subject refers to an activity (*una fiesta, un baile, una conferencia*) rather than an object or a person (*la mesa, María*), only *ser* is used, and has the meaning "to take place," "to be held" (second example).

TRANSLATION

1. Where is Andrés?
   Where is the dance?
2. The dinner was (*imperf.*) on the table.
   The dinner was being held at (in) the Grand Hotel.[16]
3. The president was (*pret.*) here.
   The coup d'état was (*pret.*) here.
4. The guest[17] is going to be here at eight.
   The lecture[18] is going to be here at eight.
5. The bride (*novia*) was going to be at (in) her aunt's house.
   The wedding was going to be at (in) Saint Joseph's Church.
6. Where will the groom (*novio*) be?
   Where will the ceremony[19] be?
7. He wouldn't be in the back yard.[20]
   The wedding wouldn't be in the back yard.
8. I don't want anybody to be here.
   I don't want the party to be here.
9. Luz María wanted Flaco to be at (in) her party.
   Luz María wanted the party to be held at the country club.[21]
10. I hope (*ojalá*) Dolores is there.
    I hope the lecture is there.
11. I wish you were here.
    I wish the picnic were here.
12. As if the generals were everywhere!
    As if the lectures were everywhere!

---

[16] *El hotel.*   [17] *Invitado.*   [18] *Conferencia.*   [19] *Ceremonia.*   [20] *Patio.*   [21] *El country club.*

1. ¿Dónde va a estar la orquesta?
   _____el baile?
   _____fue_____
   _____la conferencia?
   _____era_____
   _____ustedes?

2. El profesor está en la casa.
   La fiesta_____
   _____iba a ser_____
   Yo_____
   _____aquí.
   El examen_____

3. Ojalá que el examen sea en este cuarto.
   _____ mi libro_____
   _____en la escuela.
   _____ estuviera_____
   _____la fiesta_____

81.   *The* tú *command forms*[22]

	Affirmative		Negative	
-ar	Habla (tú).	Talk.	No hables (tú).	Don't talk.
-er	Bebe (tú).	Drink.	No bebas (tú).	Don't drink.
-ir	Escribe (tú).	Write.	No escribas (tú).	Don't write.

-ar	Hablad (vosotros).	No habléis (vosotros).
-er	Bebed (vosotros).	No bebáis (vosotros).
-ir	Escribid (vosotros).	No escribáis (vosotros).

A. The *affirmative tú* command forms are the same as those of the third person singular present indicative.

El habla inglés; habla tú inglés también.
El bebe mucho; bebe tú mucho también.
El escribe bien; escribe tú bien también.

B. The *negative tú* command forms are the same as the *tú* forms of the present subjunctive.

No quiero que hables. ¡No hables!
Es malo que bebas. ¡No bebas!
No es necesario que escribas. ¡No escribas!

C. A few common verbs have irregular *affirmative tú* command forms.

hacer:	**Haz** algo.	*Do something.*
tener:	**Ten** paciencia.	*Be patient.*
poner:	**Pon** atención.	*Pay attention.*

---

[22] For the reasons given in Chapter 2 (page 32), *tú* verb forms have not, in general, been emphasized in this book. Correspondingly, the purpose of the following explanations and exercises is not to enable you to use the *tú* command forms actively yourself, but only to enable you to recognize them when you encounter them in speech or writing.

decir:	**Di** algo.	*Say something.*
venir:	**Ven** acá.	*Come here.*
salir:	**Sal** de aquí.	*Get out of here.*
ser:	**Sé** bueno.	*Be good.*
ir:	**Ve** a tu casa.	*Go home.*

The *negative tú* commands of these verbs are formed as described in the previous paragraph: *No hagas nada, No tengas paciencia,* etc.

D. The *affirmative vosotros* commands are formed by replacing the final *r* of the infinitive with a *d.* All these forms are regular.

ir:	**Id.**	*Go.*
ser:	**Sed** buenos.	*Be good.*

The *negative vosotros* command forms are the same as the *vosotros* forms of the present subjunctive.

> No quiero que vayáis. ¡No vayáis!
> No quiero que seáis malos. ¡No seáis malos!

E. The position of object pronouns with respect to *tú* command forms is the same as for the *usted, ustedes,* and *nosotros* command forms. That is, object pronouns follow affirmative command forms (and are attached to them in writing), but precede negative command forms.

Mándamelo.	*Send it to me.*
No **me lo** mandes.	*Don't send it to me.*

Díselo.	*Tell it to him.*
No **se lo** digas.	*Don't tell it to him.*

WRITTEN TRANSLATION

Use a *tú* command in the second clause of each sentence.

1. If he calls, you call too.
2. If he learns, you learn too.
3. If Luz María gets married, you get married too.
4. If Mr. Gómez sells his house, you sell your house too.
5. If he bathes, you bathe too.
6. If your godmother writes to you, you write to her too.

COMPLETION

Write completions containing negative *tú* commands, using the same verb and addressing the commands to Juanito, as in the model.

1. Hable usted, señor, pero...
   no hables tú, Juanito.
2. Cásese usted, tía Marta, pero...
3. Lea usted, don Pedro, pero...
4. Quédese usted aquí, señora, pero...
5. Acuéstese usted, doña María, pero...
6. Escríbale usted a ella, señor, pero...

Use *tú* commands only.

1. Don't come now, come tomorrow.
2. Do me a favor, will you?[23] Don't do anything.
3. Don't put that on the table, put it here.
4. Be good, don't be foolish.
5. Leave in the morning, don't leave now.
6. Come here. Don't come to me with stories.
7. Don't be afraid (don't have fear); have patience.
8. Don't tell me lies, tell me the truth.

LISTENING COMPREHENSION

Listen to the following sentences with books closed. Then give the meaning of each in English.

1. Ven acá, Pedro, y siéntate.
2. Cállate, hazme el favor, ¿quieres?
3. No seas malo, sé un hombre bueno toda la vida.
4. Dile a María que te devuelva el libro.
5. ¡No quiero verte más! ¡Sal de aquí!
6. Ve a cualquier parte, pero vete. ¡Vete, por el amor de Dios!
7. Ponte algo en la cabeza si vas a entrar a la iglesia.
8. Diez años más, María, eso es todo. Ten paciencia, y dime que me esperarás. ¡Dímelo!

Reading

El Index de los mayas

Soy por disposición una persona alegre y confiada, y mis años de servicio de secretario del Club de los Optimistas en Kansas City son un comprobante de esta feliz condición humana. Sin embargo, comencé a perder algo de esta cualidad cuando llegué a Puerto Delgado, ciudad pacífica de ambiente colonial o viceversa, tal vez. Me era lo mismo; yo vine con un solo propósito: encontrar el Index de los mayas. Según mi estimado mentor, el profesor alemán Reichmann, existen en un archivo de Puerto Delgado unos documentos en quiché que descifran el misterio de la decadencia de la gran cultura maya y que datan del siglo ocho o nueve. Decían algunos que Reichmann estaba loco, pero para mí, él era un

gran hombre; además, yo necesitaba desesperadamente encontrar un modo de ganarme un ascenso en mi universidad.

Bueno, llegué de la capital en uno de estos viejos autobuses que llevaban más gallinas que gente. Paramos en la plaza principal, típica con sus palmeras graves y la estatua de bronce de algún general a caballo sudando bajo el calor de un sol infernal. La calle hervía cuando llegué por fin al hotel "El Sevillano". Detrás de las gruesas paredes de adobe y a la sombra de palmeras me senté en el patio, gocé de la brisa del mar y acepté unos vasos con jugo de papaya. Delicioso. El dueño, un andaluz solitario, se sentó a mi lado y me habría contado por lo menos un tercio de

---

[23] *Quieres.*

la historia de su vida si no le hubiera dicho que había venido con una misión muy urgente y que necesitaba salir en seguida para encontrar el archivo. Me miró con sospecha, y yo sabía que me creía uno de estos anglosajones de película, exploradores locos con dientes postizos y pipa apagada que salen a la calle cuando toda persona cuerda duerme la siesta, y que se acuestan cuando las personas salen a gozar del fresco de la noche. Bueno, a mí, ¿qué me importaba? No había venido a este puerto castigado por la fiebre amarilla y un clima implacable para tocar una guitarra y dar serenatas bajo algún balcón que se estaba cayendo con el peso combinado de dos o tres bellezas locales. El andaluz, quien se rascaba la cabeza, por fin me dijo en su acento español:

—Mire, caballerito. Archivo aquí no tenemos. Pué[24] ser que usté busca la casa e[25] la familia Peñafiel. Queda en la calle Otero pasando la vieja iglesia. Pero a esta hora, debe estar cerrao.

Le agradecí la información y me puse en marcha. El sol estaba en lo más alto y las calles se encontraban sin vida. Ni una tienda, ni una puerta o ventana abierta. Ambiente colonial, de reyes y virreyes católicos. Poco me importaba. Yo tenía mi misión, y el Index de los mayas no permitía tardanzas o siestas tropicales. Encontré la iglesia, pobre ejemplo de la arquitectura plateresca, y continué por Otero, calle curva y angosta, de casas antiquísimas con rejas y paredes despintadas. Nada de bibliotecas ni archivos. Otero terminaba en el puerto. Justo antes de la última esquina vi una casa tan vieja que temía que las paredes se vinieran abajo. Al acercarme noté una placa de metal oxidado que decía:

Museo Peñafiel
1893

El grueso portón de madera semipodrida estaba firmemente cerrado. Suspiré. Mi instinto me decía que en esta ruina había algo que me iba a servir como el tesoro de los incas. Del puerto venían unos olores fétidos y calientes, y de repente mis piernas aflojaban bajo el terrible calor de este sol matador. Llegué al hotel sudado y temblando. El andaluz, que al parecer nunca dormía, me dijo que podía haber sufrido una insolación y me preparó una combinación de jugo de piña, guayaba y un poquito de ron, que tenía un gusto maravilloso. Después del cuarto vaso me quedé dormido un ratito. Cuando desperté estaba semioscuro. La ciudad se había transformado: las calles estaban llenas de vida, se oía música de radio mezclada con las campanas vespertinas. En las tiendas se habían prendido las luces y la gente entraba o salía a montones. Esta vez la calle Otero ofrecía otro espectáculo. Las ventanas y puertas estaban abiertas y detrás de ellas muchos pares de ojos parecían fijarse en mi pelo rubio-gris y mis pasos apresurados. Esta vez el portón del "Museo Peñafiel" estaba entreabierto. Sin vacilar un segundo me metí adentro donde sorprendí a una gorda de unos cuarenta años hablando a un viejo criado. El viejo me dio una mirada llena de dignidad:

—El horario para el público, caballero, es de once a doce, del lunes al jueves.

—Mire —le dije—, he viajado seis mil kilómetros para ver el Index de los mayas y no me voy de aquí hasta que haya examinado la biblioteca.

La gordita estaba indecisa; para hacerla salir de su indecisión, le grité.

—¡La biblioteca o no respondo de mis actos!

Dos minutos después los tres estábamos en la biblioteca. Era una pieza bastante pequeña y pobremente amueblada. Había dos estantes con libros de toda clase. Vi inmediatamente que la gran mayoría eran ediciones baratas de autores franceses y españoles del siglo pasado. A la derecha, dos colecciones de enciclopedias, y más abajo unas historias del Nuevo Mundo, en cuero muy gastado, entre ellas una de Diego de Landa con fecha de 1569.

—Nada —dije dándome vuelta. Los dos no me quitaban los ojos de encima.

—¡El Index de los mayas! —grité—, ¿dónde está? —Siete mil kilómetros para ver el Index, y nada. ¿Ni unas páginas sueltas, hojas dibujadas, cortezas con impresiones?

---

[24]*Puede.* [25]*De.*

La gorda se puso pálida. Yo creí que ella se iba a desmayar y salí apresuradamente. Una vez en la calle, me encaminé tranquilamente hacia la Plaza y pregunté cuándo salía el próximo autobús para la capital. Me dijeron que a las ocho de la mañana. Continué caminando a mi hotel, lentamente para que el viejo criado que me seguía no me perdiera de vista. La cena era a las diez pero yo pedí algo de comer a las ocho; y el andaluz, que comía a la española, es decir a las once, me trajo un plato de huevos fritos.

A las ocho de la mañana me trajo lo mismo. Estaba tomando mi café cuando se presentó un señor flaco en un traje blanco muy gastado; detrás de él venía el viejo criado del "Museo". El flaco tenía un discurso de protesta preparado. Tomó más de veinte minutos y estaba repleto de palabras como "falta de respeto", "dignidad", "honor de la familia", "pobre niña indefensa" (refiriéndose a la gorda) y "de hombre a hombre". Después hablé yo. Le mostré mis documentos de historiador, mencioné mi gran interés por el pasado del ilustre país, en especial por el Index de los mayas, y mi admiración por el "Museo Peñafiel"; pedí mil disculpas a la "niña" ausente, y por último anuncié mi decisión irrevocable de donar cien dólares al "Museo". Después de diez minutos de protestas el dinero cambió de mano.

—El "Museo" y yo estamos a su entera disposición —me dijo el flaco.

—Gracias —contesté—, de verdad me gustaría muchísimo llevar un pequeño recuerdo de mi viaje a Puerto Delgado, ciudad magnífica e inolvidable.

—A sus órdenes, caballero.

—Tal vez uno de estos viejos tomos como el de Diego de Landa, historiador tan original —dije.

—¿Cuándo se va usted?

—En el autobús de las ocho.

—Perfecto; José le llevará el libro a la Plaza.

Se despidió. Pagué la cuenta, le dije adiós al andaluz y salí con la maleta hacia la Plaza. Eran las 9:35. A las 9:45 llegó el autobús. Me instalé en un asiento al lado de la ventanilla abierta. Dos minutos más tarde el viejo criado apareció y me entregó el libro por la ventanilla. Di un suspiro. En mis rodillas descansaba una crónica inédita de nada menos que Diego de Landa, que representaba un ascenso y valía una fortuna. A las diez en punto partió el autobús de las ocho a la capital, y yo sentí renacer mi viejo optimismo.

DISCUSSION

1. Describa Puerto Delgado.
2. Indique algunas diferencias culturales entre los Estados Unidos y América Latina, según se observa en el cuento.
3. ¿Qué piensa usted de la actitud del personaje principal del cuento?

[*To be followed by* LISTENING COMPREHENSION–SPEAKING EXERCISE]

Appendix

Regular Verbs

1. cantar *to sing*

PRESENT PARTICIPLE	cantando
PAST PARTICIPLE	cantado
PRESENT INDICATIVE	canto, cantas, canta, cantamos, cantan, (cantáis)
PRESENT SUBJUNCTIVE and COMMAND (usted)	cante, cantes, cante, cantemos, canten, (cantéis)
IMPERFECT	cantaba, cantabas, cantaba, cantábamos, cantaban, (cantabais)
PRETERIT	canté, cantaste, cantó, cantamos, cantaron, (cantasteis)
PAST SUBJUNCTIVE	cantara, cantaras, cantara, cantáramos, cantaran, (cantarais)
FUTURE	cantaré, cantarás, cantará, cantaremos, cantarán, (cantaréis)
CONDITIONAL	cantaría, cantarías, cantaría, cantaríamos, cantarían, (cantaríais)
COMMAND (tú; vosotros)	canta, no cantes; cantad, no cantéis

2. beber *to drink*

PRESENT PARTICIPLE	bebiendo
PAST PARTICIPLE	bebido
PRESENT INDICATIVE	bebo, bebes, bebe, bebemos, beben, (bebéis)
PRESENT SUBJUNCTIVE and COMMAND (usted)	beba, bebas, beba, bebamos, beban, (bebáis)
IMPERFECT	bebía, bebías, bebía, bebíamos, bebían, (bebíais)
PRETERIT	bebí, bebiste, bebió, bebimos, bebieron, (bebisteis)
PAST SUBJUNCTIVE	bebiera, bebieras, bebiera, bebiéramos, bebieran, (bebierais)
FUTURE	beberé, beberás, beberá, beberemos, beberán, (beberéis)
CONDITIONAL	bebería, beberías, bebería, beberíamos, beberían, (beberíais)
COMMAND (tú; vosotros)	bebe, no bebas; bebed, no bebáis

3. vivir *to live*

PRESENT PARTICIPLE	viviendo
PAST PARTICIPLE	vivido
PRESENT INDICATIVE	vivo, vives, vive, vivimos, viven, (vivís)
PRESENT SUBJUNCTIVE and COMMAND (usted)	viva, vivas, viva, vivamos, vivan, (viváis)
IMPERFECT	vivía, vivías, vivía, vivíamos, vivían, (vivíais)
PRETERIT	viví, viviste, vivió, vivimos, vivieron, (vivisteis)
PAST SUBJUNCTIVE	viviera, vivieras, viviera, viviéramos, vivieran, (vivierais)
FUTURE	viviré, vivirás, vivirá, viviremos, vivirán, (viviréis)
CONDITIONAL	viviría, vivirías, viviría, viviríamos, vivirían, (viviríais)
COMMAND (tú; vosotros)	vive, no vivas; vivid, no viváis

Stem-changing Verbs

Forms with vowel changes are shown in **boldface**. Tenses in which no vowel alternation occurs are omitted.

e ⟶ ie

4. pensar (ie) *to think; to intend*

PRESENT INDICATIVE	**pienso, piensas, piensa,** pensamos, **piensan,** (pensáis)
PRESENT SUBJUNCTIVE and COMMAND (usted)	**piense, pienses, piense,** pensemos, **piensen,** (penséis)
COMMAND (tú)	**piensa, no pienses**

5. perder (ie) *to lose*

PRESENT INDICATIVE	**pierdo, pierdes, pierde,** perdemos, **pierden,** (perdéis)
PRESENT SUBJUNCTIVE and COMMAND (usted)	**pierda, pierdas, pierda,** perdamos, **pierdan,** (perdáis)
COMMAND (tú)	**pierde, no pierdas**

6. sentir (ie, i)   *to feel; to regret, be sorry*

PRESENT PARTICIPLE	sintiendo
PRESENT INDICATIVE	siento, sientes, siente, sentimos, sienten, (sentís)
PRESENT SUBJUNCTIVE and COMMAND (usted)	sienta, sientas, sienta, sintamos, sientan, (sintáis)
PRETERIT	sentí, sentiste, sintió, sentimos, sintieron, (sentisteis)
PAST SUBJUNCTIVE	sintiera, sintieras, sintiera, sintiéramos, sintieran, (sintierais)
COMMAND (tú)	siente, no sientas

e ⟶ i

7. pedir (i)   *to ask*

PRESENT PARTICIPLE	pidiendo
PRESENT INDICATIVE	pido, pides, pide, pedimos, piden, (pedís)
PRESENT SUBJUNCTIVE and COMMAND (usted)	pida, pidas, pida, pidamos, pidan, (pidáis)
PRETERIT	pedí, pediste, pidió, pedimos, pidieron, (pedisteis)
PAST SUBJUNCTIVE	pidiera, pidieras, pidiera, pidiéramos, pidieran, (pidierais)
COMMAND (tú)	pide, no pidas

o ⟶ ue

8. contar (ue)   *to count; to tell*

PRESENT INDICATIVE	cuento, cuentas, cuenta, contamos, cuentan, (contáis)
PRESENT SUBJUNCTIVE and COMMAND (usted)	cuente, cuentes, cuente, contemos, cuenten, (contéis)
COMMAND (tú)	cuenta, no cuentes

9. volver (ue)   *to return*

PRESENT INDICATIVE	vuelvo, vuelves, vuelve, volvemos, vuelven, (volvéis)
PRESENT SUBJUNCTIVE and COMMAND (usted)	vuelva, vuelvas, vuelva, volvamos, vuelvan, (volváis)
COMMAND (tú)	vuelve, no vuelvas

10. dormir (ue, u) *to sleep*

PRESENT PARTICIPLE	**durmiendo**
PRESENT INDICATIVE	**duermo, duermes, duerme,** dormimos, **duermen,** (dormís)
PRESENT SUBJUNCTIVE and COMMAND (usted)	**duerma, duermas, duerma, durmamos, duerman,** (durmáis)
PRETERIT	dormí, dormiste, **durmió,** dormimos, **durmieron,** (dormisteis)
PAST SUBJUNCTIVE	**durmiera, durmieras, durmiera, durmiéramos, durmieran,** (durmierais)
COMMAND (tú)	**duerme, no duermas**

u ⟶ ue

11. jugar (ue) *to play, gamble*

PRESENT INDICATIVE	**juego, juegas, juega,** jugamos, **juegan,** (jugáis)
PRESENT SUBJUNCTIVE and COMMAND (usted)	**juegue, juegues, juegue,** juguemos, **jueguen,** (juguéis)
COMMAND (tú)	**juega, no juegues**

Irregular Verbs

Only those tenses having irregular forms are shown, and these forms are printed in **boldface.** Past subjunctive forms are not listed, since they have the same stem—regular or irregular—as the preterit forms. Stem vowel alternation, if any, is indicated parenthetically after the infinitive. Irregular verbs that are not treated in the grammar sections of the textbook are not included in these verb charts. Also not shown are regularly formed negative *vosotros* commands.

12. andar *to walk, go*

PRETERIT	**anduve, anduviste, anduvo, anduvimos, anduvieron,** (anduvisteis)

13. caer *to fall*

PRESENT INDICATIVE	**caigo,** caes, cae, caemos, caen, (caéis)
PRESENT SUBJUNCTIVE and COMMAND (usted)	**caiga, caigas, caiga, caigamos, caigan,** (caigáis)

14. conocer *to know, be acquainted with; to meet*

PRESENT INDICATIVE **conozco,** conoces, conoce, conocemos, conocen, (conocéis)
PRESENT SUBJUNCTIVE and
   COMMAND (usted) **conozca, conozcas, conozca, conozcamos, conozcan, (conozcáis)**

15. dar *to give*

PRESENT INDICATIVE **doy,** das, da, damos, dan, (dais)
PRESENT SUBJUNCTIVE and
   COMMAND (usted) **dé, des, dé, demos, den, (deis)**
PRETERIT **di, diste, dio, dimos, dieron, (disteis)**

16. decir (i) *to say, tell*

PAST PARTICIPLE **dicho**
PRESENT INDICATIVE **digo,** dices, dice, decimos, dicen, (decís)
PRESENT SUBJUNCTIVE and
   COMMAND (usted) **diga, digas, diga, digamos, digan, (digáis)**
PRETERIT **dije, dijiste, dijo, dijimos, dijeron, (dijisteis)**
FUTURE **diré, dirás, dirá, diremos, dirán, (diréis)**
CONDITIONAL **diría, dirías, diría, diríamos, dirían, (diríais)**
COMMAND (tú) **di**

17. estar *to be*

PRESENT INDICATIVE **estoy, estás, está,** estamos, **están,** (estáis)
PRESENT SUBJUNCTIVE and
   COMMAND (usted) **esté, estés, esté,** estemos, **estén,** (estéis)
PRETERIT **estuve, estuviste, estuvo, estuvimos, estuvieron, (estuvisteis)**

18. haber *to have*

PRESENT INDICATIVE **he, has, ha, hemos, han,** (habéis)
PRESENT SUBJUNCTIVE **haya, hayas, haya, hayamos, hayan, (hayáis)**
PRETERIT **hube, hubiste, hubo, hubimos, hubieron, (hubisteis)**
FUTURE **habré, habrás, habrá, habremos, habrán, (habréis)**
CONDITIONAL **habría, habrías, habría, habríamos, habrían, (habríais)**

19. hacer *to do; to make*

PAST PARTICIPLE	**hecho**
PRESENT INDICATIVE	**hago,** haces, hace, hacemos, hacen, (hacéis)
PRESENT SUBJUNCTIVE and COMMAND (usted)	**haga, hagas, haga, hagamos, hagan,** (hagáis)
PRETERIT	**hice, hiciste, hizo, hicimos, hicieron,** (hicisteis)
FUTURE	**haré, harás, hará, haremos, harán,** (haréis)
CONDITIONAL	**haría, harías, haría, haríamos, harían,** (haríais)
COMMAND (tú)	**haz**

20. ir *to go*

PRESENT PARTICIPLE	yendo°
PRESENT INDICATIVE	**voy, vas, va, vamos, van,** (vais)
PRESENT SUBJUNCTIVE and COMMAND (usted)	**vaya, vayas, vaya, vayamos, vayan,** (vayáis)
IMPERFECT	**iba, ibas, iba, íbamos, iban,** (ibais)
PRETERIT	**fui, fuiste, fue, fuimos, fueron,** (fuisteis)
COMMAND (tú)	**ve**

21. oír *to hear*

PRESENT INDICATIVE	**oigo, oyes, oye,** oímos, **oyen,** (oís)
PRESENT SUBJUNCTIVE and COMMAND (usted)	**oiga, oigas, oiga, oigamos, oigan,** (oigáis)

22. poder (ue) *to be able*

PRESENT PARTICIPLE	**pudiendo**
PRETERIT	**pude, pudiste, pudo, pudimos, pudieron,** (pudisteis)
FUTURE	**podré, podrás, podrá, podremos, podrán,** (podréis)
CONDITIONAL	**podría, podrías, podría, podríamos, podrían,** (podríais)

23. poner *to put*

PAST PARTICIPLE	**puesto**
PRESENT INDICATIVE	**pongo,** pones, pone, ponemos, ponen, (ponéis)

° *Yendo* is listed only to show its spelling. It is actually regular.

PRESENT SUBJUNCTIVE and COMMAND (usted)	ponga, pongas, ponga, pongamos, pongan, (pongáis)
PRETERIT	puse, pusiste, puso, pusimos, pusieron, (pusisteis)
FUTURE	pondré, pondrás, pondrá, pondremos, pondrán, (pondréis)
CONDITIONAL	pondría, pondrías, pondría, pondríamos, pondrían, (pondríais)
COMMAND (tú)	pon

24. querer (ie)   *to want; to love*

PRETERIT	quise, quisiste, quiso, quisimos, quisieron, (quisisteis)
FUTURE	querré, querrás, querrá, querremos, querrán, (querréis)
CONDITIONAL	querría, querrías, querría, querríamos, querrían, (querríais)

25. saber   *to know*

PRESENT INDICATIVE	sé, sabes, sabe, sabemos, saben, (sabéis)
PRESENT SUBJUNCTIVE and COMMAND (usted)	sepa, sepas, sepa, sepamos, sepan, (sepáis)
FUTURE	sabré, sabrás, sabrá, sabremos, sabrán, (sabréis)
CONDITIONAL	sabría, sabrías, sabría, sabríamos, sabrían, (sabríais)

26. salir   *to go out*

PRESENT INDICATIVE	salgo, sales, sale, salimos, salen, (salís)
PRESENT SUBJUNCTIVE and COMMAND (usted)	salga, salgas, salga, salgamos, salgan, (salgáis)
FUTURE	saldré, saldrás, saldrá, saldremos, saldrán, (saldréis)
CONDITIONAL	saldría, saldrías, saldría, saldríamos, saldrían, (saldríais)
COMMAND (tú)	sal

27. ser   *to be*

PRESENT INDICATIVE	soy, eres, es, somos, son, (sois)
PRESENT SUBJUNCTIVE and COMMAND (usted)	sea, seas, sea, seamos, sean, (seáis)
IMPERFECT	era, eras, era, éramos, eran, (erais)
PRETERIT	fui, fuiste, fue, fuimos, fueron, (fuisteis)
COMMAND (tú)	sé

28. tener (ie) *to have*

PRESENT INDICATIVE	**tengo,** tienes, tiene, tenemos, tienen, (tenéis)
PRESENT SUBJUNCTIVE and COMMAND (usted)	**tenga, tengas, tenga, tengamos, tengan, (tengáis)**
PRETERIT	**tuve, tuviste, tuvo, tuvimos, tuvieron, (tuvisteis)**
FUTURE	**tendré, tendrás, tendrá, tendremos, tendrán, (tendréis)**
CONDITIONAL	**tendría, tendrías, tendría, tendríamos, tendrían, (tendríais)**
COMMAND (tú)	**ten**

29. traer *to bring*

PRESENT INDICATIVE	**traigo,** traes, trae, traemos, traen, (traéis)
PRESENT SUBJUNCTIVE and COMMAND (usted)	**traiga, traigas, traiga, traigamos, traigan, (traigáis)**
PRETERIT	**traje, trajiste, trajo, trajimos, trajeron, (trajisteis)**

30. valer *to be worth*

PRESENT INDICATIVE	**valgo,** vales, vale, valemos, valen, (valéis)
PRESENT SUBJUNCTIVE and COMMAND (usted)	**valga, valgas, valga, valgamos, valgan, (valgáis)**
FUTURE	**valdré, valdrás, valdrá, valdremos, valdrán, (valdréis)**
CONDITIONAL	**valdría, valdrías, valdría, valdríamos, valdrían, (valdríais)**
COMMAND (tú)	**val**

31. venir (ie, i) *to come*

PRESENT INDICATIVE	**vengo,** vienes, viene, venimos, vienen, (venís)
PRESENT SUBJUNCTIVE and COMMAND (usted)	**venga, vengas, venga, vengamos, vengan, (vengáis)**
PRETERIT	**vine, viniste, vino, vinimos, vinieron, (vinisteis)**
FUTURE	**vendré, vendrás, vendrá, vendremos, vendrán, (vendréis)**
CONDITIONAL	**vendría, vendrías, vendría, vendríamos, vendrían, (vendríais)**
COMMAND (tú)	**ven**

32. ver *to see*

PAST PARTICIPLE	**visto**
PRESENT INDICATIVE	**veo,** ves, ve, vemos, ven, (veis)
PRESENT SUBJUNCTIVE and COMMAND (usted)	**vea, veas, vea, veamos, vean, (veáis)**
IMPERFECT	**veía, veías, veía, veíamos, veían, (veíais)**

Summary of the Forms of a Sample Verb: *aprender,* to learn

1. Ana aprende inglés.	*Ana learns, is learning, will learn English.*
2. Ana está aprendiendo inglés.	*Ana is learning English.*
3. Ana va a aprender inglés.	*Ana is going to learn English.*
4. Ana ha aprendido inglés.	*Ana has learned English.*
5. Ana ha estado aprendiendo inglés.	*Ana has been learning English.*
6. Ana aprendió inglés.	*Ana learned English.*
7. Ana aprendía inglés.	*Ana used to learn, was learning English.*
8. Ana estaba (estuvo) aprendiendo inglés.	*Ana was learning English.*
9. Ana había aprendido inglés.	*Ana had learned English.*
10. Ana había estado aprendiendo inglés.	*Ana had been learning English.*
11. Ana iba a aprender inglés.	*Ana was going to learn English.*
12. Aprenda usted inglés, Ana.	*Learn English, Ana.*
13. Aprende tú inglés, Ana.	*Learn English, Ana.*
14. (Ojalá que) Ana aprenda inglés.	*(I hope) Ana learns English.*
15. (Ojalá que) Ana aprendiera inglés.	*(I wish) Ana would learn English.*
16. (Ojalá que) Ana haya aprendido inglés.	*(I hope) Ana has learned English.*
17. (Ojalá que) Ana hubiera aprendido inglés.	*(I wish) Ana had learned English.*
18. Ana aprenderá inglés.	*Ana will learn English.*
19. Ana aprendería inglés.	*Ana would learn English.*
20. Ana habría aprendido inglés.	*Ana would have learned English.*
21. Si Ana aprendiera inglés	*If Ana should learn English*
22. Si Ana hubiera aprendido inglés	*If Ana had learned English*

Vocabularies

Gender is indicated for all nouns except masculine nouns ending in -o and feminine nouns ending in -a. The vowel alternation of stem-changing verbs is given in parentheses after the infinitive. A number in parentheses following the infinitive of an irregular verb refers to the paradigm in the Appendix (page 287) for the conjugation of that verb or a verb with the same irregularity.

The English-Spanish Vocabulary includes all words and expressions used in the basic dialogs and supplements, the grammatical charts, the exercises, and the listening passages. The Spanish-English Vocabulary includes all Spanish words and expressions used in the text except exact cognates, personal proper nouns, and the names of most places.

Abbreviations

adj	adjective	f	feminine noun	pl	plural
adv	adverb	m	masculine noun	pp	past participle
dim	diminutive	n	noun	sing	singular

English-Spanish Vocabulary

A

a un, una
able: to be — poder (ue, u) (22)
abound abundar
about de, acerca de, sobre; como (approximately)
abroad en el extranjero
absurd absurdo
accent acento
accept aceptar
accompany acompañar
according to según
account cuenta; **on — of** por, a causa de
accumulate acumular

accustom acostumbrar
accustomed: be — acostumbrar; **become —** acostumbrarse
ache dolor m
achieve realizar
acquisition adquisición f
action acción f
active activo
activity actividad f
adapt adaptar
add agregar
addition: in — to además
adequate adecuado
adjective adjetivo
administrative administrativo
admiral almirante m
advance avanzar

advantage ventaja; **take —** aprovechar
affection cariño
affirmative afirmativo
afford (give, provide) dar
afraid: to be — tener miedo
after después (de)
afternoon tarde f; **good —** buenas tardes
afterwards después
again otra vez; **— and —** una y otra vez
against contra
age edad f
agency agencia, servicio
ago: (ten years) — hace (diez años)

agree estar de acuerdo; **— to** quedar en
agreement acuerdo; concordancia (grammatical)
agricultural agrícola
ahead: get — adelantarse
aid ayuda
alarm alarmar; alarma
alike igual, parecido
all todo
almost casi
alms limosna
alone solo
alongside al lado de
alphabet alfabeto
alphabetical alfabético
already ya
also también
although aunque
always siempre
America América; **Spanish —** Hispanoamérica; **Central — ** Centroamérica
American americano
among entre
amusing divertido
an un, una
and y, e
Anglo-Saxon anglosajón, -ona
angry enojado; resentido; furioso; **get —** enojarse; resentirse (ie, i)
annoy molestar
another otro
answer contestar
anthropologist antropólogo
any cualquier; alguno; ninguno (after negative)
anybody alguien; nadie (after negative)
anyone alguien; nadie (after negative)
anything cualquier cosa; nada (after negative)
anyway de todos modos
appeal apelar
appear aparecer (14)
appearance apariencia
apple manzana
apply aplicar
approach acercarse
approval aprobación *f*
approximately aproximadamente
April abril *m*
Argentinean argentino

argue discutir
arise surgir
arm brazo
armed armado
arrive llegar
art arte *m*
article artículo
artist artista *m*
as como; a medida que; **— for (me)** en cuanto a (mí)
ask preguntar; pedir (i)
aspect aspecto
assimilate asimilar
at en; a
Atlantic Atlántico
attain obtener (ie) (28)
attend asistir; atender (ie) (wait on, look after)
attitude actitud *f*
attract atraer (29)
August agosto
aunt tía
authority autoridad *f*
avoid evitar
away: right — inmediatamente

B

baby bebé *mf*
bachelor soltero
back espalda
bad malo
bag bolsa
baker panadero
bamboo bambú *m*
banana banano (tree)
band banda
bank banco; orilla (shore)
barbarianism barbarie *f*
barber peluquero; **— shop** peluquería
barrier barrera
base base *f*
basic básico
basket canasta; **shopping —** canasta de las compras
bass bajo
bath baño; **take a —** bañarse
bathe bañarse
bathroom baño
be estar (17); ser (27)
beach playa
bean frijol *m*

beautiful lindo; bello
because porque; **— of** a causa de
become ponerse (23); hacerse (19)
bed cama; **go to —** acostarse (ue)
bedroom cuarto
beer cerveza
before antes (de)
beforehand de antemano
beggar mendigo
begin comenzar (ie); empezar (ie)
behalf: on — of a favor de
behind atrás; detrás (de)
being ser *m*
belligerent beligerante
belong pertenecer (14)
below abajo
bench banco
beside al lado de
besides además (de)
best mejor
bet apostar (ue)
better mejor
better-off acomodado
between entre
beyond más allá
big grande
bill cuenta
biology biología
bird pájaro
birthday cumpleaños *m sing*
bit: a little — un poco
bitter amargo
black negro
bless bendecir (16, but *pp* bendecido)
block bloque *m*
blond rubio
blouse blusa
blue azul
board tabla
Bogotá: person from bogotano
boiling hirviendo
Bolivian boliviano
bookstore librería
bored aburrido; **get —** aburrirse
boring aburrido
born: be — nacer (14)
both ambos; los dos
bother molestar
bottle botella

bottom fondo
bourgeosie burguesía
boy muchacho; chico; **little —** niño
Brazil (el) Brasil
bread pan *m*
breakfast desayuno
bring traer (29); **— about** causar; **— closer** estrechar
broth caldo
brother hermano
brother-in-law cuñado
brown café; de color café; marrón; pardo; castaño; habano
brunette de pelo negro
budget presupuesto
build construir
building edificio
bull toro
bullfight corrida de toros
bum sinvergüenza *m*
bus autobús *m*
busy ocupado
but pero; sino (que)
butcher carnicero; **— shop** carnicería
butter mantequilla
buy comprar
by por; para

C

cabinet gabinete *m*
calendar calendario
call llamar
can poder (ue, u) (22)
candle vela
canvas lona
capable capaz
capital capital *f* (city)
captain capitán *m*
car carro; coche *m*
caravel carabela
cardboard cartón *m*
cardinal cardinal
care cuidado
career carrera
carefully con cuidado
Caribbean Caribe *m*
carpenter carpintero
carry llevar
case caso

cat gato, gata
catch: **a great —** un gran partido
cause causar; causa
cease cesar
cemetery cementerio
center centro
central central; **Central America** Centroamérica; **Central American** centroamericano
century siglo
ceremony ceremonia
certain cierto
chair silla
chance oportunidad *f*
change cambiar; cambio
chapter capítulo
character carácter *m;* personaje *m*
charge: **take —** encargarse; **in —** encargado
chat conversar
chauffeur chofer *m*
cheap barato
cheerful alegre
cheese queso
chemical químico
chemistry química
chicken pollo; gallina (hen)
child niño, niña; hijo, hija
Chilean chileno
choose escoger; elegir (i); optar (por)
chop picar
church iglesia
cigarette cigarro, cigarrillo
circulate circular
circumstance circunstancia
citizen ciudadano
city ciudad *f*
civic cívico
civilization civilización *f*
civilize civilizar
clarinet clarinete *m*
class clase *f*
clause cláusula
clean limpiar; limpio
cleaner: **dry —'s shop** tintorería
clear claro
close cerrar (ie)
close **(to)** cerca (de); **pay — attention** poner mucha atención
closer: **bring —** estrechar

clothes ropa
cloud nube *f*
club club *m*
coast costa
coat abrigo
Coca Cola Coca-Cola
coffee café *m;* **— shop** cafetería
cold frío; **to be —** (weather) hacer frío; **to be (feel) —** tener frío; resfrío (illness)
collect cobrar
collector cobrador *m*
college universidad *f; adj* universitario
Colombian colombiano
colonel coronel *m*
colony colonia
colossus coloso
Columbus Colón
comb peinar; **— one's hair** peinarse
come venir (ie, i) (31); **— about** ocurrir; **— back** regresar, volver (ue); **how is (he) coming along?** ¿cómo sigue (él)?
comfort confort *m*
comfortably cómodamente
command mando; imperativo (grammatical)
comment comentar; comentario
commit cometer
commonly comúnmente
Communism comunismo
community comunidad *f; adj* comunal
companion compañero
comparison comparación *f*
complain quejarse
complaint queja
complement complemento
compose componer (23)
conceive concebir (i)
concentrate concentrar
concentration concentración *f*
concept concepto
concert concierto
conditional condicional
condolence pésame *m*
conduct conducta
confess confesar (ie)
confidence confianza
conflict conflicto
confuse confundir

conglomeration conglomeración *f*
congratulate felicitar
congress congreso
consequently por consiguiente; consecuentemente; por consecuencia
consider considerar
consolation consuelo
consonant consonante *f*
constant constante
constitute constituir
construction construcción *f*
contain contener (ie) (28)
continent continente *m*
continually continuamente
continuously continuamente
contract contraer (29)
contraction contracción *f*
contradict contradecir (16)
contrast contraste *m;* **in —** en cambio
contribute contribuir
control controlar; control *m*
controversy controversia
convenience comodidad *f*
conversation conversación *f*
convert convertir (ie, i); **be — to** convertirse en
convertible convertible
convince convencer
cook cocinar; cocinero, cocinera
cooperation cooperación *f*
corner rincón *m* (of room); esquina (of street)
correct correcto
corresponding correspondiente
cost costar (ue); costo
Costa Rican costarricense; tico (nickname)
count contar (ue)
country país *m;* campo
countryside campo
coup d'état golpe de estado *m*
course (class) curso; **—** (of an evening, etc.) transcurso; **of —** cómo no, claro
cousin primo, prima; **first —** primo hermano
cover tapar, cubrir
cow vaca
crazy loco; **go —** volverse loco
create crear
creditor acreedor *m*
crew tripulación *f*

crime delito
cross cruzar
cry llorar
cultivate cultivar
cultural cultural
culture cultura
cup taza
curiosity curiosidad *f*
curious curioso
curse maldecir (16, but *pp* maldecido)
custom costumbre *f*
customer cliente *m*
cut cortar
cute simpático

D

dad papá *m*
daily diario
dance baile *m*
dangerous peligroso
date fecha; cita (appointment); **make a —** citarse
daughter hija
day día *m*
deal: a great — mucho
dean decano
dear querido, estimado, recordado
dearest adorado, queridísimo
death muerte *f*
debt deuda
decade década
deceive engañar
December diciembre *m*
decent decente
decide decidir
declare declarar
decompose descomponer (23)
defect defecto
definite definido
delayed: be — atrasarse
delicious delicioso
demand exigir; exigencia
democratic democrático
demonstration demostración *f;* manifestación *f*
demonstrative demostrativo
depart partir
department departamento
depend (on) depender (de)
derive provenir (ie, i) (31)
descriptive descriptivo

desire desear; ganas *f pl*
desolate desolado
despair desesperación *f*
desperate desesperado
despite a pesar de
dessert postre *m*
detail detalle *m*
detain detener (ie) (28)
develop desarrollar
dialog diálogo
dictate dictar
dictator dictador *m*
dictatorial dictatorial
dictatorship dictadura
die morir (ue, u)
difference diferencia
different distinto, diferente
differentiate diferenciar
difficulty dificultad *f*
dignity dignidad *f*
dining room comedor *m*
dinner comida
diplomatic diplomático
direct dirigir; directo
disappear desaparecer (14)
disappointed decepcionado
discover descubrir
discoverer descubridor *m*
discovery descubrimiento
discuss discutir
dish plato
displease disgustar
distance distancia
distrust desconfianza
divide dividir
divine divino
divorce divorcio; **get a —** divorciarse
do hacer (19)
doctor médico; doctor *m*
dog perro
dollar dólar *m*
dominate dominar
door puerta
dormitory dormitorio
dot: on the — en punto
doubt duda; **without a —, no — ** sin duda
downtown centro
draw (out) extender (ie)
dream soñar (ue); sueño
dress vestir (i); vestido
drink beber, tomar; **soft —** refresco
drive manejar

driver automovilista *m;* chofer
  m; **taxi —** taxista *m*
drought sequía
drum tambor *m;* **set of —s**
  batería
duel duelo
dull apagado
dumb tonto
dumbbell tonto
during durante
dust polvo
duty deber *m;* **to do (my) —**
  cumplir con (mi) deber

E

each cada; **— other** el uno al
  otro
ear oído (inner); oreja (outer)
earache dolor de oídos
early temprano
earn ganar
easily con facilidad;
  cómodamente
Easter Pascuas; **— Week**
  Semana Santa
eat comer
educational educativo
educator educador *m*
effectively eficazmente
efficient eficiente
effort esfuerzo
effusiveness efusión *f*
egg huevo
eight ocho
eighteen dieciocho
eighth octavo
eight hundred ochocientos
eighty ochenta
either o; ni; tampoco (after
  negative)
elastic elástico
elect elegir (i)
electrician electricista *m*
electricity electricidad *f*
elegant elegante
eleven once
else más
elude eludir
embassy embajada
emerge surgir
emotion emoción *f*
empirical empírico
employee empleado, empleada

empty vacío; **— table** mesa
  desocupada
enchant encantar
end terminar; acabar
English inglés *m; adj* inglés,
  -esa
English speaker inglés-hablante
  m
enjoy disfrutar; gozar (de)
enormous enorme
enter entrar
enterprising emprendedor, -ra
entertain entretener (ie) (28)
enthusiasm entusiasmo
entire entero
environment ambiente *m*
envy envidiar
epoch época
equal igual
equality igualdad *f*
era era
erroneous erróneo
error error *m*
especially especialmente
essentially esencialmente
establish establecer (14)
Europe Europa
European europeo
even parejo; hasta; **not —** ni
  (siquiera); **— though** aunque
evening tarde *f;* noche *f;* **good**
  — buenas noches
event acontecimiento
ever siempre; jamás (after
  negative); nunca (after
  negative)
every todos; cada (each)
everybody todo el mundo; todos
everyone todo el mundo; todos
everything todo
everywhere por todas partes; en
  todas partes
exact exacto
exaggerate exagerar
exam examen *m*
examine examinar
example ejemplo
excellent excelente
except exceptuar; excepto
exception excepción *f*
exclaim exclamar
excuse excusa
exercise ejercicio
exhibit exposición *f*
exile exilio

exist existir
existence existencia
expense gasto
expensive caro
explain explicar
explanation explicación *f*
explorer explorador *m*
export exportación *f*
express expresar
expression expresión *f*
extension extensión *f*
extreme extremo; *adj* extremado
eye ojo
eyeglasses gafas

F

fabric tela
face enfrentarse; cara; **in the —**
  of ante
facility facilidad *f*
fact hecho, dato
factor factor *m*
faint desmayarse
fall caída; otoño (season)
fame fama
family familia
famous famoso
far lejos; **— from** lejos de
farewell: say — despedirse (i)
farm finca
farmer agricultor *m*
fast *adj* rápido, veloz; *adv*
  rápidamente
fat gordo
father padre *m*
fatherland patria
favor favor *m*
fear temor *m;* miedo
feat hazaña
feature aspecto
February febrero
fed: be — up estar hasta la
  coronilla
feel sentir (ie, i); **— like** tener
  ganas (de)
feeling sentimiento; sentido
fellow chico
few pocos, pocas
ficticious ficticio
field campo
fifteen quince
fifth quinto
fifty cincuenta

figure figura; cifra
filial filial
film película
finally finalmente; por fin
financial económico
find encontrar (ue); — **out** averiguar
fine bien
finger dedo
fire despedir (i)
firm firma
first primero; — **cousin** primo hermano
five cinco
five hundred quinientos
flat plano
flirt flirtear
flood inundación *f*
floor piso
flower flor *f*
follow seguir (i)
following siguiente
food comida
fool tonto
foot pie *m*
footstep paso
for por; para
force fuerza
foreign extranjero
forget olvidar, olvidarse de
fork tenedor *m*
form formar; forma
formal formal
formality formalidad *f*
formation formación *f*
former aquél; *adj* antiguo
formidable formidable
formula fórmula
forth: and so — etcétera
fortunate afortunado
forty cuarenta
found fundar
four cuatro
four hundred cuatrocientos
fourteen catorce
fourth cuarto
fraternity fraternidad *f*
free gratis; libre
freedom libertad *f*
French francés *m; adj* francés, -esa
Frenchman francés *m*
frequent frecuente
frequently frecuentemente; a menudo

fresh fresco; atrevido (bold)
Friday viernes *m*
friend amigo, amiga
friendship amistad *f*
from de; desde; — **(table) to (table)** de (mesa) en (mesa)
front: in — of delante de, enfrente de; frente a
fruit fruta
fry freír
frying pan sartén *f*
full lleno
fun alegría
furious furioso
future porvenir *m;* futuro

G

gamble jugar (ue)
gap abismo
garden jardín *m*
gardener jardinero
garlic ajo
gather reunir(se)
gathering reunión *f*
gender género
general general
generally por lo general
generic genérico
generous generoso
genius genio
Genoa Génova
gentleman señor *m;* caballero
geographical geográfico
geography geografía
German alemán *m;* alemán, -ana
Germanic germánico
Germany Alemania
gesture gesto
get conseguir (i); obtener (ie) (28); recibir; — **off (a bus)** bajar; — **ready** alistarse; — **somewhere** llegar; — **up** levantarse
girl muchacha, chica; **little —** niña
girlfriend amiga; novia
give dar (15); regalar
glad: be — alegrarse
gladly con mucho gusto
glass vaso
glove guante *m*

go ir (20); andar (12); — **all out** echar la casa por la ventana; — **around** andar; — **away** irse; — **in** entrar; — **on** seguir (i); — **out** salir; — **through the light** pasarse la luz
God Dios *m*
godfather padrino
godmother madrina
godson ahijado
golden dorado
good bueno
good-bye adiós; **say —** despedirse (i)
government gobierno
gown traje *m;* **wedding —** traje de boda
grammar gramática; *adj* gramatical
granddaughter nieta
grandmother abuela
granny abuelita
grape uva
gray gris
great grande
greater mayor
green verde
greens verduras
greet saludar
greeting saludo
ground molido
group grupo
grow crecer (14)
Guatemalan guatemalteco; chapín *m* (nickname)
guest invitado
guitar guitarra
guy tipo

H

habit hábito; costumbre *f*
hacienda hacienda
haggle regatear
hair pelo
half mitad *f; adj* medio
hand mano *f;* **on the other —** en cambio; por otra parte
happen ocurrir, pasar
happy alegre, contento, feliz
hard duro
hardly apenas
hard-working trabajador, -ra

haste prisa
hat sombrero
hate detestar; odio
have tener; haber; —
    (something to eat) tomar;
    one has to (study) hay que
    (estudiar); to have to
    (leave) tener que (salir)
he él
head cabeza; jefe *m* (leader)
hear oír
heart corazón *m;* by — de
    memoria
heat calentar (ie); calor *m*
height altura
hello aló
help ayudar; ayuda
hemisphere hemisferio
hence de ahí
her la; le; ella; su
here aquí
hers suyo
herself se
hesitation cavilación *f*
hi hola
hide esconder
high alto; — up arriba
high school colegio, (escuela)
    secundaria; — student
    estudiante secundario
highway camino
him lo; le; él
himself se
hint indirecta
his su; suyo
historical histórico
history historia
holiday feriado
home casa; be — estar en
    casa; go — ir a casa
homely feo
homesick: be — estar con mal
    de patria
Honduran hondureño
honest honrado
hope esperar; esperanza
horse caballo
hot caliente; picante (spicy); to
    be — (weather) hacer
    calor; to be (feel) — tener
    calor
house casa
household hogar *m*
housewife ama de casa
housing vivienda

how cómo; — much cuánto;
    — many cuántos; — (nice)!
    ¡qué (bueno)!
however sin embargo
hug abrazo
human humano
humble humilde
humidity humedad *f*
humor humor *m*
hundred ciento
hunger hambre *f*
hungry: be — tener hambre
hurry: to be in a — tener prisa;
    estar de prisa
hurt resentido
husband marido; esposo

I

I yo
Iberian ibérico
idea idea
ideal ideal
identify identificar
if si; even — aunque
ill grave; enfermo
illegitimate ilegítimo
illness mal *m*
illogical ilógico
imagine imaginarse
imitate imitar
immediate inmediato
immigrant inmigrante *m*
impenetrable impenetrable
imperfect imperfecto
impersonal impersonal
importance importancia
important importante; to be
    — importar
impose imponer (23)
impossible imposible
impression impresión *f*
impressive impresionante
impulse impulso
in en; de (after superlative)
inasmuch as como
incidentally a propósito
increase aumentar
independence independencia
independent independiente
Indian indio
indication indicación *f*
indicative indicativo
indirect indirecto

individual individuo
individualism individualismo
individualistic individualista
industry industria
inexact inexacto
inexpensive barato
inevitable inevitable
infinite infinito
infinitive infinitivo
inform avisar
information información *f*
ingredient ingrediente *m*
inhabitant habitante *m*
initial inicial
initiate iniciar
inside dentro (de)
insist insistir
insolent insolente
install instalar
instance ocasión *f;* for — por
    ejemplo
instead en vez de
institution institución *f*
intelligent inteligente
intend pensar (ie)
intense intenso
interest interés *m*
interested: become — (in)
    interesarse (en)
interesting interesante
interior interior
interminable interminable
interrogative interrogativo
interrupt interrumpir
intervene intervenir (ie, i) (31)
intervention intervención *f*
introduce presentar
investigation investigación *f*
invitation invitación *f*
invite invitar
iron planchar; hierro
irregular irregular
island isla
it lo, la; él, ella
Italian italiano
Italy Italia
its su

J

jail cárcel *f*
January enero
Japan (el) Japón
jealous celoso

job oficio; empleo
join unirse (a)
jointly conjuntamente
joke bromear; chiste *m;* broma
judge juzgar; juez *m*
judgment juicio
juice jugo
July julio
jump saltar
June junio
jungle selva
junta junta
just justo; nada más; **to have —**
(**gone out**) acabar de (salir)

K

keep mantener (ie) (28)
kill matar
kilogram kilo
kilometer kilómetro
kind amable; especie *f,* clase *f*
king rey *m*
kiss besar; beso
kitchen cocina
knife cuchillo
know saber (25); conocer (14)
knowledge conocimiento

L

labor trabajo
lack faltar; falta
lady señora; **young —** señorita
lake lago
land tierra
language lengua, idioma *m;*
lenguaje *m*
large grande
largely en gran parte
last durar
last último; **— name** apellido;
at — por fin; **— night**
anoche; **— week** la semana
pasada
late tarde
Latin latín *m;* latino
Latin America la América
Latina, Latinoamérica
Latin American
latinoamericano
laundress lavandera

law ley *f;* **— school** facultad
de derecho
lawyer abogado
lead dirigir; **— a life** llevar
una vida
learn aprender
least menor; **at —** al menos,
por lo menos
leave salir (26); irse (20)
lecture conferencia
left izquierda; *adj* izquierdo
leg pierna
legal legal
legendary legendario
lend prestar
length longitud *f*
lesson lección *f*
let dejar
letter carta; letra, carácter *m*
(of the alphabet)
lettuce lechuga
level nivel *m*
liberator libertador *m*
library biblioteca
license licencia; **driver's —**
licencia de manejar
lie mentira
lieutenant teniente *m*
life vida
light encender (ie); luz *f*
like: (I) — these (me) gustan
estos
like como; **— that** así
limit limitar
linguistic lingüístico
Lisbon Lisboa
listen escuchar
liter litro
literature literatura
little poco; **— by —** poco a
poco; pequeño
live vivir; *adj* vivo
living *adj* residente; **— room**
sala
local local
located situado
long largo; **how —** cuánto
tiempo; **so —** hasta luego
look parecer (14); **— after**
atender (ie), guardar; **— at**
mirar; **— for** buscar; **they**
— alike son parecidos
lose perder (ie)
lot: a — mucho
lottery lotería

love querer (ie) (24); amor *m;* **in**
— with enamorado de
low bajo
loyalty lealtad *f*
luck suerte *f*
lucky dichoso; afortunado; con
suerte
lunch almuerzo
luxury lujo

M

mad: get — enojarse; resentir
(ie, i)
magazine revista
maid criada
maiden: — aunt tía soltera
mailman cartero
main principal
maintain mantener (ie) (28)
maintenance mantención *f*
major mayor *m*
majority mayoría
make hacer (19)
man hombre *m*
mango mango
mankind humanidad *f*
manner manera; trato; **in (this)**
— de (esta) manera
manual manual
many muchos
March marzo
marimba marimba
market mercado
marriage casamiento
marry casarse (con)
marvelous maravilloso
mass masa
master señor *m*
mathematics matemáticas *f pl*
matter importar; asunto;
cuestión *f;* **what's the —?**
¿qué pasa?
maybe tal vez
me me; mí
mean significar; malo
meaning significado
means medio
meantime: in the — mientras
tanto
measure medir (i)
meat carne *f*
mechanical mecánico
meddle meterse

Mediterranean Mediterráneo
meet conocer (14); recibir
memory memoria
mention mención *f*
mess desastre *m*
method método
Mexican mexicano
middle medio
midnight medianoche *f*
migratory migratorio
military militar
milk leche *f*
milkman lechero
million millón *m*
mine mi; mío
miniature miniatura
minimum mínimo
minister ministro
minute minuto
miss señorita
missionary misionero
mister señor
mobility movilidad *f*
modern moderno
modest modesto
modify modificar
moment momento
monarch monarca *m*
Monday lunes *m*
money dinero
month mes *m*
monthly mensual
morals moral *f*
more más
morning mañana; **good —**
   buenos días
mortality mortalidad *f*
most la mayor parte
mother madre *f*
mother-in-law suegra
motive motivo
mountain montaña
mouth boca; **make (his) —**
   water hacer(le) la boca
   agua
move mover(se) (ue); mudarse
   (de casa) (to another
   house)
moved: be — conmoverse (ue)
movies cine *m*
much mucho; **how —?**
   ¿cuánto?
municipal municipal
must deber
myself me

N

nail clavar
name nombrar; nombre *m;* **last**
   — apellido; **(my) — is**
   (me) llam(o)
napkin servilleta
nation nación *f*
nationalism nacionalismo
nationalistic nacionalista
nationality nacionalidad *f*
native nativo
naturally naturalmente
nature naturaleza
navigation navegación *f*
near cerca (de)
nearly casi
necessary necesario; **it is —**
   hay que (followed by
   infinitive)
need necesitar
negative negativo
neighborhood barrio
neither tampoco; **— . . . nor**
   ni... ni
nephew sobrino
never nunca
new nuevo
news noticias; noticia (item)
newspaper periódico
New York Nueva York
next próximo; **— to (him)** a
   (su) lado
nice simpático; **how —** ¡qué
   bien!
nickname apodo
niece sobrina
night noche *f;* **last —** anoche;
   — before last anteanoche
nine nueve
nine hundred novecientos
nineteen diecinueve
ninety noventa
ninth noveno
no no; ninguno
nobody nadie, ninguno
nominalization substantivación *f*
none ninguno
nonsense tontería
no one nadie, ninguno
norm norma
normal normal
north norte *m*
North American norteamericano
nose nariz *f*

not no
note notar
notebook cuaderno
notes apuntes *m pl*
nothing nada
notice notar; fijarse (en); **give**
   — avisar
noun substantivo; **— clause**
   cláusula substantiva
November noviembre *m*
now ahora
nowadays hoy en día
number número
numerous numeroso
nursemaid niñera

O

obedience obediencia
obey obedecer (14)
obligate obligar
obscure obscuro
observe observar
obtain obtener (ie) (28)
obvious obvio
occident occidente *m*
occupy ocupar
occur ocurrir
o'clock: it is (two) — son las
   (dos); **it is one —** es la una
October octubre *m*
of de
offer ofrecer (14)
office oficina
officer oficial *m*
official funcionario; *adj* oficial
oil aceite *m*
okay bien; **if it's — (with you)**
   si (te) parece bien
old viejo
oligarchy oligarquía
on en, sobre
once una vez
one uno
onion cebolla
only solamente, sólo, nada más;
   único; **not — . . . but also**
   no sólo... sino también
open abrir; abierto
opinion opinión *f;* **to venture**
   an — opinar
opponent oponente *m*
opportunity oportunidad *f*
oppose oponer (23)

optimism optimismo
or o
orange anaranjado (color); naranja (fruit)
order pedir (i); **in — to** para
ordinal ordinal
ordinary corriente
organize organizar
orient oriente *m*
originate (in) provenir (de) (ie, i) (31)
ostentation ostentación *f*
other otro
our nuestro
ours nuestro
outdoors al aire libre
outing paseo
outside fuera (de)
outskirts afueras *f pl*
over sobre; más (more); — **there** allá
overcoat abrigo
overthrow destituir, derrocar
ow! ¡ay!
owe deber
own tener (ie) (28); propio
owner dueño
ox buey *m*

P

pain dolor *m*
pair par *m*
pan: frying — sartén *f*
Panama Panamá; **— Canal** Canal de Panamá
Panamanian panameño
pants pantalones *m pl*
paper papel *m;* periódico (newspaper)
paragraph párrafo
Paraguayan paraguayo
parallel paralelo
parcel parcela
parent madre *f,* padre *m;* —s padres
park parque *m*
part parte *f*
particle partícula
particularly especialmente, particularmente
party fiesta; partido (political)
pass pasar
passage pasaje *m*

past pasado; (five) — (twelve) las (doce) y (cinco)
patience paciencia
patron patrón *m*
pay pagar; — **attention** poner atención, hacer caso; — **a visit** hacer una visita
payment pago
peace paz *f*
peanuts maní *m*
pear pera
peasant campesino
pen pluma
pencil lápiz *m*
peon peón *m*
people gente *f;* pueblo
pepper pimienta; chile *m;* ají *m*
percentage porcentaje *m*
perhaps tal vez
period época, período
perseverance perseverancia
person persona
personal personal
Peru (el) Perú
phenomenon fenómeno
phone teléfono
phrase frase *f*
physics física
piano piano
picnic paseo; picnic *m*
picture cuadro
picturesque pintoresco
piece pedazo
pig cerdo
pity lástima
place lugar *m*
plan plan *m*
plane avión *m*
plantation plantación *f*
plate plato
play jugar (ue) (game); tocar (music)
pleasant agradable; simpático
please gustar; por favor
plenty mucho
plus más; y
point punto; — **of view** punto de vista; — **out** señalar
political político
politics política
pool piscina
poor pobre
poorly mal
population población *f*
port puerto

Portuguese portugués *m; adj* portugués, -esa
position posición *f*
possessive posesivo
possibility posibilidad *f*
possible posible
postpone posponer (23)
potato papa
pound libra
power poder *m*
practically prácticamente
practice práctica
prairie llanura
precisely precisamente
predecessor predecesor *m*
prepare preparar
preposition preposición *f*
present presentar; *adj* presente, actual; actualidad *f;* — (tense) presente *m;* — **perfect (tense)** antepresente *m*
president presidente *m*
press planchar
prestige prestigio
pretend aparentar
preterit pretérito
pretext pretexto
pretty bonito
prevail prevalecer (14)
prevailing prevaleciente
prevent prevenir (ie, i) (31)
price precio
principal principal
privilege privilegio
privileged privilegiado
probability probabilidad *f*
probably probablemente
problem problema *m*
produce producir
product producto
professor profesor, profesora
progress progreso
progressive progresivo
project proyecto
prominent prominente
promise prometer; promesa
pronoun pronombre *m*
pronounce pronunciar
pronunciation pronunciación *f*
propose proponer (23)
protection protección *f*
protest protestar
proverb refrán *m*
provide proveer

provided that con tal que
province provincia
provoke provocar
psychology psicología
punctuality puntualidad *f*
punishment castigo
purple morado
purpose fin *m;* **for the — of**
  para
purse cartera
push empujar
put poner (23); **— in** meter; **—
  on (clothing)** ponerse

Q

quality calidad *f;* cualidad *f*
quarter cuarto
queen reina; **the king and —**
  los reyes
question pregunta; cuestión *f;*
  frase interrogativa
quite bastante

R

radio radio *f* (broadcast); radio
  m (apparatus)
rain llover (ue)
raincoat impermeable *m*
rainfall lluvia
rapid rápido
rare raro
rate: at any — de todos modos,
  de cualquier modo
rather mejor dicho; **— than** en
  vez de
reach llegar
reaction reacción *f*
read leer
ready listo; **get —** alistarse
reality realidad *f*
realization realización *f*
realize darse cuenta de
really de veras; realmente
reason razón *f;* motivo
reasonable razonable
reasoning razonamiento
rebel rebelar
rebellion rebelión *f*
recipe receta
recognize reconocer (14)
recourse recurso, remedio

red rojo
reduction rebaja
reflexive reflexivo
refuge refugio; **take —**
  refugiarse
regard recuerdo
regime régimen *m*
region región *f*
regret sentir (ie, i)
regular regular
reject rechazar
relating (to) relativo (a)
relation relación *f*
relationship relación *f*
relative pariente *m; adj* relativo
relaxed relajado
religion religión *f*
remain quedar (to be left);
  quedarse (to stay)
remember recordar (ue)
remind recordar (ue)
repeat repetir (i)
repetition repetición *f*
replace reponer (23)
reply responder; respuesta
represent representar
representative representante *m*
republic república
require requerir (ie, i); pedir (i)
resemblance semejanza
resign renunciar
resource recurso
respect respetar; respeto
  (esteem or regard); **in this
  —** a este respecto; **with —
  to** respecto a
respectable respetable
respective respectivo
responsibility responsabilidad *f*
responsible responsable
rest descansar; resto
result resultar; resultado
retain retener (ie) (28)
return regresar, volver (ue);
  devolver (ue) (give back an
  object)
review repaso
rhythm ritmo
rice arroz *m*
rich rico
right derecha; derecho (privilege); *adj* derecho; **be —**
  tener razón; **— away** ahora
  mismo; **turn —** doblar a
  la derecha

riot disturbio
ripe maduro
river río
road camino
robber bandido
rock piedra
role papel *m*
Roman romano
romance romance
romantic romántico
roof techo
room cuarto
rooster gallo
round redondo
route ruta
routine *adj* rutinario
rule regla
ruling *adj* dominador, -ra
rumor rumor *m*
run correr
running corriente
rural rural

S

sad triste
sail navegar
sailor marinero
saint santo, santa; **—'s day** día
  del santo, santo
sake: for Pete's — caramba
salad ensalada
salary sueldo
salty salado
Salvadoran salvadoreño
same igual, mismo; **in the —
  way** de la misma manera;
  the — as igual a, igual que
sandwich sandwich *m*
satisfied contento
Saturday sábado
sauce salsa
savage salvaje *m*
save salvar
say decir (i) (16) **that is to —**
  es decir
saying dicho
Scandinavian escandinavo
scarce escaso
scene escena
scholarship beca
school escuela; **high —**
  colegio, (escuela) secundaria
scientifically científicamente

scoundrel canalla *m*
sea mar *m*
seaman marinero
seamstress costurera
seaport puerto
search buscar; busca
season estación *f*
seat sentar (ie); asiento
second segundo
secondary secundario
see ver (32); **I'll — you** chao
seek buscar
seem parecer (14)
seize usurpar
select elegir (i)
-self mismo; **(him) —** (él) mismo
sell vender
semester semestre *m*
send mandar
sensational sensacional
sentence frase *f*
sentimental sentimental
sentimentalism sentimentalismo
separate separar
September septiembre *m*
sergeant sargento
serious serio
servant sirviente, sirvienta
serve servir (i)
service servicio
set: — the table poner la mesa
settle establecerse (14)
settler colonizador *m*
seven siete
seventeen diecisiete
seventh séptimo
seventy setenta
several varios
sex sexo
shack choza
shade sombra; **in the —** a la sombra
share compartir
shave afeitarse
she ella
ship barco
shipwrecked: be — naufragar
shirt camisa
shoe zapato; **— store** zapatería
shoemaker zapatero
shoeshine boy limpiabotas *m sing*
shopping: go — ir (andar) de compras

short corto; bajo (stature); pequeño (small); **in —** en fin, en breve
shorten acortar
shortening acortamiento
shout gritar
shouting griterío
show mostrar (ue)
shrimp camarón *m*
shut up callarse
sick enfermo, grave
side lado
sight divisar; vista
sign muestra; **stop —** alto
signal señal *f*
silly tonto
silverware cubiertos
similar parecido
simple simple
simply simplemente
since pues; ya que
sing cantar
single solo; soltero (unmarried)
sir señor
sister hermana
sit sentarse (ie)
sitting sentado
situated situado
situation situación *f*
six seis
six hundred seiscientos
sixteen dieciséis
sixth sexto
sixty sesenta
skill pericia, habilidad *f*
sky cielo
sleep sueño
sleepy: be — tener sueño
slender delgado
slightest menor
slim flaco
small pequeño
smart-aleck chistoso
smile sonreír; sonrisa
smoke fumar; humo
snow nevar (ie); nieve *f*
so así; **— and —** tal por cual; **— called** llamado; **— long** hasta luego; **— much** tanto; **— that** para que; **— they say** según dicen
soap jabón *m*
social social
society sociedad *f*
socio-economic socio-económico

sociologist sociólogo
sock calcetín *m*
soft suave
some alguno
somebody alguien, alguno
someone alguien, alguno
something algo
sometimes algunas veces, a veces, unas veces
son hijo
soon pronto
sorry: to be — sentir (ie, i)
sort estilo; **and of the —** y por el estilo
soul alma
sound sonido
soup sopa
south sur *m*
southern sur, al sur
Spain España
Spanish español *m; adj* español, -la; **— America** Hispanoamérica; **— American** hispano-americano
spare: to — de sobra
speak hablar
speech lenguaje *m;* discurso
spell escribir; **the word is —ed** la palabra se escribe
spelling ortografía; *adj* ortográfico
spend pasar (time); gastar (money)
spite: in — of a pesar de
splendorous esplendoroso
sponsor patrocinar
spoon cucharita (teaspoon); cuchara (tablespoon)
spot sitio (place)
spring primavera
stability estabilidad *f*
stage etapa
stand estar de pie; aguantar (tolerate)
standing de pie; **social —** status social
stand (someone) up dejar plantado (a alguien)
start empezar (ie), comenzar (ie); ponerse a; principio; **from the —** desde un principio
starve morirse de hambre
state estado

statistic estadística
stay quedarse
steal robar
step paso
stick palo
still todavía
stinking cochino
stocking media
stomach estómago
stop detener(se) (ie) (28), parar-
    (se); — **sign** alto
store tienda
story cuento, historia
straight derecho
strange extraño
street calle *f*
stressed acentuado
strict estricto
strike huelga; **on** — en huelga
strong fuerte
struggle lucha
student estudiante; alumno,
    alumna
study estudiar; estudio
stupid estúpido
subdivide subdividir
subject sujeto (grammatical);
    school — materia
subjective subjetivo
subjunctive subjuntivo
subordinate subordinario; *adj*
    subordinado
subordination subordinación *f*
success éxito
such (a) tal
suddenly de repente
suffer sufrir
suffering mal *m*
sufficiently suficientemente
suffix sufijo
sugar azúcar *m*
suggest sugerir (ie, i)
suit convenir (ie, i) (31); traje *m*
suitable: be — convenir (ie, i)
    (31)
suitor pretendiente *m*
sullenly de mala gana
summer verano
Sunday domingo
supper cena
support apoyo
suppression supresión *f*
sure seguro; cómo no
surprise sorprender
swear jurar

sweep barrer
sweet dulce
sweetheart novio, novia
swimming: — **pool** piscina
syllable sílaba
synonymous sinónimo
system sistema *m*

T

table mesa
tablecloth mantel *m*
tablespoon cuchara
tact tacto
tailor sastre *m;* — **shop**
    sastrería
take tomar; — **charge**
    encargarse; — **out** sacar
talk hablar, conversar
tall alto
task tarea
taste saber; probar (ue)
tax impuesto
taxi taxi *m;* — **driver** taxista *m*
tea té *m*
teach enseñar
teacher maestro, maestra
teaspoon cucharita
technical técnico
tell decir (i) (16) — **time** decir
    la hora
temporarily temporalmente
ten diez
tend tender (ie)
tendency tendencia
tennis tenis *m*
tense tiempo; *adj* tenso
tenth décimo
term término
terrible terrible
terrific fenomenal
territorial territorial
than que; de
that ese, esa; aquel, aquella;
    ése, ésa; aquél, aquélla; eso;
    aquello; que; — **is to say**
    es decir; —**'s why** por eso
the el, la, los, las
their su
theirs suyo
them los, las; les; ellos, ellas
theme tema *m*
themselves se
then entonces, luego

there allí; — **is,** — **are** hay
therefore por consiguiente, por
    eso
these estos, estas; éstos, éstas
thesis tesis *f*
they ellos, ellas
thin delgado
thing cosa; **how are** —**s?** ¿qué
    tal?
think pensar (ie)
third tercero
thirst sed *f*
thirsty: be — tener sed
thirteen trece
thirty treinta; media (telling
    time): **two** — las dos y
    media
this este, esta; éste, ésta; esto
those esos, esas; aquellos,
    aquellas; ésos, ésas; aquéllos,
    aquéllas
though: even — aunque
thousand mil
three tres
three hundred trescientos
throat garganta; **sore** — dolor
    de garganta
through a través de; por; **go** —
    (the light) pasarse (la luz)
throw echar
Thursday jueves *m*
thus así, así pues
ticket: lottery — pedacito de
    lotería
tie corbata
till hasta
time tiempo; vez *f;* **at a** —
    a la vez; **at** —**s** a
    veces; **in** — con el
    tiempo; **on** — a tiempo;
    what — **is it?** ¿qué hora
    es?
tin lata
tiny diminuto
tired cansado; **get** — cansarse
to a
today hoy, hoy día
together junto con; juntos
tomato tomate *m*
tomorrow mañana; —
    (morning) mañana por
    (la mañana)
too demasiado; — **much**
    demasiado; — **many**
    demasiados

tooth diente *m;* muela (molar)
toothache dolor de muelas
top: on — of encima (de)
touch tocar
touchy delicado
toward hacia
towel toalla
town pueblo
trade comercio
tradition tradición *f*
traffic tráfico, tránsito
train tren *m*
tranquillity tranquilidad *f*
transition transición *f*
trap atrapar
treat tratar
tree árbol *m*
trend tendencia
trivial trivial
tropical tropical
tropics trópico
trouble pena; dificultad; **the —
is** lo malo es; **to be worth
the —** valer la pena
true verdadero; **it is —** es
verdad, es cierto
trumpet trompeta
truth verdad *f*
try tratar (de); probar (ue)
Tuesday martes *m*
tune afinar
turn doblar; **to — out** resultar
twelve doce
twenty veinte
twin gemelo, gemela
twist torcer (ue)
two dos
two hundred doscientos
typical típico

U

ugly feo
umbrella paraguas *m sing*
uncle tío
under bajo; debajo de
undergo sufrir
underline subrayar
understand comprender,
entender (ie)
understandable comprensible
undesirable indeseable
undoubtedly indiscutiblemente
uneven disparejo

unfortunate desafortunado
unfortunately desgraciadamente
ungrateful ingrato
unite unir
United States Estados
Unidos
university universidad *f; adj*
universitario
unless a menos que
unlike al contrario de
unmarried soltero
unpleasant antipático
unripe verde
unspecified no especificado
unstressed inacentuado
until hasta; hasta que
up arriba; **— to** hasta
urban urbano
us nos; nosotros
use usar; uso
used to acostumbrado
(accustomed)
usefulness utilidad *f*
usual corriente; acostumbrado;
as — de costumbre
utilize utilizar

V

vacation vacaciones *f pl*
vegetation vegetación *f*
vender vendedor *m*
Venezuelan venezolano
verb verbo; *adj* verbal
very muy
vice vicio
victim víctima
view vista
violin violín *m*
Virgin Islands Islas Vírgenes
virtue virtud *f*
visit visitar; visita; **to pay a —**
hacer una visita
visiting: to be — estar de visita
visitor visita; visitante *m*
vote voto
vowel vocal *f*
voyage viaje *m*

W

wait esperar; **— on** atender (ie)

waitress mesera
walk andar (12), caminar
wall pared *f*
wallet cartera
want querer (ie) (24)
war guerra
warn advertir (ie, i); prevenir
(ie, i) (31)
warning advertencia *f*
wash lavar; **get —ed** lavarse
waste desperdiciar
watch mirar; reloj *m*
water agua
wave ola
way manera, modo; **by the —**
a propósito; **in this —** de
esta manera; **this —** para
acá; **that —** para allá; **—
over there** allá lejos
weapon arma; **—s** armamentos
weaver tejedor *m*
wedding boda
Wednesday miércoles *m*
week semana
welcome: you're — de nada
well bien
what qué, cuál; lo que (that
which); **— else?** ¿qué
más? **— for?** ¿para qué?
whatever cualquier, cualquiera
when cuando; cuándo
whenever cuando
where donde; dónde
wherever donde
whether si
which cuál; qué; que
while rato; **a little —** un poco;
mientras, mientras que
white blanco
who quién; que
whom quién; quien; que
whose cuyo; de quién
why por qué
wide ancho
wife esposa, mujer
willing dispuesto
win ganar
wind viento
window ventana
windy: it is — hace viento
wine vino
winter invierno
wish deseo; **I —** ojalá
with con
without sin; sin que

woman mujer *f;* **young —** señorita
wonder: and no — y con razón
wool lana
word palabra
work trabajar; trabajo
worker obrero
world mundo; *adj* mundial
worn out gastado
worried preocupado
worry preocuparse
worse peor
worst peor
worth: be — valer (30)

write escribir
writer escritor *m*
writing escritura

Y

year año
yellow amarillo
yes sí
yesterday ayer; **day before —** anteayer
yet todavía
you tú, vosotros, usted, ustedes;

te, os, lo, la, los, las; te, os, le, les; ti, vosotros, usted, ustedes
young joven
your tu, vuestro, su
yours tuyo, vuestro, suyo
yourself te, se; *pl* os, se
youth juventud *f*

Z

zero cero
zone zona

Spanish-English Vocabulary

A

a to; at
abajo below
abierto, -a open; *pp of* **abrir**
abogado lawyer
abrazo embrace, hug
abrigo overcoat
abril *m* April
abrir to open; **—se paso** to make one's way
absurdo, -a absurd
abuela grandmother
abuelo grandfather
aburrido, -a bored; boring
aburrirse to get bored
acá here; **para —** this way
acabar to finish, end; **— (pagando)** to end up (paying); **— de (salir)** to have just (left)
acalorado, -a heated (discussion or argument)
accidente *m* accident
aceite *m* oil; olive oil
aceptar to accept
acercarse to approach
acompañar to accompany
acostarse (ue) to go to bed
acostumbrado, -a accustomed, used to
acto act

acuerdo accordance, agreement; **de — con** in accordance with
adelantarse to get ahead
además (de) besides
adiós good-bye
admirar to admire
adoptar to adopt
adorado, -a dearest, adored
advertir (ie, i) to warn; to advise
afeitarse to shave
aflojar to weaken
afueras *f pl* outskirts
agosto August
agradable pleasant
agradecer to be grateful, thank
agradecido, -a grateful
agregar to add
agrupar to group
agua water
ahijada goddaughter
ahijado godson
ahora now; **— mismo** right now
ahorrar to economize, save
ajeno, -a another's; foreign
ají *m* pepper (green)
ajo garlic
al to the; at the
alcanzar to reach
alegrarse to be glad

alegre happy, gay
alemán, -ana German
alfabeto alphabet
algo something
alguien someone, anyone, anybody
alguno (algún), -a some, any; someone
alma soul
almirante *m* admiral
almuerzo lunch
aló hello
alrededor (de) around
alto, -a *adj* tall; *m* stop sign
alumno, alumna student
allá there, over there; **para —** that way (in that direction)
allí there
ama de casa housewife
amable kind
amanecer *m* dawn
amargo, -a bitter
amarillo, -a yellow
ambicioso, -a ambitious
ambiente *m* atmosphere, environment
ambulante traveling; **vendedor —** street vender
americano, -a American
amiga friend, girlfriend
amigo friend
amor *m* love

amplio, -a large, wide
amueblado, -a furnished
análisis *m* analysis
anaranjado, -a orange
andaluz, -za Andalusian
andar (12) to walk, go; **— de compras** to go shopping
anglosajón, -ona Anglo-Saxon
angosto, -a narrow
anoche last night
ansioso, -a anxious
anteanoche night before last
anteayer day before yesterday
antepasado ancestor
antes (de) before
antiguo, -a old, ancient; *before noun,* former
antipático, -a unpleasant, disagreeable
antiquísimo, -a *superlative of* **antiguo**
anunciar to announce
añadir to add
año year
apagado, -a extinguished, out (fire or light); dull
aparecer (14) to appear
apariencia appearance
apartamento apartment
apellido surname
apenas barely
aplauso applause
aplicar to apply
apogeo peak, high point
apostar (ue) to bet
aprender to learn
apresurado, -a hasty, hurrying
apropiado, -a appropriate, suitable
aprovechar to take advantage
aproximadamente approximately
aproximarse (a) to approach
apuntar to point
apuntes *m pl* notes
aquí here
árbol *m* tree
archivo archives
arquitectónico, -a architectural
arquitectura architecture
arreglar to arrange, straighten up
arriba up, upward, up high
arrojar to throw
arroz *m* rice

arruinar to ruin
arte *m* art
artes *f pl* arts, skills, crafts
ascenso promotion
así thus, so, like that, this way
asiento seat
asombrar to astonish
astronauta *m* astronaut
atención *f* attention
atraer (29) to attract
atrasarse to lag behind, be delayed
atrevido, -a fresh, insolent
aumento increase
aunque although, even though
autobús *m* bus
autor *m* author
autoridad *f* authority
avanzar to advance
avenida avenue
averiguar to find out, ascertain
avión *m* airplane
avisar to warn, inform, give notice
ayer yesterday
ayuda help, aid
ayudar to help
azúcar *m* sugar
azul blue

B

bachiller *m* high school graduate
bailar to dance
baile *m* dance
bajo, -a *adj* low, short; *m* bass
balcón *m* balcony
banco bank; bench
banda band
bandido robber
bañar to bathe; **—se** to take a bath
baño bathroom
barato, -a cheap, inexpensive
barbaridad: ¡qué —! how terrible!
barco boat, ship
barrer to sweep
barril *m* barrel
básico, -a basic
bastante enough; quite, fairly
bastón *m* cane

batería set of drums
bello, -a beautiful
bendecir (i) (16) to bless
beso kiss
biblioteca library
bicicleta bicycle
bien well, okay
binóculos *m pl* binoculars
biología biology
blanco, -a white
blusa blouse
boca mouth
bocina automobile horn
boda wedding
bogotano, -a from Bogotá, Colombia
bolsa bag
bolsillo pocket
bonito, -a pretty
bota boot
botella bottle
boxeo boxing
brazo arm
brillo shine
brisa breeze
broma joke
brusco, -a brusque
bueno (buen), -a good, nice; **buenos (buenas)** common response to **buenos días, buenas tardes, buenas noches**
buey *m* ox
bulto bundle
buscar to look for

C

caballo horse
cabeza head
caer (13) to fall
café *m* coffee, cafe; *adj* brown
cafetería coffee shop
cajero cashier
calcetín *m* sock
calcular to calculate, estimate
caldo broth
calentar (ie) to heat
calidad *f* quality
caliente hot
calma calm
calor *m* heat; **hacer —** to be warm (of weather); **tener**

— to be, feel, warm (of persons)

callarse to be quiet, shut up
callo callous
cama bed
camarón *m* shrimp
cambiar to change, exchange
cambio change
camino road
camión *m* truck
camisa shirt
campana bell
campeón *m* champion
campesino, campesina peasant, farm worker
campo country; field
canalla *m* scoundrel
canasta canasta; market basket
canguro kangaroo
cansado, -a tired
cansarse to get tired
cantar to sing
cañón *m* cannon
capilla chapel
capitán *m* captain
cara face
carácter *m* character, nature
característica characteristic
caramba for Pete's sake
cariño affection
carne *f* meat
carnicero butcher
caro, -a expensive
carpintero carpenter
carretera highway
carro car
carta letter
cartera purse, wallet
carterista *m* pickpocket
cartero mailman
casa house, home; **en —** at home; **(ir) a —** (to go) home
casar to marry, marry off; **—se (con)** to marry, get married (to)
caso case; **hacer —** to pay attention
castigar to punish
castillo castle
catástrofe *f* catastrophe
catedral *f* cathedral
catorce fourteen
causa cause
cayo islet, key

caza hunt
cazador *m* hunter
cebolla onion
celebrar to celebrate
celoso, -a jealous
cementerio cemetery
cena supper
centavo penny
céntimo penny
centro center; downtown
cerca (de) near, nearby
cercano, -a near
cerdo pig
cero zero
cerrar (ie) to close
cerro hill
certificado certificate
cerveza beer
cielo sky
ciencia science
ciento (cien) one hundred
cierto, -a certain, true
cigarro cigar, cigarette
cinco five
cincuenta fifty
cine *m* movies
circular to move about
ciudad *f* city
ciudadano citizen
clarinete *m* clarinet
claro, -a clear; **¡—!** of course!
clase *f* class
clasificar to classify
clima *m* climate
cobrador *m* collector
cocina kitchen; stove
cocinera cook
cocodrilo crocodile
coctel *m* cocktail
coche *m* car
coger to seize; to catch; to pick up; to pick, harvest
colaborar to collaborate
colombiano, -a Colombian
Colón Columbus
comedor *m* dining room
comer to eat, dine
cometer to commit; **— un error** to make an error
comida meal, food, dinner
como like, as
cómo how; **¿— es (ella)?** what is (she) like? **— no** of course; **¿— se dice?** how do you say?

compañía company; **— de Jesús** Society of Jesus, Order of Jesuits
compasión *f* compassion
completo, -a complete
complicado, -a complicated
componente *m* component
componer (23) to compose; to fix
compra purchase; **andar de —s** to go shopping
comprar to buy
comprobante *m* proof
comunismo Communism
con with; **— tal que** provided that
conducta conduct
conferencia lecture
confesar (ie) to confess
confiado, -a confident
conmigo with me
conocer (14) to know, be acquainted with; to meet
conquistar to conquer
consecuencia consequence
conseguir (i) to get, obtain
consejos *m pl* advice
consentido, -a pampered, spoiled
conservador, -ra conservative
considerar to consider
consiguiente: por — therefore
consonante *f* consonant
constitución *f* constitution
constituir to constitute
construir to build
contar (ue) to tell; to count
contener (ie) (28) to contain
contento, -a content, happy, satisfied
contestar to answer
contigo with you
continuar to continue
contra against
contradecir (i) (16) to contradict
contraer (29) to contract; **—se** to shrink
contrario opponent; **al —** on the contrary
convenir (ie, i) (31) to suit; to be suitable
conversar to converse, chat
convertir (ie, i) to change
copa crown (of a hat)

corbata necktie
cordillera cordillera, mountain range
coro choir
coronel *m* colonel
correctamente correctly
correo mail
corrida de toros bullfight
cortar to cut
cortina curtain
corto, -a short
cosa thing
costa coast
costar (ue) to cost
creer to believe
crema cream
criada maid
criado servant
crimen *m* crime
crisantemo chrysanthemum
crisis *f* crisis
Cristo Christ
crónica chronicle
cuaderno notebook
cuál which, what
cualidad *f* quality
cualquier(a) any, whatever; *pl* **cualesquiera**
cuando when; whenever
cuándo when
cuánto, -a how; how much; *pl* how many; **— lo siento** I'm very sorry; **¿— tiempo?** how long?
cuarenta forty
cuarto, -a fourth; *m* room, bedroom; quarter (of an hour)
cuatro four
cuatrocientos, -as four hundred
cubiertos *m pl* silverware
cubrir to cover
cuchara tablespoon
cucharada tablespoonful
cucharita teaspoon
cuchillo knife
cuento story
cuerdo, -a sane
cuero leather
cuerpo body; corps
cuestión *f* question, matter
cuidado care, caution; **¡—!** be careful! **tener —** to be careful
cuidar to take care of

culpa guilt, blame; **tener la —** to be to blame
cultivo cultivation
cumpleaños *m sing* birthday
cumplir to fulfill; **— con (mi) deber** to do (my) duty
cuñada sister-in-law
cuñado brother-in-law
cuota dues; quota, share

CH

chao so long (from Italian *ciao*)
chapín nickname for Guatemalan
cheque *m* check
chico, -a *adj* small; *n* boy, girl, child
chileno, -a Chilean
chilito hot pepper
chino, -a Chinese
chiquita little girl
chiste *m* joke
chistoso, -a *adj* funny; *m* smart-aleck
chofer *m* driver
choque *m* collision; shock

D

dama lady
dar (15) to give; **—se cuenta de** to realize; **—se vuelta** to turn around
datar to date
de from; of; about
debajo de under
deber must; to owe; *m* duty
decadencia decline
decente decent, nice
decidir to decide
décimo, -a tenth
decir (i) (16) to say, tell
dedicarse to devote oneself
dedo finger; **— del pie** toe
defensa defense
del from the; of the; about the
delgado, -a slender
delicioso, -a delicious, delightful
demás rest (remaining)
denominar to name, refer to
dentro (de) inside

derecha right
derecho, -a *adj* right; *m* right (privilege); law; **facultad de —** law school; *adv* straight; **seguir todo —** to go straight ahead
derivar to derive
derrocar to overthrow
desaparecer (14) to disappear
desarrollar to develop
desarrollo development
desastre *m* disaster; mess
desayuno breakfast
descender (ie) to descend
descendiente *m* descendant
descifrar to decipher
descomponer (23) to decompose; break down
desconfianza mistrust
desconocido, -a unknown
describir to describe
descubrir to discover
desde from; since
desesperado, -a desperate, in despair
desfile *m* parade
deshacer (19) to tear down
desmayarse to faint
desnutrido, -a undernourished
desocupado, -a unoccupied, free
despedir (i) to fire; **—se (de)** to say good-bye (to)
desperdiciar to waste, throw away
despintado, -a faded
después afterwards; **— de** after
detalle *m* detail
detener (ie) (28) to detain, stop; **—se** to stop, come to a stop
detrás (de) behind
devolver (ue) to return
devoto, -a devout
día *m* day; **al —** a day, per day; **buenos —s** good morning
diablo devil
diario, -a daily
dibujar to draw
diccionario dictionary
diciembre *m* December
dictadura dictatorship
dicho *pp of* **decir; mejor —** rather
dichoso, -a lucky

diecinueve nineteen
dieciocho eighteen
dieciséis sixteen
diecisiete seventeen
diente *m* tooth
diferencia difference
diferente different
difícil difficult; **es —** it is
    unlikely
dificultad *f* difficulty
dinero money
Dios *m* God
dirigirse (a) to go toward;
    to address
disculpar to forgive
discurso talk, speech
discutir to argue, discuss
dispensar to excuse
disposición *f* disposal
distinguido, -a distinguished
diverso, -a different
divertido, -a amusing, funny
divino, -a divine
divorciarse to get a divorce
doblar to turn; to fold
doce twelve
dolor *m* pain, ache
domesticado, -a domesticated
domingo Sunday
don a title used with masculine
    first names
donar to donate
donde where
dónde where
doña a title used with
    feminine first names
dos two; **en un — por tres** in
    a jiffy
doscientos, -as two hundred
dueño, dueña owner, boss
dulce sweet
durante during
durar to last
duro, -a hard

E

e and
ecuación *f* equation
ecuatoriano, -a Ecuadorian
edad *f* age
edificio building
eficiente efficient
ejemplo example

ejercicio exercise
ejército army
el the; *pl* **los**
él he; him; it
electricista *m* electrician
elefante *m* elephant
ella she; her; it
ellos they; them
embajador *m* ambassador
embargo: sin — however
empeñar to pawn
empezar (ie) to begin
empleado, empleada employee
empleo job
en in; on; at
enamorado, -a (de) in love
    (with)
encaminarse (hacia) to make
    one's way (toward)
encantado, -a charmed,
    delighted; delighted to meet
    you
encantar to charm
encender (ie) to light
encima (de) on top of, above
enchilada Mexican dish, tortilla
    stuffed with meat or other
    filling and baked in
    chile-seasoned sauce
encontrar (ue) to find
endosar to endorse
enero January
enfermo, -a sick
enfrente (de) in front (of)
engañar to deceive
enojado, -a angry
enojarse to get angry
enorme enormous
ensalada salad
entender (ie) to understand
entero, -a whole, entire
entonces then
entrar to enter
entre between, among
entreabierto, -a partially open
entretener (ie) (28) to entertain
entusiasmo enthusiasm
época epoch, period
equivalente *m* equivalent
errático, -a erratic
escala scale, degree
escandinavo, -a Scandinavian
escasez *f* shortage
escaso, -a scarce
escenario scene

esclavo slave
escoger to choose
escribir to write
escuchar to listen
escuela school
ese, -a that; *pl* **esos, -as** those
ése, ésa that one; *pl* **ésos, ésas**
    those
esfuerzo effort
eso that; **por —** therefore,
    that's why
espacio space
espantoso, -a frightening
español, -la *adj* Spanish; *n*
    Spanish; Spaniard
especial special
espectáculo spectacle
espectador *m* spectator
esperar to hope; to wait
esposa wife
esposo husband
esquina corner
esquivar to dodge
establecer (14) to establish;
    —se to settle
estación *f* station; season
estadio stadium
estado state
Estados Unidos United States
estadounidense *m* inhabitant of
    the United States
estante *m* shelf
estar (17) to be; **— mal (de**
    salud) to be ill
estatua statue
este, -a this; *pl* **estos, -as** these
éste, ésta this one; the latter; *pl*
    éstos, éstas these; the latter
estilo style
estimado, -a dear, esteemed
esto this
estómago stomach
estrecho, -a *adj* narrow; *m* strait
estricto, -a strict
estudiar to study
eterno, -a eternal; interminable
exaltadamente excitedly
examen *m* test, exam
examinar to examine
excepción *f* exception
exclamar to exclaim
excusa excuse
exigir to demand
exilio exile
expresión *f* expression

extender (ie) to extend
extinto, -a extinct
extraer (29) to extract

F

fácil easy
facultad *f* school (of a university); **— de derecho** law school
famoso, -a famous
fantástico, -a fantastic, wonderful
farmacia pharmacy
fe *f* faith
febrero February
fecha date
felicitar to congratulate
feliz happy
fenomenal great, terrific
fenómeno phenomenon
feo, -a ugly
feriado holiday
ferrocarril *m* railroad
fiebre *f* fever
fiesta party
fijarse (en) to fix (upon), notice
filosofía philosophy
fin: por — at last
finalmente finally
finca farm
finlandés, -esa *adj* Finnish; *n* Finnish; Finn
firma signature; firm
físico, -a physical
flaco, -a slim
flor *f* flower
fondo bottom; **en el —** at heart
francés, -esa *adj* French; *n* French; Frenchman
Francia France
franco, -ca frank
freír to fry
fresco, -a cool; fresh
frío, -a *adj* cold; *m* cold
frito, -a fried
fruta fruit
fuera (de) outside
fuerte *adj* strong; *adv* hard
fuerza force; **—s aéreas** air force
fumar to smoke
furioso, -a furious
fusión *f* fusion

G

gafas *f pl* eyeglasses
gallina hen
ganar to earn; to win
gastado, -a worn-out
gastar to spend
gata cat
gemelo twin
genio genius
gente *f* people
gobierno government
golpe *m* blow; **— de estado** coup d'état
golpear to knock
gordo, -a fat
gozar (de) to enjoy
gracias *f pl* thanks
grado grade
gramática grammar
grande (gran) big, large; great
grandioso, -a grandiose
grave ill
Grecia Greece
griego, -a Greek
gris gray
gritar to shout
grito scream, shout
grueso, -a thick
guante *m* glove
guapo, -a handsome, good-looking
guardar to keep
guardia guard; **— civil** policeman
guayaba guava
guitarra guitar
gustar to be pleasing
gusto pleasure, taste; **con mucho —** gladly; **mucho — glad to meet you**

H

habano, -a brown
haber (18) to have
habilidad *f* ability, skill
habitante *m* inhabitant
hábito habit
habla speech
hablar to speak
hacer (19) to do; to make; **hace (buen) tiempo** the weather is (good); **— caso** to pay attention; **hace (dos años)**

(two years) ago; **hace (sol)** it is (sunny)
hacia toward
hambre *f* hunger
hasta until, up to; even; **— mañana** see you tomorrow
hay there is, there are; **— que** it is necessary; **¿qué — de nuevo?** what's new?
hemisferio hemisphere
hermana sister
hermano brother
hermoso, -a beautiful
hermosura beauty
hervir (ie, i) to boil
hija daughter
hijito *dim of* **hijo**
hijo son *pl* children
hipótesis *f* hypothesis
historia history
histórico, -a historical
hoja leaf; page, sheet
hola hi
hombre *m* man
honrado, -a honest
honrar to honor
hora hour; **¿qué — es?** what time is it?
hoy today
huevo egg
humedad *f* humidity
humillar to humiliate
humor *m* humor; mood

I

ida departure
idioma *m* language
iglesia church
igual same, alike
ilegal illegal
ilustre illustrious
impacto impact
imperio empire
impermeable *m* raincoat
imponente impressive
imponer (23) to impose
importar to import; to matter, be of importance
imposible impossible
impuesto tax
inacentuado, -a unaccented
inca Inca
inclusive including

indeciso, -a undecided
indefenso, -a defenseless
indicar to indicate
indio Indian
inédito, -a unpublished
inevitable inevitable
infantería infantry
infeliz unhappy, unfortunate
ingeniero engineer
ingenioso, -a clever, ingenious
inglés, -esa *adj* English; *m*
English; Englishman
ingrato, -a *adj* ungrateful; *n*
ingrate
ingrediente *m* ingredient
inicial *f* initial
iniciar to start, begin
inmediatamente immediately
inmigrar to immigrate
insistir to insist
insolación *f* sunstroke
inspirar to inspire
instalarse to settle down
institución *f* institution
insultar to insult
inteligente intelligent
interés *m* interest
interesante interesting
interesarse to become interested
intersección *f* intersection
intervenir (ie, i) (31) to
intervene
intimidar to intimidate
intromisión *f* intrusion, butting
in
inútil useless, futile
investigar to investigate
invierno winter
invitar to invite
ir (20) to go
irresponsable irresponsible
isla island
italiano, -a Italian
izquierdo, -a left

J

jabón *m* soap
japonés, -esa Japanese
jardín *m* garden
jardinero gardener
jefe *m* head, chief, leader, boss
Jesucristo Jesus Christ
joven young
jueves *m* Thursday

jugar (ue) to play; to gamble
jugo juice
julio July
junio June
jurar to swear

K

kilo kilogram (approximately
2.2 pounds)

L

la the; it, her, you; *pl* them,
you
lado side; **al — (de)** beside,
alongside
ladrón *m* thief
lago lake
lágrima tear; **llorar a — viva**
to cry one's eyes out
lápiz *m* pencil
largo, -a long
lástima pity
lata nuisance
lavandera laundress
lavar to wash; **—se** get
washed
le you; (to, for) him, her, you,
it; *pl* (to, for) them, you
leche *f* milk
lechero milkman
lechuga lettuce
leer to read
lejos (de) far (from)
lengua tongue; language
lenguaje *m* language
lentamente slowly
león *m* lion
letra letter (of the alphabet)
levantar to lift, raise; **—se** to
get up
leyenda legend
libra pound
librería bookstore
libro book
licencia license; **— de manejar**
driver's license
licenciado title conferred upon
a graduate of a law school
limón *m* lemon
limosna alms
limosnita *dim of* **limosna**
limpiabotas *m sing* shoeshine
boy

limpiadita cleaning, shine
limpiar to clean
limpio, -a clean
lindo, -a pretty, nice
lingüístico, -a linguistic
lío mess
litro liter
lo him, it, you; *pl* them, you;
the; **— que** that which,
what
loco, -a crazy
lógico, -a logical
lotería lottery
luego presently, immediately,
next; later; then
lugar *m* place
lujo luxury
lunes *m* Monday
luz *f* light

LL

llamar to call; **—se** to be
called, named
llegar to arrive
lleno, -a full
llevar to carry; to wear
llorar to weep; **— a lágrima
viva** to cry one's eyes out
llover (ue) to rain
lluvia rain

M

madera wood
madre *f* mother
madrina godmother
maduro, -a ripe; mature
maestro, maestra teacher
magnífico, -a magnificent
maíz *m* corn
mal *m* illness; evil; **— de
patria** homesickness; *adv*
badly, poorly
maldecir (i) (16) to curse
maleta suitcase
malo (mal), -a bad; ill
mamá mama
mamacita *dim of* **mamá**
mandar to send; to command
manejar to drive; to manage
maní *m* peanuts
mano *f* hand
mantel *m* tablecloth
mantener (ie) (28) to maintain

mantequilla butter
manzana apple
mañana morning; tomorrow; — por la — tomorrow morning
mar *m* sea
maravilloso, -a marvelous
marido husband
marimba marimba
marina navy
mariscal *m* marshal
marrón, -ona brown
martes *m* Tuesday
marzo March
más more
matador *m* matador; *adj* murderous
matar to kill
matemáticas *f pl* mathematics
materno, -a maternal
máximo, -a *adj* maximum; *m* maximum
maya Maya, Mayan
mayo May
mayor *m* major; *adj* older, bigger
me me; (to, for) me; myself
media stocking
mediados: a — (de) about the middle of (a period of time)
medicina medicine
médico doctor
medio, -a *adj* half, half a; middle; *m* means, way
medir (i) to measure
mejor better; best
mejorar to improve
melódico, -a melodic
memoria memory
mencionar to mention
mendigo beggar
menos less; minus; al — at least
mentir (ie, i) to lie
mentira lie; ¡—! that's not true!
mentor *m* mentor, teacher
mercado market
mes *m* month
mesera waitress
mesero waiter
mestizo, -a mestizo, born of Indian and white parents
meter to put in; —se en to get inside
mexicano, -a Mexican

mezcla mixture
mezclar to mix
mi my
mí me
miedo fear; ¡qué —! what a scare! tener — to be afraid
miembro member
miércoles *m* Wednesday
mil *m* thousand
milagro miracle
milla mile
millón *m* million
millonario millionaire
mina mine
minuto minute
mirar to look, look at
mismo, -a same
moda fashion
modo way, manner; de todos —s anyway
molido, -a ground
momento moment
monopolio monopoly
montaña mountain
montar to mount; — a caballo to ride horseback
montón *m* pile, stack, heap; a montones in crowds
morado, -a purple
morir(se) (ue, u) to die
moro, -a Moorish
mostrar (ue) to show
motivo reason, motive
muchacha girl
muchacho boy
mucho plenty, much, a lot; *pl* many
mudarse to move (to another house)
muela tooth (molar)
muerto, -a *adj* dead; *m* dead man; *pp of* morir
mujer *f* woman; wife; "dear"
mulato mulatto
mundo world; todo el — everybody
música music
muy very

N

nacer (14) to be born
nada nothing; anything (after negative); de — you're welcome; — más only

nadie no one, nobody; anyone (after negative)
naranja orange
nariz *f* nose
naturaleza nature; por — by nature
Navidad *f* Christmas
necesidad *f* necessity
necesitar to need
negro, -a black
nene *m* baby
nervioso, -a nervous
ni neither, nor; not even
nieta granddaughter
ninguno (ningún), -a no, none, no one; any, anyone (after negative)
noche *f* night
nómada *f* nomad; *adj* nomadic, wandering
nombre *m* name
normando Norman
nosotros, nosotras we
novecientos, -as nine hundred
noveno, -a ninth
noventa ninety
novia sweetheart, fiancée, girlfriend; bride
noviembre *m* November
novio sweetheart, fiancé, boyfriend; bridegroom
nueve nine
nuevo, -a new
número number
nunca never; ever (after negative)

O

o or
obedecer (14) to obey
obediencia obedience
observar to observe
obtener (ie) (28) to obtain
obvio, -a obvious
occidental western
octavo, -a eighth
octubre *m* October
ocupado, -a occupied, busy
ocurrir to occur
ochenta eighty
ochocientos, -as eight hundred
odio hatred
oficial *m* officer
oficina office
oído (inner) ear

oír (**21**) to hear
ojalá I wish, I hope
ojo eye
olvidar to forget
once eleven
opinar to express an opinion
oponer (**23**) to oppose
opresión *f* oppression
orden: a sus órdenes how do you do
oriente *m* east
origen *m* origin
originarse to originate
orquesta band, orchestra
orquídea orchid
oscurecer (**14**) to get dark
oscuridad *f* darkness
oscuro, -a dark
otoño autumn
otro, -a other, another

P

pacífico, -a peaceful
padre *m* father; *pl* parents
padrino godfather
paella saffron-flavored rice cooked with seafood, chicken, and other ingredients
pagar to pay (for)
país *m* country
pájaro bird
palabra word; word of honor
pálido, -a pale
palmera palm tree
palo pole, stick
pan *m* bread
panadería bakery
panadero baker
panameño, -a Panamanian
pantalones *m pl* pants
papa potato
papá *m* papa
papel *m* paper
par *m* pair
para for; in order to; to; by (a certain time); **— que** so that
parada parade
paraguas *m sing* umbrella
parar to stop
pardo, -a brown
parecer (**14**) to seem
parecido, -a alike, similar
pared *f* wall

pariente *m* relative
parte *f* part; **la mayor —** most; **por — de (padre)** on (my father's) side
partido: un gran — a great catch
partir to depart
pasado, -a *adj* past, last; *m* past
pasaje *m* passage
pasar to happen; to pass; to spend (time); **—se una luz** to go through a traffic light
paseo walk, drive, outing, picnic
paso step
paterno, -a paternal
pecado sin
pedacito small piece
pedazo piece
pedir (**i**) to ask for
peinarse to comb one's hair
pelele *m* punk
película film
pelo hair
peluquería barber shop
peluquero barber
pena trouble
pensar (**ie**) to think; to intend; **— de** to think of (have an opinion); **— en** to think of (bring to mind)
peón *m* manual laborer
peor worse; worst
pequeño, -a small, short
pera pear
perder (**ie**) to lose; **— de vista** to lose sight of
perdón *m* pardon
perdonar pardon
periódico newspaper
permiso permission; **con —** excuse me
permitir to permit
pero but
perro dog
persa *mf* Persian
perseverancia perseverance
persona person
personaje *m* character
pertenecer (**14**) to belong
peruano, -a Peruvian
pesar to weigh; *m* sorrow; **a — de** in spite of
pescar to fish
piano piano
picado, -a chopped, minced

picante hot (spicy)
pie *m* foot; **a —** on foot
piedra stone, rock
pierna leg
pimienta pepper
pintoresco, -a picturesque
piña pineapple
pipa pipe
piscina swimming pool
piso floor, story (of a building)
planchar to iron, press
planeta *m* planet
plateresco, -a platheresque, fancifully ornamented
platicar to chat
plato dish, plate
playa beach
pleno, -a full, complete; **en — (verano)** in the middle of (summer)
pluma pen
población *f* population, people; town
pobre poor
poco, -a *adj* little, scanty; *pl* few; *m* a little; **un —** a little bit; *adv* little, in a small degree; **— a —** little by little
poder (**ue**) (**22**) to be able, can
poderío might
policía *f* police (department); *m* policeman
polvo dust
pollo chicken
poner (**23**) to put; **— la mesa** to set the table; **—se** to put on (clothing); to become
popular of the people
poquito *dim of* **poco**
por by; for; through; along; per; as; on account of, because of; **— favor** please; **— (la mañana)** in (the morning); **— qué** why
porque because
portón *m* large, heavy door
porvenir *m* future
posponer (**23**) to postpone
postizo, -a false
postre *m* dessert
práctico, -a practical
precario, -a precarious
predominar to predominate
preferir (**ie, i**) to prefer
preguntar to ask

prender to catch; to turn on (a light)
preocupado, -a worried
preocuparse to worry
preparar to prepare
presencia presence; appearance
presidente *m* president
prestar to lend
presupuesto budget
pretencioso, -a haughty
pretendiente *m* suitor
prevenir (ie, i) (31) to prevent; to warn
primavera spring
primo, prima cousin; — **hermano** first cousin
prisa speed, haste; **estar de —** to be in a hurry; **tener —** to be in a hurry
probar (ue) to taste, try
problema *m* problem
procedente (de) coming (from)
proceder to proceed
procedimiento procedure
procesión *f* procession
profe *m* short for **profesor,** "Prof"
profesor *m* professor
progreso progress
promesa promise
prometer to promise
pronto soon
pronunciar to pronounce
proponer (23) to propose
propósito purpose; **a —** by the way, incidentally
provenir (de) (ie, i) (31) to originate (in)
próximo, -a next
pueblo people; town
puerta door
pulga flea
punto point; **en —** on the dot

Q

que that, which; who, whom; than; **lo —** that which, what
qué what, which; **¿— tal?** hi, how are you? **¿— tal es (ella)?** what is (she) like? *in exclamations,* how: **¡— (bueno)!** how (nice)!

quedar to remain, be left over; **—se** to stay, remain
quejarse to complain
quemar to burn
querer (ie) (24) to want; to love
querido, -a dear
queso cheese
quien who, whom
quién who, whom
quince fifteen
quinientos, -as five hundred
quinto, -a fifth
quitar to remove, take away; **—se** to take off (clothing)
quiteño, -a from Quito, Ecuador

R

radio *f* radio (broadcast); *m* radio (apparatus)
ranchero, -a ranch-style
rapidez *f* rapidity
rápido, -a rapid, fast
raro, -a strange
rascar to scratch
ratito *dim of* **rato**
rato while
rayo flash
razón *f* reason; **tener —** to be right
razonable reasonable
reaccionar to react
rebajo reduction
receta recipe
recién recently
reciente recent
recipiente *m* container, dish
recoger to pick up, gather, collect
recomendar (ie) recommend
recordado, -a dear (in greeting of a letter)
recordar (ue) to remember; to remind
recuerdo memory; souvenir; *pl* regards
referirse (ie, i) to refer
refugiarse to take refuge
regalar to give
regalo gift
regatear to haggle
regla rule
regresar to return
regular regular; so-so
rehusar to refuse
reja wrought iron grillwork

relajado, -a relaxed
relativamente relatively
reloj *m* watch; clock
reluciente shiny
remediar to help, remedy
remoto, -a remote
renacer (14) to be reborn
repetir (i) to repeat
repleto, -a full
reponer (23) to replace
representante *m* representative
representar to represent; to perform
reptil *m* reptile
república republic
requerir (ie, i) to require
resentido, -a angry, hurt
resentirse (ie, i) to become angry or hurt
resfrío cold (illness)
resolver (ue) to solve
respecto respect
respetar to respect
restaurante *m* restaurant; *also* **restorán, restaurán**
resto rest (remainder)
resultado result
retener (ie) (28) to retain
revelar to reveal
revista magazine
rezar to pray
río river
risa laughter; **¡qué —!** what a joke!
robar to steal
roca rock
rodear to surround
rodilla knee
rogar (ue) to beg
rojo, -a red
romano, -a Roman
ron *m* rum
ropa clothing, clothes
rótulo sign
rubio, -a blond
rubio-gris grayish blond
ruidoso, -a noisy
rumano, -a Rumanian
rumbo direction; **sin —** aimlessly
ruso, -a Russian

S

sábado Saturday
saber (25) to know

sacar to take out
sacerdote *m* priest
saco suit jacket
sal *f* salt
sala living room
salado, -a salty
salir (26) to go out
salsa sauce
saltar to jump
saludar to greet, say hello
saludo greeting
salvaje *m* savage; *adj* wild
salvar to save
sanguíneo, -a *adj* blood
sanito, -a *dim of* **sano**
sano, -a healthy
sánscrito Sanskrit
santo (san) saint; saint's day
sargento sergeant
sartén *f* frying pan
sastrería tailor shop
satisfecho, -a satisfied
se himself, herself, yourself,
  oneself, itself, yourselves,
  themselves
secar to dry
seco, -a dry; unemotional
sed *f* thirst; **tener —** to be
  thirsty
seguida: en — at once
seguir (i) to follow; to continue;
  — (hablando) to keep on
  (talking); **¿cómo sigue
  (Juan)?** how is (John)
  coming along?
según according to
segundo, -a second; *m* second
seis six
seiscientos, -as six hundred
selva jungle
semana week
sembrar (ie) to sow, plant
semioscuro, -a dim
semipodrido, -a half rotten
sentarse (ie) to sit down
sentir (ie, i) to feel; to regret
señal *f* signal
señor Mr.; *m* gentleman
señora Mrs.; lady
señorita Miss; girl
separar to separate
septiembre *m* September
séptimo, -a seventh
sequía drought
ser (27) to be
serenata serenade

serio, -a serious
serpiente *f* serpent, snake
servicial helpful
servidor *m* servant
servilleta napkin
servir (i) to serve
sesenta sixty
setecientos, -as seven hundred
setenta seventy
sexto, -a sixth
si if
sí yes
siempre always
siete seven
siglo century
simpático, -a nice, pleasant,
  charming
sin without; **— que** without
sinvergüenza *m* bum
siquiera at least; **ni —** not
  even
sirviente, sirvienta servant
sistema *m* system
situado, -a situated, located
sobre on, upon, about; *m*
  envelope
sobrecama bedspread
sobrina niece
sobrino nephew
sociedad *f* society
sol *m* sun; **hace —** it is sunny
solamente only
solo, -a alone
sólo only
soltero, -a unmarried
sombra shade
sombrero hat
sonar (ue) to sound; to blow
sonido sound
soñar (ue) (con) to dream
  (about)
sopa soup
sorprender to surprise
sospecha suspicion
su your, his, her, its; their
suave soft
súbitamente suddenly
sucio, -a dirty
sudar to sweat
suegra mother-in-law
suegro father-in-law
suelto, -a loose
sueño dream; sleep; **tener —**
  to be sleepy
suerte *f* luck
suficiente enough, sufficient

sugerir (ie, i) to suggest
suicidarse to commit suicide
supuesto: por — of course
surgir to arise
suspirar to sigh

T

tal such, such a; **con — que**
  provided that; **¿qué —?**
  how are things? **¿qué —
  es (ella)?** what is (she)
  like? **— vez** perhaps
tamal *m* Mexican dish,
  chile-seasoned meat or other
  filling steamed in soft cornmeal casing
también too, also
tampoco neither; either (after
  negative)
tan so, as
tanque *m* tank
tanto, -a so much, as much; *pl*
  so many, as many; *adv* so
  much, to such an extent
tardanza delay
tarde *f* afternoon; **buenas —s**
  good afternoon, good
  evening; *adv* late; **llegar —**
  to be late
taxista *m* taxi driver
taza cup
té *m* tea
teatro theater
técnicamente technically
tecnología technology
techo ceiling; roof
teléfono telephone
temer to fear
templo temple
temprano, -a early
tendencia tendency
tenedor *m* fork
tener (ie) (28) to have; **—
  calor** to be (feel) warm; **—
  hambre** to be hungry; **— la
  culpa** to be to blame; **—
  miedo** to be afraid; **—
  prisa** to be in a hurry; **—
  que (trabajar)** to have to
  (work); **— razón** to be
  right; **— sed** to be thirsty
teniente *m* lieutenant
tenis *m* tennis
tequila tequila, liquor made
  from distilled juices of the

Mexican century plant

tercero (tercer), -a third
tercio third
terminar to finish, end; close
término term
tesoro treasure
testigo witness
ti you
tía aunt
tico, -a nickname for Costa Rican
tiempo time; weather; **a —** on time
tienda store
tierra land
tigre *m* tiger
timbre *m* bell
tímido, -a timid
tintorería dry cleaner's shop
tío uncle
típico, -a typical
tipo type; guy
tirar to throw; to draw, pull; **— la casa por la ventana** to go all out
toalla towel
tocar to touch; to play (music); **— la puerta** to knock at the door, ring the bell
todavía still, yet
todo, -a *adj* all; every; *m* all; whole; everything; *pl* everybody, all
tolteca-azteca Toltec-Aztec
tomar to take; to drink; to eat
tomate *m* tomato
tomo volume
tontería nonsense
tonto, -a dumb, silly
toro bull
tortilla thin cornmeal pancake (Mexican)
tostar (ue) to toast, roast; **—se** to get a tan
trabajar to work
trabalenguas *m sing* tongue twister
traer (29) to bring
tragedia tragedy
traje *m* suit; gown
transformar to transform
transitado, -a busy (as a street)
tránsito traffic
tras after
trasero, -a back

tratar (de) to try (to)
través: a — de in the course of; across; through
trece thirteen
treinta thirty
tren *m* train
tres three
trescientos, -as three hundred
tribu *f* tribe
triste sad
trompeta trumpet
tropa troop
tu your
tú you
tumbar to knock down
tumulto tumult
tuyo, -a your, yours, of yours

U

último, -a last
único, -a unique, only
universidad *f* university; college
uno (un), -a one; a; *pl* some
usted you
usurpación *f* usurpation
uva grape

V

vaca cow
vacaciones *f pl* vacation
vacilar to hesitate
vacío, -a empty
valer (30) to be worth
válido, -a valid
valor *m* value
variado, -a varied
variar to vary
vaso glass
vehículo vehicle
veinte twenty
vela candle
velocidad *f* speed
vender to sell
venir (ie, i) (31) to come
ventana window
ver (32) to see
verano summer
veras: de — really
verdad *f* truth; ¿—? isn't that so? right?
verdadero, -a real, true
verde green; unripe

verduras *f pl* greens
vespertino, -a evening, vesper
vestido dress
vestir (i) to dress; **—se** to get dressed
vez *f* time; **algunas (unas) veces** sometimes; **en — de** instead of; **muchas veces** often; **tal —** perhaps
viaje *m* trip
vicio vice
víctima victim
vida life
viejita little old lady
viejo, -a old
viento wind; **hace —** it is windy
viernes *m* Friday
villa town; **— miseria** conglomeration of hovels and shacks which house the poor in many Latin American countries
violar to violate
violento, -a violent
violín *m* violin
virrey *m* viceroy
visita visit; visitor
vista view, sight; **la — fija al frente** looking straight ahead
viuda widow
vivir to live
vivo, -a live, lively, alive
volver (ue) to return; **—se loco** to go crazy
vosotros, vosotras you

Y

y and; plus
ya now; yet; already; still; **— no** no longer, not any more; **— que** since
yo I

Z

zambo, -a born of black and Indian parents
zapatero shoemaker
zapato shoe
zona zone, region

Index

Abbreviations

adj	adjective	indic	indicative	pres	present
adv	adverb, adverbial	indir	indirect	pret	preterit
art	article	inf	infinitive	prog	progressive
cond	conditional	interrog	interrogative	pron	pronoun
const	construction	irr	irregular	refl	reflexive
def	definite	obj	object	sing	singular
dir	direct	perf	perfect	subj	subject
fn	footnote	pers	person	subjunc	subjunctive
fut	future	pl	plural	vs	versus
imperf	imperfect	prep	preposition(s)		

a: + el ⟶ al, 41 fn, 89; after entrar, 69 fn; ir a + inf, 52; as
personal particle, 55 fn, 87,
110 fn, 276 fn; in prepositional
phrases, 108, 110; with verbs
of motion, 228

[a], 5–6

a menos que, subjunc after, 241

acabar + pres participle, 205 fn

acabar de + inf, 86, 93, 162 fn

accent mark: on adv with -mente
suffix, 16 fn; on capital letters,
23 fn, 67 fn; on demonstrative
pron, 67; as indicator of stress,
15–16, 53; on pres participle
with obj pron attached, 108;
on pret forms, 157, 158

adjective: agreement of, with
nouns, 27–28, 30; demonstrative, 66; nominalization of,
145; past participles as, 191;
position of, 28, 79 fn; possessive, 143–44; shortened forms
of, 177–78

adjective clause, 244; indic in, 244;
subjunc in, 244, 274–75

adverb: with -mente suffix, 16 fn,
196–97

adverb clause, 240; indic in, 241–
43; subjunc in, 241–43, 274–75

affirmative words, 175–76

agreement: see adjective; article;
gender; number

al: from a + el, 41 fn, 89

alphabet, 12

antes (de) que, subjunc after, 241

-ar verb: commands, 206–07, 281–
82; cond, 257; fut, 278–79;
imperf, 159; past participle,
190; past subjunc, 258–59;
pres, 68; pres participle, 71,
191; pres subjunc, 209–10;
pret, 157–58; stem-changing,
104, 139

article: agreement with noun, 27,
30; lo, 247; with sing nouns
beginning with stressed [a],
44 fn, 222 fn; see also article,
definite

article, definite, 27, 30; before
más and menos, 195; before
numbers indicating the hour,
50; generic use of, 245; with
days of week, 70; with geographical names, 114 fn; with
names and titles of persons,
88; with names of languages,
135 fn; with things possessed,
119 fn; see also article

article, indefinite, 27, 30; see also
article

aunque, indic and subjunc after,
242–43

[b]: spelled b, 9 fn, 13, 80; spelled
v, 6 fn, 9 fn, 13, 80; vs [β], 81

[β], 81; vs [b], 81

c: see [k], [s]

capitalization: and accent mark,
23 fn, 67 fn; of days of week,
70; of months of year, 107; of
names of languages, 24 fn,
135 fn; of nationalities, 24 fn,
135 fn

cardinal numeral: see numeral,
cardinal

Castilian pronunciation: see pronunciation

ch, 13

cognate, 16

command: compared to subjunc,
210; position of obj pron in,
208–09, 282; tú and vosotros

321

command (*continued*)
   forms of, 281–82; **usted, -es,**
   and **nosotros** forms of, 206–07
como, indic after, 241
como si, subjunc after, 260
cómo, 33–34
comparison: of equality, 261; of
   inequality, 194–95; superlative, **-ísimo** suffix, 196–97
con tal que, subjunc after, 241
conditional: forms, 257, 279; in
   "if" clauses, 259–60
conjugation: *see* verb conjugation
conjunction: **e** for **y,** 162 fn
conocer vs **saber,** 90
contractions: **a + el ⟶ al,** 41 fn,
   89; **de + el ⟶ del,** 55 fn
correspondence: familiar closings
   in, 198; familiar openings in,
   197
cuál, -es, 33–34
cuando, indic and subjunc after,
   242–43
cuánto, -a, -os, -as, 33–34

[d], 7–8; vs [đ], 7–8
[đ], 7–8; vs [d], 7–8
date, 107
days of week, 70
de: + el ⟶ del, 55 fn; in comparisons of inequality, 194–95;
   in dates, 107; to express possession, 143; in time of day, 50
definite article: *see* article, definite
demonstrative: accent mark with,
   67; adj, 66; neuter, 68; pron,
   67
después (de) que, indic and subjunc
   after, 242–43
diminutive: **-ito, -cito** suffix, 61 fn,
   196
diphthong: with final glide, 154–
   55; and syllable, 6
direct object: *see* object
discourse: indir vs dir, 112
donde, indic and subjunc after,
   242–43
dónde, 33–34
"double *r*": *see* **rr**

[e], 5–6
el: *see* article; article, definite
él: as pron after prep, 106; as
   subj pron, 31–32

ella: as pron after prep, 106; as
   subj pron, 31–32
ellos, -as: as pron after prep, 106;
   as subj pron, 31–32
-er verb: commands, 206–07, 281–
   82; cond, 257; fut, 278–79;
   imperf, 159; past participle,
   190; past subjunc, 258–59;
   pres, 84; pres participle, 71,
   191; pres subjunc, 209–10;
   pret, 157–58; stem-changing,
   104, 139
ese, -a, -os, -as: *see* demonstrative
estar: in past perf prog, 224–25;
   past prog, 224; pres, 46; in pres
   perf, 191, 224; in pres prog,
   70–71; pret, 172–73
este, -a, -os, -as: *see* demonstrative

[f], 14
feminine: *see* gender
future, 278–79; *see also* **ir a** + inf;
   present

g, 12; *see also* [g]; [ǥ]; [h]
[g], 12, 81; in combination with
   vowels, 13–14; vs [ǥ]
[ǥ], 81; vs [g], 81
gender: of adj, 27–28; of art, 27; of
   noun, 26; of possessive adj,
   143
gu: *see* [g]; [gu]; [gw]
[gu], 12
gustar, 246
[gw], 12

h, 6 fn, 13, 63 fn
[h]: spelled **g,** 12, 13, 101; spelled
   j, 13, 101
haber: hay que + inf, 228–29;
   impersonal forms of, 193–94;
   past perf, 224–25; pres perf,
   190–91; pret perf, 225; prog,
   191; subjunc, 210
hacer: in expressions of time, 264–
   65
hasta que, indic and subjunc after,
   242–43
hour, 50

[i], 5–6; spelled **y,** 14
imperative: *see* command
imperfect, 159; vs pret, 160–61;
   see also verb conjugation
indefinite article: *see* article

indicative: in adj clause, 244; in
   adv clause, 240–43; in "if"
   clause, 259–60; vs subjunc, 211
indirect discourse: *see* discourse
indirect object: *see* object pronoun
infinitive, 52; after **acabar de,** 86;
   after **ir a,** 52; prep before, 52,
   92; after **tener que,** 86; as
   verb complement, 52, 228–29
interrogative word, 33–34
ir: imperf, 159; pres, 51; pret,
   172–73
ir a + infinitive, 52, 93, 224–26;
   meaning of in imperf and pret,
   226
-ir verb: commands, 206–07, 281–
   82; cond, 257; fut, 278–79;
   imperf, 159; past participle,
   190; past subjunc, 258–59;
   pres, 84; pres participle, 71,
   191, 226–27; pres subjunc,
   209–10; pret, 157–58; stem-
   changing, 104, 122, 139,
   226–27
irregular verb: *see* verb conjugation

j, 6 fn, 34 fn; *see also* [h]

[k]: in combination with vowels,
   13–14; spelled **c,** 12, 53;
   spelled **qu,** 7 fn, 53, 158

[l]: at end of word, 100–01
la: *see* article; article, definite;
   object pronoun
le: *see* object pronoun
letter writing: *see* correspondence
ll, 63 fn; *see also* [y]
lo: as art, 247; *see also* object pronoun
lo más...posible: *as...as possible,*
   263
los: *see* article; article, definite;
   object pronoun

más: as comparative word, 194–95;
   position of, 262
masculine: *see* gender
mayor, 195
me: as refl pron, 123–24; *see also*
   object pronoun
mejor, 195
menor, 195

C 3
D 4
E 5
F 6
G 7
H 8
I 9
J